The Lone Star Gardener's Book of Lists

The Lone Star Gardener's

BOOK OF LISTS

William D. Adams and Lois Trigg Chaplin

Series Editor
Lois Trigg Chaplin

TAYLOR TRADE PUBLISHING
Lanham • New York • Oxford

Designed by David Timmons

Published by Taylor Trade Publishing
An Imprint of the Rowman & Littlefield Publishing Group
4501 Forbes Blvd., Suite 200
Lanham, Maryland 20706

Distributed by National Book Network
1-800-462-6420

Library of Congress Cataloging-in-Publication Data

Adams, William D.
   The lone star gardener's book of lists / William D. Adams and Lois Trigg Chaplin.
            p.   cm.
   Includes bibliographical references.
   ISBN 0-87833-174-3 (pbk.)
      1. Landscape plants—Texas. 2. Landscape gardening—Texas. I. Chaplin, Lois
   Trigg. II. Title
   SB408 .A33 2000
   635'.09764—dc21   00-042587

Printed in the United States of America

CONTENTS

ACKOWLEDGMENTS

The Lone Star Gardener's Book of Lists is, first of all, a team effort. If it weren't for the contributions of so many knowledgeable Texas gardeners, this would have been a much lesser work. Linda Gay, chief horticulturist at the Mercer Arboretum (Northeast Harris County), did yeoman duty on the perennial and fern lists. She also made major contributions to the ornamental grass list and reviewed the book in its entirety. Mark Fox contributed multiple lists of bay plants. Clyde Cannon and Field Roebuck are responsible for most of the rose information. Bob Riffle's encyclopedic knowledge of plants, especially tropicals, proved invaluable.

Many other contributors were involved, and they are included in the numerous quotes throughout the book. My wife Debbi's love and devotion kept me going through the disappointments. She transcribed so many lists of plant names, she has developed quite a scientific vocabulary. Her vocation may be securities accounting, but she can spout a lot of Latin when called on to do so. She is also a good organizer and isn't even a tiny bit afraid of a computer. The book would have taken years to complete without her help.

You may now be wondering, as I have, what my role in this project was. My credentials include a M.S. in horticulture from Oklahoma State University; my mother, Marge, insisted I take two years of typing in high school (thanks, Mom); and I've grown a lot of plants in my twenty-nine years as a County Extension horticulture agent in Harris County. Most importantly, I have many wonderful friends in the horticulture industry. A lot of new friendships were cultivated in the last few years; these two years I've spent as Master Gardener coordinator have been the best of my career.

Extension professionals and Master Gardeners are well represented in this book. It's a better book for their passionate contributions. Nursery professionals, landscape designers and architects, and folks who love to garden are represented. Mostly I've tried to be the captain of this team, encouraging, even pestering the best in this industry to make a contribution. This book might have taken a year longer to produce if it weren't for e-mail. It's possible to garden without being "connected," but I wouldn't recommend it.

Finally, I would like to dedicate this book to my wife, Debbi, for the unwavering support she gave to this project. I would like to dedicate it as well to the late Lynn Lowrey, a good friend, mentor, and one of America's great plantsmen.

William D. Adams

Thanks to Bill Adams for the wonderful job he has done in adapting my original title, The Southern Gardener's Book of Lists, to Texas. Although I am listed as coauthor here because I am the author of the original title, Bill Adams did all the work on this Texas version and deserves all credit. I trust this text will be helpful to gardeners for years to come.

Lois Trigg Chaplin

INTRODUCTION

I t's difficult not to use the word "BIG" when discussing Texas. Just consider that it is over 900 miles from the northern border of the Panhandle to Brownsville in the Rio Grande Valley and more than 800 miles from Texarkana to El Paso. It's easy to drive all day and not get out of Texas. Not only are there wide ranges of temperatures in this expansive land, but there are distinct differences between East and West Texas—mostly high rainfall in East Texas and very little in West Texas. This also means that pH is a factor, mostly alkaline in West Texas and acid in East Texas.

Soils that are sandy in areas of high rainfall (more than 30 inches per year) tend to become acid. These soils often need lime to raise the pH. Heavy, clay soils in these same areas are usually neutral to slightly alkaline in pH because basic or alkaline ions aren't leached out the way they are in sandy soil. In West Texas these basic ions (calcium, magnesium, sodium, etc.) stay put and result in a high pH, and in many cases they contribute to a high soluble salt problem as well. Adding lots of organic matter to garden beds and leaching the soil with irrigation water helps.

Soil depth is another consideration. Rainfall helps to weather rocks and deposit the smaller particles as deep alluvial soils along rivers and streams. This means that deep soils are more typical of East Texas than West Texas. In fact, in Far West Texas, finding any substance that resembles topsoil can be a challenge. Raised beds with lots of organic matter can be constructed anywhere, but at some point sanity has to prevail. Installing an azalea bed in Van Horn, Texas, might get you into the *Guinness Book of World Records* as the World's Craziest Gardener, but is it worth it?

Wind is a major factor for Texas gardening, especially on the open plains. Texas has many plains areas. According to the dictionary, a plain is an extensive treeless land region. In Texas, the High Plains and Rolling Plains make up the panhandle. The South Texas Plains extend from Uvalde to the Rio Grande Valley. To add to the confusion, some people refer to the area south of Plainview and north of the Hill Country as the South Plains (see "Trees for the South Plains"). These relatively flat, treeless areas are often subjected to extended periods of high winds. Farmers used to say on the Texas Plains: "You can throw your hat up on the side of the barn, and it will stay there all day." That's windy and very drying. Think how the plants must suffer in these areas without some protection.

Wherever you live in Texas, it's best to start any gardening or landscape project with a soil test. Do several soil tests if necessary. First, come up with a composite sample that represents the basic soil on your lot. Take four to six samples from areas in the landscape with similar soils, mix them together, and send in about one pint of the mix. Then you may want to collect separate soil samples from suspected problem areas or areas with significantly different soil types. This will give you a basis from which to work as you're improving these soils with organic matter and fertilizer. The Texas A&M University Extension Soils Lab at College Station is the main facility where people have their soil tested. Many agricultural universities, even community colleges, may offer soil testing for a small fee as well. Also check with your local nursery—they may offer soil tests. See the "Resources" section of this book for the Texas A&M Soils Lab address.

EVENING
PRIMROSE

All this bigness and the variations in soil and climate mean that Texas gardeners have a tremendous selection of plants to choose from and more than a few ideas about how those choices should be made. Consider, for example, that Beaumont on the east end of the Gulf Coast often gets 60 inches of rain in a year, while El Paso gardeners are lucky to get 15 inches.

Texas native plants are becoming increasingly popular, and well they should. Texas has contributed a number of species that are now common garden plants. Most recently, Japanese plant breeders have taken the Texas bluebell, *Eustoma grandiflorum*, renamed it *Lisianthus,* and developed a wide range of varieties with new colors, picotee edges, double flowers, and variable plant height. Bluebells in the wild are mostly blue to purple, with an occasional white. Now we have reds, yellows, blues, pinks, whites, and bicolors. Plant breeders have also worked wonders with Texas native columbines (especially *Aquilegia longissima*), annual phlox (*Phlox drummondii*), *Gaillardia* spp., *Coreopsis,* and *Salvia farinacea.* What's next? Pink, white, and Aggie Maroon bluebonnets have been selected from wild populations and grown as separate colors in isolated fields, so these pure colors are now available in addition to the regular blue bluebonnets. Could a burnt-orange one be on the horizon? Not likely, but University of Texas graduates can still dream.

One might deduce that it would be easy enough to take all the good lists of plants developed in other books in this series and just use them in Texas, what with our wide range of conditions. The main factor that precludes us from doing that is the extremely variable Texas climate. In the Panhandle, winter temperatures may be similar to those in the northeastern states, but these temperatures are typically combined with extreme drought and sudden changes in temperature—an early and hard freeze in the fall plus mild winter weather followed by a late and brutal spring freeze. Plants have to be tough to survive in Texas gardens year round, or we plant them as annuals and enjoy them in season. At least a Texas garden doesn't have to be boring!

THE PLANT LISTS

Coming up with consistent and up-to-date scientific names for the plant lists in this book has been a real challenge. We've used *Hortus Third* as a primary reference, but it is getting old and a lot of names have been changed over the last thirty years. It's also not very useful for a lot of native plants, many of which are just now being discovered in the landscape industry. Poring through other references, we have seen different names or spellings used in the same book for the same plant. There are often so many variations in terminology for the same plant, it's not difficult to understand how this happens. We've tried to list the most current scientific name first, with outdated names in brackets [ ] if they are still in use.

The first word of the scientific name is the *genus* (the taxonomic name ranking below family) followed by the *species.* The abbreviation *spp.* is used to indicate most of the species within a genus. Plants within a species are generally capable of interbreeding, so they are closely related. Beyond this, we have included cultivar names if they have significant attributes compared to the common species. The terms *cultivar* and *variety* are often used synonymously, although cultivar is the most recent of the terms. It is used to designate a horticulturally derived form of a plant, as distinguished from a natural (or found) variety. Cultivar names are usually enclosed in single quotation marks. For example, 'Profusion' Zinnia (*Zinnia elegans* X *angustifolia*).

Other designations you will encounter in plant names are *x* and *hyb.* Both abbreviations indicate a hybrid. When it comes to perennials and woody plants, the hybrid designation typically means that two dissimilar plants were crossed to produce a superior offspring. This often occurs within a single generation, although rose hybrids often involve several generations and a more complex family tree.

Hybrid vegetable varieties and annual flower hybrids are developed as separate inbred parents. One marigold may have big flowers but poor plant form. The other parent may have disease resistance but small flowers. They are combined to produce seed that will have most of the good characteristics from both parents in one plant (the F1 generation). If you save seed of these varieties, the offspring in this next generation (F2 generation) will be wildly different. It's not a good idea to save seed from hybrid petunias or tomatoes, for example. Since perennials and woody plants are usually not propagated from seed, we don't have to worry about this divergence of genetic characteristics. We just grow them from cuttings, divide them, or propagate them by grafting or budding them to seedling rootstock. They're clones, in other words. Deciding whether to apply x or hyb. to the names of these plants is mostly a matter of tradition (what is most common in the literature).

In a number of the lists you will see plants with "Annual" or "Tropical" included in the zone description. This means that they are used as annuals in the zones not specifically mentioned. Generally, if you see

"Annual" in the zone description, it indicates a perennial that is worth using as an annual. Some perennials are too expensive or hard to come by; others don't mature and bloom quickly enough to be worth trying as annuals. Plants with "Tropical" added to the zone description would be long-lasting perennials or woody plants in the tropics, but because they bloom quickly or have attractive foliage, they are worth using farther north as summer annuals.

A SHOPPING LIST

This book is designed to be a shopping list. In most cases you won't find all the information you will need about a particular plant in this book. If we had included all the details, this book would be the size of Texas and would come with its own cart. It was often hard to hold back contributors. They wanted to include every little detail. As much as possible we've honored their lists, but some material has gone onto the editorial "cutting-room floor."

The important thing is that this book gives you someplace to start. The title of each list indicates the use category. The list gives you a plant's common and scientific names, usually followed by the gardening zones in which the plant will do well. Common names can be confusing. We've tried to use the most common "common name," but don't be surprised if there are a few inconsistencies. Some plants have several common names that are used frequently.

The Internet is a wonderful place to research more information on plants. Texas A&M's http://aggie-horticulture.tamu.edu is one of the best sources of information on plants for Texas, and it includes lots of wonderful links, too.

Also check out the library. Texas and the South are much better represented by books and magazines than they used to be. Rather own the books? Check with local book stores, or you can buy almost any book, including many that are out of print, through Internet suppliers like Amazon.com and BN.com.

BOOKS FOR YOUR GARDEN LIBRARY

In the past, gardeners south of the Mason-Dixon line had to extrapolate information from books written for England or New England. Then a few regional books began to appear on the shelves, and now a number of books have been written specifically for the needs of Texas gardeners. However, it's still typical to walk into a bookstore and find that the majority of garden books are still written for New England or the Midwest. Savvy gardeners are rebelling, though. Even regional books are shunned in favor of books written by local authors. To help you learn more about the plants and techniques listed in this book, consider the following titles for your gardening library.

Must Have for Basic Reference
Adams, William D., and Thomas LeRoy. *Commonsense Vegetable Gardening for the South*. Dallas, Texas: Taylor
    Publishing, 1995.
Drees, Bastiaan M., and John A. Jackman. *A Field Guide to Common Texas Insects*. Houston, Texas: Gulf
    Publishing, 1998.
Odenwald, Neil, and James Turner. *Southern Plants*. Baton Rouge, Louisiana: Claitor's Publishing, 1987.
    (Available from Claitor's by writing to them at Box 3333, Baton Rouge, LA 70821.)
Welch, William C. *Perennial Garden Color*. Dallas, Texas: Taylor Publishing, 1989.
Simpson, Nan Booth, and Patricia Scott McHargue. *Great Garden Sources for Texans*. Portland, Oregon:
    TACT, 1999.
Sperry, Neil. *Neil Sperry's Complete Guide to Texas Gardening*. Dallas, Texas: Taylor Publishing, 1991.
Wasowski, Sally, with Andy Wasowski. *Native Texas Plants: Landscaping Region by Region*. Houston, Texas:
    Gulf Publishing, 1991.

Others for Special Interests
Ajilvsgi, Geyata. *Butterfly Gardening for the South*. Dallas, Texas: Taylor Publishing, 1990.
Armitage, Allan M. *Herbaceous Perennial Plants*, 2nd ed. Champaign, Illinois: Stipes Publishing, 1998.
Bowen, Mark, with Mary Bowen, *Habitat Gardening for Houston and Southeast Texas*. Houston, Texas: River
    Bend Publishing, 1998.
Evans, Douglas B. *Cactuses of Big Bend Park*. Austin, Texas: University of Texas Press, 1998.

Gentry, Howard Scott. *Agaves of Continental North America*. Flagstaff, Arizona: University of Arizona Press, 1982.

Gouge, Dawn H., Kirk A. Smith, and Don Wilkerson. *Field Guide to the Insects, Mites and Mollusks of Nursery, Floral and Greenhouse Crops B-6089*. College Station, Texas: Texas A&M University, 1999.

Hatch, Stephan L. *Checklist of the Vascular Plants of Texas*. College Station, Texas: Texas A&M University, 1990.

Hill, Madeline, and Gwen Barclay. *Southern Herb Growing*. Houston, Texas: Shearer Publishing, 1987.

Hunter, C. D. *Suppliers of Beneficial Organisms in North America* (1994 ed.). California EPA, Dept. of Pesticide Regulation, 1020 N. Street, Room 161, Sacramento, CA 95814-5604; 916-324-4100.

Hutson, Lucinda. *The Herb Garden Cookbook*. Houston, Texas: Gulf Publishing, 1998.

Jones, David L. *Encyclopedia of Ferns*. Portland, Oregon: Timber Press, 1997.

Jones, David L., and Dennis Stevenson. *Cycads of the World*. Washington, D.C.: Smithsonian Institution Press, 1993.

Meerow, Alan W. *Betrocks Guide to Landscape Palms*. Library binding, 1992.

Mickel, John. *Ferns for American Gardens*. New York: Macmillan, 1994.

Nash, Helen, with Steve Stroupe. *Plants for Water Gardens: The Complete Guide to Aquatic Plants*. New York: Sterling Publishing, 1998.

Ogden, Scott. *Gardening Success with Difficult Soils—Limestone, Alkaline Clay, and Caliche*. Dallas, Texas: Taylor Publishing, 1992.

Palmer, Stanley J. *Palmer's Hibiscus in Colour*. Queensland, Australia: Lancewood Publishing, 1997.

Pope, Thomas, Neil Odenwald, and Charles Fryling Jr. *Attracting Birds to Southern Gardens*. Dallas, Texas: Taylor Publishing, 1993.

Riffle, Robert Lee. *The Tropical Look: An Encyclopedia of Dramatic Landscape Plants*. Portland, Oregon: Timber Press. 1998.

Simpson, Benny J. *A Field Guide to Texas Trees*. Austin, Texas: Texas Monthly Press. 1988.

Squire, Sally McQueen. *A Gardener's Guide to Growing Bulbs on the Gulf Coast*. Houston, Texas: River Bend Publishing, 1998.

Tveten, John, and Gloria Tveten. *Butterflies of Houston and Southeast Texas*. Austin, Texas: University of Texas Press, 1996.

Tveten, John, and Gloria Tveten. *Wildflowers of Houston*. Houston, Texas: Rice University Press, 1993.

Vanderplank, John. *Passion Flowers*. Boston, Massachusetts: MIT Press, 1996.

Welch, William C. *Antique Roses for the South*. Dallas, Texas: Taylor Publishing, 1990.

Weniger, Dell. *Cacti of Texas and Neighboring States*. Austin, Texas: University of Texas Press, 1984.

MAGAZINES

Texas gardeners are fortunate to have two magazines devoted to gardening in the state. Both of them should be on your "to order" list.

Chris Corby's *Texas Gardener*, P.O. Box 9005, Waco, TX 76714.
Neil Sperry's *Gardens and More*, P.O. Box 864, McKinney, TX 75070-0864.

Another magazine published in Texas is *Pecan South*, P.O. Drawer CC, College Station, TX 77841.

ADDITIONAL HELP

The Texas Agricultural Extension Service, a division of the Texas A&M University system, is represented in virtually every county in the state. It has knowledgeable people, bulletins, and fact sheets to help you with your gardening questions. Also check with area nurseries, landscape designers, botanical gardens, and plant societies.

If you're new to an area, it shouldn't take more than a few weeks to find out who the local plant enthusiasts are. They are relatively easy to find. Check the local paper—chances are if there's a gardening column, the author is one of the local gardening experts. Also, call the County Extension Office. They can help with many of your gardening questions, and in the urban counties there may be a horticulturist on the staff. Find out if they offer a Master Gardener program. If they do, you'll have located lots of garden enthusiasts and potential new friends. Ask the Extension Agent or Master Gardeners about plant societies. In larger towns and cities, you'll find hibiscus groups, daylily groups, and orchid and camellia enthusiasts. A native plant society may be close by, and garden clubs are everywhere. Ask about garden seminars and local plant experts at the nursery, too. Chances are, the nursery sponsors workshops several times a year.

Not every plant listed in this book is readily available. Most should be, but it takes time to bring a plant from discovery to availability. A number of sources are listed in the "Resources" section at the back of this book, but companies and organizations come and go. Don't forget the Internet. If you can't find it there, it may not exist beyond someone's plant collection.

A gardener's book of lists can never be complete. There will always be new plant varieties, and current varieties may fade away. Our greatest fear is that we may have overlooked the obvious. Fortunately, with so many contributors, the potential for this flaw is minimized. The lists in this edition are exhaustive. Still, as this project is coming to a close, we can't help wishing we had another year to work on it, or maybe two or three.

THE ZONE MAP

The accompanying Texas zone map was developed from the U.S. National Arboretum website version of the USDA Plant Hardiness Zone Map. It's meant to be a simplified, practical map of Texas growing zones that works for most plants. Tropical plants and plants that are marginal because of their sensitivity to heat or to soil factors such as pH or salt concentration no doubt need a more sophisticated system, but even the most detailed zone map won't work all the time for all plants. Zone maps are guidelines, and plants (like all biological systems) are difficult to explain in mathematical terms.

The North (N) zone on our map includes USDA zones 6a, 6b, and 7a. The Central (C) zone includes zones 7b and 8a. The Coastal South (CS) region takes in 8b and 9a. The Rio Grande Valley (V) is 9b. Qualifiers like "n" (north, or upper) and "s" (south, or lower) help to delineate which portion of the zone a plant is most likely to survive in.

Additional qualifiers "e" (east) and "w" (west) have been added to this book's zone designations to reflect the importance of rainfall and soil pH. Most soils in East Texas are neutral to acid in pH. In West Texas the soils tend to be alkaline. The east and west qualifiers are very significant for Texas. East Texas gardeners can grow far more species than gardeners in West Texas. In Far West Texas, the lack of rainfall can play a significant roll in plant hardiness. It generally stays dry in the fall, so plants aren't pushed into the first hard freeze while making a lush spurt of growth. The opposite often happens in the east and along the upper Gulf Coast. Eucalyptus species are a good example of plants that have limited use in Texas because of their tendency to burst forth in a rainy fall only to get zapped by the first hard freeze.

Plant stress caused by drought, pest infestations, or low soil fertility can affect a plant's hardiness, too. Moreover, temperate climate plants need a certain amount of chilling in the winter to cause them to break dormancy. Fruit trees, in particular, are often referred to by their chill-hour requirements—the number of hours below 45 degrees F but above freezing. Other plants usually aren't referred to by their chill-hour requirements, but they are affected to some extent. Peonies, for example, aren't likely to ever be grown in the Valley—or in Houston, for that matter.

Gardeners are famous for creating microclimates. The microclimate could be as simple as an area on the south side of the house, protected from wind and moderated from cold, or it could be a conservatory. Lots of new homes have atriums—a genuine, packaged microclimate. Even tall trees and shrub borders contribute to the microclimate effect. Raised beds, rich with organic matter and fitted out with an irrigation system, improve the soil microclimate.

Heat, humidity, depth of topsoil, and impenetrable subsoils are all factors that affect our ability to grow specific plants. Some of them we can deal with; others we can't. The USDA has a new Heat Zone map, and in the future it will prove to be a valuable tool in determining where a plant will grow. Currently it hasn't been used enough to categorize many plants by heat zone.

Most plants in the book are coded to the zones indicated on the accompanying map. Annuals aren't, and some tropicals are listed as annuals or tropicals, since they aren't reliably hardy anywhere in Texas. Some specialty lists don't have codes. Some lists, such as "High Plains Daylilies" and "Trees for West Texas," are for specific areas. Plants included in the Coastal Bay lists will grow close to the coast from Orange to Brownsville but not necessarily on the beachfront. These plants will grow in other areas of Texas, too, and are included in many lists with the appropriate zones listed.

Within the four basic zones, the following combinations might exist:

North, N	Nn (6b plus 6a), Ns (7a)
Central, C	Cn (7b), Cs (8a), Cw, Ce, Csw, Cse, Cnw, Cne
Coastal South, CS	CSn (8b), CSs (9a), CSw, CSe, CSsw, CSse, CSnw, CSne
Rio Grande Valley, V	V (9b)

If the qualifiers seem a bit confusing, take comfort in the fact that they aren't used much. Personally, our favorites are Ns for North southern, and Nn for North northern. They sound funny, but it's a simpler abbreviation than N (upper) or N (lower).

Geographically, the following cities are located within these specific hardiness zones. If a plant description includes this zone, there is a good chance the plant will grow here. However, it should not be presumed that only plants with these specific zone codes are suitable for these cities. Cities can be located in a specific zone, but plants are adapted to much wider zones, in all cases. For example, plants designated CS will grow fine in Houston even though they are not specifically coded CSse. Dallas–Fort Worth is difficult to code because it falls essentially on the zone line for north and south. It should be noted that in some cases, success with a particular plant is contingent on special soil preparation with extra organic matter and pH adjustment.

		Houston	CSse
Amarillo	Nn	Lubbock	Ns
Beaumont	CSse	Midland–Odessa	Cnw
Brownsville	V	Nacogdoches	Cse
Dallas–Fort Worth	Ce	San Antonio–Austin	CSnw
El Paso	CSw	Tyler	Cse

MIMOSA

Remember, this book is a shopping list. There is a lot more to learn about every plant listed on these pages. Talk to nursery professionals, landscape designers, Extension Agents, Master Gardeners, and the most prized of all—the plant enthusiast. Many of them are credited in this book; many others are yet to be discovered. Often they can be found in plant society groups like The Hemerocallis Society, The Cactus and Succulent Society, The Camellia Society, The Orchid Society, The Hibiscus Society, and similar organizations. Don't hesitate to make notes in this book. There are bound to be a few mistakes and lots of disagreements, so customize your edition to reflect your experiences.

Some twenty-nine years ago one of the authors of this book blurted out on a local TV show, "You can't grow apples in Houston." A week later, a one-sentence letter arrived that said, "You otta see the apples on West 18th Street!" Telling gardeners they can't grow something is likely to prove embarrassing in the long run, though we're still tempted to say, "You can't grow peonies in Houston." Zone designations aren't definitive statements about where the determined gardener can force something to grow; they're just guidelines.

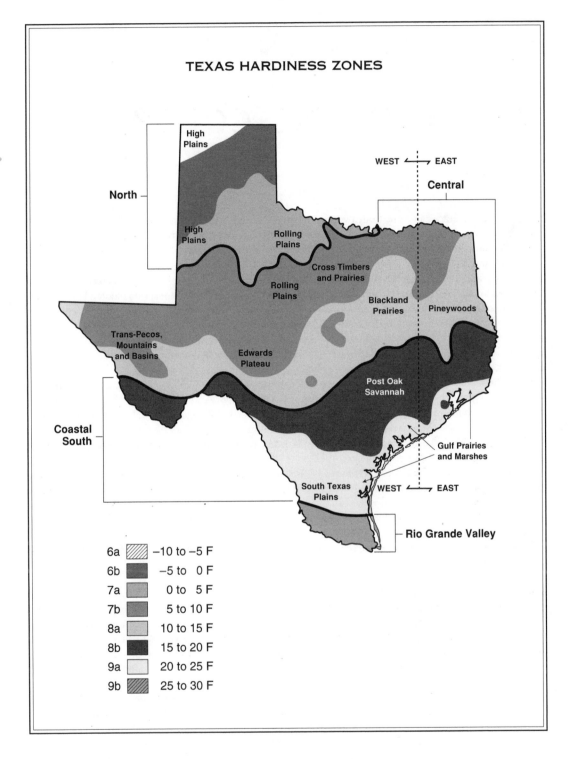

TEXAS HARDINESS ZONES

ANNUAL COLOR

Annual color can come from a variety of plants. Not all of the plants listed in this chapter are annuals in a botanical sense. It has become very popular, for example, to use tropicals just for the summer, knowing that you will have to move them into the greenhouse or lose them with the first freeze.

Some plants that are perennial in other climates—for example, delphiniums—can be grown along the Gulf Coast as annuals. However, this requires that they be planted in the fall for spring bloom. Then they die out in the summer heat. This only works in areas of Texas where winter temperatures are not extreme—basically in the Coastal South and Valley regions. Other perennials act more like short-lived perennials or annuals in Texas gardens. For example, columbines (*Aquilegia*) are considered perennial in most areas of the country, but in Texas even native columbines are treated more like annuals that sometimes come back and often reseed. Foxglove (*Digitalis*) is more of an annual for us, too.

Lots of annual color relies on the foliage. Coleus (*Solenostemon* or *Coleus*) varieties, especially the new sun-tolerant types like 'Alabama Sunset,' are very popular these days. Annual amaranth (*Amaranthus*) is spectacular as a background plant, even if it is a first cousin to pigweed. Polka-dot plant (*Hypoestes*) looks super in shade or partial shade. Many tropicals can be grown for annual color. Some, like the pentas, are grown for bright flowers; others, like Persian shield (*Strobilanthes*), are grown for their foliage (see Gary Outenreath's list, "The Foliage of Moody Gardens").

A great many bulbs can be used for annual color in Texas gardens, but some of the traditional bulbs like tulips and hyacinths need to be coaxed with special treatment if they are going to perform in warm-winter areas. Tulips and most hyacinths grow best in these areas if they are chilled in the refrigerator for sixty to ninety days before planting. The absolute reference on this topic is Sally McQueen Squire's *A Gardener's Guide to Growing Bulbs on the Gulf Coast*.

Because the lists in this chapter are of plants used as annuals, hardiness zone designations are not included.

Basic Cultural Requirements
- Good soil preparation is basic to any garden endeavor. Either mix 6 to 8 inches of compost with the existing soil or build raised beds 8 to 12 inches deep and fill them with a soil mix bought in bulk from a local supplier. It's always a good idea to have your soil tested before planting, whether you're planting in raised beds or regular ground beds (see the "Resources" section in this book for soil testing information).
- Select annuals based on their cool- or warm-season requirements. Cool-season annuals would include pansies, snapdragons, dianthus, larkspur, cornflower, poppies, and sweetpeas. These are planted in the fall in most areas of the state, except Far North Texas. Petunias, nigella, allysum, flowering tobacco, geraniums, nasturtiums, baby's breath, and calendulas like cool weather but won't stand a hard freeze. Planted in the fall, they'll do fine in a mild winter from the Gulf Coast south, but in a hard winter they may freeze all the way to the Valley. From the South Plains north, they are planted in the early spring after the danger of frost has passed, for early summer color. Almost everything else is planted in the spring for summer bloom. Some plants like periwinkles, caladiums, and tropicals used as annuals insist on being planted after the soil has thoroughly warmed up.
- Try using slow-release fertilizer tablets or pellets one inch under transplants at planting time to ensure season-long growth. The new fertilizer sprayers that attach to a hose are great as well. They can be used

to supplement slow-release fertilizers, or use them biweekly throughout the season. If you use soluble, granular fertilizers, be careful to keep them away from the base of the plant, and water them in immediately after application.

- Remove spent flowers (deadhead) before they go to seed to encourage continuous blooming.
- Start early to control weeds, insects, and disease pests before they negate your efforts.
- Install a low-volume irrigation system (drip or micro-sprinkler) and mulch, mulch, mulch!

ANNUALS FOR ALKALINE SOIL

Many Texas gardens are based on alkaline soils. Adding lots of organic matter in the form of compost is a good idea, but the alkalinity tends to creep back in. Sure, you can mix in up to five pounds of sulfur per 100 square feet of bed area, and some apple growers in the Hill Country even tried to ward off Cotton Root Rot with sulfuric acid applications, but eventually the roots grow out of the acidified zone or the alkalinity comes back. Scott Ogden, who lives and gardens in New Braunfels has compiled an excellent text entitled *Gardening Success in Difficult Soils—Limestone, Alkaline Clay, and Caliche*. To learn more about growing plants in soils with high pH, and how and why pH affects plants, I would recommend his book.

For Fall Planting
Bachelor's-Button (*Centaurea cyanus*)
Larkspur (*Consolida* spp.)
Calliopsis (*Coreopsis tinctoria*)
California Poppy (*Escholzia californica*)
Lisianthus (*Eustoma grandiflorum*)
Blanket Flower (*Gaillardia pulchella*)
Scarlet Flax (*Linum grandiflorum*)
Sweet Alyssum (*Lobularia maritima*)
Money Plant (*Lunaria annua*)
Texas Bluebonnet (*Lupinus texensis*)
Stock (*Matthiola incana*)
Love-in-a-Mist (*Nigella damascena*)
Opium Poppy (*Papaver somniferum*)
Annual Phlox (*Phlox drummondii*)

For Spring Planting
Arkansas Lazy Daisy (*Aphanostephus skirrhobasis*)
Cleome (*Cleome hasslerana*)
Cosmos (*Cosmos bipinnatus*)
Klondike (*Cosmos sulphureus*)
Dahlberg Daisy (*Dyssodia tenuiloba*)
Gomphrena (*Gomphrena globosa*)
Melampodium (*Leucanthemum* [*Melampodium*] *paludosum*)
Tahoka Daisy (*Machaeranthera tanacetifolia*)
Gloriosa Daisy (*Rudbeckia hirta*)
Mexican Sunflower (*Tithonia rotundifolia*)
Narrowleaf Zinnia (*Zinnia angustifolia*)
Zinnia (*Zinnia elegans*)
Chippendale Daisy (*Zinnia haageana*)

BACHELOR'S-
BUTTON

Scott Ogden, the author of *Gardening Success in Difficult Soils: Limestone, Alkaline Clay, and Caliche*, notes that spring planting is not appropriate for some annuals. "The harsh, dry conditions typical of limestone soils in summer are too brutal for many moisture-loving plants to endure....Such annuals reverse the season: they germinate in fall, grow through the winter months, flower in spring, and go dormant in summer."

ANNUALS FOR BEGINNERS

First-time gardeners need some early successes. Otherwise they may give up and never realize how fascinating and therapeutic a garden can be. These flowers are super tough. Most are best if grown from transplants, but even rank beginners can grow zinnias from seed.

Plants marked with an asterisk (*) should be planted in the cool-season garden—fall for most Texas gardens, early spring in North Texas.

Abelmoschus (*Abelmoschus moschatus*)
Ageratum (*Ageratum houstonianum*)
Snapdragon (*Antirrhinum majus*)*

Wax-Leaf Begonia (*Begonia* x *semperflorens*)
Madagascar Periwinkle (*Catharanthus roseus*)
Cleome (*Cleome hasslerana*)

Coleus (*Coleus* x *hybridus*)
Annual Dianthus (*Dianthus* spp.)*
Blue Daze (*Evolvulus glomeratus* [*nuttalianus*])
Gomphrena (*Gomphrena globosa*)
Touch-Me-Not (*Impatiens balsamina*)
Impatiens (*Impatiens wallerana*)
Lantana (*Lantana* spp.)
Melampodium (*Leucanthemum* [*Melampodium*] *paludosum*)
Pentas (*Pentas lanceolata*)

Petunia (*Petunia* x *hybrida*)
Annual Phlox (*Phlox drummondii*)*
Moss Rose (*Portulaca grandiflora*)
Annual Salvia (*Salvia splendens*)
Wishbone Flower (*Torenia fournieri*)
Verbena (*Verbena* x *hybrida*)
Pansy (*Viola* x *wittrockiana*)*
Narrowleaf Zinnia (*Zinnia angustifolia*)
'Profusion' Zinnia (*Zinnia elegans* x *angustifolia*)

Norm Arnold, owner of Glorious Gardens Inc. in Houston, is a master at creating colorful gardens with a variety of annuals and perennials. "Fall/winter/spring is one long season to me," he says. "After the initial fall flourish of color, there are about six weeks in the winter when the snaps just sort of set there, the foxgloves and hollyhocks just fill out but not up, and a few other plants don't seem to do much. During that period, pansies, kale and a few other winter lovers carry the show. Then, magically, spring takes hold and everything bursts into life."

BULBS FOR CENTRAL TEXAS

Phil Huey, who provided these bulb lists for Central Texas, has tucked many a bulb into the soil during his career as a horticulturist and former assistant director for the Dallas Parks and Recreation Department. "The only way to really know if a bulb is adaptable to your area is to grow it in your own garden," Phil points out. "Don't be afraid to grow new, untried varieties. You just might be pleasantly surprised." The following are some of his favorites.

Fragrant Daffodils
Hundreds of readily available daffodils are adapted to Central Texas, with a wide choice of color, size, shape, and fragrance. "Make a point to select some daffodils for your garden based on fragrance alone," Phil Huey advises. "You won't be disappointed! Many varieties are available either through local garden centers or catalogue sources. Look particularly for daffodils in Division 7 and 8—these two of the twelve daffodil divisions include the bulk of the fragrant daffodils." (For a complete list and explanation of daffodil divisions, see the box accompanying this list.) Colors can be yellow, white, or combinations of both, and some have cups of a contrasting color—particularly orange. Phil recommends the following daffodils for their fragrance.

Autumn Colors
Avalanche
Cheerfulness
Early Pearl
Erlicheer
Falconet
Geranium

Golden Dawn
Grand Primo
Highfield Beauty
Hoopoe
Indian Maid
Intrigue
Jonquila Simplex

Motmot
Paperwhite Narcissus, Ziva and
  Galilee
Sir Winston Churchill
Soleil d'Or
Sweetness
Wendover

Caladiums
According to Phil Huey, "The most frequently planted bulb for summer color in the shade in Central Texas is the caladium. It is always a dependable plant to brighten shady spots in the garden." These are Phil's favorite caladium varieties.

Aaron
Candidum
Candidum Junior
Frieda Hemple

Gingerland
Jackie Suthers
Lady of Fatima

Pink Symphony
White Queen
White Wing

Daffodil/Narcissus Divisions

The classification of daffodils and narcissus established by the Royal Horticultural Society of Great Britain—and adopted by the American Daffodil Society and worldwide bulb growers—breaks *Narcissus* into the basic groups, or divisions, described below.

- Division 1. Trumpet daffodil—One large flower to a stem; cup (trumpet) is as long or longer than the petals (perianth); 13 to 19 inches high.
- Division 2. Large-cup daffodil—One large flower to a stem; cup *more than* one-third of the total length of the petals; 14 to 20 inches high.
- Division 3. Small-cup daffodil—One flower per stem; cup less than one-third of the length of the petals; 14 to 18 inches high.
- Division 4. Double daffodil—All types that have more than one layer of petals with the appearance of double flowers; one or more flowers per stem.
- Division 5. *Triandrus Narcissus*—The hybrid descendants of the species N. *triandrus*; one to six dainty flowers per stem; slender foliage; 8 to 15 inches tall.
- Division 6. *Cyclamineus Narcissus*—The hybrid descendants of the species N. *cyclamineus*; one nodding flower with a tiny tubelike cup per stem with petals curving back from the wavy-edged cup; 8 to 15 inches tall.
- Division 7. *Jonquilla Narcissus*—The descendants of N. *jonquilla*; two to six sweetly scented flowers on long, slender stems; narrow foliage; cup between one-third and two-thirds the length of a petal; 11 to 17 inches high.
- Division 8. *Tazetta Narcissus*, or *Poetaz Narcissus*—Descendants of species N. *tazetta*; clusters of four to eight sweetly scented flowers; cups shorter than the length of the petals; 15 to 17 inches high.
- Division 9. *Poeticus Narcissus*, or 'Poet's Narcissus'—One fragrant flower per stem; flattened, shallow cup.
- Division 10. Species and wild forms and wild hybrids.
- Division 11. Corona daffodils of garden origin.
- Division 12. Miscellaneous daffodils—All daffodils not falling into any other division.

Tulips

Two groups of tulips can be grown successfully in Texas from Central Texas north. The first group consists of botanical or species tulips. These are mostly low-growing, small-flowered tulips that will multiply and rebloom each year. The following are some of Phil Huey's recommendations for botanical or species tulips.

'Lilac Wonder' *Tulip bakeri*	T. *kolpakowskiana*	T. *saxatilis*
T. *clusiana*	T. *acuminata*	

Some of the May-flowering tulips bloom well in Central Texas. Precooling of the bulbs for 45 days prior to planting is recommended. These tulips are tall, up to 28 inches, with large flowers. Even though they may rebloom for a few seasons, they should be considered annuals. Phil recommends the following varieties.

Grand Style	Maureen	Mrs. John Scheepers
Halcro	Menton	Renown
Kingsblood		

ANNUALS FOR SUNNY, HOT, DRY PLACES

The plants in this list are the really tough ones. Some, lantana for example, may need pruning back a time or two through the season, but otherwise the plants on this list need almost no care except for weeding the beds. If too many old flowers begin to look unsightly, deadheading (removing the old blooms) can make the planting look new again within a few weeks.

Several of these plants, like lantana and firebush, are tropical or semi-tropical perennials, but they are most commonly used in Texas gardens as annuals.

Abelmoschus (*Abelmoschus sakensis*)
Amaranth, Joseph's-Coat (*Amaranthus tricolor*)
Angel Mist, Angel Flower (*Angelonia angustifolia*)
Dutchman's-Pipe (*Aristolochia* spp.)
Wax-Leaf Begonia (*Begonia* x *semperflorens*)
Plume Cockscomb (*Celosia cristata 'plumosa'*)
Flamingo Feather (*Celosia spicata*)
Cleome (*Cleome hasslerana*)
Alabama Sunset Coleus, Red Ruffles Coleus (*Coleus alabamensis* x *hybridus*)
Firefly Cuphea (*Cuphea hybridum*)
Cigar Plant (*Cuphea micropetala*)
Blue Daze (*Evolvulus glomeratus* [*nuttallianus*])
Blanket Flower (*Gaillardia pulchella*)
Gomphrena (*Gomphrena* spp.)
Firebush (*Hamelia patens*)
Red Shield Hibiscus (*Hibiscus acetosella*)
Impatiens (*Impatiens wallerana*)
Moonflower (*Ipomoea alba*)
Cypress Vine (*Ipomoea quamoclit*)
Morning Glory (*Ipomoea tricolor*)
Hyacinth Bean (*Lablab purpurea* [*Dolichos lablab*])
Lantana (*Lantana* spp.)

Lavender Popcorn Lantana (*Lantana trifolia*)
Blackfoot Daisy (*Melampodium leucanthum*)
Mina (*Mina lobata*)
Pavonia (*Pavonia lasiopetala, P. praemorsa*)
Purple Fountain Grass (*Pennisetum setaceum 'rubrum'*)
Pentas (*Pentas lanceolata*)
Moss Rose (*Portulaca grandiflora*)
Purslane (*Portulaca oleracea*)
Castor Bean (*Ricinus communis*)
Gloriosa Daisy (*Rudbeckia hirta*)
Mexican Bush Sage (*Salvia leucantha*)
'Blue Wonder' Scaevola (*Scaevola aemula*)
Dahlberg Daisy (*Thymophylla* [*Dyssodia*] *tenuiloba*)
Mexican Sunflower (*Tithonia rotundifolia*)
'Summer Wave' Blue Wishbone Flower (*Torenia fournieri*)
Peruvian Verbena (*Verbena peruviana*)
Narrowleaf Zinnia (*Zinnia angustifolia*)

MEXICAN SUNFLOWER

ANNUALS FOR THE BEACH

The key to selecting annuals for a beach home is choosing those that can withstand battering winds and salt spray. (Imagine growing wispy spikes of larkspur at sea.) The ocean breeze blows swiftly and consistently, but the plants in this list can take it. Their neat, low habit, sturdy stems, and rugged or waxy leaves have been proven to withstand salty air.

Of course, you can always cheat and grow your beach annuals behind protective walls in microclimates. But mixing lots of compost with the soil helps. Chances are, you will have plenty of seaweed to work with, and there are stables everywhere in Texas, even at the beach.

Ageratum (*Ageratum houstonianum*)
Wax-Leaf Begonia (*Begonia* x *semperflorens*)
Ornamental Cabbage (*Brassica oleracea 'acephala'*)
Calendula (*Calendula officinalis*)
Mexican Heather (*Cuphea hyssopifolia*)
Yellow Ice Plant (*Delosperma cooperi*)
Blanket Flower (*Gaillardia pulchella*)
Gazania (*Gazania rigens*)

Lantana (*Lantana* spp.)
Sweet Alyssum (*Lobularia maritima*)
Annual Phlox (*Phlox drummondii*)
Moss Rose (*Portulaca grandiflora*)
Purslane (*Portulaca oleracea*)
Dusty-Miller (*Senecio cineraria*)
Verbena (*Verbena* x *hybrida*)

 Moss rose, or portulaca (***Portulaca grandiflora***), is a heat-tolerant, spreading annual that grows 4 to 6 inches tall. According to Kathy Huber, garden editor of the *Houston Chronicle,* "Portulaca comes in all colors except blue. The brilliantly colored flowers sit slightly above needle-like succulent foliage and may be single or double. The flowers open in sun and close in the afternoon. At least one variety, 'Afternoon Delight,' remains open longer." Kathy says to give these annuals sun and a sandy soil for the best results. "Purslane (***Portulaca oleracea***) is a relative with broader succulent foliage and single, colorful flowers. It is especially suitable for the coastal garden."

COOL-SEASON ANNUALS

Too many gardeners fail to take advantage of the tremendous cool-season flowers that we can grow. This list gets pretty short in Amarillo—maybe pansies protected by a coldframe during the winter—but for gardeners in the lower half of the state, most of these flowers are easy to grow and have fewer weeds and other pests.

Don't forget that cool-season flowers need fertilizer. Using slow-release plant tabs under the transplants is a good idea, but you may also want to get out the foliar fertilizer sprayer for a quick boost when we have long periods of mild winter weather.

If a hard freeze threatens, get out old blankets, hay, or straw and cover the beds for a night or two. A new product called a frost blanket is especially handy. Also, plants need moisture to survive cold temperatures. We often have a rain just before the cold front settles in, but if it is dry and windy, water thoroughly.

Will sprinkler irrigation really save tender plants from a freeze? Yes, but the parameters are narrow. The irrigation must continue through the freezing period and then continue until the temperature warms up above freezing. If temperatures drop below the mid 20s F, you may create ice sculptures. Never go out the morning after a hard freeze and hose off your plants. The rapid change in temperature can cause cells to rupture. Plants marked with an asterisk (*) in this list are tolerant of the hardest frosts.

Snapdragon (*Antirrhinum majus*)
English Daisy (*Bellis perennis*)*
'Bright Lights' Swiss Chard (*Beta vulgaris*)
Osaka Mustard (*Brassica* spp.)
Ornamental Cabbage and Kale (*Brassica oleracea 'acephala'*)*
Calendula (*Calendula officinalis*)
Bachelor's-Button (*Centaurea cyanus*)
Wallflower (*Cherianthus cheiri*)
Rocket Larkspur (*Consolida ambigua*)
Cyclamen (*Cyclamen* spp.)
Cardoon (*Cynara cardunculus*)
Chinese Forget-Me-Not (*Cynoglossum amabile*)
Belladona Delphinium (*Delphinium elatum* x *Delphinium grandiflorum*)
Dianthus (*Dianthus chinensis*)*

Foxglove (*Digitalis purpurea*)
Sweet Pea (*Lathyrus odorata*)
Linaria, Toadflax (*Linaria maroccana*)
Sweet Alyssum (*Lobularia maritima*)
Stock (*Matthiolla* x *hybrida*)
Forget-Me-Not (*Myosotis sylvatica*)*
Poppy (*Papaver* spp.)
Hardy Geranium (*Pelargonium* x *hortorum*)
Petunia (*Petunia* x *hybrida*)
Annual Phlox (*Phlox drummondii*)
German Primrose (*Primula obconica*)
Nasturtium (*Tropaeolum majus*)
Viola (*Viola cornuta*)*
Johnny-Jump-Up (*Viola tricolor*)*
Pansy (*Viola* x *wittrockiana*)*

WAIT TILL IT'S REALLY WARM TO PLANT THESE

A few plants can't stand the cool of early spring. If you set them out too early, they just won't grow. Sometimes the plants are stunted; sometimes the problem is a soil-borne disease. Periwinkles, for example, are much more susceptible to Aerial Phytophthora when planted before April or May. Wait until two to three weeks after the last frost before you plant the following.

Firetail (*Acalypha pendula, A. repens*)
Love-Lies-Bleeding (*Amaranthus caudatus*)
Joseph's-Coat (*Amaranthus tricolor*)
Caladium (*Caladium* x *hortulatum*)
Madagascar Periwinkle (*Catharanthus roseus*)
Crested Cockscomb (*Celosia cristata*)

Gomphrena (*Gomphrena globosa*)
Cat's Whiskers (*Orthosiphon stamineus*)
Wishbone Flower (*Torenia fournieri*)
Narrowleaf Zinnia (*Zinnia angustifolia*)
Zinnia (*Zinnia elegans*)

"Irresistible and pest-free, torenia (*Torenia fournieri*) is a must for the summer garden. The foot-tall plants produce small, deeply cupped flowers that are white rimmed in rose, purple, or blue, or are pale blue with deep blue rims. The throat is splashed with yellow. The stamens form a wishbone, therefore the common name 'wishbone flower.' Torenia also is known as the summer pansy. This small plant blooms nonstop in partial sun or bright shade in a fertile, moist garden soil, and the plants reseed eagerly. The blooms are ideal for small vases."
—Kathy Huber, garden editor, *Houston Chronicle*

TEXAS SPECIALTY CUT FLOWERS

Frank and Pamela Arnosky, owners of Texas Specialty Cut Flowers, generate an impressive gross income from their eight acres of cutting flowers near Blanco. They also generate a lot of perspiration, and expenses can run to 80 percent of gross. The profits come mostly from sales in Austin and San Antonio, so not only do the flowers have to be grown and harvested with considerable effort, but they have to be delivered. Fast delivery is hard work, but it also gives them an advantage. Because these locally grown flowers are delivered the same day they are picked, they are more beautiful and last longer than cut flowers that have been shipped long distances. Frank and Pam are sticklers about quality. That's why they have been so willing to help other folks interested in the cut flower business. They don't want people to buy a Texas-grown cut flower and be disappointed. If the consumer is dissatisfied with the product, it hurts everyone's business in the long run.

The Arnoskys deal with some hardships, but they savor their independent lifestyle. In years past, many of our productive, hard-working members of society got their start on a farm. They had chores to do in addition to homework, and it all helped to build a strong work ethic. Even with all the hard work, the Arnoskys still have to remind themselves occasionally: "We live in the beautiful Texas Hill Country, and we're making a living."

Frank and Pam are constantly trying new flowers and new varieties. The following are some of their most reliable favorites.

'Colorado,' 'Credo' Yarrow (*Achillea millefolium*)
'Blue Horizon' Ageratum (*Ageratum houstonianum*)
'Spring Giant' Snapdragon (*Antirrhinum majus*)
'Chief Mix' Crested Cockscomb (*Celosia cristata*)
'Giant Imperial' Larkspur (*Consolida ambigua*)
Calliopsis (*Coreopsis tinctoria*)
'Magnus' Echinacea (*Echinacea purpurea*)
'Echo Series' Lisianthus (*Eustoma grandiflorum*)

Gladiolus (*Gladiolus* x *hortulanus*)
Gomphrena (*Gomphrena globosa*)
'Sunbright' Sunflower (*Helianthus annuus*)
Single Mexican Tuberose (*Polianthes tuberosa*)
'Indian Summer' Rudbeckia (*Rudbeckia hirta*)
Mexican Sage (*Salvia leucantha*)
'Gold Coin' African Marigold (*Tagetes* spp.)
'Benary's Giant' Zinnia (*Zinnia elegans*)

ANNUALS FOR FRAGRANCE

Fragrance can make an indelible mark on one's impression of a garden. Most garden fragrances come out at night—they're the siren calls for moths and other night pollinators. Four-o'clocks, moonvine, and night-blooming jasmine have a wonderful, intense sweetness. Moths, it would seem, have good taste in fragrances. By the light of day there are petunias, sweet peas, sweet alyssum, and banana shrub (*Michelia*) to lure you into the garden.

For Spring Fragrance
Pink (*Dianthus* spp.)
Sweet William (*Dianthus barbatus*)
Heliotrope (*Heliotropium arborescens*)
Sweet Pea (*Lathyrus odoratus*)
Sweet Alyssum (*Lobularia maritima*)
Stock (*Matthiola* spp.)
Petunia, especially white (*Petunia* x *hybrida*)

For Summer Fragrance
Moonflower (*Ipomoea alba*)

Four-O'clock (*Mirabilis jalapa*)
Flowering Tobacco (*Nicotiana alata*)
Argentine Nicotiana (*Nicotiana sylvestris*)
Petunia, heat tolerant (*Petunia* x *hybrida*)

SWEET PEA

For Fall Fragrance
Sweet Alyssum (*Lobularia maritima*)
Petunia (*Petunia* x *hybrida*)

KATHY HUBER'S FAVORITE SUMMER ANNUALS

Kathy Huber, garden editor for the *Houston Chronicle*, recommends the plants in this list as the summer annuals that have performed most consistently. Most are easy to grow. For prolific bloomers, Kathy recommends angelonia: "This Mexican native likes a well-draining soil and sun to partial sun. Mature height is 15 to 24 inches. Prune lightly to shape, if needed, and to encourage another full round of blooms." In warm winters, angelonia may prove a tender perennial.

Pentas have a long bloom season. "Pest-free and long-flowering, pentas produce rounded clusters of tiny, star-shaped flowers in shades of pink, violet, red, or white against large, dark-green leaves, spring to frost. Given an organically enriched, well-draining soil, they require little attention. Plant en masse for more effective showing. Pentas also work well in pots. Butterflies love them. Morning sun to bright shade is best. Mature height is 2 to 3 feet, but the showy pink dwarf varieties and the more subtle lavender dwarfs are attractive."

Angelonia (*Angelonia* spp.)	purple spires, spring to frost
Blue Daze (*Evolvulus glomeratus* [*nuttalianus*])	bright blue flowers, gray-green foliage
Caladium (*Caladium* × *hortulanum*)	fancy foliage in combination colors
Periwinkle (*Catharanthus roseus*)	pink, rose, red, lavender, or white pinwheel flowers
Plume Celosia (*Celosia cristata* '*plumosa*')	red, yellow, rosy-lavender, or buff plumes
Crested Cockscomb (*Celosia cristata*)	flamboyant red, yellow, orange, or purple plumes
Cleome (*Cleome hasslerana*)	unusual protruding stamens, seed capsules
Coleus (*Coleus* × *hybridus*)	colorful foliage, spring to frost
Cosmos (*Cosmos sulphureus*)	orange, yellow, white, or pink flowers
'Batface' Cuphea (*Cuphea llavea*)	flowers with reddish-orange ears, dark purple face
Globe Amaranth, Gomphrena (*Gomphrena globosa*)	purple, red, orange, lavender-pink, or white clover-like flowers
Impatiens (*Impatiens wallerana*)	red, pink, orange, lavender, or white flowers
Melampodium, Medallion Plant (*Leucanthemum* [*Melampodium*] *paludosum*)	yellow daisy-like flowers, bright-green foliage
Pentas (*Pentas lanceolata*)	pink, violet, red, or white star-shaped flowers
Moss Rose, Portulaca (*Portulaca grandiflora*)	brilliant flowers, needle-like succulent foliage
Chocolate Plant (*Pseuderanthemum alatum*)	silver-splotched brown foliage, brilliant purple flowers
Torenia (*Torenia fournieri*)	white cupped flowers rimmed in rose, purple, or blue; or pale blue with deep blue rims
'Crystal White,' 'Profusion Orange,' 'Profusion Cherry' Zinnia (*Zinnia angustifolia*)	prolific blooms, mounding plants

For colorful foliage, Kathy Huber, garden editor of the *Houston Chronicle*, recommends caladiums and coleus. "Caladiums were once a shade-garden item only, but some varieties of these leafy tuberous plants have shown some tolerance for sun. Plant after the soil warms in spring in an organically enriched, well-draining soil. Keep the soil moist during the growing season. Remove flowers when they appear. Plants mature to 1 or 2 feet. When the foliage declines, some gardeners lift the tubers, air dry, and store in sawdust in a cool, well-ventilated place." Caladiums sport foliage combinations of pink, red, white, and green.

"Coleus, an old standby, has attracted attention in more recent years as many colorful cultivars for sun and shade have become available," advises Kathy. "Hard to beat for easy growth and color spring to frost. Just water as needed, remove flower stalks—it's great foliage you're after—and pinch to promote bushiness. Mix various varieties in a bed, or work in with summer flowers. Look for lower-growing, spreading ducksfoot varieties—the shape of the foliage resembles that of a duck—as well as upright types with larger leaves. Heights vary from 1 to 3 feet."

EVERLASTING FLOWERS

These flowers are the perfect way to extend the gardening season. Their petals are tough and papery, so they are easy to air dry and keep around the house for years. Most need to be cut when the blossoms are partially open and should be tied in bundles and hung to dry. In the humid eastern part of the state, they will need to be dried indoors. Colors will fade slightly, but the flowers retain a pastel look that is reminiscent of gardens and days gone by.

Winged Everlasting (*Ammobium alatum*)
Safflower (*Carthamus tinctorius*)
Cockscomb (*Celosia argentea*)
'Flamingo Feather' Cockscomb (*Celosia spicata*)
Drumstick Flower (*Craspedia chrysantha*)
Globe Amaranth (*Gomphrena globosa*)
Strawflower (*Helichrysum* spp.)

Statice (*Limonium sinensis*)
Money Plant (*Lunaria annua*)
Bells-of-Ireland (*Molucella laevis*)
Love-in-a-Mist (*Nigella damascena*)
Poppy (seed pods) (*Papaver somniferum*)
Star Flower (*Scabiosa stellata*)

ANNUALS THAT DO WELL IN THE SHADE

FLOWERING TOBACCO

Shade is such a relative thing. Most shade-loving annuals really like a little dappled sun if they can get it. For really deep shade, stick with impatiens, tropicals like chocolate plant and Persian shield, and light-colored caladiums. The caladium varieties on this list are complex hybrids. The strap-leaf varieties (with the exception of 'Pink Symphony') can take full sun in high-rainfall areas and include some *Caladium picturatum* genetics.

Winter shade offers special opportunities, especially in the Coastal South and the Rio Grande Valley. Deciduous trees lose their leaves, providing sun in areas that may have been heavily shaded in the summer, and it's a gentler winter sun, shorter in duration and at a lower angle than the sun in summer.

Plants in this list that do well in partial shade are marked with an asterisk (*). Partial shade means dappled shade through scattered trees, or areas with morning sun. The rest of the plants in this list would tolerate full shade all day.

Summer Annuals for Shade
Achimenes (*Achimenes* x *hybrida*)*
Wax-Leaf Begonia (*Begonia* x *semperflorens*)*
Strap-Leaf Caladium (*Caladium* x *hortulanum*)*
Caladium (*Caladium* x *hortulanum*)
Cleome (*Cleome hasslerana*)
Coleus (*Coleus* x *hybridus*)*
Foxglove (*Digitalis purpurea*)*
Gerbera Daisy (*Gerbera jamesonii*)
Polka-Dot Plant (*Hypoestes phyllostachya*)
Impatiens (*Impatiens wallerana*)
Jacobinia (*Justicia carnea*)

Flowering Tobacco (*Nicotiana alata, N. sylvestris*)*
Pentas (*Pentas lanceolata*)*
Plectranthus (*Plectranthus* spp.)
Chocolate Plant (*Pseuderanthemum alatum*)
Scarlet Sage (*Salvia splendens*)*
Persian Shield (*Strobilanthes dyeranus*)
Black-Eyed Susan Vine (*Thunbergia alata*)*
Wishbone Flower (*Torenia fournieri*)*

Cool Season Annuals for Shade
Cyclamen (*Cyclamen persicum*)
Forget-Me-Not (*Myosotis* spp.)
Johnny-Jump-Up (*Viola tricolor*)

ANNUALS YOU CAN PLANT IN THE HEAT OF SUMMER

It's surprising, but some plants that really suffer in the summer are capable of getting started at this time if set out as seedlings. No doubt seedling vigor and regular attention are factors in making this happen, but it does seem a bit strange. Hybrid marigolds are usually covered with spider mites in the summer from a spring planting, but small plants or seeds planted in the heat seem to miss the window for infestation and perform beautifully in the fall.

Plants in this list that are followed by an asterisk (*) may also be grown from seed sown directly in the garden. Caladiums, impatiens, and wishbone flower (*Torenia fournieri*) will need some shade.

Abelmoschus (*Ablemoschus moschatus*)
Joseph's-Coat (*Amaranthus tricolor*)
Wax-Leaf Begonia (*Begonia semperflorens*)
Caladium (*Caladium* x *hortulanum*)
Ornamental Pepper (*Capsicum annuum*)

Madagascar Periwinkle (*Catharanthus roseus*)
Wheat or Feather Cockscomb (*Celosia spicata*)
Cleome (*Cleome hasslerana*)*
Coleus (*Coleus* x *hybridus*)
Mexican Heather (*Cuphea hyssopifolia*)

Blue Daze (*Evolvulus glomeratus* [*nuttalianus*])
Indian Blanket (*Gaillardia pulchella*)
Gomphrena (*Gomphrena globosa*)*
Sunflower (*Helianthus annuus*)*
Impatiens (*Impatiens wallerana*)
Moonflower (*Ipomoea alba*)*
Morning Glory (*Ipomoea purpurea*)*
Hyacinth Bean (*Lablab purpurea* [*Dolichos lablab*])*
Lantana (*Lantana camara*)
Melampodium (*Leucanthemum* [*Melampodium*]
    paludosum)

Ornamental Basil (*Ocimum basilicum*)*
Pentas (*Pentas lanceolata*)
Plectranthus (*Plectranthus* spp.)
Moss Rose (*Portulaca grandiflora*)*
Purslane (*Portulaca oleracea*)
Black-Eyed Susan (*Rudbeckia hirta*)
Marigold (*Tagetes* spp.)
Dahlberg Daisy (*Thymophylla* [*Dyssodia*] *tenuiloba*)
Mexican Sunflower (*Tithonia rotundifolia*)*
Wishbone Flower (*Torenia fournieri*)
'Profusion' Zinnia (*Zinnia elegans* × *angustifolia*)*

"Soil preparation is the key to success anywhere in Texas, but along the Brazos River bottom we have everything from sand to clay gumbo. The soil is often striped or multi-layered, and it takes 6 to 8 inches of organic matter worked into these soils to make them friable enough to grow beautiful flowers. Once you've added the organic matter, clay soils are great for holding nutrients and water."
—Stephanie Gebhardt, horticulturist, Sealy

ANNUALS FOR HANGING BASKETS

This list is mainly composed of annuals, but there are some short-lived perennials and tropicals included. All of these plants have a trailing growth habit that is perfect for hanging pots and baskets—a pleasing focal point for deck, patio, or porch.

Strawberry Firetail (*Acalypha pendula*)
Golden Sprite Allamanda (*Allamanda cathartica* ×
    neriifolia)
Lazy Daisy (*Aphanostephus skirrhobasis*)
Angel-Wing Begonia (*Begonia* × *argenteo-guttata*)
Bougainvillea (*Bougainvillea* × *buttiana*)
Periwinkle (*Catharanthus roseus*)
Dwarf Plumbago (*Ceratostigma plumbaginoides*)
Spider Plant (*Chlorophytum comosum*)

Ornamental Sweet Potato (*Ipomoea batatas*)
Lantana (*Lantana camara*)
Ivy Geranium (*Pelargonium peltatum*)
Petunia (*Petunia* × *hybrida*)
Plectranthus (*Plectranthus* spp.)
Trailing Rosemary (*Rosmarinus officinalis*)
Scaevola (*Scaevola aemula*)
'Blue Princess' Verbena (*Verbena* × *hybrida*)
Narrowleaf Zinnia (*Zinnia angustifolia linearis*)

TALLEST ANNUALS FOR THE BACK OF A BORDER

The rules of garden design tell us to plant the tallest annuals in the back of a bed so that we don't hide smaller plants. If the bed is viewed from all sides, then you will probably want to put your tallest annuals in the center of the bed. Actually, the vegetable garden is a great place for tall annuals, especially any that need staking or those that are planted for use as cut flowers. Interestingly, plant breeders are working to make annuals shorter, not taller, because of the trend toward smaller lots. Smaller annuals are also easier to handle in cell packs. This is important to commercial growers and retailers because big plants outgrow their small pots quickly. However, if you're a gardener looking for tall flowers (3 to 4 feet) to create that cottage garden look, here are a few.

Hollyhock (*Alcea rosea*)
'Powderpuff Mix' Hollyhock (*Alcea rosea*)
Joseph's-Coat (*Amaranthus tricolor*)
'Rocket Hybrid Mix' Snapdragon (*Antirrhinum
    majus*)

Wheat or Feather Cockscomb (*Celosia spicata*)
Cornflower, Bachelor's-Button (*Centaurea cyanus*)
Cleome (*Cleome hasslerana*)
Cosmos (*Cosmos bipinnatus*)
Delphinium, fall planted (*Delphinium* × *cultorum*)

Foxglove (*Digitalis purpurea*)
Sunflower (*Helianthus annuus*)
Red Shield Hibiscus (*Hibiscus acetosella*)
'Zebrina' Compact Hollyhock (*Malva sylvestris*)
Argentine Nicotiana (*Nicotiana sylvestris*)

Purple Fountain Grass (*Pennisetum setaceum* 'rubrum')
Castor Bean (*Ricinus communis*)
Mexican Sunflower (*Tithonia rotundifolia*)

Cleome (*Cleome hasslerana*) are favorites of Kathy Huber, garden editor of the *Houston Chronicle*, who says that this tall, old-fashioned annual adds 3 to 5 feet of height to the back of the border. "The unusual flower has extremely long, protruding stamens, therefore the common name 'spider flower.' The petals curl up as day passes. Slender seed capsules follow the blooms. If allowed to dry on the plant, the pod will split and several seedlings will follow. Or allow the pods to dry on the plant, then collect for future sowing. Sun or partial sun and a well-draining soil help ensure success."

ANNUALS FOR NATURALIZING

Annuals that reseed can be a blessing or a nuisance. The cornflowers (bachelor's-buttons) that came up behind Grandpa's tool shed were nice because they bloomed their heads off in the spring and didn't require any care. The purslane that reverts to a tiny-flowered weed is, however, a weed! The following are more blessing than nuisance, and most are easy to get rid of if you tire of them.

Bidens (*Bidens* spp.)
Bachelor's-Button (*Centaurea cyanus*)
Cleome (*Cleome hasslerana*)
Rocket Larkspur (*Consolida ambigua*)
Calliopsis (*Coreopsis tinctoria*)
Cosmos (*Cosmos bipinnatus*)
Blanket Flower (*Gaillardia pulchella*)
Gomphrena (*Gomphrena globosa*)

Melampodium (*Leucanthemum* [*Melampodium*] *paludosum*)
Bluebonnet (*Lupinus texensis*)
Old-Fashioned Petunia (*Petunia violaceae*)
Annual Phlox (*Phlox drummondii*)
Black-Eyed Susan (*Rudbeckia hirta*)
Mexican Sunflower (*Tithonia rotundifolia*)
Johnny-Jump-Up (*Viola tricolor*)
Zinnia (*Zinnia elegans*)

THE FOLIAGE OF MOODY GARDENS

Moody Gardens is located on 156 acres adjacent to Galveston Bay. Because of its sheltered location, many plants thrive here that would be tender in Houston only sixty miles to the north. Tropical plants that would be too tender even for this protected oasis are brought out of the Moody Gardens greenhouses to flourish in the summer landscape. One of the main horticultural features is the Rainforest Pyramid. Butterflies, birds, and tropical fish share this greenhouse environment with exotic plants from around the world. Gary Outenreath, the horticulturist at Moody Gardens, uses plants from every ecosystem imaginable. There are plenty of blooming plants at Moody—tropical hibiscus, oleanders, and annual flowers of every description—but Gary is famous for his use of bright and colorful foliage plants.

Moody Gardens uses a wide variety of evergreen and seasonal plants that have colorful foliage. These complement the numerous flowering plant varieties such as oleanders, hibiscus, jatropha, lantana, and crape myrtle. Of special note are the many varieties of coleus and copper plant (*Acalypha*). Generally speaking, the foliage plants are more durable and longer lasting than most of the seasonal flowering plants. The following list, compiled by Gary Outenreath, includes the majority of the colorful foliage on display at Moody Gardens.

Yellow or White Variegations
Copper Plant (*Acalypha godseffiana* 'heterophylla')
'Hoffmanii,' 'Java White,' 'Marginata,' 'Tahiti' Copper Plant (*Acalypha wilkesiana*)
Variegated Shell Ginger (*Alpinia zerumbet* 'variegata')

Joseph's-Coat (*Alternanthera ficoidea*)
'Raspberry Ice' Bougainvillea (*Bougainvillea spectabilis*)
Snowbush (*Breynia nervosa*)
Croton (*Codiaeum* spp.)
Coleus (*Coleus* x *hybridus*)

Golden Banyan (*Ficus altissima 'variegata'*)
'Snow Queen' Hibiscus (*Hibiscus rosa-sinensis*)
Variegated Tapioca (*Manihot esculenta 'variegata'*)
'Mrs. Runge' Oleander (*Nerium oleander*)
Pseuderanthemum spp.
Sanchezia nobilis 'glaucifolia'
Dwarf Variegated Schefflera (*Schefflera arboricola 'variegata'*)
'Texas Gold' Wedelia (*Wedelia trilobata*)

Purples
Copper Plant (*Acalypha 'moorea'*)
Ornamental Pepper (*Capsicum annuum*)
Coleus (*Coleus × hybridus*)
Ti Plant (*Cordyline* spp.)
Basil (*Ocimum* spp.)
Purple Fountain Grass (*Pennisetum setaceum 'rubrum'*)
Pseuderanthemum atropurpureum
Persian Shield (*Strobilanthes dyeranus*)

Grays and Silvers
Wormwood (*Artemisia* spp.)
Mexican Blue Palm (*Brahea armata*)
Dusty-Miller (*Centaurea cineraria*)
Silverthorn (*Elaeagnus pungens*)
Trailing Gazania (*Gazania uniflora*)
Texas Sage (*Leucophyllum frutescens*)
Silver Form Saw Palmetto (*Sabal urseana*)
Stemodia (*Stemodia tomentosa*)
Variegated Vitex (*Vitex trifolia 'variegata'*)

Pinks, Whites, Reds, and Oranges
'Rosy Frills' Copper Plant (*Acalypha godseffiana*)
'Ceylon,' 'Macafeana,' 'Macrophylla,' 'Orange Giant' Copper Plant (*Acalypha wilkesiana*)
Joseph's-Coat (*Alternanthera ficoidea*)
Amaranthus, Cultivated Pigweed, Joseph's Coat (*Amaranthus*)
Caladium (*Caladium × hortulanum*)
Crotons (*Codiaeum* spp.)
Ti Plant (*Cordyline* spp.)
'Waimea' Calico Plant (*Graptophyllum pictum*)
Hibiscus cooperi

"Colorful tropical foliage plants are much underused as seasonal plants along the Gulf Coast, especially in view of the fact that for seven months of the year, the climate here is almost an exact duplicate of the areas these plants originate from."
—Gary Outenreath, Horticulturist, Moody Gardens, Galveston

SUPER EASY FLOWERS FROM A PACKET OF SEEDS

These are a few of the flowers you can pick up at your favorite garden shop, or even the grocery store, in a seed packet for $2 or less. They are easy to start as seed because they sprout quickly, bloom within a few months, and most of the seeds are big enough to handle easily. They are great for kids. The ones marked with an asterisk (*) are for cool-season planting. That also happens to be the best season for starting school projects.

Bachelor's-Button (*Centaurea cyanus*)*
Larkspur (*Consolida ambigua*)*
Calliopsis (*Coreopsis tinctoria*)
Cosmos (*Cosmos bipinnatus*)
Klondike Series Cosmos (*Cosmos sulphureus*)
Gomphrena (*Gomphrena globosa*)
Sunflower (*Helianthus annuus*)
Morning Glory (*Ipomoea* spp.)
Moonflower (*Ipomoea alba*)
Cypress Vine (*Ipomoea quamoclit 'cardinalis'*)

Cardinal Climber (*Ipomoea × multifida 'cardinalis'*)
Hyacinth Bean (*Lablab purpurea* [*Dolichos lablab*])
Sweet Pea (*Lathyrus odoratus*)*
Scarlet Runner Bean (*Phaseolus coccineus*)
Annual Phlox (*Phlox drummondii*)
Marigold (*Tagetes* spp.)
Black-Eyed Susan Vine (*Thunbergia alata*)
Mexican Sunflower (*Tithonia rotundifolia*)
Nasturtium (*Tropaeolum majus*)*
Zinnia (*Zinnia elegans*)

"The multicolored, old-fashioned 'Cut and Come Again' zinnias are still a favorite," says Kathy Huber, garden editor of the *Houston Chronicle,* "but mildew can be a problem in the more humid areas of the state. Those with this problem—or any gardener—should be pleased with the narrow-leaf zinnias. *Zinnia angustifolia* 'Crystal White,' a 1997 All America Selections Winner, produces prolific blooms on a mounding 10-inch plant. No pinching, pruning, or deadheading required. The 1999 AAS Gold Medal winners 'Profusion Orange' and 'Profusion Cherry' are also disease-resistant and freely produce 2- to 3-inch single blooms on mounded plants 12 to 18 inches tall. The warm season annuals have a spread slightly broader than their height. Best results with all zinnias occur in full sun and a well-draining soil. Mass them in the garden with gomphrena or coleus, or plant them in pots."

ANNUALS THAT BLOOM FROM SPRING TO FROST
IF YOU DEADHEAD

Deadheading and cutting back are two methods that can help gardeners extend an annual's bloom period. Deadheading is removing old blooms, whereas cutting back removes the leggy stem tissue that accumulates with rapid growth. Deadheading would usually be accomplished with shears, while hedge trimmers are more appropriate for cutting back.

In Texas, deadheading or cutting back annuals isn't always as successful as it is in other parts of the country. It's the weather extremes that short-circuit the effort. Cut back petunias in late spring and they are faced with few leaves and 100 degree weather. The new trailing varieties are more heat resistant and respond better, but most of the standard varieties never survive to see the cooler temperatures of fall.

Deadheading combined with a few weeks under fiber row cover might help some flowers recover, but the stuff is rather ugly in the landscape. Foliar feeding with one of the new hose-on fertilizer sprayers is a better idea. It's an easy and safe way to give these plants a boost.

Ageratum (*Ageratum houstonianum*)
Cleome (*Cleome hasslerana*)
Cosmos (*Cosmos bipinnatus*)
Blanket Flower (*Gaillardia pulchella*)
Sunflower, multibranched (*Helianthus annuus*)
Black-Eyed Susan (*Rudbeckia hirta*)

Mealycup Sage (*Salvia farinacea*)
Annual Salvia (*Salvia splendens*)
Copper Canyon Daisy (*Tagetes lemmonii*)
Mexican Sunflower (*Tithonia rotundifolia*)
Wishbone Flower (*Torenia fournieri*)
Zinnia (*Zinnia elegans*)

PLANTS THAT BLOOM UNAIDED FROM SPRING
UNTIL FROST

Blooming from spring until frost is a tall order for flowers subjected to Texas weather extremes. No plant will be at its peak all season, but with a little fertilizer every two to four weeks and an occasional shearing, the plants in this list will just keep going and going.

'Bella' Flowering Maple (*Abutilon hybridum*)
Wax-Leaf Begonia (*Begonia x semperflorens*)
Mexican Bachelor's-Button (*Centratherum punctatum [camporum]*)
Mexican Heather (*Cuphea hyssopifolia*)
Gomphrena (*Gomphrena* spp.)
Impatiens (*Impatiens wallerana*)
Moonflower (*Ipomoea alba*)

Morning Glory (*Ipomoea tricolor*)
Lantana (*Lantana* spp.)
'Derby,' 'Showstar' Melampodium (*Leucanthemum [Melampodium] paludosum*)
Cup Flower (*Nierembergia hippomanica*)
Pentas (*Pentas lanceolata*)
Annual Phlox (*Phlox drummondii*)
Wishbone Flower (*Torenia fournieri*)
Yellow Sage Rose, Cup-of-Gold (*Turnera ulmifolia*)
Narrowleaf Zinnia (*Zinnia angustifolia*)
'Profusion' Zinnia (*Zinnia elegans x angustifolia*)

MORNING
GLORY

GREG GRANT'S SUREFIRE ANNUALS AND BULBS

Greg Grant, horticulturist and lecturer with the Stephen F. Austin State University Arboretum in Nacogdoches, has a lot to say about gardening in Texas:

- "If a plant is rare, it's either ugly or won't grow."
- "I never met a plant I didn't like—only plants that didn't like me."
- "When it comes to bulbs in Texas, we're closer to Hell than Holland!"
- "If I had a choice between all the lilacs in the world or one crape myrtle, I'd take a one-gallon crape myrtle."
- "Most seed-grown annuals belong in the North and Europe. Our best stuff is from the tropics, from cuttings."
- When choosing *Narcissus* for Texas, don't choose the big daffodils. Better to go with early blooming, small-flowered, cluster-blooming species and old hybrids."
- "If you don't like cannas and you live in the South, you'd better learn to like them."
- "You grow peonies in the North. We grow crinums in the South."

Greg is a no-nonsense kind of guy, and the following are no-nonsense plants. If your green thumb has been looking a little brown, these lists may be the place for you to start. If you fail with these flowers, consider taking up ceramics or some other hobby.

Hardiness zones are indicated for the perennial bulbs.

Super Tough Annuals
Copper Plant (*Acalypha wilkesiana*)
Mexican Heather (*Cuphea hyssopifolia*)
Ornamental Sweet Potato (*Ipomoea batatas* cvs.)
Bush Morning Glory (*Ipomoea fistulosa*)
Lantana (*Lantana* x *hybrida*)
Purple Fountain Grass (*Pennisetum setaceum* '*rubrum*')
Pentas (*Pentas lanceolata*)
Laura Bush VIP Petunia (*Petunia violaceae*)
Purslane (*Portulaca oleracea*)
Purple Heart (*Setcreasea pallida*)
Persian Shield (*Strobilanthes dyeranus*)

Eternal Perennial Bulbs
Canna (*Canna* x *generalis*), All

Crinum Lily (*Crinum* hybs.), CS, V
Byzantine Gladiolus (*Gladiolus byzantinus*), CS, V
'Kwansa' Double Orange Daylily (*Hemerocallis fulva*), All
St. Joseph's Lily (*Hippeastrum* x *johnsonii*), CS, V
'Tropical Giant' Spider Lily (*Hymenocallis caribaea*), CS, V
Snowflake (*Leucojum aestivum*), All
'Grand Primo' Narcissus (*Narcissus tazetta*), All
Campernelle Jonquil (*Narcissus* x *odorus*), All
Oxblood Lily (*Rhodophiala bifida*), C, CS, V

PENTAS

BULBS ALL YEAR ROUND

Sally McQueen Squire, who wrote *A Gardener's Guide to Growing Bulbs on the Gulf Coast*, has been growing bulbs in the Houston area longer than she will admit. "The one big piece of advice I have to give novice bulb gardeners is to build your garden beds high and fill them with good, well-drained soil full of humus and sand (if you garden in an area of heavy soil) and to select carefully your bulbs from ones known to grow in your area. Garden shops, nurseries, and catalogs are full of beautiful pictures of bulb flowers, but they cannot always tell you if those particular bulbs will grow in your garden. Know your own garden, know your bulbs, and you cannot go wrong. Bulbs are very forgiving, if given half the chance."

The bulbs in this list by Sally are arranged by season of bloom. Be sure to investigate the specific needs for these bulbs and when to plant them, so that they will bloom in the proper season.

Winter (December–February)
Amaryllis (*Hippeastrum*)
Cyclamen
Dutch, Roman Hyacinths
    (*Hyacinthus*)
Leucojum
Tazettas Narcissus (*Narcissus*)
    'Paperwhite'
    'Chinese Sacred Lily'
    'Soleil d'Or'
    'Geranium'
Early-Blooming Narcissus (*Narcissus*)
    'Avalanche'
    'Barret Browning'
    'Erlicheer'
    'Golden Harvest'
    'Jack Snipe'
    'Tete à Tete'
'Apricot Beauty' Single Early
    Tulip (*Tulipa*)
Emperor Series Fosteriana Tulip
    (*Tulipa*)

Spring (March–May)
Amaryllis (*Hippeastrum*)
Anemone
Calla
Clivia
Crinodonna
Crocus
Cyclamen
Dahlia
Eucharis

Freesia
Gladiolus
Gloriosa Lily (*Gloriosa*)
Dutch, Louisiana, Bearded Iris
    (*Iris*)
Ixia
Leucojum
Lily (*Lilium*)
Muscari
Nerine
Ornithogalum
Ranunculus
Scilla (*Scilla campanulata,
    S. peruviana*)
Sparaxis
Triteleia uniflora
Tulip (*Tulipa*)
    Darwin Hybrid
    Triumph
    Single and Double Late
    Lily-Flowering
Veltheimia
Watsonia

Summer (June–August)
Achimenes
Acidanthera
Agapanthus
Allium
Alstroemeria
Bletilla
Caladium
Canna
Crinum

Crocosmia
Eucomis
Gingers
Gladiolus
Haemanthus
Hemerocallis
Hosta
Hymenocallis
Lily (*Lilium*)
Montbretia (*Crocosmia*)
Oxalis
Rain Lily (*Zephyranthes, Habranthus*)
Sprekelia
Tigridia
Tritonia
Tulbaghia

Fall (September–November)
Allium
Caladium
Canna
Colchicum
Crinum
Lycoris
Oxalis
Sternbergia

All-Year Backbone Bulbs
Aspidistra
Liriope
Monkey Grass (*Ophiopogon*)
Rain Lily (*Zephyranthes, Habranthus*)

PERENNIALS

The perennial border as one might experience it in New England or the Pacific Northwest isn't as widespread in Texas landscapes. It's possible to have a beautiful perennial border here, but it will usually come at a different time of the year than it will in other parts of the country. Let's face it: Midsummer weather almost anywhere in Texas is unpleasant. Some hot weather devotees may disagree, but most people stay pretty close to the air conditioner in midsummer.

Our spectacular perennial displays come in late winter or very early spring. During mild winter years they may flourish again in the fall and early winter. Perennial beds almost always include annuals for seasonal color, too. Or we use perennials that are short-lived anyway, so they really function as annuals. (See the chapter on "Annual Color" for more plant ideas and for information on most bulbs.)

Basic Requirements
- Make a plan. Perennials vary significantly in height and spread. There's no point in placing a low-growing dianthus in the back of the border. Besides, this is the fun part. Lay out the bed to scale on graph paper and overlay tracing paper so you can doodle to your heart's content. When all is well, stop erasing and draw your final work plan.
- The gardener with the most compost wins! Build rich, organic planting beds using a minimum of 6 to 8 inches of compost, rotted manure, or the best organic matter you can find. Dig or till everything in and then send a composite soil sample off to the Texas A&M University soil testing lab in College Station (see the "Resources" section in this book). Based on the soil test, add any recommended fertilizer or lime and work it in before planting.
- Incorporate a low-volume irrigation system: drip irrigation, microsprinklers, microbubblers, or one of the leaky-tube systems. Then hook it up to a timer so you can go on vacation or water at night during water restrictions (assuming that's legal).
- Mulch, mulch, mulch! Mulch conserves water, keeps down weeds, keeps the soil cooler, and looks good.
- Plant the best varieties. This book should help you choose wisely, but don't hesitate to ask the plant enthusiasts in your area which perennials they recommend.
- Divide most perennials every two to three years. Daylilies and Louisiana iris quickly become overcrowded.

PERENNIALS FOR SUNNY BORDERS

Perennials might not seem to have the landscape tradition in Texas gardens that they have in other parts of the country, but sometimes we forget how many perennials we actually depend on. Some like salvias, Louisiana iris, and cannas are almost invasive. Others such as columbines (*Aquilegias*), black-eyed Susans, coneflowers (*Rudbeckia/Echinacea*), and pinks (*Dianthus*) fall into the short-lived category. They give us two to three seasons and then they are gone. If we're lucky, they reseed. Bear's-breech (*Acanthus*), peony (*Paeonia*), foxglove (*Digitalis*), and balloon flower (*Playtocodon*) may die without surviving their first Texas summer.

Bear's-Breech (*Acanthus montanus, A. mollis*), All
Yarrow (*Achillea millifolium*), All
Lily-of-the-Nile (*Agapanthus africanus*), CS, V
Agave (*Agave* spp.), CS, V

Garlic Chives (*Allium tuberosum*), All
Flame Anisacanthus (*Anisacanthus* spp.), Cw, CSw, V
Columbine (*Aquilegia* spp.), All

Butterfly Weed (*Asclepias tuberosa*), Ce, CSe
Hardy Blue Aster (*Aster oblongifolius*), All
False Indigo (*Baptisia australis*), All
Shrimp Plant (*Beloperone guttata*), All
Canna (*Canna* x *hybrida*), All
Chrysanthemum (*Chrysanthemum* spp.), All
'Nana' Dwarf Coreopsis (*Coreopsis auriculata*), Ce, CSe
Coreopsis (*Coreopsis grandiflora*), All
Montbretia (*Crocosmia* spp.), CS, V
'David Verity' Cigar Plant (*Cuphea* x *hybrida*), V, Annual
Sotol (*Dasylirion texanum*), All
Pink (*Dianthus* spp.), All
Foxglove (*Digitalis*) spp., C, CS
Purple Coneflower (*Echinacea purpurea*), All
Perennial Ageratum (*Eupatorium coelestinum*), All
Blanket Flower (*Gaillardia* x *grandiflora*), All
Gaura (*Gaura lindheimeri*), All
Byzantine Gladiolus (*Gladiolus byzantinus*), All
Swamp Sunflower (*Helianthus angustifolius*), Ce, CSe
Maximilian Sunflower (*Helianthus maximiliani*), All
Downy Sunflower (*Helianthus mollis*), CS, V
Daylily (*Hemerocallis* x *hybrida*), All
Red Yucca (*Hesperaloe parviflora*), All
Hardy Hibiscus (*Hibiscus moscheutos, H. coccineus, H. grandiflorus*), Ce, Cse
Confederate Rose (*Hibiscus mutabilis*), CSs, V
Sedum (*Hylotelephium* [*Sedum*] *spectabile*), All
Giant Star Grass (*Hypoxis decumbens*), C, CS, V
Louisiana Copper Iris (*Iris fulva*), All
Bearded Iris (*Iris* x *hybrida*), N, Cw, CSw

FOXGLOVE

Lantana (*Lantana* x *hybrida*), CS, V, Annual
Snowflake (*Leucojum aestivum*), N, C, CS
Gayfeather (*Liatris* spp.), All
Blue Baby-Tears, Angel Tears (*Lindernia grandiflora* [*Ilysanthes floribunda*]), C, CS, V
Loosestrife (*Lythrum virgatum*), N, C, CS
Horse Mint (*Monarda* spp.), All
Bear Grass (*Nolina texana*), CS, V
Wood-Sorrel (*Oxalis crassipes*), All
Peony (*Paeonia* x *hybrida*), N, C
Rock Rose (*Pavonia lasiopetala*), All
Penstemon (*Penstemon* spp.), All
Russian Sage (*Perovskia atriplicifolia*), N, C, CS
Phlox (*Phlox* spp.), All
Obedient Plant (*Physostegia virginiana*), All
Balloon Flower (*Platyocodon* spp.), All
Plumbago (*Plumbago auriculata* [*capensis*]), CSs, V
Mexican Oregano (*Poliomentha longiflora*), CS, V
Oxblood Lily (*Rhodophiala bifida*), C, CS, V
Black-Eyed Susan (*Rudbeckia fulgida*), All
Mexican Petunia (*Ruellia* spp.), All
Salvia, Sage (*Salvia* spp.), All
Mexican Mint Marigold (*Tagetes lucida*), CSs, V, Annual
Verbena (*Verbena* spp.), All
'Blue Princess' Verbena (*Verbena* x *hybrida*), All
Ironweed (*Vernonia altissima, V. baldwinii, V. lindheimeri*), All
Speedwell (*Veronica* spp.), N, C, CS
Yucca (*Yucca* spp.), All
Rain Lily (*Zephyranthes* spp., *Habranthus* spp.), C, CS, V

DROUGHT-TOLERANT PERENNIALS

Every gardener in Texas at some time faces a drought. Even in the rainy eastern third of the state, summers are quite dry. This list of drought-tolerant plants is from Linda Gay, chief horticulturist at the Mercer Arboretum in Humble. These perennials can take it once established, but don't presume you can plant them, water them in, and walk away. They will need regular watering for the first growing season, and a mulch would help to conserve moisture.

Yarrow (*Achillea millifolium*), All
African Mallow (*Anisodontea hypomandarum*), CSs, V
Silver King Artemisia (*Artemisia ludoviciana*), N, Cw, CSw
Indigo (*Baptisia australis* 'alba'), All
Bulbine (*Bulbinopsis* spp.), CS, V
Bird-of-Paradise (*Caesalpinia gilliesii*), CSs, V
Pride-of-Barbados (*Caesalpinia pulcherrima*), CSs, V
Square-Stemmed Primrose (*Calylophus* spp.), N, Cw, CSw, V

Garden Pinks (*Dianthus plumarius*), All
Coral Bean (*Erythrina herbacea*), All
Blanket Flower (*Gaillardia* x *grandiflora*), All
'Dauphine Island,' 'Siskiyou Pink,' 'Whirling Butterflies' Gaura (*Gaura*), All
White Gaura (*Gaura lindheimeri*), All
Sculptural Pinwheel (*Hectia texensis*), CSs, V
Rough-Leaf Sunflower (*Heliopsis hirsutus*), All
Red Yucca (*Hesperaloe parviflora*), All
Pink Indigo (*Indigofera kirilowii*), CSe
Mexican Morning Glory (*Ipomoea fistulosa*), CSs, V

Bush Lantana (*Lantana camara, L. horrida*), CS, V, Annual

'Irene,' 'Dallas Red,' 'Silver Mound' Lantana (*Lantana* hyb.) , CS, V, Annual

'Delhomme White' Dwarf Lantana (*Lantana* hyb.), CS, V, Annual

Lantana (*Lantana montevidensis*), CS, V, Annual

Manfreda (*Manfreda* spp.), Cs, CS, V

Bear Grass (*Nolina texana*), CS, V

Yellow Evening Primrose (*Oenothera drummondii*), C, CS, V

Pink Evening Primrose (*Oenothera speciosa*), All

Garden Phlox (*Phlox paniculata*), All

Arkansas Phlox (*Phlox pilosa*), Ce, CSe

'Goldsturm' Rudbeckia (*Rudbeckia fulgida*), ⏷

Giant Coneflower (*Rudbeckia maxima*), Ce, (

Silver Sage (*Salvia argentea*), CSw, V

Autumn Sage (*Salvia greggii*), All

'Butterfly Blue' Pincushion Flower (*Scabiosa columbaria*), C, CS

Wooly Stemodia (*Stemodia tomentosa*), All

Copper Canyon Daisy (*Tagetes lemmonii*), CSs, V, Annual

Yucca (*Yucca* spp.), All

"Most perennials greatly benefit from fall planting," advises Dawn Parish, a research associate working on ornamental crops evaluation with the SFA Mast Arboretum, Stephen F. Austin State University, Nacogdoches. **"When planted in the fall, perennials are able to establish their roots well before the hostile conditions of the summer arrive. This doesn't mean you won't have to water in the summer, but perennials planted in the fall won't be as susceptible to drought stress as ones planted in the spring."** Dawn recommends planting perennials after the summer heat subsides and at least four to six weeks before expected freezes.

THE MOST POPULAR DAYLILIES IN TEXAS

Daylilies, also known by their scientific name, *Hemerocallis*, are immensely popular. They are easy to grow, they produce bushels of flowers in a wide variety of colors, and the flowers are even edible. The following daylilies are Texas favorites, based on an American Hemerocallis Society (AHS) poll. At the AHS website, www.daylilies.org, you can find more information about these plants and information about visiting display gardens in your area.

The daylilies in this list from Diane Ballentine, a Harris County Master Gardener, are adapted to just about all of Texas, although adding organic matter and lots of water will be a must in most areas of West Texas. Plants marked with an (S) are semi-evergreen, and those marked with an (E) are evergreen. The rest go completely dormant.

Always Afternoon (S)	mauve with purple eye	early
Barbara Mitchell (S)	pink	mid-season
Bright Eyed (E)	yellow with purple eye	mid-season
Daring Dilemma (S)	pink with plum eye	mid-season
Dragon's Eye (S)	pink with red eye	mid to late season
Elizabeth Salter (S)	pink	mid-season
Jason Salter (E)	yellow with purple eye	early to mid-season
Jedi Dot Pierce (S)	pink with rose eye	early to mid-season
Jolyene Nichole (E)	rose blend	mid-season
Midnight Magic (E)	red	early to mid-season
Paper Butterfly (S)	peach with violet eye	early
Pirate's Patch (E)	cream with purple eye	early to mid-season
Smoky Mountain Autumn	rose with lavender halo	early
Strawberry Candy (S)	pink with red eye	early to mid-season
Texas Sunlight	gold	mid-season
Touched By Midas (E)	gold	early to mid-season
True Pink Beauty (E)	pink	mid-season
Wedding Band (S)	cream with yellow edge	mid-season
Wind Frills (E)	pink	early to mid-season

"Daylilies make wonderful perennials. They're easy to grow, many have evergreen foliage, and they produce loads of flowers in a myriad of colors. One of my favorite variety names is 'Concrete Blond' because it so aptly describes the toughness and ease of culture associated with daylilies."
—Diane Ballentine, Harris County Master Gardener, Houston

SHADE-PERFORMING PERENNIALS

Shade plants still need some light for growth, so pruning and removal of native trees will allow more sunlight to penetrate for maximum performance. Other factors to consider are competition from tree roots, soil fertility, and the amount of organic matter in the soil.

This list of perennials that do well in shady areas of the garden is from Linda Gay, chief horticulturist with the Mercer Arboretum, Humble. She notes, "Shade beds are often built underneath mature trees whose feeder roots can fill the bed quickly, being very opportunistic! The more a bed is amended by adding compost, not only do the shade plants benefit, but the tree or shrub roots respond very quickly to fill up the new soil area with feeder roots. Tilling with a small Mantis-type tiller helps keep the roots at bay. Competition can be fierce with smaller plants growing in the root zone of large trees. Any time I plant in shade beds, I use my tiller to remove the roots, amend with compost or mulch, plant, and water in with a cocktail of Superthrive and Peters 15-30-30, giving the new plants a really good start. In beds that are completely planted, spring tilling around the plants will stimulate new growth and vigor of the existing plants."

For more plants that do well in shade, also see Linda's list of "Perennials That Thrive in Wet, Shady Areas."

Bush Ardisia (*Ardisia crenata*), CS, V
Cast-Iron Plant (*Aspidistra elatior*), C, CS, V
Hardy Begonia (*Begonia grandis*), C, CS, V
Ground Orchid (*Bletilla striata*), All
Palm Grass (*Curculigo capitata*), CS, V
Butterfly Iris (*Dietes bicolor, D. vegeta*), CSs, V
'Orange Drop' Dietes (*Dietes vegeta*), CSs, V
Snow Poppy (*Eomecon chionantha*), All
'Claridge Druce' (*Geranium* x *oxonianum*), N, C, CS
Rain Lily (*Habranthus robustus*), C, CS, V
Yellow-Eyed Grass (*Hypoxis hirsuta*), All
'Nada' Crested Iris (*Iris japonica*), CSs, V
'Thelma's Pink' Jacobinia (*Justicia carnea*), CS, V

'Silverspot,' 'Alva,' 'Satin Checks,' 'Mansonii' Peacock Ginger (*Kaempferia* hybs.), CS, V
Asian Crocus (*Kaempferia rotunda*), CS, V
Cardinal Flower (*Lobelia cardinalis*), All
Native Turk's-Cap (*Malvaviscus arboreus* 'drummondii'), All
Firespike (*Odontonema strictum*), CSs, V, Annual
Root-Beer Plant (*Piper auritum*), CSs, V
Perennial Foxglove (*Rehmannia angulata*), CS
Lipstick Sage (*Salvia miniata*), V, Annual
Strawberry Geranium (*Saxifraga stolonifera*), N, C, CS
Toad Lily (*Tricyrtis formosana*), All
Hairy Toad Lily (*Tricyrtis hirta*), N, C, CS

PERENNIALS THAT THRIVE IN WET, SHADY AREAS

Linda Gay, chief horticulturist with the Mercer Arboretum in Humble, provided this list. Garden areas that are both wet and shady are very difficult to work with. Shady sites need sun for plant growth, so tree removal, thinning, and pruning may be required to allow sun to filter through all day or at least create a four-hour window of direct light for maximum plant performance. Most of the plants on this list are evergreen year round and will adapt to sunnier areas. Plants marked with an asterisk (*) will grow directly in water. (Also see the list of "Perennials That Tolerate Boggy Conditions.")

Variegated Sweetflag (*Acorus calamus 'variegatus'*),* All
Japanese Sweetflag (*Acorus gramineus 'variegatus'*),* All

Dwarf Golden Acorus (*Acorus minimus 'aureus'*),* All
'Pink Sunset,' 'Tropicana,' 'Pretoria' Canna (*Canna* hyb.),* All

Birdfoot Sedge (*Carex conica*), All
Blue Sedge (*Carex glauca*), All
Inland Sea Oats (*Chasmanthium latifolium*), All
Elephant Ears (*Colocasia esculenta*), CS, V
Umbrella Grass (*Cyperus alternifolius*),* CS, V, Annual
Joe Pye Weed (*Eupatorium maculatum*), All
Snakeroot (*Eupatorium rugosum*), All
White Butterfly Ginger (*Hedychium coronarium*),* Cs, CS, V
Spider Lily (*Hymenocallis liriosme*),* C, CS, V
Louisiana Copper Iris (*Iris fulva*),* All
Fleur-de-Lis (*Iris pseudacorus*),* All

Marsh Mallow (*Kosteletzkya virginica*), All
Cardinal Flower (*Lobelia cardinalis*), All
Creeping Jenny (*Lysimachia nummularia*),* All
Flamingo Plant, Water Celery (*Oenanthe javanica* 'Flamingo'), N, C, CS
Ribbon Grass (*Phalaris arundinacea* 'variegata'), All
'Chi-Chi,' 'Katie's Compact' Ruellia (*Ruellia brittoniana*),* C, CS, V
Bog Sage (*Salvia uliginosa*), C, CS, V

CARDINAL
FLOWER

PERENNIALS FOR THE HIGH PLAINS

The northern West Texas High Plains area presents some special conditions that need to be incorporated into any garden plan, but the area also produces long seasons of color in the garden and a place for birds and other wildlife, as well as a place where garden lovers can perfect their craft. This area is a transition zone and sometimes gets an extra measure of whatever weather condition is passing through. Planting species that require extra cold on the north side of the house and those which need more warmth when temperatures become cold on the south can widen the selection of plant materials available to the gardener.

The water supply as well as the quality have become key issues. Selections that have performed the best are plants that use less water, are resistant to wind, and have sturdy blooms and foliage. Perennials have many of these characteristics, and some are just perfect for our sandy soil, weather, and water. The plants in this list are varieties that Judith Wilmington, a horticulturist with the Texas Tech Horticulture Gardens, has worked with over the years and found to be the most successful. These plants are also relatively available in area nurseries. It's always disappointing when plants are recommended for an area and yet aren't available.

Silvery Yarrow (*Achillea clavennae*)
Cloth of Gold (*Achillea filipendula*)
'Colorado' Yarrow (*Achillea millefolium*)
'Catlin's Giant,' 'Burgundy Glow,' 'Green,' 'Metallica Crispa Bronze' Ajuga (*Ajuga reptans*)
'Chater's Double Mix,' 'Single Mix,' 'Single Nigra' Hollyhock (*Alcea rosea*)
'Blue Bird,' 'Cardinal,' 'Texas Gold' Columbine (*Aquilegia*)
'Songbird' Hybrid Columbine (*Aquilegia*)
'Colorado Blue' Columbine (*Aquilegia caerulea*)
Sea Pinks, Thrift (*Armeria maritima*)
'Powis Castle,' 'Silver King' Artemisia (*Artemisia ludoviciana*)
'David's Choice' Artemisia (*Artemisia pycnocephala*)
'Silver Mound' Artemisia (*Artemisia schmidtiana*)
'Silver Brocade' Artemisia (*Artemisia stellerana*)
'Monch' Aster (*Aster* x *frikartii*)
'Black Knight,' 'Lavender,' 'Pink,' 'White' Buddleia (*Buddleia davidii*)
'Sungold' Buddleia (*Buddleia davidii weyeriana*)
'Nanho Blue,' 'Nanho Purple' Buddleia (*Buddleia nanhoensis*)
'Mme. Galen' Trumpet Vine (*Campsis* x *tagliabuana*)
'Tropical Red,' 'Tropical Rose' Canna (*Canna* x *generalis*)

'Red Valerian,' 'White Valerian' Jupiter's Beard (*Centranthus ruber*)
Dwarf Plumbago (*Ceratostigma plumbaginoides*)
'Nana' Coreopsis (*Coreopsis auriculata*)
'Domino,' 'Early Sunrise,' 'Flying Saucers,' 'Badengold' Coreopsis (*Coreopsis grandiflora*)
'Moonbeam' Coreopsis (*Coreopsis verticillata*)
Purple Ice Plant (*Delosperma cooperii*)
'Blue Butterfly' Delphinium (*Delphinium elatum*)
'Magic Fountains Mix' Delphinium (*Delphinium grandiflorum*)
'Encore,' 'Heather,' 'Sundoro,' 'Sunny Morning,' 'Yellow Sarah' Chrysanthemum (*Dendranthema* x *grandiflora*)
Yellow Foxglove (*Digitalis ambigua* [*grandiflora*])
'Excelsior' Foxglove (*Digitalis purpurea*)
'Strawberry' Foxglove (*Digitalis* x *mertonensis*)
'Magnus Purple,' 'White Swan' Coneflower (*Echinacea purpurea*)
'Bowles Mauve' Wallflower (*Erysimum* spp.)
Myrtle Spurge (*Euphorbia myrsinites*)
'Goblin' Gaillardia (*Gaillardia grandiflora*)
'Siskiyou Pink' Gaura (*Gaura lindheimeri*)
'Happy Festival,' 'White Festival' Gypsophila (*Gypsophila paniculata*)
'Texas Red' Yucca (*Hesperaloe parvifolia*)

'Palace' Coral Bells (*Heuchera micrantha*)

Stonecrop (*Hylotelephium* [*Sedum*] *brevifolium*)

'Silverfox' Stonecrop (*Hylotelephium* [*Sedum*] *reflexum*)

'Blaze of Fulda,' 'Green,' 'Tricolor' Stonecrop (*Hylotelephium* [*Sedum*] *spurium*)

'Vera Jameson' Stonecrop (*Hylotelephium* [*Sedum*] *telphium*)

'Flamenco' Red Hot Poker (*Kniphofia uvaria*)

'Hidcote Blue,' 'Munstead' Lavender (*Lavandula angustifolia*)

'Ester Reed,' 'Snow Lady' Shasta Daisy (*Leucanthemum* x *superbum* [*Chrysanthemum maximum*])

'Kobold Kansas' Gayfeather (*Liatris spicata*)

'Pixie Buff,' 'Pixie Butter,' 'Pixie Crimson,' 'Pixie Orange' Dwarf Asiatic Lily (*Lilium* x *hybrida*)

Statice, Sea Lavender (*Limonium latifolium*)

'Texas Purple' Honeysuckle (*Lonicera japonica*)

'Morden's Pink' Lythrum (*Lythrum virgatum*)

Brave Heart (*Malva sylvestris*)

Blackfoot Daisy (*Melampodium leucanthum*)

'Grandview Scarlet,' 'Marshall's Delight' Monarda (*Monarda didyma*)

Evening Primrose (*Oenothera berlandieri*, *O. missouriensis*)

'Pauline's Pink' Oxalis (*Oxalis crassipes*)

'Iron Cross' Oxalis (*Oxalis tetraphylla*)

Rock Rose (*Pavonia lasiopetala*)

'Husker's Red' Penstemon (*Penstemon digitalis*)

'Blue Spring' Penstemon (*Penstemon heterophyllus*)

'Pineleaf Beard Tongue' Penstemon (*Penstemon pinifolius*)

Russian Sage (*Perovskia atriplicifolia*)

'Louisiana Purple,' 'Clouds of Perfume,' 'London Grove' Phlox (*Phlox divaricata*)

'Alpha' Phlox (*Phlox maculata*)

'Bright Eyes,' 'David,' 'Starfire' Garden Phlox (*Phlox paniculata*)

'Texas Pink' Old-Fashioned Garden Phlox (*Phlox paniculata*)

'Summer Snow,' 'Vivid' False Dragonhead (*Physostegia speciosa*)

'Fuji Blue,' 'Sentimental Blue' Platycodon (*Platycodon grandiflorus*)

Potentilla (*Potentilla neumanniana*)

'Goldsturm' Rudbeckia (*Rudbeckia fulgida*)

'Chi Chi,' 'Katie's Compact,' 'Purple Showers' Mexican Petunia (*Ruellia brittoniana*)

Salvia (*Salvia greggii*)

Mexican Bush Sage (*Salvia leucantha*)

'Blue Queen' Salvia (*Salvia superba*)

Santolina (*Santolina virens, S. chamaecyparissus*)

'Blue Butterfly' Pincushion Flower (*Scabiosa columbaria*)

Pink Skullcap (*Scutellaria suffrutescens*)

'Icicle,' 'Rojin,' 'Lavender and Old Lace' Hen-and-Chicks (*Sempervivum tomentosum*)

Lamb's-Ears (*Stachys byzantina*)

Homestead Germander (*Teucrium chamaedrys*)

Trailing Verbena (*Verbena canadensis*)

'Fire of Peru' Verbena (*Verbena peruviana*)

'Sunny Border Blue' Veronica (*Veronica longifolia*)

Vinca (*Vinca major*)

'Royal Robe' Viola (*Viola odorata*)

"I am constantly amazed at how many plants are compatible with the High Plains climate and the long-lasting durability that is evident in the long period we are able to sustain color in the Texas Tech Horticulture Gardens."
—Judith Wilmington, horticulturist, Texas Tech Horticulture Gardens

A GINGER PRIMER FOR BEGINNERS

Gingers may be hot and spicy in culinary dishes, but they're even hotter in the garden. The peak season for gingers is June, July, and August, when most other plants have given up, dried up, and finally been pulled up! These plants thrive in our horrid heat and high humidity with no pest problems and virtually no care after proper bed preparation.

Linda Gay, chief horticulturist with the Mercer Arboretum, Humble, put together this introductory list of gingers and their characteristics. People are just discovering the wondrous beauty of these garden jewels. Some offer exotic leaf patterns with iridescent flowers, while others titillate the senses with their delicate perfume. Gingers have fleshy roots that allow them to overwinter in most of Texas, but these tubers will rot while in dormancy (during the winter) if not planted in well-drained soil.

The following is a beginner's list of gingers that you will find appealing and enchanting. They belong in the Coastal South (CS) and Valley (V) zones, and *Kaempferias* will likely survive in the lower half of the Central (C) zone. In other areas, they can be grown in porous ceramic pots sunk into the soil, then moved into the garage or greenhouse for the winter.

Dwarf Cardamom (*Alpinia nutans*)	18–24 inches	fragrant foliage
'Jungle Gold' Ginger (*Cornukaempferia*)	4 inches	ground cover
Crepe Ginger (*Costus speciosus*)	4–6 feet	red cone, white flowers
Variegated Spiral Ginger (*Costus speciosus 'variegatus'*)	3–6 feet	variegated foliage
Aussie Plume Ginger (*Curcuma australasica*)	6–8 feet	spring, summer bloom
Giant Plume Ginger (*Curcuma elata*)	6–8 feet	spring bloom, before foliage
Orange Brush Ginger (*Hedychium coccineum*)	4 feet	orange bottlebrush flowers
White Butterfly Ginger (*Hedychium coronarium*)	4–8 feet	white fragrant flowers
'Mansonii' Peacock Ginger (*Kaempferia pulchra*)	4 inches	ground cover
'Silverspot' Silver Peacock Ginger (*Kaempferia pulchra*)	4 inches	ground cover
Shampoo Ginger (*Zingiber zerumbet*)	4 feet	red cone

GLEN GRAVES'S FAVORITE LOUISIANA IRIS

According to Glen Graves, a Harris County Master Gardener in Houston, "It's hard to find a better perennial for East Texas than the Louisiana iris. If you add enough water and lots of peat moss or compost, you can even push its limit a good bit west of a line from Dallas to Houston, but moisture and an acid pH is necessary to insure good growth of this wonderful flower. Some gardeners have even gone to the extreme of digging a shallow pond, lining it with plastic, and filling it with an organic soil. The liner makes it easy to keep the soil wet even in a climate that is too dry."

Because Louisiana iris do most of their growing from October to May, Glen stresses that water, sunlight, and fertilizer during this period are critical. "Often beds that have deciduous trees will have enough light in the winter for Louisianas. During the summer it's important to keep up the watering during dry spells and cover the beds with mulch to keep the shallow rhizomes from baking. In late summer or fall, dig the extras and share them with friends."

Glen points out that there are a number of Louisiana iris breeders around the country, and one very successful breeder in Australia. "As a result, new varieties with different colors, different flower forms, and heights from 16 inches to chest high come out each year."

Acadian Miss	white	Handmaiden	pink
Bob Ward	very pale violet	Justa Reflection	lavender tones
Brazos Gold	rich yellow	Kirk Strawn	red
Bryce Leigh	lavender	Laughing Budda	yellow
Charlene Strawn	large purple	Mac's Blue Heaven	violet with white
Charlie's Tress	rose-purple	Marie Caillet	dark blue-violet
Clara Goula	ruffled white	Mighty Rich	ruby red
Colorific	purple with white	Mrs. Ira Nelson	blue-violet
Crisp Lime	white with green	Pegaletta	light purple
Delta Butterfly	pale rose-pink	President Hadley	golden yellow
Delta Dawn	lavender with apricot-pink center	Professor Paul	light lavender-blue
		Ruth Holleyman	soft blue
Dixie Deb	sulphur yellow	Sea Wisp	wisteria blue
Faenelia Hicks	medium rose		

"There seems to be no limit to the color range in Louisiana iris. Their colors include the purest form of red of any iris species. Purples and blues are the most common colors, but Louisiana iris also come in white, yellow, brown, and bicolor combinations. Flower forms vary from flat to flaring, and the flowers may be single or semidouble; sizes vary from 3 to more than 7 inches across. The flowers are produced on stalks from 1 to 5 feet tall. Though each flower lasts only a few days, the entire spike may be in flower for two weeks."
—Glen Graves, Harris County Master Gardener, Houston

SALVIAS FOR TEXAS

Sage advice from Suzzanne Chapman, greenhouse manager of the Harris County Mercer Arboretum: There are salvias for all Texas gardens. Many are Texas natives but some of the perennials have to be treated as annuals in the northern (N) part of the state. Salvias are in the mint family, *Lamiaceae*, and while their flowers are scent free, most have fragrant foliage. With flowers that vary from deep, rich blues to pale corals, this genus offers lots of variety in color and form. Some of the herbaceous plants tower at 6 feet. Forsythia sage (*Salvia madrensis*) can reach 7 feet tall. Others are ground covers, such as bicolor sage (*Salvia sinaloensis*), which has dark blue flowers and wine-colored foliage. All attract butterflies, bees, and hummingbirds. Another big plus is that neither the foliage nor flowers appeal to grazing deer or rabbits!

Flower color

Silver Sage (*Salvia argentea*)	white	CSw, V
Blue Sage (*Salvia azurea*)	blue	All
Eyelash Sage (*Salvia blepharophylla*)	rosy red	C, CS, V
Tropical Sage (*Salvia coccinea*)	red, white, coral	CSs, V, Annual
Pineapple Sage (*Salvia elegans*)	red	C, CS, V
Engelmann's Sage (*Salvia engelmannii*)	lavender-blue	C, CS, V
Mealy-Cup Sage (*Salvia farinacea*)	blue, white	C, CS, V
Jupiter's Distaff (*Salvia glutinosa*)	yellow with brown spots	All
Autumn Sage (*Salvia greggii*)	red, white, pink, purple	All
Anise-Scented Sage (*Salvia guaranitica*)	light and dark blue, purple	CS, V
Yugoslavian Sage (*Salvia jurisicii*)	violet-blue and white	All
Mexican Bush Sage (*Salvia leucantha*)	white, purple	CS, V
Canyon Sage (*Salvia lycioides*)	blue	C, CS, V
Forsythia Sage (*Salvia madrensis*)	yellow	C, CS, V
Mexican Sage (*Salvia mexicana*)	blue-purple	CS, V
Graham's Sage (*Salvia microphylla*)	red, pink	C, CS, V
Neurepia Sage (*Salvia microphylla*)	red	C, CS, V
Lipstick Sage (*Salvia miniata*)	velvety red	V, Annual
Garden Sage (*Salvia officinalis*)	blue	All
Mountain Sage (*Salvia regla*)	clear red	C, CS, V
Cedar Sage (*Salvia roemeriana*)	dark red	C, CS, V
Bicolor Sage (*Salvia sinaloensis*)	dark blue	CS, V
Van Houttei Sage (*Salvia splendens*)	maroon or red	CS, V
Scarlet Sage (*Salvia splendens*)	various	Annual
Texas Sage (*Salvia texana*)	blue	C, CS, V
Bog Sage (*Salvia uliginosa*)	sky blue	C, CS, V

"Many salvias bloom over a long period of time, so they blend well with old roses, daylilies, and grasses in mixed borders. Salvias look great featured in rock gardens with rain lilies (*Zephyranthes*) at their feet. Also try combining them with native composites like purple coneflower and black-eyed Susans. In addition, salvias are a natural in the herb garden with trailing oregano and thyme."
—Suzzanne Chapman, greenhouse manager, Harris County Mercer Arboretum, Spring

PERENNIALS THAT RESEED THEMSELVES

Plants that reseed themselves give us our money's worth or "lagniappe," which means something for nothing, and when working within a budget, this can be a great plus. Many perennials must be propagated asexually, as they are sterile or do not produce seed. An abundance of easy to propagate perennials in the garden makes for great swapping material with other gardeners. Garden folk call these "pass along plants." This list comes from Linda Gay, chief horticulturist with the Mercer Arboretum in Humble.

Peruvian Lily (*Alstroemeria psittacina*), CS, V
Columbine (*Aquilegia* spp.), All
Sea Pink, Thrift (*Armeria maritima*), N, C, CS
Hardy Begonia (*Begonia grandis*), C, CS, V
Blackberry Lily (*Belamcanda chinensis*), All
Inland Sea Oats (*Chasmanthium latifolium*), All
Oxeye Daisy (*Chrysanthemum leucanthemum*), All
Perennial Coreopsis (*Coreopsis* spp.), All
Purple Coneflower (*Echinacea purpurea*), All
Palm-Leaf Mist Flower (*Eupatorium greggii*), All
Texas Star Hibiscus (*Hibiscus coccineus*), CS, V,
 Annual

Philippine Lily (*Lilium formosanum*), C, CS
Cardinal Flower (*Lobelia cardinalis*), All
Rose Campion (*Lychnis coronaria*), N, C, CS
'Moudry' Black Fountain Grass (*Pennisetum
 alopecuroides*), All
Gulf Coast Penstemon (*Penstemon tenuis*), Ce, CSe
'Goldsturm' Rudbeckia (*Rudbeckia fulgida*), All
Cut-Leaf Coneflower (*Rudbeckia lacinata*), All
'Katie's Compact' Ruellia (*Ruellia brittoniana*), C,
 CS, V
Tropical Sage (*Salvia coccinea*), CSs, V, Annual
Stokes' Aster (*Stokesia laevis*), All

HIGH PLAINS DAYLILIES

Judith Wilmington, a horticulturist with the Texas Tech Horticulture Gardens, offers this list of hybrid daylilies (*Hemerocallis*) that do well in the West Texas High Plains. For other perennials that do well in High Plains conditions, see the list of "Perennials for the High Plains." For more daylilies, see "The Most Popular Daylilies in Texas."

Ann Warner
Autumn Red
Breathless Beauty
Chicago Apache
Flying Saucer
Frans Hals
Happy Return
Hazel Sawyer
Hyperion
Joan Senior
Lullaby Baby

Mary Reed
Morocco Red
Pardon Me
Pastel Pink
Purple Water
Rajah Orange
Star Struck Yellow
Stella D'Oro
Sunray
Wine Delight

DAYLILY

PERENNIALS FOR THE COASTAL BAY AREA

Coastal Bay regions are essentially those areas from Orange to Brownsville that are near the coast but don't include beachfront landscapes. These coastal areas are subject to salinity problems, high humidity, and at times horrendous rainfall as well as strong winds. Plants have to be tough to survive here outside of specially constructed microclimate gardens. The plants in this list, from Mark D. Fox, owner of Mark Fox Landscape Co. in Baycliff, are all good choices. Also see the separate list of "Perennials That Tolerate Bayside Conditions."

Low (under 3 feet)
Dwarf Cardamom (*Alpinia nutans*)
Columbine (*Aquilegia* spp.)
Calylophus (*Calylophus drummondii*)
Blue Carex Sedge (*Carex glauca*)
Chrysanthemum, Mum (*Chrysanthemum* spp.)
'Ryan's Pink,' 'Country Girl' Mum (*Chrysanthemum
 zawadskii*)
Damianita (*Chrysactinia mexicana*)
Crinum (*Crinum* spp.)
Perennial Dianthus (*Dianthus gratianopolitanus*)
Palm-Leaf Eupatorium (*Eupatorium greggii*)
Heart-Leaf Hibiscus (*Hibiscus cardiophyllus*)
Halberd Hibiscus (*Hibiscus militaris*)
Hybrid Amaryllis (*Hippeastrum* x *hybrida*)

Four-Nerve Daisy (*Hymenoxys scaposa*)
Gayfeather (*Liatris* spp.)
Manfreda (*Manfreda* spp.)
'New Look' Dwarf Pentas (*Pentas lanceolata*)
Russian Sage (*Perovskia atriplicifolia*)
Coneflower (*Rudbeckia fulgida*)
Eyelash Sage (*Salvia blepharophylla*)
Pink Skullcap (*Scutellaria suffrutescens*)
Stokes' Aster (*Stokesia laevis*)
Dahlberg Daisy (*Thymophylla* [*Dyssodia*] *tenuiloba*)
Verbena (*Verbena* spp.)
Rain Lily (*Zephyranthes* spp., *Habranthus* spp.)

Tall (3 feet and higher)
'Ella Mae' Lily-of-the-Nile (*Agapanthus africanus*)

Sky-Drop Fall Aster (*Aster patens*)
Hardy Blue, False Red Agave (*Beschorneria decosteriana*)
Angel Trumpet (*Brugmansia arborea*)
Ginger (*Curcuma* spp., *Hedychium* spp.)
Coral Bean (*Erythrina herbacea*)
Fragrant Mist Flower (*Eupatorium havanesis*)
Hummingbird Bush (*Hamelia patens*)
Hardy Hibiscus (*Hibiscus coccineus, H. grandiflorus, H. moscheutos, H. mutabilis*)
Jacobinia (*Jacobinia carnea*)
Loosestrife (*Lythrum salicaria*)
Native Turk's-Cap (*Malvaviscus arboreus 'drummondii'*)
'Sarabande' Miscanthus Grass (*Miscanthus sinensis*)

Seep Muhly Grass (*Muhlenbergia reverchonii*)
Firespike (*Odontonema strictum*)
Dwarf Fountain Grass (*Pennisetum alopecuroides*)
Purple Fountain Grass (*Pennisetum setaceum 'rubrum'*)
Blue Plumbago (*Plumbago auriculata [capensis]*)
Single Mexican Tuberose (*Polianthes tuberosa*)
Mealy-Cup Sage (*Salvia farinacea*)
'Indigo Spires' Salvia (*Salvia farinacea* × *longispicata*)
Anise-Scented Sage (*Salvia guaranitica*)
'Lollie Jackson,' 'Frank Jackson' Mexican Salvia (*Salvia mexicana*)
Copper Canyon Daisy (*Tagetes lemmonii*)
Mexican Mint Marigold (*Tagetes lucida*)
'Angustata' Yellow Bells (*Tecoma stans*)

PERENNIALS FOR BAYSIDE CONDITIONS

The extremes of wind and salt are especially severe close to the ocean. Palm trees, oleanders, and a few beach grasses are the typical plantings where landscapes are close to the beach, and there are even fewer adapted plants as landscapes near the oceanfront. "Think of creating microclimates when planning a bayside landscape," advises Mark D. Fox, owner of Mark Fox Landscape Co., Baycliff. "Use evergreen shrubs like elaeagnus, pineapple guava, Texas sage, Mediterranean fan palm, or sago palm to create a shield from the wind. Then use perennials like Texas pavonia, pink skullcap, zexmenia, or angelonia in front for interest."

Low (under 3 feet)
Lily-of-the-Nile (*Agapanthus africanus*)
Angelonia (*Angelonia salicariifolia*)
Bulbine (*Bulbine* spp.)
Coreopsis (*Coreopsis* spp.)
Crinum (*Crinum* spp.)
Mexican Heather (*Cuphea hyssopifolia*)
Blanket Flower (*Gaillardia* spp.)
Daylily (*Hemerocallis* spp.)
Dwarf Lantana (*Lantana* × *hybrida*)
Shasta Daisy (*Leucanthemum* × *superbum* [*Chrysanthemum maximum*])
Gulf Muhly Grass (*Muhlenbergia capillaris*)
Rudbeckia (*Rudbeckia* spp.)
Coral Blow Russelia (*Russelia* 'San Carlos')
Pink Skullcap (*Scutellaria suffrutescens*)
Mexican Feather Grass (*Stipa tenuissima*)
Society Garlic (*Tulbaghia violacea*)
Zexmenia (*Wedelia* [*Zexmenia*] *hispida*)

Tall (3 feet and higher)
Mexican Butterfly Weed (*Asclepias curassavica*)
Cigar Plant (*Cuphea micropetala*)
'David Verity' Cigar Plant (*Cuphea* × *hybrida*)
Hybrid Coral Bean (*Erythrina* × *hybrida bidwillii*)
Hummingbird Bush (*Hamelia patens*)
Shrimp Plant (*Justicia brandegeana* [*ovata*])
Lantana (*Lantana* × *hybrida*)
Mexican Turk's-Cap (*Malvaviscus arboreus* 'mexicanus' ['penduliflorus'])
Lindheimer Muhly Grass (*Muhlenbergia lindheimeri*)
Star Flower, Pentas (*Pentas lanceolata*)
'Chi-Chi' Ruellia (*Ruellia brittoniana*)
Coral Fountain Plant (*Russelia equisetiformis*)
Mexican Bush Sage (*Salvia leucantha*)
Bog Sage (*Salvia uliginosa*)
Silverbush (*Sophora tomentosa*)

"Plants that will tolerate the most brutal, right-on-the-bay situations include purslane (an annual), angelonia, wedelia, stemodia (a ground cover), bulbine, Mexican feather grass, lantana, silverbush (*Sophora tomentosa*), and Yeddo hawthorne (a tall shrub)."
—Mark D. Fox, owner of Mark Fox Landscape Co., Baycliff

FORT WORTH TRIAL GARDEN PERENNIALS

What would we do without places like the Fort Worth Botanic Garden? Not only does it display spectacular plants, but it also conducts wonderful plant trials. Though these results are reported for this specific garden, the plants on this list can be used across a wide area of North Central Texas.

	Height (inches)	Peak bloom
Hardy Blue Aster (*Aster oblongifolius*)	36	Oct–Nov
'The President' Canna (*Canna*)	48	Sept–Nov
'Dark Knight' Blue Mist Spiraea (*Caryopteris clandonensis*)	36	June–Sept
'Golden Gain' Tickseed (*Coreopsis*)	18	June–Sept
Tickseed (*Coreopsis rosea*)	12	July–Sept
'Moonbeam' Tickseed (*Coreopsis verticillata*)	10	July–Oct
'Zagreb' Tickseed (*Coreopsis verticillata*)	14	June–Sept
Hardy Ice Plant (*Delosperma cooperi*)	3	Apr–Oct
Gaura (*Gaura lindheimeri*)	24	Apr–May; Aug–Sept
'Corrie's Gold' Gaura (*Gaura lindheimeri*)	24	June–Nov
'Anne Arundel' Rose Mallow, Hibiscus (*Hibiscus*)	66	June–Sept
'Lady Baltimore' Rose Mallow, Hibiscus (*Hibiscus*)	72	June–Sept
'Lord Baltimore' Rose Mallow, Hibiscus (*Hibiscus*)	96	June–Oct
'Moy Grande' Rose Mallow, Hibiscus (*Hibiscus*)	72	June–Sept
'Red River' Rose Mallow, Hibiscus (*Hibiscus*)	66	June–Sept
'Brilliant' Sedum (*Hylotelephium* [*Sedum*] *spectabile*)	12	Oct–Nov
'Dropmore Purple' Loosestrife (*Lythrum virgatum*)	36	June–Sept
'Purple Spires' Loosestrife (*Lythrum virgatum*)	28	June–Sept
Blackfoot Daisy (*Melampodium leucanthum*)	12	Apr–Oct
Pink Oxalis, Wood-Sorrel (*Oxalis crassipes*)	10	Apr; Sept–Nov
Russian Sage (*Perovskia atriplicifolia*)	30	June–Oct
'Herbstonne' Black-Eyed Susan (*Rudbeckia*)	42	July–Sept
'Viette's Little Suzy' Black-Eyed Susan (*Rudbeckia*)	18	July–Aug
'Chi Chi' Ruellia (*Ruellia brittoniana*)	32	May–Sept
'Katie's Compact' Ruellia (*Ruellia brittoniana*)	9	June–Oct
'Victoria' Mealy Blue Sage (*Salvia farinacea*)	18	Apr–June; Sept–Oct
'Coral' Autumn Sage (*Salvia greggii*)	32	Apr–Nov
'Pink' Autumn Sage (*Salvia greggii*)	36	Apr–Nov
'Red' Autumn Sage (*Salvia greggii*)	30	Apr–Aug; Oct–Nov
'White' Autumn Sage (*Salvia greggii*)	32	Apr–May; Oct
Anise-Scented Sage (*Salvia guaranitica*)	42	May–July; Sept–Oct
'Indigo Spires' Perennial Sage (*Salvia*)	48	May–Aug; Oct–Nov
'Blue Queen' Perennial Sage (*Salvia nemorosa*)	12	Apr–June; Oct–Nov
'East Friesland' Perennial Sage (*Salvia nemorosa*)	8	Apr; Sept–Oct
'May Night' Perennial Sage (*Salvia nemorosa*)	12	Apr–Aug
'Snow Hill' Perennial Sage (*Salvia nemorosa*)	12	May–Nov
'Red Velvet' Perennial Sage (*Salvia*)	36	Apr–Oct
Pink Skullcap (*Scutellaria suffrutescens*)	14	May–Nov
Purple Heart (*Setcreasea pallida*)	18	Aug–Oct
Texas Betony (*Stachys coccinea*)	15	Apr–Sept
Mexican Mint Marigold (*Tagetes lucida*)	42	Oct
'Blue Princess' Verbena (*Verbena*)	18	May–Sept
'Evelyn Scott' Verbena (*Verbena*)	14	Apr–July
'Homestead Purple' Verbena (*Verbena*)	15	Mar–Apr; July–Aug
'Taylortown Red' Verbena (*Verbena*)	10	Apr–July
'Tiger Rose' Verbena (*Verbena*)	18	Apr–Oct

'Purple' Verbena (*Verbena tenuisecta*)	10	Apr–Oct
'Barcarolle' Speedwell (*Veronica*)	4	July–Sept
Zexmenia (*Wedelia* [*Zexmenia*] *hispida*)	18	June–Oct

"Ornamental grasses are absolutely beautiful in the landscape! They add wonderful texture and interest to a garden and require a minimum of care. They can be used as individual specimens or in masses or sweeps. They go beautifully with perennials and antique roses and could even be used in a bed of just grasses with their different heights, colors, textures, flower plumes, and spikes."
—Heidi Sheesley, president, Treesearch Farms, Inc., Houston

ORNAMENTAL GRASSES

Using tall, clump-forming grasses in the landscape is a relatively new idea for Texas landscape designers. Though this interest has been building for some time in other regions of the country, many of the grass species that flourish in New England don't last a year in Texas. Maidengrass (*Miscanthus sinensis*) works in most gardens north of the upper Gulf Coast. Pampas grass (*Cortaderia selloana*) and fountain grass (*Pennisetum alopecuroides*) also have their uses.

Most of these grasses will look better if they are sheared back in late winter. Some of the really tough ones like pampas grass may require a weed trimmer with a metal blade. Emerald zoysia (*Zoysia japonica* x *tenuifolia*), which is normally recommended as a turf grass, makes an excellent ground cover. When unmowed, it develops a wavy ocean-like characteristic that creates the appearance of a water feature in the landscape. Even when it turns brown in the winter, it has a nice appearance. In late winter, just before it starts to grow, mow it or use a line trimmer to renew it for the next growing season.

For more grasses, see the list of "Native Texas Grasses" in this chapter.

FEATHER REED GRASS

Variegated Sweetflag (*Acorus calamus 'variegatus'*), All
'Oborozuki' Sweetflag (*Acorus gramineus*), All
'Ogon' Sweetflag (*Acorus gramineus*), All
Dwarf Sweetflag (*Acorus gramineus minimus 'aureus'*), All
Broomsedge (*Andropogon virginicus*), Ce, CSe, V
Giant Variegated Reed (*Arundo donax 'variegata'*), All
'Karl Foerstor' Feather Reed Grass (*Calamagrostis*), N, C, CS
Carex (*Carex cherokeensis*), CS, V
Chocolate Grass (*Carex comans*), All
Blue Sweetflag (*Carex glaucescens*), All
Pampas Grass (*Cortaderia selloana*), All
'Silver Comet' Variegated Pampas Grass (*Cortaderia selloana*), All
Dwarf Pampas Grass (*Cortaderia selloana 'pumila'*), All
Umbrella Grass (*Cyperus alternifolius*), CS, V, Annual
Variegated Chinese Water Chestnut (*Eleocharis dulcis 'variegata'*), Container, protect
Eel Grass (*Eleocharis monteridensis*), CS, V

Horsetail (*Equisetum hyemale*), All
Sugarcane Plumegrass (*Erianthus giganteus*), Ce, CSe
Blue Fescue (*Festuca ovina 'glauca'*), N
Blue Avena Grass (*Helictotrichon sempervirens*), N
Galleta (*Hilaria jamesii*), N
Japanese Blood Grass (*Imperata cylindrica*), N
Maidengrass (*Miscanthus sinensis*), All
'Adagio,' 'Cabaret,' 'Cosmopolitan,' 'Goliath,' 'Morning Light,' 'Sarabande,' 'Yaku Jima' Maidengrass (*Miscanthus sinensis*), All
Porcupine Grass (*Miscanthus sinensis 'strictus'*), All
Variegated Maidengrass (*Miscanthus sinensis 'variegata'*), All
Bamboo Muhly (*Muhlenbergia dumosa*), C, CS, V
Burgundy Giant Fountain Grass (*Pennisetum* spp.), Tropical
Black Fountain Grass (*Pennisetum aloepecuroides*), CS, V
'Cassian,' 'Moudry' Fountain Grass (*Pennisetum aloepecuroides*), CS, V

Purple Fountain Grass (*Pennisetum setaceum* 'rubrum'), CSs, V
Dwarf Feathertop (*Pennisetum villosum*), CS, V
Ribbon Grass (*Phalaris arundinacea* 'picta'), All
Ruby (Natal) Grass (*Rhynchelytrum repens*), CS, V
Ravenna Grass (*Saccharum [Erianthus] ravennae*), CS, V

Giant Purple Fountain Grass (*Saccharum officinarum*), CS, V
Knotroot Bristlegrass (*Setaria geniculata*), All
Palm Grass (*Setaria palmifolia*), V, Annual
Vetiver Grass (*Vetiveria zizanioides*), V, Annual
Emerald Zoysia (*Zoysia japonica* x *tenuifolia*), CSs, V

"Native Texas grasses are my favorites—sometimes you find them in your own backyard. Otherwise they can be hard to find in nurseries. Check the native plant nurseries in places like Austin, New Braunfels, and anywhere else you see natives advertised. You never know where you might find a few grasses. In some cases you may have to harvest your own seed."
—Ruby Summers, Harris County Master Gardener, Spring Branch

NATIVE TEXAS GRASSES

Ruby Summers, a Harris County Master Gardener in Spring Branch, helped compile this list. Native Texas grasses are just being discovered and made available in the nursery trade. Gulf muhly (*Muhlenbergia capillaris*), with its spectacular pink blooms, no doubt inspired this interest, and hopefully Texas nurseries will continue to search out and propagate our native species. Most of the grasses on this list will look better if sheared back in late winter.

For introduced grass species that do well in Texas, see the "Ornamental Grasses" list.

Big Bluestem (*Andropogon gerardii*), N, Cw, CSw
Bushy Bluestem (*Andropogon glomeratus*), All
Split-Beard Bluestem (*Andropogon ternarius*), Ce, CSe
Longspike Silver Bluestem (*Bothriochloa saccharoides* 'longipaniculata'), Ce, CSe, V
Sideoats Grama (*Bouteloua curtipendula*), N
Blue Grama (*Bouteloua gracilis*), N, Cw
Inland Sea Oats (*Chasmanthium latifolium*), All
Canada Wild Rye (*Elymus canadensis*), All
Sand Lovegrass (*Eragrostis tricodes*), N, C
Curly Mesquite (*Hilaria belangeri*), All
Gray Rush (*Juncus effusus*), Ce, CSe
Ear Muhly (*Muhlenbergia arenacea*), C, CS, V
Gulf Muhly (*Muhlenbergia capillaris*), C, CS, V
Weeping Muhly (*Muhlenbergia dubiodes*), C, CS, V
Bull Muhly (*Muhlenbergia emersleyi*), CSw
Lindheimer Muhly (*Muhlenbergia lindheimerii*), C, CS, V
Seep Muhly (*Muhlenbergia reverchoni*), C, CS, V
Deer Muhly (*Muhlenbergia rigens*), C, CS, V
Bear Grass (*Nolina texana*), CS, V

Indian Ricegrass (*Oryzopsis hymenoides*), N
Switch Grass (*Panicum virgatum*), N, C, CS
Texas Bluegrass (*Poa arachnifera*), N
Little Bluestem (*Schizachyrium scoparium*), All
Burrograss (*Scleropogon brevifolius*), N, Cw, CSw
Yellow Indiangrass (*Sorghastrum nutans*), N, C, CS
'Sioux Blue' Indiangrass (*Sorghastrum nutans*), N, C, CS
Sand Dropseed (*Sporobolus cryptandrus*), N
Giant Sacaton (*Sporobolus wrightii*), N
Mexican Feather Grass (*Stipa tenuissima*), CS, V
Two-Flowered Trichlorus (*Trichlorus crinita*), Cw, CSw
Eastern Gamagrass (*Tripsacum dactyloides*), All

GRAY RUSH

"During our mild winters, 'Homestead Purple' verbena has been a semi-evergreen," says Steve Huddleston, senior horticulturist at the Fort Worth Botanic Garden. "During the growing season, shear this plant regularly to stimulate flowering. Pink skullcap (*Scuttelaria suffrutesens*) is a compact, tidy little plant that loves the heat. An occasional shearing keeps this plant looking especially nice."
    According to Steve, "*Salvia greggii,* autumn sage, is one of our best performers. It blooms especially strong in the spring and fall and lighter, though continually, during the summer." For a plant that looks particularly good in a xeriscape or rock garden, Steve recommends wedelia. "The holly-looking leaves of *Wedelia hispida* (formerly *Zexmenia hispida*) have a rough, sandpaper-like texture that I like. The small,

PERENNIALS THAT TOLERATE BOGGY CONDITIONS

Mark D. Fox, owner of Mark Fox Landscape Co. in Baycliff, recommends these tough perennials for wet areas in the garden. Most do well in shade.

'Oborozuki' Sweetflag (*Acorus gramineus*), All
Dwarf Golden Sweetflag (*Acorus gramineus minimus 'aureus'*), All
Daylily (*Hemerocallis* spp.), All
Louisiana Iris (*Iris* × *hybrida*), All
Cardinal Flower (*Lobelia cardinalis*), All

Tuckahoe (*Peltandra virginica*), All
Gulf Coast Penstemon (*Penstemon tenuis*), Ce, CSe
Obedient Plant (*Physostegia virginiana*), All
Bog Sage (*Salvia uliginosa*), C, CS, V
Calla Lily (*Zantedeschia aethiopica*), CS, V

DEER-RESISTANT PLANTS

Deer are beautiful animals, but they can be very damaging to landscapes—both rural and urban. Deer-resistant plants are often thorny, poisonous, or taste bad. Cactus and tough succulents are obvious examples. (See the chapter of "Tropicals, Succulents, and Exotics" for lists of cactus and succulents.) The plants on this list are resistant to damage from deer, but a very hungry whitetail will eat almost anything, including these. Deer also nibble on tender young shoots in the spring that they might not bother after the plants toughen up in the summer. Pay attention to where deer usually travel and avoid planting there if possible.

Bear's-Breech (*Acanthus mollis*), All
Yarrow (*Achillea* spp.), All
Lily-of-the-Nile (*Agapanthus africanus*), CS, V
Agave (*Agave* spp.), CS, V
Aloe (*Aloe* spp.), CS, V
Flame Acanthus (*Anisacanthus wrightii*), Cw, CSw, V
Columbine (*Aquilegia* spp.), All
Wormwood (*Artemisia* spp.), All
Cast-Iron Plant (*Aspidistra elatior*), C, CS, V
Bamboo (*Bambusa* spp.), CSs, V
Coreopsis (*Coreopsis* spp.), All
Crocus (*Crocus* spp.), N, C, CS
Sotol (*Dasylirion* spp.), All
Foxglove (*Digitalis* spp.), C, CS
Coneflower (*Echinacea angustifolia*), All
Freesia (*Freesia* × *hybrida*), All
Blanket Flower (*Gaillardia lanceolata*), All
Daylily (*Hemerocallis* × *hybrida*), All
Red Yucca (*Hesperaloe parviflora*), All
Iris (*Iris* spp.), All

Red-Hot Poker (*Kniphofia uvaria*), All
Bluebonnet (*Lupinus texensis*), C, CS, V, Annual
Manfreda (*Manfreda* spp.), Cs, CS, V
Blackfoot Daisy (*Melampodium leucanthum*), C, CS, V
Daffodil (*Narcissus* spp.), All
Bear Grass (*Nolina texana*), CS, V
Oriental Poppy (*Papaver orientale*), N, C, CS
Fountain Grass (*Pennisetum* spp.), All
Moss Pink (*Phlox subulata*), All
Mexican Poppy (*Romneya coulteri*), C, CS, V
Black-Eyed Susan (*Rudbeckia hirta*), All
Salvia (*Salvia* spp.), All
Santolina (*Santolina* spp.), N, Cw, CSw
Copper Canyon Daisy (*Tagetes lemmonii*), CSs, V, Annual
Mexican Mint Marigold (*Tagetes lucida*), CSs, V, Annual
Verbena (*Verbena* spp.), All
Wedelia (*Wedelia* [*Zexmenia*] *hispida*), C, CS, V

LINDA GAY'S GINGERS FOR THE HOUSTON AREA

Linda Gay, chief horticulturist of the Mercer Arboretum in Humble, contributed this list (as well as "A Ginger Primer for Beginners" elsewhere in this chapter). Gingers offer lots of variety. Shell gingers, *Alpinia*, range from 5 to 10 feet in height and have major landscape value due to their different forms, varying heights, and tropical foliage. This group blooms on previous season's growth in the spring, so select a site that will offer frost protection. If your plants don't freeze back, do not cut them to the ground.

Butterfly gingers, *Hedychium*, are the most fragrant gingers, and the flowers resemble butterflies. This group reaches a height of 6 to 8 feet in medium sun and 4 feet in full sun. Growing them in the full summer sun causes the foliage to bleach out to a yellowish-green, but this doesn't affect their flowers. They won't bloom if grown in too much shade, which causes them to grow horizontal to the ground; they need at least 4 hours of sun to stand up tall and bloom well. Butterfly gingers are very tolerant of wet or heavy soils, and some can adapt to aquatic situations, growing directly in the water.

Spiral gingers, *Costus*, are a very diverse group that includes sun lovers and shade lovers, and they range in height from 3 to 8 feet. Known as spirals for the spiral growth habit of the stems, some produce crepey flowers out of terminal cones, while others produce plastic-looking tubes. The cones are very attractive even after they have finished blooming. The flowers are not fragrant, but they are long lasting.

Dancing ladies, *Globba*, reach only 1 to 2 feet in height and are true shade lovers. They require morning or filtered sun, but no direct sun or the leaves will burn. Well-drained soil keeps the rhizomes from rotting in the winter while they are dormant.

The common edible gingers, *Zingiber*, have two types of growth habits: either erect with 1-inch narrow leaves, or arching with dark, glossy green leaves. Most *Zingiber* produce basal (from the ground) blooms in mid to late summer and contain a gel that is very fragrant and used in shampoos. Give them medium sun to afternoon shade.

More gingers are listed in the "Ferns and Ground Covers" and the "Tropicals, Succulents, and Exotics" chapters.

Shell Gingers

Pinstripe (*Alpinia formosana 'variegata'*)	pinstripe leaves, flowers on erect stems
Dwarf Cardamom (*Alpinia nutans*)	fragrant leaves, flowers on erect stem
Shell Ginger, Porcelain Ginger (*Alpinia zerumbet*)	white flowers, yellow or red throats
Variegated (*Alpinia zerumbet 'variegata'*)	yellow and green foliage

Butterfly Gingers

'Double Eagle' (*Hedychium*)	coppery flowers, fragrant
'Elizabeth' (*Hedychium*)	raspberry-pink flowers
'Gold Flame' (*Hedychium*)	lightly fragrant
'Hawaiian Pink' (*Hedychium*)	pink summer flowers
'Lemon Sherbert' (*Hedychium*)	yellow flowers, pink stamens
'Tara' (*Hedychium*)	vivid orange flower, red stamens
Red Butterfly (*Hedychium coccineum*)	red flowers resemble a bottlebrush
White Butterfly (*Hedychium coronarium*)	sweet fragrance
'Robustum' Ginger (*Hedychium coronarium* X *coccineum*)	variegated leaf
Yellow Butterfly (*Hedychium flavescens*)	yellow fall flowers
'Kahili' Ginger (*Hedychium gardnerianum*)	large yellow flowers, orange stamens
White Pincushion (*Hedychium thrysiforme*)	starburst flowers, wavy leaves.

Spiral Gingers

Costus amazonicus	green and white foliage
'Red Tower' (*Costus barbatus*)	red cone, yellow flowers
Costus curvibracteatus	orange waxy flowers, long terminals
'Green Mountain' (*Costus curvibracteatus*)	reddish-orange bracts, green tips

Oxblood Ginger (*Costus erythrophyllus*)	forest-green leaves, burgundy undersides
Costus pulverulentus	long orange/red flowers.
Crepe Ginger (*Costus speciousus*)	red cones, white crepe blooms
Variegated (*Costus speciosus 'variegatus'*)	soft, fuzzy leaves

Dancing Ladies

Purple Globe (*Globba globulifera*)	purple flowers, globe shape
Yellow Dancing Lady (*Globba shomburgkii*)	blooms constantly, reproduces readily
Mauve Dancing Lady (*Globba winitii*)	exotic purple and yellow bloom
White Dragon (*Globba winitii*)	solid-white bloom

Edible Gingers

'Milky Way' (*Zingiber*)	white cones
Zingiber mioga	single yellow flowers
Common Edible Ginger (*Zingiber officinale*)	green cones turn red when mature
Red Spotted Ginger (*Zingiber rubens*)	red and white spotted flowers
Shampoo Ginger (*Zingiber zerumbet*)	arching stems, dark-green foliage

"When preparing the soil for gingers, a good ratio of pine bark mulch (not hard-wood), compost or organic matter, and coarse sand will give you good aeration and soil porosity. Building beds for the first time, you would remove the turf, till the area to break up the existing soil, add the three amendments, and till in to create a well-drained soil. This practice should raise the level of the bed 4 to 6 inches, allowing quick establishment of plants. Taking the time to prepare good beds will reward you with an abundance of flowers, fragrance, and overall plant production. Always mulch your gingers in the fall with pine bark mulch or pine straw to protect rhizomes from potential winter damage."
—Linda Gay, chief horticulturist, Mercer Arboretum, Humble

A SAMPLER OF PERENNIAL BLOOM THROUGH THE SEASONS

These lists indicate the main season of bloom or the start of the season. Some overlap is likely.

Winter/Very Early Spring
Hardy Cyclamen (*Cyclamen hederifolium*)
Candytuft (*Iberis sempervirens*)
Summer Snowflake (*Leucojum aestivum*)
Daffodil, Narcissus (*Narcissus* spp.)
Moss Pink, Creeping Phlox (*Phlox subulata*)
German Primrose (*Primula obconica*)
Sweet Violet (*Viola odorata*)

Louisiana Iris (*Iris* spp.)
Yellow-Flag Iris (*Iris pseudacorus*)
Shasta Daisy (*Leucanthemum* × *superbum* [*Chrysanthemum maximum*])
Louisiana Phlox (*Phlox divaricata*)
Mexican Petunia (*Ruellia* spp.)
Verbena (*Verbena* spp.)
Calla Lily (*Zantedeschia* spp.)

Spring
Yarrow (*Achillea* spp.)
Columbine (*Aquilegia* spp.)
Oxeye Daisy (*Chrysanthemum leucanthemum*)
Coreopsis (*Coreopsis* spp.)
Pink (*Dianthus* spp.)
Coneflower (*Echinacea angustifolia*)
St. Joseph's Lily (*Hippeastrum* × *johnsonii*)
Iris (*Iris* spp.)

Summer
Angel Plant (*Angelonia angustifolia*)
Butterfly Weed (*Asclepias tuberosa*)
Crinum Lily (*Crinum* spp.)
Mexican Heather (*Cuphea hyssopifolia*)
Purple Coneflower (*Echinacea purpurea*)
Gaura (*Gaura lindheimeri*)
Firebush (*Hamelia patens*)
Daylily (*Hemerocallis* spp.)

Rose Mallow (*Hibiscus coccineus*)
Swamp Hibiscus (*Hibiscus militaris*)
Mallow (*Hibiscus moscheutos*)
Shrimp Plant (*Justicia brandegeana*)
Lantana (*Lantana* spp.)
Shasta Daisy (*Leucanthemum* x *superbum*
    [*Chrysanthemum maximum*])
Philippine Lily (*Lilium formosanum*)
Cardinal Flower (*Lobelia cardinalis*)
Native Turk's-Cap (*Malvaviscus arboreus*
    '*drummondii*')
Old-Fashioned Garden Phlox (*Phlox paniculata*)
Obedient Plant (*Physostegia virginiana*)
Plumbago (*Plumbago auriculata*)
Yellow Coneflower (*Rudbeckia fulgida*)
Black-Eyed Susan (*Rudbeckia hirta*)
Mexican Petunia (*Ruellia* spp.)
Sage (*Salvia* spp.)
Rain Lily (*Zephyranthes, Habranthus* spp.)

Autumn
Autumn Aster (*Aster oblongifolius*)
Tartarian Daisy (*Aster tartaricus*)
Philippine Violet (*Barleria cristata*)
Chrysanthemum (*Chrysanthemum* spp.)
Cigar Plant (*Cuphea micropetala*)
Hardy Ageratum (*Eupatorium coelestinum*)
Joe Pye Weed (*Eupatorium maculatum*)
Swamp Sunflower (*Helianthus angustifolia*)
Confederate Rose (*Hibiscus mutabilis*)
Showy Sedum (*Hylotelephium* [*Sedum*] *spectabile*)
Gayfeather (*Liatris* spp.)
Red Spider Lily (*Lycoris radiata*)
Oxblood Lily (*Rhodophiala bifida*)
Mexican Bush Sage (*Salvia leucantha*)
Goldenrod (*Solidago* spp.)
Sternbergia (*Sternbergia lutea*)
Copper Canyon Daisy (*Tagetes lemmonii*)
Mexican Mint Marigold (*Tagetes lucida*)
Toad Lily (*Tricyrtus formosana*)
Society Garlic (*Tulbaghia violacea*)

FERNS AND
GROUND COVERS

Ferns are a real mystery to most gardeners. We tend to imagine them growing in lush tropical forests, and thus we sometimes overwater them. Many ferns actually need dry spells, and most species want good drainage. Ferns create a subtle, almost understated effect. They contribute to a soothing, tranquil, green experience in the garden and give an impression of cool even when temperatures soar into the 90s F. Ferns are like the greenery in a flower arrangement. They complement the other landscape elements like annuals, perennials, and flowering shrubs, but they deserve a closer look for the textures, mood, and color that they contribute. Ferns may not produce flowers, but they have a feathery grace and lacy elegance that no other plant can duplicate.

Linda Gay, chief horticulturist of the Mercer Arboretum in Humble, compiled the fern lists in this chapter except for the staghorns, and there's something here for almost everyone: tall ferns, evergreen ferns, ferns for dry areas, even ferns that like sun (mostly morning sun).

Also in this chapter are lists of ground covers that do well in Texas. Gardeners never have enough ground-cover options. These are the plants that will grow where turf won't (because of too much shade), and they can be low maintenance. Ground covers can also be weedy, ragged-looking features in the landscape, so be sure you want and need a nonturf ground cover before you start planting. Ground covers won't take traffic the way turf will when it's growing in full sun, but turf won't take much traffic in heavy shade. If heavy shade is a problem, use the appropriate ground cover and construct necessary pathways with bark mulch, crushed granite, or other materials.

Ground covers should never be planted without extensive soil preparation. Start with a soil test (see the "Resources" section in this book). Even though these plants are often quite vigorous, they rarely have the ability to choke out the most persistent weeds. You may first want to spray the area to be developed as a ground-cover bed with a nonselective herbicide like glyphosate. This should kill most actively growing weeds, including perennials, but it won't destroy weed seeds. Preemergence herbicides labeled for landscape use will help to keep the weed seeds from germinating after you've planted the ground cover. Wait to incorporate these materials until you've tilled in 4 to 6 inches of organic matter (preferably compost) and 1 to 2 pounds of a complete fertilizer like 15-5-10 per 100 square feet.

Turf areas rarely benefit from this kind of soil preparation. Usually a builder hires the low bidder to level the yard and spread some sod. The leveling is often done with bank sand. This is a bad technique because it creates a loose, permeable layer (often over clay) that dries out quickly and won't hold nutrients. If you are having a house constructed, tell the builder you'll take the monetary credit and do it yourself. Work 2 to 4 inches of compost into the soil along with 15 pounds of 15-5-10 per 1,000 square feet (use a slow-release fertilizer or an organic, if you prefer). Then plant your grass and make plans for the "Yard of the Month" sign you'll be awarded on a regular basis. You should also have fewer pests to contend with and a deep-rooted turf that will be easier to water. If you mow regularly and don't pick up the clippings, you will find that fertilizing once a year in late spring should be adequate. See the "Texas Turf Grasses" list for more information.

LINDA GAY'S FAVORITE FERNS

Dwarf Hawaiian Tree Fern (*Blechnum gibbeum*), CSs, V

Australian Tree Fern (*Cyathea cooperi*), CSs, V

Vegetable Fern (*Diaplazium esculentum*), CSs, V

Shaggy Shield Fern (*Dryopteris cycadina*), N, C, CS

Lace Fern (*Microlepia strigosa*), CSs, V

Spreading Sword Fern (*Nephrolepis cordifolia*), CSs, V

Chinese Brake Fern (*Pteris vittata*), CSs, V

Japanese Beech Fern (*Thelypteris decursive-pinnata*), All

The following codes are used in most of the fern lists to describe how ferns grow. It is important to consider these growth characteristics before using ferns in the landscape.

CR Short, creeping rhizome that produces many fronds that appear as a tight, full clump.

R Long, creeping rhizome that spreads quickly to form extensive colonies.

CF Produces a crown with fronds out of the top of the crown.

CL Produces a clump, then spreads to produce another clump.

FERNS FOR DRY GROUND

Ferns are really tougher than most gardeners realize. These ferns will continue to look good even during periods of drought when other understory plants begin to show stress. They will also thrive with good growing conditions. Ferns on this list that are marked with an asterisk (*) prefer a higher soil pH.

Fern	Code	Region
Foxtail Fern (*Asparagus densiflorus 'meyeri'*)	CF	CSs, V
Asparagus Fern (*Asparagus densiflorus 'sprengeri'*)	CF	CSs, V
Ebony Spleenwort (*Asplenium platyneuron*)*	CL	N, C, CS
Hairy Lip Fern (*Cheilanthes lanosa*)*	CR	N, C, CS
Holly Fern (*Cyrtomium falcatum*)	CF	C, CS, V
Shaggy Shield Fern (*Dryopteris cycadina*)	CF	N, C, CS
Bramble Fern (*Hypolepis punctata*)	R	CSs, V
Lace Fern (*Microlepia strigosa*)	CF	CSs, V
Spreading Sword Fern (*Nephrolepis cordifolia*)	R	CSs, V
Wavy Cloak Fern (*Notholoena sinuata*)*	CR	CS, V
Purple Cliff Brake (*Pellaea atropurpurea*)*	CR	All
Bracken Fern (*Pteridium aquilinum*)	R	All
Chinese Brake Fern (*Pteris vittata*)	CF	CSs, V
Leatherleaf Fern (*Rumohra adiantiformis*)	CR	CSs, V
Arborvitae Fern (*Selaginella pallescens*)*	CL	CSs, V
Japanese Beech Fern (*Thelypteris decursive-pinnata*)	CF	All

FERNS THAT LIKE WATER

Most of these ferns like the soil environment to be moist but well drained. At least partial shade and a soil rich with decaying organic matter are also prerequisites. Many will grow along streams and ponds, a few in flood zones. Mosquito fern and water clover are aquatic plants.

For Moist Sites With Good Drainage

Fern	Code	Region
Five-Finger Maidenhair (*Adiantum pedatum*)	CR	N, C, CS
East Indian Holly Fern (*Arachniodes simplicior 'variegata'*)	CR	C, CS, V
Maidenhair Spleenwort (*Asplenium trichomanes*)	R	All

Autumn Fern (*Dryopteris erythrosora*)	CL	N, C, CS
Goldie's Wood Fern (*Dryopteris goldiana*)	CR	N, C, CS
Marginal Shield Fern (*Dryopteris marginalis*)	CF	N, C, CS
Leatherleaf Fern (*Rumohra adiantiformis*)	CR	CSs, V

For Moist Sites

Southern Maidenhair Fern (*Adiantum capillus-veneris*)	CR	Cs, CS, V
Walking Maidenhair (*Adiantum caudatum*)	n/a	CSs, V
Rosy Maidenhair (*Adiantum hispidulum*)	CR	CSs, V
Lady Fern (*Athyrium filix-femina*)	CF	N, C, CS
Japanese Painted Fern (*Athyrium niponicum 'pictum'*)	CF	N, C, CS
Toothed Wood Fern (*Dryopteris carthusiana*)	CF	N, C, CS
Japanese Climbing Fern (*Lygodium japonicum*)	n/a	C, CS, V
Climbing Fern (*Lygodium palmatum*)	n/a	Ce
Sensitive Fern (*Onoclea sensibilis*)	R	All
Cinnamon Fern (*Osmunda cinnamomea*)	CF	All
Royal Fern (*Osmunda regalis*)	CF	All
Sword Fern (*Polystichum munitum*)	CF	C, CS, V
Chain Fern (*Woodwardia areolata*)	R	All
Virginia Chain Fern (*Woodwardia virginica*)	R	All

For Swampy, Boggy Sites

Lady Fern (*Athyrium filix-femina*)	CF	N, C, CS
Mosquito Fern (*Azolla caroliniana*)	n/a	All
Water Clover (*Marsilea macropoda*)	R	All
Sensitive Fern (*Onoclea sensibilis*)	R	All
Cinnamon Fern (*Osmunda cinnamomea*)	CF	All
Royal Fern (*Osmunda regalis*)	CF	All
Marsh Fern (*Thelypteris palustris*)	R	All
Chain Fern (*Woodwardia areolata*)	R	All
Virginia Chain Fern (*Woodwardia virginica*)	R	All

"No matter what region of Texas you live in, winter protection of the roots and crowns of ferns is essential," advises Linda Gay, chief horticulturist of the Mercer Arboretum in Humble. "As ferns are frozen back or natural dormancy occurs, it is beneficial to leave the dead fronds on the plants. They act as a shield or insulator to the crown and to the root zone, protecting the plant from subsequent frost damage. Additional protection can be obtained by using pine-straw or pine-bark mulch, leaves, or peat moss; these items retain moisture in the soil in regions that don't receive winter rains, and they also help to keep a constant soil temperature in the root zone." Linda points out that ferns are shallow-rooted plants. She recommends top-dressing ferns with compost or humus twice a year during the growing season to add fertility and increase vigor and growth.

FERNS FOR SUN

Not all ferns grow in the deep, shaded forest. Many thrive on filtered sun, and most of the ferns on this list appreciate at least four hours of direct morning sun. The natives—sensitive fern, cinnamon fern, royal fern, bracken fern, and chain fern—as well as Japanese climbing fern and wavy cloak fern, will grow in full sun as long as they have ample soil moisture. This environment typically occurs along the edge of a stream or pond. If in full sun, sensitive fern, cinnamon fern, royal fern, and chain fern require a constant source of moisture, such as at the water's edge of a pond or creek.

Foxtail Fern (*Asparagus densiflorus 'meyeri'*)	CF	CSs, V
Asparagus Fern (*Asparagus densiflorus 'sprengeri'*)	CF	CSs, V
Japanese Painted Fern (*Athyrium niponicum 'pictum'*)	CF	N, C, CS
Silvery Glade Fern (*Athyrium thelypteroides* [*Deparia acrostichoides*])	CR	All
Toothed Wood Fern (*Dryopteris carthusiana*)	CF	N, C, CS
Log Fern (*Dryopteris celsa*)	CF	All
Goldie's Wood Fern (*Dryopteris goldiana*)	CF	N, C, CS
Japanese Climbing Fern (*Lygodium japonicum*)	n/a	C, CS, V
Lace Fern (*Microlepia strigosa*)	CF	CSs, V
Spreading Sword Fern (*Nephrolepis cordifolia*)	R	CSs, V
Wavy Cloak Fern (*Notholoena sinuata*)	CR	CS, V
Sensitive Fern (*Onoclea sensibilis*)	R	All
Cinnamon Fern (*Osmunda cinnamomea*)	CF	All
Royal Fern (*Osmunda regalis*)	CF	All
Bracken Fern (*Pteridium aquilinum*)	R	All
Chinese Brake Fern (*Pteris vittata*)	CF	CSs, V
Japanese Beech Fern (*Thelypteris decursive-pinnata*)	CF	All
Southern Shield Fern (*Thelypteris kunthii*)	R	CSs, V
Chain Fern (*Woodwardia areolata*)	R	All

EVERGREEN FERNS

Not all ferns are evergreen, and the region they're growing in makes a lot of difference. Ferns that are evergreen in Houston may survive in Dallas, but some will be frozen to the ground. Some ferns, such as the wood fern (*Thelypteris kunthii*), go dormant regardless of frost. Most of the ferns in this list, however, are evergreen most of the year.

East Indian Holly Fern (*Arachnoides simplicior 'variegata'*)	CR	C, CS, V
Ebony Spleenwort (*Asplenium platyneuron*)	CL	N, C, CS
Maidenhair Spleenwort (*Asplenium trichomanes*)	CL	All
Holly Fern (*Cyrtomium falcatum*)	CF	C, CS, V
Toothed Wood Fern (*Dryopteris carthusiana*)	CF	N, C, CS
Crested Shield Fern (*Dryopteris cristata*)	CR	N, C, CS
Shaggy Shield Fern (*Dryopteris cycadina* [*atrata*])	CF	N, C, CS
Autumn Fern (*Dryopteris erythrosora*)	CR	N, C, CS
Goldie's Wood Fern (*Dryopteris goldiana*)	CR	N, C, CS
Evergreen Wood Fern (*Dryopteris intermedia*)	CF	N, C, CS
Florida Shield Fern (*Dryopteris ludoviciana*)	CR	C, CS, V
Marginal Shield Fern (*Dryopteris marginalis*)	CF	N, C, CS
Christmas Fern (*Polystichum acrostichoides*)	CF	All
Tassel Fern (*Polystichum polyblepharum*)	CF	N, C, CS
Korean Rock Fern (*Polystichum tsus-sinense*)	CF	C, CS, V
Chinese Brake Fern (*Pteris vittata*)	CF	CSs, V
Leatherleaf Fern (*Rumohra adiantiformis*)	CR	CSs, V
Oriental Chain Fern (*Woodwardia orientalis*)	CF	CSs, V

FERNS FOR ROCK WALLS

Ferns tucked into rock crannies soften the effect of a harsh element like a wall. They also work great in a rock garden. The ferns listed here for moist rocks are particularly good close to waterfalls that provide an abundance of spray and evaporation. The ferns for dry rocks need lots of sun and a limited amount of moisture. Those marked with an asterisk (*) need alkaline conditions such as limestone or concrete. Alkaline soil between the rocks will also get the job done. The others grow in either neutral or acid soil.

For Moist Rocks

Southern Maidenhair (*Adiantum capillus-veneris*)	CR	Cs, CS, V
Five-Finger Maidenhair (*Adiantum pedatum*)	CR	N, C, CS
Ebony Spleenwort (*Asplenium platyneuron*)*	CL	N, C, CS
Maidenhair Spleenwort (*Asplenium trichomanes*)	R	All
Chinese Brake Fern (*Pteris vittata*)	CF	CSs, V
Arborvitae Fern (*Selaginella pallescens*)	CL	CSs, V

For Dry Rocks

Hairy Lip Fern (*Cheilanthes lanosa*)*	CR	N, C, CS
Wavy Cloak Fern (*Notholaena sinuata*)*	CR	CS, V
Purple Cliff-Brake (*Pellaea atropurpurea*)*	CR	All
Spider Brake Fern (*Pteris multifida* [*serrulata*])	CF	C, CS, V

Not all ferns are the delicate babies we think they are. With the exception of a few dry-land species, most need lots of fertilizer, and they are not too picky about where they get it. In other words 15-5-10 lawn fertilizer (no weed killers) will work as well as Peruvian bat guano. Lee Marsters, longtime garden columnist with the *Houston Post,* used to fertilize his staghorn fern (*Platycerium bifurcatum),* a tropical fern grown on cork or wood slabs, with ammonium sulfate (21-0-0). He simply mixed up a tablespoon per gallon and drenched the plant with it. The staghorn was magnificent!

TALL FERNS

Use these fern species for backdrops or accent plants. Try many different combinations with the tall ferns, such as rhizomatous and cane begonias, bromeliads, caladiums, alocasias, and plants with vertical spear-like foliage such as butterfly iris (*Moraea* spp.), aspidistra (*Aspidistra* spp.), crinums (*Crinum* spp.), and gingers. The tall running ferns can be kept in bounds by using 4-inch steel edging. This keeps them from running over other desirable plants in the landscape.

ROYAL FERN

Glade Fern (*Athyrium* [*Diplazium*] *pycnocarpon*)	CR	All
Silvery Glade Fern (*Athyrium thelypteroides* [*Deparia acrostichoides*])	CR	All
Vegetable Fern (*Diaplazium* [*Anisogonium*] *esculentum*)	CR	CSs, V
Log Fern (*Dryopteris celsa*)	CR	All
Florida Shield Fern (*Dryopteris ludoviciana*)	CR	C, CS, V
Bramble Fern (*Hypolepis punctata*)	R	CSs, V
Lace Fern (*Microlepia strigosa*)	CF	CSs, V
Giant Sword Fern (*Nephrolepis biserrata*)	R	V
Sword Fern (*Nephrolepis exaltata*)	R	CSs, V
Cinnamon Fern (*Osmunda cinnamomea*)	CF	All
Royal Fern (*Osmunda regalis*)	CF	All
Bracken Fern (*Pteridium aquilinum*)	R	All
Southern Shield Fern (*Thelypteris kunthii*)	R	CSs, V
Mariana Maiden Fern (*Thelypteris* [*Macrothelypteris*] *torresiana*)	CR	CSs, V

Ferns don't produce seeds. Instead they produce spores, which are a bit more difficult to start. Fortunately, a fern usually can be propagated by division or by tissue culture. Though most gardeners won't bother trying to grow their own ferns from spores, they often become concerned about the spore-bearing structures called sori. These structures, found on the underside of the leaf, may look like insect or disease damage. Ferns can have insect or disease problems, too, but they will be more random over the leaf surface. The sori are usually in rows or along the edge of the leaf.

TREE FERNS

Tree ferns can be grown along the lower Coastal South (CSs) and in the Valley (V). These ferns produce trunks like palms. The three listed here can be grown successfully in Houston and further south; you just need to know where to plant them and the care required.

Australian tree fern can put on 1 to 3 feet of trunk per year when happy. Locate underneath a tree canopy for shade in summer and frost protection in winter. A light frost will not kill this tree fern. Winter protection (covering) should be implemented during hard frosts. The Australian tree fern can be winter protected just as we protect banana trunks from freezing to the ground. Cut off the fronds to the trunk, wrap the trunk with fabric at least 1-inch thick, then cover with plastic and tie. Use pine-straw mulch around the base, piled about 1 foot, and tuck it up and around the base of the tree fern. This keeps the trunk from being frozen during periods of freezing weather.

The Tasmanian tree fern is very slow growing, coarse leafed, and very cold hardy (notice the species name). Due to its slow growth habit, if you want this tree fern with a trunk, you should purchase it with a trunk. It doesn't need winter protection, but it needs well-drained organic soil and plenty of moisture year round, even in the winter.

The dwarf Hawaiian tree fern likes to grow in filtered light or morning sun (with afternoon shade) in a well-drained soil. It produces a 6-inch slender trunk in about three years, spreading about 18 to 24 inches. It's rated for USDA hardiness zone 9, so it needs frost protection. Generally, you'll find this fern available only in small, 4-inch pots.

Australian tree fern (*Cyathea [Sphaeropteris] cooperi*)   Dwarf Hawaiian tree fern (*Blechnum gibbeum*)
Tasmanian tree fern (*Dicksonia antarctica*)

STAGHORN FERNS

The staghorns are tropical ferns that hang from trees in their native habitats. To simulate these growing conditions, gardeners tie them to slabs of wood or cork, or they can be grown in hanging baskets. They need protection in the winter, so you will need to bring them into the greenhouse or—in a pinch—keep them in the garage. In Far South Texas (Brownsville, Weslaco), staghorns may survive a mild winter outdoors. Staghorn fern (*Platycerium bifurcatum*), the most commonly used staghorn, is the most hardy and will stand brief dips into the 20s F, but others like the disc staghorn (*Platycerium coronarium*) don't like it when temperatures dip into the 50s. All of the staghorns like filtered sun through the trees or morning sun and afternoon shade.

Staghorn Fern (*Platycerium bifurcatum*)   Ridley's Staghorn (*Platycerium ridleyi*)
Disc Staghorn (*Platycerium coronarium*)   Australian Staghorn (*Platycerium superbum*)
Australian Staghorn (*Platycerium grande*)   New Guinea Staghorn (*Platycerium wandae*)
Elk's-Horn Fern (*Platycerium hillii*)

FERNS WITH COLORFUL FOLIAGE

Believe it or not, some ferns are quite colorful. The Japanese painted fern blends purples and lavender with its gray-green foliage. East Indian holly fern has a yellow band down the center of the leaflet. Others have distinct white bands. Cinnamon fern develops a beautiful orange fall color, while royal fern turns a beautiful golden yellow. This type of colorful foliage is short-lived because it occurs prior to dormancy, but it signals the change in seasons, a feature often lacking in southern landscapes. Japanese painted fern and autumn fern are evergreen.

East Indian Holly Fern (*Arachnoides simplicior*)	dark green with yellow band down center of leaflet	C, CS, V
Japanese Painted Fern (*Athyrium niponicum 'pictum'*)	silver, burgundy, and dark-green variegation	N, C, CS
Mosquito Fern (*Azolla caroliniana*)	turns red-purple in cold	All

Autumn Fern (*Dryopteris erythrosora*)	bronze new growth against darker green fronds	N, C, CS
Cinnamon Fern (*Osmunda cinnamomea*)	orange fall color	All
Royal Fern (*Osmunda regalis*)	golden-yellow fall color	All
Cretan Brake Fern (*Pteris cretica 'albolineata'*)	green, some with broad white midrib band	CSs, V
Victorian Brake Fern (*Pteris ensiformis 'victoriae'*)	variegated with white midrib band	V

FERNS FOR GROUND COVER

Turf grass and many ground covers aren't happy in dense shade, but most ferns are. These are the ones that spread rapidly, providing an easy-to-maintain greenspace where you might otherwise be left with bare dirt. Notice that most of these species are in the R category; they have long, creeping rhizomes that spread quickly to form extensive colonies. The ferns on this list that are marked with an asterisk (*) will grow in a swampy, boggy area.

Lady Fern (*Athyrium filix-femina*)	CL	N, C, CS
Glade Fern (*Athyrium [Diplazium] pycnocarpon*)	CR	All
Holly Fern (*Cyrtomium falcatum*)	CL	C, CS, V
Florida Shield Fern (*Dryopteris ludoviciana*)	CR	C, CS, V
Bramble Fern (*Hypolepis punctata*)	R	CSs, V
Spreading Sword Fern (*Nephrolepis cordifolia*)	R	CSs, V
Sensitive Fern (*Onoclea sensibilis*)*	R	All
Bracken Fern (*Pteridium aquilinum*)	R	All
Broad Beech Fern (*Thelypteris [Phegopteris] hexagonoptera*)	R	All
Southern Shield Fern (*Thelypteris kunthii*)	R	CSs, V
Marsh Fern (*Thelypteris palustris*)*	R	All
Chain Fern (*Woodwardia areolata*)*	R	All
Virginia Chain Fern (*Woodwardia virginica*)*	R	All

"There's a tremendous difference in the ferns that will grow in Houston and those that will grow north of the city in Montgomery County, seemingly only a few miles away. Ferns are a trial-and-error group of plants. Sometimes a species you think wouldn't have a chance will surprise you and flourish, especially if it survives a few years and gets established."
—Walter E. Hesson, president of the Texas Gulf Coast Fern Society, Houston

GROUND COVERS FOR THE COASTAL BAY AREA

A great deal is expected of ground covers. They are supposed to produce a lush vegetation cover, and they should be free of weeds. In some cases we expect them to do this in the shade. Near the bay, with salt spray and wind as factors to contend with, we're asking for even more. Mark D. Fox, owner of Fox Landscaping in Baycliff, recommends the following plants. According to Mark, these plants are tough but still appreciate good soil preparation. Before planting, mix 4 to 6 inches of organic matter with the soil, plus 2 to 3 pounds of a complete fertilizer per 100 square feet. Weed the bed diligently until the ground cover is established. Mark's list indicates the plants' sun or shade requirements.

Rosy Pink Yarrow (*Achillea* spp.), sun/some shade
Creeping Ardisia (*Ardisia japonica*), some sun
Asparagus Fern (*Asparagus densiflorus*), shade
Carex Sedge (*Carex* spp.), shade/morning sun

Inland Sea Oats (*Chasmanthium latifolium*), shade
Silver-and-Gold (*Chrysanthemum pacificum*), sun
Pink Ice Mum (*Chrysanthemum* X *morifolium*), sun
Pink Ice Plant (*Delosperma cooperi, D. nucifolia*), sun

Uruguayan Firecracker (*Dicliptera suberecta*), sun
Creeping Snake Herb (*Dyschoriste linearis*), sun
Palm-Leaf Eupatorium (*Eupatorium greggii*), shade/sun
Peacock Ginger (*Kaempferia* spp.), shade
Lantana (*Lantana camara*), sun
Dwarf Barbados Cherry (*Malpighia glabra*), sun/some shade
Dwarf Mondo Grass, Kyoto Dwarf (*Ophiopogon japonicus 'nana'*), shade/morning sun
Louisiana Phlox (*Phlox divaricata*), shade/some sun
Pinella (*Pinella tripartita*), shade/morning sun
Magic Carpet Polygonum (*Polygonum capitatum*), shade/sun with irrigation
Scurfy Pea (*Psoralea* spp.),
Pigeonberry (*Rivina humilis*), shade/some sun
'Chi-Chi,' 'Katie's Compact' Ruellia (*Ruellia brittoniana*), sun/some shade

'Blue Shade' Mexican Petunia (*Ruellia squarrosa*), shade
Lyre-Leaf Salvia (*Salvia lyrata*), sun
Bicolor Sage (*Salvia sinaloensis*), sun/some shade
Bouncing Bet (*Saponaria officinalis*), sun/some shade
Lizard's-Tail (*Saururus cernuus*), shade/morning sun
Strawberry Begonia (*Saxifraga stolonifera*), shade
Sedum (*Sedum* spp.), sun
Stemodia (*Stemodia tomentosa*), sun
Wood Fern (*Thelypteris* spp.), shade
Thyme (*Thymus* spp.), sun
Asiatic Jasmine (*Trachelospermum asiaticum*), sun or shade
Verbena (*Verbena* spp.), sun
Violet (*Viola* spp.), shade
Creeping Australian Violet (*Viola hederacea*), shade/some sun

 Before choosing a ground cover, be sure to check the amount of sun that a bed receives throughout the day. A sun-loving ground cover planted in a shady bed will become a real eyesore. Ground covers for full sun will require six to eight hours of sun to make good growth. On the other hand, shade lovers like *Ajuga* will melt away where they receive six hours of afternoon sun.

GROUND COVERS FOR FULL SUN

Landscape designers just can't get enough ground covers—they solve so many problems. Most of all they cut down on the high maintenance required to keep high-quality turf. They are also a valuable landscape element in terms of texture, color, and form.

Lots of plant types can qualify as ground covers: grasses, perennials, shrubs, roses, and vines. Emerald zoysia grass is a potential turf grass from the Gulf Coast south, but unmowed it makes a beautiful, wavy ground cover. It almost becomes a water feature. Even in the winter when it turns brown, it looks good as a ground cover. Try to mow it for turf and you better have a sharp mower because it gets tough and wiry in the summer, often looking worse after mowing than before.

The plants in this list are ones to choose as an alternative to grass. They have to be tough to survive in full Texas sun. English ivy can be a wonderful ground cover in the shade, but if you plant it in a sunny location in the fall, it will probably look great until the first summer. Then it will just gradually melt away.

DIANTHUS

Dwarf Abelia (*Abelia* x *grandiflora 'prostrata'*), All
Pygmy Bamboo (*Arundinaria* [*Sasa*] *pygmaea*), CS, V
Dwarf Variegated Bamboo (*Arundinaria viridistriata*), CS, V
Frikarti Aster (*Aster* x *frikartii*), C, CS
Compact Gold Calylophus (*Calylophus drummondii*), N, Cw, CSw, V
Dwarf Plumbago (*Ceratostigma plumbaginoides*), CS, V
Clara Curtis Chrysanthemum (*Chrysanthemum zawadskii*), C, CS
Green-and-Gold (*Chrysogonum virginianum*), All
'Early Sunrise' Coreopsis (*Coreopsis grandiflora*), All

Barberry Cotoneaster (*Cotoneaster dammeri*), N, Cw, CSw
Rockspray Cotoneaster (*Cotoneaster horizontalis*), N, Cw, CSw
Willowleaf Cotoneaster (*Cotoneaster salicifolius 'repens'*), N, Cw, CSw
Dwarf Umbrella Grass (*Cyperus alternifolius 'nana'*), CS, V, Annual
'Bath's Pink' Dianthus (*Dianthus gratianopolitanus*), N, C, CS
Elephant's Footprint (*Elephantopus tomentosus*), C, CS, V
Wintercreeper (*Euonymus fortunei*), N, C

Hardy Gynura (*Gynura bicolor*), CS, V
Daylily hybrids (*Hemerocallis*), All
Chameleon Plant (*Houttuynia cordata 'chameleon'*), N, C
Four-Nerve Daisy (*Hymenoxys scaposa*), CS, V
Creeping St. John's Wort (*Hypericum calycinum*), C
Star Grass (*Hypoxis stellata*), CSs, V
Sargent Juniper (*Juniperus chinensis 'sargentii'*), N, C
'Blue Pacific' Shore Juniper (*Juniperus conferta*), N, C, CS
'Blue Rug' Creeping Juniper (*Juniperus horizontalis*), N, C
Dwarf Juniper (*Juniperus procumbens 'nana'*), N, C
Trailing Lantana (*Lantana montevidensis*), CS, V
Blue Baby-Tears, Angel Tears (*Lindernia grandiflora* [*Ilysanthes floribunda*]), C, CS, V
Liriope (*Liriope muscari, L. spicata*), All
Golden Globes (*Lysimachia congestiflora*), C, CS, V
Maidengrass (*Miscanthus sinensis*), All
Siberian Catmint (*Nepeta sibirica*), All
Yellow Evening Primrose (*Oenothera drummondii*), C, CS, V

Fountain Grasses (*Pennisetum* spp.), All
Ribbon Grass (*Phalaris arundinacea 'picta'*), All
Moss Pink, Creeping Phlox (*Phlox subulata*), All
Three-Toothed Cinquefoil (*Potentilla tridentata*), N, C
Formosa Firethorn (*Pyracantha koidzumii*), All
'Katie's Compact' Ruellia (*Ruellia brittoniana*), C, CS, V
Bicolor Sage (*Salvia sinaloensis*), CS, V
Pink Skullcap (*Scutellaria suffrutescens*), Ns, C, CS, V
Stemodia (*Stemodia tomentosa*), CS, V
Creeping Thyme (*Thymus* spp.), All
Society Garlic (*Tulbaghia violacea*), CSs, V
Trailing Purple Verbena (*Verbena bipinnatifida*), CS, V
Moss Verbena (*Verbena tenuisecta*), C, CS, V
Zexmenia (*Wedelia* [*Zexmenia*] *hispida*), C, CS, V
Wedelia (*Wedelia trilobata*), CSs, V
Emerald Zoysia, unmowed (*Zoysia japonica* x *tenuifolia*), CSs, V

GROUND COVERS FOR LIGHT TO MEDIUM SHADE

Gardeners are always on the lookout for ground covers to use in the shade, especially in East Texas. This need can occur almost anywhere, however. Add heat and drought, and the challenge to find a suitable ground cover is daunting. Since trees are usually involved, it is important to water thoroughly. Microsprinklers in the ground-cover beds can do the job. A more tedious but almost as effective technique is letting a hose run slowly overnight, moving it daily until the area is soaked 10 to 12 inches deep. Lots of ferns will work as a ground cover for shady areas. A few are included here, but for more possibilities, see the fern lists in this chapter.

Many of the plants in this list can be used in the colder areas of Texas by treating them as annual ground covers. In North Texas, mondo grass (*Ophiopogon japonicus*) will need protection.

Carpet Bugleweed (*Ajuga reptans*), All
Yellow Columbine (*Aquilegia chrysantha*), All
Ardisia (*Ardisia japonica*), CSs, V
Cast-Iron Plant (*Aspidistra elatior*), C, CS, V
Horseherb (*Calyptocarpus vialis*), CSe
Holly Fern (*Cyrtomium falcatum*), C, CS, V
Wood Fern, Shield Fern (*Dryopteris filix-mas*), Ce, CSe, V
Epimediums (*Epimedium* spp.), C
Creeping Fig (*Ficus pumila*), CS, V
Dwarf Gardenia (*Gardenia jasminoides 'radicans'*), Ce, CSe
Carolina Jessamine (*Gelsemium sempervirens*), C, CS, V
Algerian Ivy (*Hedera canariensis*), CS, V
English Ivy (*Hedera helix*), All
Hosta (*Hosta* spp.), N, C, CS
Crested Iris (*Iris cristata*), CSe, V
Shore Juniper (*Juniperus conferta*), N, C, CS

Silver Peacock Ginger (*Kaempferia atrovirens*), CS, V
Yellow Archangel (*Lamiastrum galeobdolon*), N
Spotted Dead Nettle (*Lamium maculatum*), All
Blue Star Creeper (*Laurentia fluviatilis*), C, CS
Liriope (*Liriope muscari, L. spicata*), All
Golden Globes (*Lysimachia congestiflora*), C, CS, V
Creeping Jenny (*Lysimachia nummularia*), All
Barbara's-Buttons (*Marshallia caespitosa*), N, C
Purple-Flowered Mazus (*Mazus reptans*), C, CS
White-Flowered Mazus (*Mazus reptans 'alba'*), C, CS
Siberian Carpet Grass (*Microbiota decussata*), N
Partridgeberry (*Mitchella repens*), Ce, CSe
'Fire Power,' 'Gulf Stream,' 'Harbour Dwarf' Dwarf Nandina (*Nandina domestica*), All
Walking Iris (*Neomarica gracilis, N. longifolia*), CSs, V
Mondo Grass (*Ophiopogon japonicus*), All
Allegheny Spurge (*Pachysandra procumbens*), C

Japanese Pachysandra (*Pachysandra terminalis*), N, C

Virginia Creeper (*Parthenocissus quinquefolia*), All

Woodland Phlox, Louisiana Phlox (*Phlox divaricata*), All

'Magic Carpet' Polygonum (*Polygonum capitatum*), CSs, V

Gumpo Azalea (*Rhododendron 'gumpo'*), Ce, CSe

Pigeonberry (*Rivina humilus*), C, CS, V

'Katie's Compact' Ruellia (*Ruellia brittoniana*), C, CS, V

Strawberry Geranium (*Saxifraga stolonifera*), N, C, CS

Asian Jasmine (*Trachelospermum asiaticum*), C, CS, V

Common Periwinkle (*Vinca minor*), N

Creeping Australian Violet (*Viola hederacea*), CS, V

Sweet Violet (*Viola odorata*), N, C, CS

Wedelia (*Wedelia trilobata*), CSs, V

 Chocolate plant (*Pseuderanthemum alatum*) makes a good short-term ground cover, according to Kathy Huber, garden editor of the *Houston Chronicle*. "Clumps of silver-splotched brown foliage and racemes of small but brilliant purple flowers on tall, slender stalks in mid and late summer are what make this shade-garden candidate distinctive. Total height is 12 to 18 inches. Since chocolate plant is a prolific reseeder, it makes a good ground cover for an established shady area during the warm months. Although mother plants will likely perish in a hard freeze, those that have flowered usually leave enough seed for more plants the next year."

GROUND COVERS FOR DEEP SHADE

One of the most frequent landscape dilemmas is what to plant under trees where the grass won't grow. St. Augustine is the most shade tolerant turf grass in Texas, and if you are gardening in East Texas, it is usually the first choice. If you can't grow St. Augustine, you will have to go to a ground cover. Another factor to consider is that in heavy shade, no ground cover is going to tolerate much traffic. If you need paths in the shade, plan to use crushed granite, bark mulch, or hard-surface walkways.

In North and Central Texas it may be possible to overseed in heavy shade with coarse fescue during the cool season to provide a ground cover. Overseeding again in the spring may even make for a good summer lawn, provided you also supply plenty of moisture.

In North Texas, dwarf yaupon (*Ilex vomitoria 'nana'*) and mondo grass (*Ophiopogon japonicus*) will need protection from cold.

Grassy-Leafed Sweetflag (*Acorus gramineus 'variegatus'*), All

Variegated Ardisia (*Ardisia japonica 'variegata'*), CSs, V

Cast-Iron Plant (*Aspidistra elatior*), C, CS, V

Japanese Painted Fern (*Athyrium niponicum 'pictum'*), N, C, CS

Miniature Variegated Sedge (*Carex conica*), All

'The Beatles' Sedge (*Carex* x *hybrida*), All

Lily-of-the-Valley (*Convallaria majalis*), N, C

Dwarf Umbrella Grass (*Cyperus alternifolius 'nana'*), Cs, V

Holly Fern (*Cyrtomium falcatum*), C, CS, V

African Iris (*Dietes vegeta, D. bicolor*), CSs, V

Sweet Woodruff (*Galium odoratum*), N

Carolina Jessamine (*Gelsemium sempervirens*), C, CS, V

English Ivy (*Hedera helix*), All

Dwarf Yaupon (*Ilex vomitoria 'nana'*), All

Crested Iris (*Iris cristata*), CSe, V

Peacock Ginger (*Kaempferia* spp.), CS, V

Yellow Archangel (*Lamiastrum galeobdolon*), N

Lilyturf (*Liriope* spp.), All

'Fire Power,' 'Gulf Stream,' 'Harbour Dwarf' Dwarf Nandina (*Nandina domestica*), All

Walking Iris (*Neomarica gracilis, N. longifolia*), CSs, V

Giant Liriope (*Ophiopogon jaburan*), CS, V

Mondo Grass (*Ophiopogon japonicus*), All

Black Mondo Grass (*Ophiopogon planiscapus 'arabicus'*), C, CS, V

Allegheny Spurge (*Pachysandra procumbens*), C

Pachysandra (*Pachysandra terminalis*), N, C

Lily-of-China, Sacred Lily (*Rohdea japonica*), All

Sarcococca (*Sarcococca hookerana 'humilis'*), All

Foamflower (*Tiarella cordifolia*), N, C

Asian Jasmine (*Trachelospermum asiaticum*), C, CS, V

Confederate Jasmine (*Trachelospermum jasminoides*), CS, V

Creeping Australian Violet (*Viola hederacea*), CS, V

Sweet Violet (*Viola odorata*), N, C, CS

If an area of your yard is too shady to grow grass, then you will have to resort to a ground cover. Unfortunately, they usually won't stand much traffic. Where you need walkways, you will have to use some type of paving such as crushed granite, flagstone, concrete stepping stones, brick, or a thick pad of bark mulch. To keep the grass or ground cover from creeping in on the walk, line the path with steel edging first and then put down the paving material. If you plan to use flagstone, put down a base of crushed granite 4 to 6 inches thick and then lay the stones. Work more granite between the stones for a very stable and attractive path.

KAEMPFERIA—PEACOCK GINGERS

Linda Gay, chief horticulturist of the Mercer Arboretum in Humble, compiled this list of *Kaempferia*, or peacock gingers, which she says make a completely hardy, shade-loving ground cover and a great substitute for hosta in the Deep South. Beautifully zoned patterns with silvers, blues, blacks, and shades of green make peacock gingers very attractive even without flowers, but iridescent purple flowers are produced over the top of the plants. If *Kaempferia* receive too much sun, the leaves will curl up, so plant in dark, shady places. Completely dormant after the second hard frost, this ground cover is actively grown from the middle of April to November.

Kaempferia angustifolia	long, narrow green leaves; purple iridescent flowers in spring and sometimes in summer
Kaempferia atrovirens, Silver Peacock	silver, black, and brown highlights; purple and white flowers
Kaempferia elegans, Green Ripple	green, rippled leaves; purple iridescent flowers
Kaempferia galanga	large green leaves flat on the ground; white flowers with fuchsia-spotted throats
Kaempferia gilbertii	green strap leaves, white margins; lilac, maroon, and white flowers
Kaempferia gilbertii '3D'	light- and dark-green leaves, white margins; white flowers with fuchsia-spotted throats
Kaempferia laotica 'Satin Checks'	dark-green leaves, black checkerboard pattern; lavender flowers
Kaempferia laotica 'Shazzam'	silver and light- and dark-green leaf patterns; purple iridescent flowers
Kaempferia mini	small, wide green leaves, silver ripples; pink flowers with dark maroon lip
Kaempferia pulchra 'Bronze'	chocolate-leaf, silver markings; purple iridescent flowers
Kaempferia pulchra 'Mansonii'	distinct patterns in spring; solid green in summer
Kaempferia pulchra 'Roscoe Pink'	black, green, and chocolate leaf patterns; purple flowers
Kaempferia pulchra 'Silverspot'	silver, turquoise, black, and dark-green patterns; purple iridescent flowers
Kaempferia rotunda 'Asian Crocus'	silver midrib accent, green and purple undersides; purple and white fragrant flowers
Kaempferia, Red Leaf	deep maroon leaves; white flowers with fuchsia spots

BAMBOO

Many cold-hardy bamboos are evergreen and do very well in Texas, but the mention of planting bamboo can strike terror in the minds of most gardeners. The running forms have a nasty reputation for taking over gardens and constantly popping up in the turf. They can be eliminated with herbicides or a sharp spade (see the Texas Bamboo Society's recommendations). The clump forming bamboos in the *Bambusa* genus are not invasive. These bamboos are highly desirable where adapted, but the plants are always in short supply because they are somewhat difficult to propagate.

The Texas Bamboo Society in Austin says that bamboos can be trimmed to a desired height to form beautiful hedges. They note that bamboo does not have to be allowed to stay at full height or left messy.

Sweetshoot bamboo (*Phyllostachys dulcis*), hairy bamboo (*Phyllostachys pubescens*), and green sulphur bamboo (*Phyllostachys viridis*) are edible species.

Tonkin Cane, Tea Stick Bamboo (*Arundinaria amabilis*), C, CS, V

Giant Canebrake (*Arundo donax*), All

Hedge Bamboo (*Bambusa multiplex* [*glaucescens*]), CSs, V

'Alphonse Karr' Hedge Bamboo (*Bambusa multiplex*), CSs, V

Oldham Timber Bamboo (*Bambusa oldhamii*), CSs, V

Weaver's Bamboo (*Bambusa textilis*), CSs, V

Punting-Pole Bamboo (*Bambusa tuldoides*), CSs, V

Buddha's-Belly Bamboo (*Bambusa ventricosa*), CSs, V

Umbrella Bamboo (*Fargesia* [*Arundinaria*] *murielae*), All

Fountain Bamboo (*Fargesia* [*Arundinaria*] *nitida*), All

Fishscale Bamboo (*Phyllostachys atrovaginata* [*congesta*]), All

Golden Bamboo (*Phyllostachys aurea*), All

Timber Bamboo (*Phyllostachys bambusoides*), C, CS, V

'Allgold' Giant Japanese Timber Bamboo (*Phyllostachys bambusoides* [*sulphurea*]), C, CS, V

'Catillon' Bamboo (*Phyllostachys bambusoides*), C, CS, V

Bisset Bamboo (*Phyllostachys bissetii*), All

Sweetshoot Bamboo (*Phyllostachys dulcis*), All

Moso Bamboo (*Phyllostachys edulis*), All

Makino Bamboo (*Phyllostachys makinoi*), All

Meyer Bamboo (*Phyllostachys meyeri*), All

Black Bamboo (*Phyllostachys nigra*), All

'Bory' Black Bamboo (*Phyllostachys nigra*), All

'Henon' Black Bamboo (*Phyllostachys nigra*), All

Hairy Bamboo (*Phyllostachys pubescens*), All

Red Margin Bamboo (*Phyllostachys rubromarginata*), All

Green Sulphur Bamboo (*Phyllostachys viridis*), All

Dwarf Greenstripe (*Pleioblastus* [*Arundinaria*] *viridistriatus*), All

CONTROL OF RUNNING BAMBOO

The Texas Bamboo Society in Austin (www.bamboo.org/abs/TexasChapterInfo.html) advises that bamboo can be controlled in a small area such as a normal city yard simply by mowing or stepping on the young shoots. Another way to control running bamboo is to use a ground barrier of concrete, metal, or very heavy plastic (60 to 120 mils). Set this at least 18 inches deep, but 24 inches is better. If a solid barrier is used, lean it outward at the top, about 30 to 45 degrees. When the rhizomes hit the barrier, they go to the surface. As they try to go over the top of the barrier, they can be pruned off.

Bamboo does not normally run under a driveway or the slab of a house. Also, bamboo will not grow into water, so a creek or fishpond will prevent growth in that direction. Many types of clumping bamboo do not run and will stay in a fairly small area. There are also very low-growing types that can be used as a ground cover and grow best in shade.

GROUND COVERS FOR DRY SITES

A ground cover has to be tough to look good on dry sites. Most of the plants in this list need some water—most are not desert plants, but rather, they tolerate the occasional dry spell. However, plants in zones with a "w" qualifier may be more desert-like. Cast-iron plant (*Aspidistra*) and Algerian Ivy (*Hedera canariensis*) are for shade only. The junipers (*Juniperus*) are for sun only. Dwarf yaupon (*Ilex vomitoria* 'nana') will need protection in North Texas gardens.

Dwarf Abelia (*Abelia* x *grandiflora* 'prostrata'), All

Artemisia (*Artemisia fridida*), CSw, V

Asparagus Fern (*Asparagus densiflorus* 'sprengeri'), CSs, V

Cast-Iron Plant (*Aspidistra elatior*), C, CS, V

Coyote Bush (*Baccharis pilularis*), CSw, V

Desert Marigold (*Baileya multiradiata*), CSw, V

California Ice Plant (*Carpobrotus chilensis*), CSw, V

Common Ice Plant (*Carpobrotus edulis*), CSw, V

Inland Sea Oats (*Chasmanthium latifolium*), All

'Blue Blanket' Clitoria (*Clitoria marian*), C, CS, V

Cotoneaster (*Cotoneaster decumbens*), N, Cw, CSw, V

Creeping Broom (*Cytisus decumbens*), Cw, CSw

Feathery Peabush (*Dalea formosa*), Cs, CS, V

Prostrate Indigo Bush (*Dalea greggii*), CS, V

Yellow Ice Plant (*Delosperma cooperi*), CSw, V

Purple Ice Plant (*Delosperma nubigenum*), Cw, CSw, V

Mock Strawberry (*Duchesnea indica*), C, CS, V

Creeping Snake Herb (*Dyschoriste linearis*), C, CS, V

Weeping Love Grass (*Eragrostis curvula*), C, CS

Palm-Leaf Eupatorium (*Eupatorium greggii*), All

Gazania (*Gazania rigens*), CSw, V

Carolina Jessamine (*Gelsemium sempervirens*), C, CS, V

Algerian Ivy (*Hedera canariensis*), CS,V

Daylily (*Hemerocallis* hybs.), All

Creeping St. John's Wort (*Hypericum calycinum*), C

Dwarf Yaupon (*Ilex vomitoria 'nana'*), All

Shore Juniper (*Juniperus conferta* cvs.), N, C, CS

Creeping Juniper (*Juniperus horizontalis* cvs.), N, C

Dwarf Juniper (*Juniperus procumbens* cvs.), N, C

Trailing Lantana (*Lantana montevidensis*), CS, V

Japanese Honeysuckle (*Lonicera japonica*), All

Creeping Mahonia (*Mahonia repens*), N, Cnw

Barbados Cherry (*Malpighia glabra*), CS, V

Blackfoot Daisy (*Melampodium leucanthum*), C, CS, V

Lindheimer Muhly Grass (*Muhlenbergia lindheimeri*), C, CS, V

'Fire Power,' 'Gulf Stream,' 'Harbour Dwarf' Dwarf Nandina (*Nandina domestica*), All

Cup Flower (*Nierembergia hippomanica*), CSw, V

Mexican Primrose (*Oenothera berlandieri*), Cw, CSw, V

Showy Evening Primrose (*Oenothera speciosa*), All

Mat Penstemon (*Penstemon caespitosus*), Cw, CSw

Ribbon Grass (*Phalaris arundinacea 'picta'*), All

Spring Cinquefoil (*Potentilla tabernaemontani*), Cw, CSw

Psorelia (*Psorelia* spp.), CS, V

Dwarf India Hawthorn (*Rhaphiolepis indica* cvs.), C, CS, V

Pigeonberry (*Rivina humilis*), C, CS, V

Rosemary (*Rosmarinus officinalis 'prostrata'*), CSs, V

Coral Fountain, Firecracker Plant (*Russelia equisetiformis*), CS, V

Lavender Cotton (*Santolina chamaecyparissus*), N, Cw, CSw

Soapwort (*Saponaria ocymoides*), N, C, CS

Sedum (*Sedum* spp.), All

Hen-and-Chicks (*Sempervivum tectorum*), C, CS, V

Lamb's-Ears (*Stachys byzantina*), Cw, CSw

Stemodia (*Stemodia tomentosa*), CS, V

Mexican Feather Grass (*Stipa tenuissima*), CS, V

Creeping Thyme (*Thymus* spp.), All

Pink Verbena (*Verbena peruviana*), C, CS

Rock Verbena (*Verbena pulchella*), Cw, CSw

Sandpaper Verbena (*Verbena rigida*), Cw, CSw

Zexmenia (*Wedelia [Zexmenia] hispida*), C, CS, V

Wedelia (*Wedelia trilobata*), CSs, V

Coontie (*Zamia floridana*), CSs, V

Ground covers may be low-maintenance plants, but they do require some care. Vigorous ground covers will look better if they are sheared back to 4 to 6 inches each year in the early spring. After shearing, use a small, hand-held fertilizer spreader to apply lawn fertilizer—but be sure it doesn't contain a weed killer that might damage the ground cover. Then water the fertilizer in thoroughly.

GROUND COVERS FOR CRACKS AND CREVICES

Cracks and crevices between the stones or bricks of a pathway or anywhere with a small pocket of soil can be a perfect setting for these really tough creepers, as long as there is not too much traffic to wear them down. They can really soften the harsh appearance of paving. A personal favorite is the emerald zoysia allowed to grow without mowing. It develops a nice wave-like growth in large patches, and it's tough enough to survive in paving designed with openings for plants. Dwarf mondo grass (*Ophiopogon japonicus 'nana'*) will need protection in North Texas.

CREEPING JENNY

Woolly Yarrow (*Achillea tomentosa*), N, C

Birdfoot Sedge (*Carex conica*), All

'The Beatles' Carex (*Carex* x *hybrida*), All

Roman Chamomile (*Chamaemelum nobile*), C, CS, V

Sweet Woodruff (*Galium odoratum*), N

Candytuft (*Iberis sempervirens*), N, Ce, CSe

Blue Baby-Tears, Angel Tears (*Lindernia grandiflora [Ilysanthes floribunda]*), C, CS, V

Creeping Jenny (*Lysimachia nummularia*), All

Mazus (*Mazus reptans*), C, CS

Dwarf Mondo Grass (*Ophiopogon japonicus 'nana'*), All

Black Mondo Grass (*Ophiopogon planiscapus 'arabicus'*), C, CS, V

Baby's-Tears (*Soleirolia soleirolii*), CS, V

American Germander (*Teucrium canadense*), All

Creeping Thyme (*Thymus* spp.), All

Creeping Speedwell (*Veronica repens*), N, C, CS

Creeping Australian Violet (*Viola hederacea*), CS, V

Emerald Zoysia (*Zoysia japonica* x *tenuifolia*), CSs, V

GROUND COVERS THAT DRAPE AND TRAIL

The ground covers in this list are wonderful for softening a wall, and they can tie areas of the landscape together. They're the sweep of free-form landscape elements.

Asparagus Fern (*Asparagus densiflorus 'sprengeri'*), CSs, V

Barberry Cotoneaster (*Cotoneaster dammeri*), N, Cw, CSw

Rockspray Cotoneaster (*Cotoneaster horizontalis*), N, Cw, CSw

Willowleaf Cotoneaster (*Cotoneaster salicifolius 'repens'*), N, Cw, CSw

Wintercreeper (*Euonymus fortunei*), N, C

English Ivy (*Hedera helix*), All

Creeping St. John's Wort (*Hypericum calycinum*), C

Candytuft (*Iberis sempervirens*), N, Ce, CSe

Sargent Juniper (*Juniperus chinensis 'sargentii'*), N, C

Shore Juniper (*Juniperus conferta* cvs.), N, C, CS

Creeping Juniper (*Juniperus horizontalis* cvs.), N, C

Dwarf Juniper (*Juniperus procumbens* cvs.), N, C

Dead Nettle (*Lamium maculatum*), All

Trailing Lantana (*Lantana montevidensis*), CS, V

Blue Baby-Tears, Angel Tears (*Lindernia grandiflora* [*Ilysanthes floribunda*]), C, CS, V

Moss Pink, Creeping Phlox (*Phlox subulata*), All

Prostrate Rosemary (*Rosmarinus officinalis 'prostrata'*), CSs, V

Stemodia (*Stemodia tomentosa*), CS, V

Creeping Thyme (*Thymus* spp.), All

'Homestead' Verbena (*Verbena hybrida*), All

Greater Periwinkle (*Vinca major*), N, C

Common Periwinkle (*Vinca minor*), N

GROUND COVERS TO STABILIZE A SLOPE

Ground covers in this category need to have a dense root system and extensive leaf cover. In order to stop heavy rains from washing away the soil on a slope, a plant must not only hold the soil tightly with a root system, but it must also break the eroding effect of the rain as it falls to the ground. Most often, these slopes occur along streams, rivers, and bayous. Thus these plants may also have to endure flooding.

Mondo grass (*Ophiopogon japonicus*) will need protection in North Texas.

Dwarf Abelia (*Abelia* x *grandiflora 'prostrata'*), All

Grassy-Leafed Sweetflag (*Acorus gramineus 'variegatus'*), All

Dwarf Golden Sweetflag (*Acorus gramineus minimus 'aureus'*), All

Five-Leaf Akebia (*Akebia quinata*), C, CS, V

Sweet Vernal Grass (*Anthoxanthum odoratum*), N

Cast-Iron Plant (*Aspidistra elatior*), C, CS, V

Cross Vine (*Bignonia capreolata*), C, CS

Sideoats Gramma (*Bouteloua curtipendula*), N

Perennial Quaking Grass (*Briza media*), N

Blue Sedge (*Carex glauca*), All

Barberry Cotoneaster (*Cotoneaster dammeri*), N, Cw, CSw

Willowleaf Cotoneaster (*Cotoneaster salicifolius 'repens'*), N, Cw, CSw

Weeping Love Grass (*Eragrostis curvula*), C, CS

Wintercreeper (*Euonymus fortunei*), N, C

Carolina Jessamine (*Gelsemium sempervirens*), C, CS

Algerian Ivy (*Hedera canariensis*), CS, V

English Ivy (*Hedera helix*), All

Daylily (*Hemerocallis* hyb.), All

Creeping St. John's Wort (*Hypericum calycinum*), C

Sargent Juniper (*Juniperus chinensis 'sargentii'*), N, C

Shore Juniper (*Juniperus conferta* cvs.), N, C, CS

Creeping Juniper (*Juniperus horizontalis* cvs.), N, C

Dwarf Juniper (*Juniperus procumbens 'nana'*), N, C

Trailing Lantana (*Lantana montevidensis*), CS, V

Liriope (*Liriope muscari, L. spicata*), All

Japanese Honeysuckle (*Lonicera japonica*), All

Muhly Grass (*Muhlenbergia* spp.), All

Showy Evening Primrose (*Oenothera speciosa*), All

Mondo Grass (*Ophiopogon japonicus*), All

Virginia Creeper (*Parthenocissus quinquefolia*), All

'Dwarf Garters' Ribbon Grass (*Phalaris arundinacea*), All

Formosa Firethorn (*Pyracantha koidzumii*), All

Memorial Rose (*Rosa wichuraiana*), C, CS, V

'Katie's Compact' Ruellia (*Ruellia brittoniana*), C, CS, V

Common Periwinkle (*Vinca minor*), N

Creeping Australian Violet (*Viola hederacea*), CS, V

Wedelia (*Wedelia trilobata*), CSs, V

Judith Wilmington, a horticulturist with the Texas Tech Horticulture Gardens, recommends several ornamental grasses for the High Plains: pampas grass (*Cortaderia selloana*), 'Elijah Blue' fescue (*Festuca glauca*), 'Dwarf Garters' ribbon grass (*Phalaris arundinacea*), gardeners' garters (*Phalaris arundinacea 'picta'*), and Mexican feather grass (*Stipa tenuissima*).

GROUND COVERS FOR MOIST, POORLY DRAINED SITES

Generally it's best to improve drainage in the landscape to avoid these areas, but in some cases they may lead into bog areas and in fact, many of these plants will flourish in a bog. Also see the "Bog Gardens" list in the chapter of "Special Lists and Gardens."

Grassy-Leafed Sweetflag (*Acorus gramineus 'variegatus'*), All

Wild Ginger (*Asarum caudatum*), All

'Snowflake' Water Hyssop (*Bacopa caroliniana*), Ce, CSe

Sedge (*Carex* spp.), All

Turtlehead (*Chelone obliqua*), Ce, CSe

Silver-and-Gold (*Chrysanthemum pacificum*), All

Green-and-Gold (*Chrysogonum virginianum*), All

Horsetail (invasive) (*Equisetum hyemale*), All

Chameleon Plant (*Houttuynia cordata 'chameleon'*), N, C

Spotted Dead Nettle (*Lamium maculatum 'variegatum'*), All

Creeping Jenny (*Lysimachia nummularia*), All

Partridgeberry (*Mitchella repens*), Ce, CSe

Wedelia (*Wedelia trilobata*), CSs, V

Yellow-Root (*Xanthorhiza simplicissima*), Ce, CSe

PARTRIDGEBERRY

GROUND COVERS FOR SUN OR SHADE

The most sought-after characteristic of a ground cover is often its toughness. Tough ones like the following will grow almost anywhere. Dwarf monkey grass (*Ophiopogon japonicus 'nana'*) will need protection in North Texas.

Wintercreeper (*Euonymus fortunei*), N, C

Liriope (*Liriope muscari, L. spicata*), All

Japanese Honeysuckle (*Lonicera japonica*), All

Creeping Jenny (*Lysimachia nummularia*), All

Manfreda (*Manfreda undulata*), Cs, CS, V

Dwarf Nandina cultivars (*Nandina domestica*), All

Dwarf Monkey Grass (*Ophiopogon japonicus 'nana'*), All

Virginia Creeper (*Parthenocissus quinquefolia*), All

Gumpo Azalea (*Rhododendron 'gumpo'*), Ce, CSe

Bouncing Bet (*Saponaria officinalis*), N, C, CS

Asian Jasmine (*Trachelospermum asiaticum*), C, CS, V

Confederate Jasmine (*Trachelospermum jasminoides*), CS, V

Wedelia (*Wedelia trilobata*), CSs, V

To add interest to a planting of Asiatic jasmine (*Trachelospermum asiaticum*), randomly plant tough daffodils like 'Fortune' throughout the bed. It won't be easy—you'll need a sharp spade to get through the tangle of stems and roots, but the daffodils will come back for years in this challenging ecosystem. Just be sure to leave the daffodil foliage on the plant until it begins to yellow. The foliage is where the daffs will store all the food reserves possible so they can compete with the aggressive jasmine.

GROUND COVERS FOR THE BEACH

Salt spray and sandy, dry soils are a real challenge for landscape plants. Add in the blazing sun and most plants turn up their toes. The plants in this list are some of the really tough ones to try. Adding organic matter to the beds and using low-volume irrigation systems (drip or soaker) will help. With luck, you'll only have to worry about the salt and sun.

These plants are even tougher than the ones listed for the Coastal Bay area, although most of them would also grow farther inland. English ivy (*Hedera helix*) and dwarf yaupon (*Ilex vomitoria 'nana'*) do best with shade.

Asparagus Fern (*Asparagus densiflorus 'sprengeri'*), CSs, V
Dwarf Natal Plum (*Carissa macrocarpa*), CSs, V
Periwinkle (*Catharanthus roseus*), CS, V
Beach Rosemary (*Ceratiola ericoides*), CS, V
Inland Sea Oats (*Chasmanthium latifolium*), All
Mexican Heather (*Cuphea hyssopifolia*), V, Annual
Creeping Snake Herb (*Dyschoriste linearis*), C, CS, V
Palm-Leaf Eupatorium (*Eupatorium greggii*), All
Blue Daze (*Evolvulus glomeratus [nuttalianus]*), V, Annual
Creeping Fig (*Ficus pumila*), CS, V
Blanket Flower (*Gaillardia pulchella*), Annual
Carolina Jessamine (*Gelsemium sempervirens*), C, CS, V
Algerian Ivy (*Hedera canariensis*), CS, V
English Ivy (*Hedera helix*), All
Beach Sunflower (*Helianthus debilis*), CS, V
Spider Lily (*Hymenocallis latifolia*), CS, V
Dwarf Yaupon (*Ilex vomitoria 'nana'*), All
Railroad Vine (*Ipomoea pes-caprae*), CS, V
Star Jasmine (*Jasminum multiflorum*), CS, V

Angel-Wing Jasmine (*Jasminum nitidum*), V, Tropical
Shore Juniper cultivars (*Juniperus conferta*), N, C, CS
Trailing Lantana (*Lantana montevidensis*), CS, V
Liriope (*Liriope muscari, L. spicata*), All
Barbados Cherry (*Malpighia glabra*), CS, V
Virginia Creeper (*Parthenocissus quinquefolia*), All
Psorelia (*Psorelia spp.*), CS, V
Dwarf India Hawthorn (*Rhaphiolepis indica*), C, CS, V
Pigeonberry (*Rivina humilis*), C, CS, V
Purple Heart (*Setcreasea pallida*), CSs, V
Cordgrass (*Spartina patens*), C, CS, V
Stemodia (*Stemodia tomentosa*), All
Asian Jasmine (*Trachelospermum asiaticum*), C, CS, V
Confederate Jasmine (*Trachelospermum jasminoides*), CS, V
Zexmenia (*Wedelia [Zexmenia] hispida*), C, CS, V
Wedelia (*Wedelia trilobata*), CSs, V
Adam's-Needle (*Yucca filimentosa*), C, CS, V
Coontie (*Zamia floridana*), CSs, V

TEXAS TURF GRASSES

The turf grass in a landscape should be considered a long-term element of the design plan. Too often, though, it is a hastily thrown in effort by the builder using a low-bid contractor. James McAfee, a turf specialist with the Texas A&M Extension Service, provided not only the lists of turf grasses, which include the newest varieties for Texas, but he has detailed the best planting techniques. If your new house includes one of those "quicky" turf installations, it is probably best to pull it up or kill it out with a product like glyphosate and start over. Think of it as a treasure hunt. You'll find pieces of lumber, bricks, mortar, and maybe even a good hammer buried under the grass.

Turf can be a spectacular feature in the landscape, or it can be a headache. If you try too hard—fertilizing every thirty days, running the sprinklers three or four times per week, and generally administering too much TLC (tender loving care)—the insects, diseases, and weeds may eat you up. Good soil preparation is a very important first step to success. You've also got to plant the right grass. Hybrid bermuda grass won't thrive in heavy shade. Even St. Augustine won't tolerate deep shade, especially if you plan to walk on it. It's frustrating to look at the neighbor's yard and see what appears to be the same amount of shade and a healthy turf while your yard is patchy and sick looking. However, a section of turf that is damaged by disease, insects, or herbicides will be very slow to recover in a shaded area. You can add more water and fertilizer to compensate for competition from trees, but you can't find a substitute for sunlight, and eventually that becomes a limiting factor (hint: see other ground-cover lists and construct walkways for traffic).

Seedbed Preparation: The seedbed should be prepared the same whether you are going to seed, sprig, plug, or sod. First, remove or control any existing weeds with a nonselective herbicide such as Roundup (glyphosate). Then till the soil down to a depth of 4 to 6 inches. This would be a good time to add some organic matter to the soil, while it is being tilled. Apply 1 to 2 inches of compost and till it in thoroughly in the top 4 to 6 inches. Level the soil, making sure there are no low areas in the seedbed, and that it slopes away from all buildings. Once the seedbed is leveled, either roll the soil or irrigate heavily to look for low areas. Add more soil to fill any low spots that show up. Apply a preplant application of a fertilizer such as 10-10-10 or 13-13-13 at 10 pounds per 1,000 square feet. The lawn is now ready for planting.

Seeding: Seeding is generally the easiest and least expensive method to establish a home lawn. When seeding a lawn, divide the total amount of seed required in half and then apply the seed in two different directions. Example, if seeding common bermuda grass, take 1 pound of bermuda grass seed and apply it in a north to south direction; then take 1 pound of bermuda grass seed and apply it in an east to west direction. This will help insure a more uniform distribution of the seed over the lawn. Next, take a garden rake and lightly rake the seed into the top quarter inch of soil. Lightly roll the lawn to firm the soil around the seed. Start watering the lawn immediately to keep the soil around the seed moist. Continue to water lightly each day until the seeds start to germinate. Once the seeds sprout and the plants are growing, cut back on the frequency of irrigation and apply more water per application.

Sodding: Once the sod is planted in the lawn, soak the lawn thoroughly. Apply enough moisture to maintain good soil moisture below the sod, but don't overdo it—the soil under the sod should not be kept saturated or you will slow root growth.

Recommended Seeding Rates

The seeding rate for buffalo grass depends on the time needed to obtain coverage and if the seed is drilled into the soil or if it is broadcast on top of the soil. The perennial and annual rye grasses are cool-season turf grasses used to overseed in the winter on dormant, warm-season lawns.

Amount per 1,000 square feet

Common bermuda grass	1 to 2 lbs.
Buffalo grass	0.5 to 6 lbs.
Centipede grass	0.25 to 0.5 lbs.
Tall fescues	6 to 8 lbs.
Kentucky bluegrasses	2 to 3 lbs.
Perennial rye grasses	5 to 7 lbs.
Annual rye grasses	10 to 12 lbs.

Recommended Seeding Dates in Texas:

Warm-season turf grasses—*Bermuda grass, buffalo grass, centipede grass*

North Texas	late May through July
Central Texas	early May through mid August
South Texas	late April through late August

Cool-season turf grasses—
Tall fescue, bluegrass, rye grass

North Texas	mid September through mid October

Rye grass for overseeding

Central Texas	late September through late October
South Texas	late October through late November

Bermuda Grass

Warm season. Heat, drought, and cold tolerant. Needs 6 to 7 hours direct sun daily. Most homeowners will want to use common varieties rather than the aggressive hybrid varieties that are better adapted to the golf course. Planted from seed.

Arizona common	Sultan	Cheyenne
Sahara	Guymon	Yuma

St. Augustine Grass

Warm season. Grows well in moderate shade to full sun; needs 4 hours direct sun daily. Drought tolerant. Floratam has very poor cold tolerance and is only recommended for the southern portions of the state, south of I-10. Varieties planted from plugs or sod:

Texas Common	Floratam	Palmetto
Raleigh	Seville	

Buffalo Grass

Warm season. Excellent heat, drought, and cold tolerance. Best adapted to fertile, well-drained, heavy clay soils and areas of low rainfall. Does not grow well in sandy soils or in shade areas. Varieties planted from plugs or sod:

Topgun	Plains	Nebraska
Texoka	Prairie	

Zoysia Grass

Warm season. Good shade tolerance (fine-textured better than coarse-textured species). Cold tolerant (coarse-textured better than fine-textured species). Traffic tolerant. Coarse-textured zoysias generally have the best drought tolerance. Varieties planted from plugs or sod:

Meyer	Palisade	Cavalier
El Toro	Crowne	Emerald

Centipede Grass

Warm season. Coarse-textured perennial. Best adapted to sandy, acid soils and average rainfall above 40 inches per year. Slow growth rate means less mowing. Moderate shade tolerance but grows best in full sun areas. Planted from seed, plugs, or sod.

Tall Fescue

Cool season. Best heat and drought tolerance of all the cool-season turf grasses, but not as heat and drought tolerant. Best in well-drained, heavy clay soils. Planted from seed.

Rebel II	Shortstop	Bonanza
Crossfire	Olympic	Vegas
Jaguar	Winchester	

Kentucky Bluegrass

Cool season. Primarily limited to the very northern portions of the panhandle. Fair shade tolerance but will not grow as well in shady areas as tall fescue. Typically planted from seed.

Baron	Glade	Touchdown
Adelphi	Nugget	Ram I

Rye Grass

Cool season. Acts as an annual in the South but can survive year round in the northern portions of the Texas panhandle, especially where moderate shade is present. Poor drought tolerance. Perennial rye grasses have better cold tolerance than annual rye grasses, but both can be killed during extremely cold winters. Planted from seed.

Gulf Rye (Annual)	Ph.D.	Prelude
Palmer	Derby	NK-200

Texas Bluegrass

Native to Texas. Excellent heat and drought tolerance. Primarily grown in south and southwestern areas of the state.

Reveille

 Recently a plant breeder at Texas A&M University released a hybrid cross between Texas bluegrass and Kentucky bluegrass. This hybrid has the dark-green, medium texture of Kentucky bluegrass and the heat and full-sun tolerance of Texas bluegrass. Water requirements are about the same as for bermuda grass. If adequate water is supplied, this new turf grass should perform well in Central to North Texas, but it does not tolerate salt very well and should not be planted where salinity is a problem. It requires 4 to 6 pounds of actual nitrogen per 1,000 square feet per year. At this time, the means of establishment for this hybrid bluegrass cross is sod.

KITCHEN GARDENS

The kitchen garden is an important element in Texas landscapes. Texans are fiercely independent, and growing some of our own food is a security factor. Even if it's only a couple of tomato plants in the flower border, it counts. For some it may involve digging up the entire backyard for vegetables or planting a pecan tree, as if the squirrels would let you harvest any. Most of us get by with a small raised bed for a few tomatoes, a jalapeño pepper, one bell pepper, and maybe a row of bush beans in the spring and summer. In the fall we grow lettuce, radishes, a row of broccoli, and a few herbs. The rest of the stuff we get at the store.

If you're a serious vegetable gardener, check out Roland Roberts's list of "Vegetables for the High Plains." Most of those varieties will do great anywhere in Texas. The big difference will be the planting times. From the Upper Gulf Coast south, fall gardening is a major event. That's when we plant cool-season crops such as broccoli, cauliflower, and other cole crops. It's when we plant root crops like beets, carrots, turnips, and radishes. It is also the time for leafy vegetables like lettuce, spinach, and chard. In a mild winter we can plant again in January and February to harvest before it gets too hot.

In March the warm-season crops like tomatoes, beans, peppers, and corn are planted. This often continues with staggered planting until late April, especially with crops like bush beans. The daring plant more warm-season crops in July and August, hoping to harvest before the first hard frost. In September and October, it's time to start the fall garden again.

Fruit trees are a special challenge. The stone fruits like peaches and plums are difficult to grow successfully without some spraying. Plum curculios (insects) and Brown Rot (a disease) are unrelenting. However, a couple of citrus trees can be care-free from Houston south if you can protect them from one or two freezes a year. Pears are pretty easy, but they do better with a few fungicide sprays to keep them from losing their leaves too early each year. Apples can be worked into the Hill Country landscape very successfully, but they are marginal in Houston. Most anyone can grow jujubes and persimmons, but not everyone cares to.

Basic Cultural Requirements for Vegetables and Herbs

- Most of these plants need full sun or at least six to eight hours of direct sunlight daily. Fruiting crops like tomatoes and squash need the most sun, root crops are intermediate, and leafy vegetables can tolerate the most shade. It's very often possible to grow leafy vegetables as a cool-season winter crop where deciduous trees drop their leaves and allow more sunlight to reach the garden. This same plot would be inadequate for summer vegetables. For best light exposure, beds should be laid out in an east to west direction, with taller plants on the north.
- Lots of organic matter, preferably compost, is always the key to good soil. Mix 6 to 8 inches with the garden soil at least three months prior to planting if possible. In addition, 2 to 3 pounds of a complete fertilizer like 15-5-10 should be mixed per 100 square feet.
- In the high rainfall areas of East Texas, the soil is worked up into ridges 12 to 18 inches high, and the plants or seeds are planted on the ridges. In Far West Texas the garden might look similar, but you'll want to plant in the furrows. If this sounds like too much work, raised beds filled with soil mix are an alternative.
- Low-volume irrigation systems are indispensable in the vegetable and herb garden. We rarely have a year in which natural rainfall comes when we need it.

- To keep weeds down, soak newspapers in water and spread them out between the rows, five to ten sheets thick, and then cover the papers with an organic mulch like pine bark or dried grass clippings to hide the papers and keep them from blowing away.
- Buy the book *Commonsense Vegetable Gardening for the South* by William D. Adams and Thomas LeRoy.

Basic Cultural Requirements for Fruit Gardens

The following recommendations refer to fruit crops across the board, whether it be a twenty-acre orchard, a dozen blueberry plants used as a landscape border, a single banana plant, strawberries in a hanging basket, or the lone peach tree.

- An orchard needs to be located where it will benefit from good air drainage. These are areas with enough slope to allow the cold to settle in low pockets away from the trees. If you have room for only one peach tree, finding a spot with good air drainage is a moot point. The most critical factor in this situation is finding a spot that has a minimum of eight hours of sunlight.
- It's a good idea to lay out the orchard on graph paper to make sure you've allowed adequate spacing and to serve as a variety template in case identification tags get lost.
- In the home landscape, protected areas can often be found on the south side of the house or buildings. This is the spot to locate your one satsuma tree, a banana plant, or any fruit that is marginally hardy.
- A deep, rich soil is important, whether you're planting strawberries or a pecan tree. The soil should be free of hard subsurface layers that cause poor drainage. Areas that flood should also be avoided.
- Large containers such as whiskey barrels or similarly sized ceramic pots can be used to grow dwarf trees, citrus trees, or other fruiting crops that require cold protection. Containers are also great for a few strawberry plants, even though they don't usually require cold protection. The exception might occur in the early spring when they're blooming and an early frost is predicted, or in a hard winter when temperatures drop into the teens or below. Even if you don't harvest a lot of strawberries, they make an attractive container plant.
- Low-volume irrigation systems are extremely critical with fruit crops. Drought stress is one of the main causes of fruit drop. Some irrigation systems can be used to reduce freeze damage. In particular, microsprinklers used within the canopy of citrus trees may save a crop that might otherwise have been lost.
- Mulch, mulch, mulch!

BEST-TASTING TOMATO VARIETIES FOR TEXAS GARDENS

Tomato lovers differ markedly in the qualities they look for in a tomato. Most like some acidity, but others like them very mild. No one seems to like them mealy, cracked, or insect damaged. Really good tomatoes have complex flavors. Tomatoes with "true tomato taste" should have a hint of sweetness combined with some acidity and a richness that makes you want to slice them in half, sprinkle them with salt, and chomp down on them while you're still in the garden. Tomato lovers know that tomatoes aren't as flavorful when they are cold. The flavors come out best at room temperature. If you store them in the refrigerator to make them keep a bit longer, at least have the decency to take them out a few hours before serving and let them warm up. Most of the flavor should return.

The tomato lovers who contributed to this list are William D. Adams, Harris County Extension Agent–Horticulture, Houston; Jerry Parsons, Area Vegetable Specialist, San Antonio; Roland Roberts, Area Vegetable Specialist, Lubbock; and George and Mary Stewart, legendary home gardeners, Missouri City. Not everyone agreed on every tomato, but this list represents a good cross-section of opinion on some good tomato varieties.

Beefmaster	big tomato, more productive than most, good flavor
Bingo	large-fruited variety, very productive and reliable if fertilized, not as acid-tasting as Celebrity
Carmello	large-fruited French variety, vigorous, with good disease resistance
Celebrity	chosen nationwide for "true tomato taste" and productivity

Champion	large fruits, always rates high on taste tests, excellent disease resistance
Dona	small-fruited French variety with very good flavor, excellent disease resistance
Enchantment	looks like a paste tomato but has flavor and juice
Heatwave	heat-setting, large-fruited variety, more traditional tomato flavor, most reliably productive, large-fruited tomato for Texas
Jackpot	requires high fertility and caging, delicious flavor
Red Sun	medium-large tomato with good flavor, not too acid, firm flesh and no white core, good disease resistance
Santiago	rich tomato flavor, deep round fruit, solid red interior, heat-setting ability
SunMaster (F1 hyb.)	heat-setting, large-fruited variety, predominately sweet flavor, solid meaty fruit
Super Bush	compact plants, nice medium-size tomatoes
Surefire	most reliably productive, medium-sized tomato for Texas, ideal for container growing, crack-resistant fruit
Sweet Chelsea	one of the best cherry tomatoes with rich tomato flavor
Whirlaway	large fruit similar in flavor to Bingo but not as susceptible to sunscald when plants are not caged or staked

George and Mary Stewart are Missouri City home gardeners who, together, have 182 years of gardening experience. When it comes to tomatoes, they recommend Bingo, Whirlaway, Celebrity, Dona, and Red Sun. "We enjoy eating vine-ripened tomatoes, but we grow far more than we can slice, cook, or put up in jars. We mostly enjoy giving them away to our friends. Of course, we give away the pretty ones and eat the culls ourselves."

"Jackpot is the best tasting of the Bingo-Whirlaway-Jackpot series of tomato varieties introduced by the Ferry Morse Seed Company," advises Jerry Parsons, a San Antonio area vegetable specialist. "Jackpot is much more determinate than Bingo or Whirlaway and must be heavily and constantly fertilized to size the abundance of fruit it produces. It is a high-maintenance tomato which produces an abundance of quality, delicious tomatoes. Bingo, Whirlaway, and Jackpot are susceptible to radial fruit cracking and curling (rolling) leaves if the plant is exposed to stress during the growing period."

BEST VEGETABLE VARIETIES FOR THE COASTAL SOUTH

The varieties included in this list are certainly not limited to Harris County. Most will grow well anywhere in Texas if they are given plenty of sun, good soil, and pest management.

Bush Beans	Contender, Topcrop, Provider, Derby, Maxibell, Roma II
Pinto Beans	Improved Pinto
Pole Beans	Kentucky Wonder, Dade, Romano
Lima Beans	Bush-Jackson, Wonder, Henderson Bush, Fordhook 242, Pole-Florida Butter, Sieva (Carolina)
Beets	Detroit Red, Green Top Bunching, Pacemaker III
Broccoli	Green Comet, Emperor, Packman
Brussels Sprouts	Jade Cross, Prince Marvel, and other hybrids
Cabbage	Early Jersey Wakefield, Savoy Hybrids, Golden Acre, Rio Verde, Ruby Ball, Green Ball
Chinese Cabbage	Jade Pagoda, Tropical Delight, China Pride
Carrots	Imperator, Danvers 126, Nantes, Orange Sherbet
Cauliflower	Snow Crown Hybrid, Snow King, Majestic
Collards	Georgia

KOHLRABI

Sweet Corn	Merit, Calumet, Florida Staysweet, Summer Sweet Hybrids, Buttersweet, Funk's G90, How Sweet It Is
White Corn	Silver Queen
Pickling Cucumbers	Victory, Liberty National Pickling, Sweet Success
Slicing Cucumbers	Poinsett, Sweet Slice, Ashley, Burpless, Suyo
Eggplant	Florida Market, Ichiban, Ping Tung Long, Thai Long Green, Listada de Gandia
Garlic	Texas White
Kohlrabi	Grand Duke Hybrid, Early White Vienna, Rapid
Leek	Titan, Unique
Leaf Lettuce	Salad Bowl, Ruby, Oakleaf, Green Ice, Red Sails
Butterhead Lettuce	Summer Bibb, Esmeralda, Buttercrunch
Romaine Lettuce	Valmaine
Mustard	Tender Green, Florida Broadleaf
Chinese Mustard	Lei Chow
Okra	Clemson Spineless, Louisiana Green Velvet, Emerald, Zeebest
Onions	Burgundy, Granex, Texas Supersweet
Green Onions	Ishikura, Summer Bunching, Evergreen White Bunching
Peas	Mississippi Silver, Blackeye No. 5, Purple Hull, Queen Ann, Cream 40, Texas Pink Eye
Snap Peas	Sugar Snap, Oregon Sugar Pod, Maestro
Peppers	Gypsy, Belltower, Big Bertha, Bell Captain, Lilac Hybrid, Golden Summer, Yellow Banana, Laparie, Aji Dulce
Hot Peppers	Super Cayenne, Tabasco, Fresno Chile, Serrano Chile, Hungarian Wax, Jalapeño, Habanero
Potatoes	Red Lasoda, Kenebec, Norgold
Radish	Cherry Belle, Early Scarlet Globe, White Icicle, Champion
Winter Radish	Black Spanish, White Chinese, Daikon
Spinach	Early Hybrid 7, Melody, Tyee, New Zealand, Malabar
Squash	Acorn, Butternut
Summer Squash	Dixie, Multipik, Hybrid Crookneck, White Bush Scallop, Zucchini Hybrids, Tromboncino, Sundance
Tomatoes	Dona, Carmello, Champion, Better Boy, Carnival, Terrific, Celebrity, Better Bush, Sweet 100 Hybrid, Chelsea, Enchantment, Texas Wild
Turnips	Purple Top White Globe, Just Right, Tokyo Cross, Royal Globe
Turnip Greens	Seven Top, Shogoin
Watermelon	Mickylee, Jubilee, Yellow Doll, Tri-x-Carousel (seedless)

TEXAS BEST CHILES

Hot peppers are a Texas tradition, and they should be included in every Texas garden. Even if you can't stand the heat, you can grow jalapeños such as Señorita or False Alarm that are almost as sweet as bell peppers and make folks think you're tough. Most of the hot stuff (capsaicin) is in the placenta or cross walls. Remove it and you can continue the illusion. The really hot ones like Habanero may still leave you breathless, and Chile Pequins may require microsurgery to remove the placenta.

Aji Dulce	Looks like a habanero but is mostly sweet.
Anaheim	Big Jim is a good standard variety; R. Naky is mild; Sandia has more spice.
Ancho	Used for chile rellenos.
Chile Pequin	Popular in vinegar sauce; a must for collard greens.
Habanero	One of the hottest peppers!
Jalapeño	TAM Mild, Señorita, and False Alarm are mild; yellow Jaloro is medium; Jalapeño Grande is plenty hot.
Serrano	Small but spicy; super for salsa.

Anchos are spicy, top-shaped peppers used for chile relleños, especially the Poblano or fresh green form. Mulato is a brown and hot variation of this pepper. Dried anchos are great in chili and stews.

The Habanero is one of the hottest peppers. A red variation, Red Savina, may be the hottest at 500,000 Scovill heat units. It has a fruity aftertaste—after you regain consciousness. Try carefully removing the cross walls and seeds before mincing to mix in fresh salsas.

Real "chileheads" put a few Serranos with fresh garlic, onion, cilantro and a bit of seasoned salt in a mini food processor to make a quick salsa. A teaspoonful in a taco or burrito will turn bland into "Arriba!"

FRUITS AND VEGETABLES WE GROW ORGANICALLY

Carol Ann Sayle and Larry Butler own and operate TDA-certified organic Boggy Creek Farms, a five-acre, historic urban farm just ten minutes east of the State Capitol building in Austin. Growing a crop of organic vegetables for fun in your backyard is challenging enough, but growing them for a living can be frightening. When asked about controlling bugs, Carol and Larry responded, "We've never met a bug we can beat. So we've changed our attitude to one of acceptance. That's made a huge difference. We now plant 90 percent for them and 10 percent for us." They also had this whimsical advice for gardeners wanting to become farmers: "Forget good water and land! Start with no debt, a marriage partner who wants to farm as much as you do, a business plan, outside income, good health, the ability to fix everything mechanical, and the serene attitude that there's always another season."

Boggy Creek Farms uses a system of successive crops. For example, they'll produce three crops of tomatoes. For the first crop, they transplant Early Girl as early as possible in late February or early March and protect from freezing with black plastic mulch, buckets of water, and a floating row cover. They harvest beginning the first of May, then in April transplant Celebrity for a second crop, which they harvest in June and July. The third crop is Heatwave and Celebrity, transplanted in July and harvested in late September and early October.

For broccoli, cauliflower, cabbage, and brussels sprouts, they sow one or more varieties in early September in a nursery bed, then bare-root transplant them in late October, harvesting during late November through December. In January they sow one or more varieties in flats in the greenhouse, transplanting them out in early March for harvesting in April and May. Carol and Larry grow brussels sprouts mostly for the leaves. "We cut the leaves and bunch them as cooking greens as soon as the plant is strong enough (about 2 feet tall) to take this affront."

Location makes a difference. "In Austin, we can grow a wide array of vegetables year round. The more variety we have, the happier our farmstand customers are." Part of the fun of having a farmstand, Carol and Larry say, is the challenge of educating folks on what vegetables are in season at a particular time. "They soon learn that there's no broccoli and lettuce in July, and there are no green beans in January. Are they happier with this knowlege? No."

If you're going to succeed at organic gardening or farming, it's important to have vigorous productive varieties. The following varieties are those that Carol and Larry depend on. To check on the weekly progress of vegetables at Boggy Creek Farms, log on to http://www.boggycreekfarm.com.

Warm-Season Crops

Tomatoes	Early Girl, Celebrity, Heatwave
Squash	Gray Zucchini, Saffron, White Scalloped
Cucumber	Supersett

Cool-Season Crops

Butter Head Lettuce	Ermosa, Optima
Cutting Lettuce for Salad Mix	Tango, Rouge d'Hiver, Winter Density, Salad Bowl, Red Salad Bowl
Greens	Italian Dandelions (red and green), Escarole, Endive Frisée, Arugula, Swiss Chard (Fordhook, Ruby Red, Bright Light), Mizuna, Broccoli Raab (Sessatina Grossa, a quick-bolting variety for "broccoli buds")
Broccoli	Packman, Marathon
Cauliflower	Snow Crown
Cabbage	Early Jersey Wakefield

| Brussels Sprouts | Jade Cross |
| Strawberries | Pájaro, Chandler |

"Surefire is the most reliably-productive, medium-sized tomato for Texans. Fruit are produced on a truly determinate plant which makes Surefire the ideal container-grown tomato. Taste panels are neutral on its taste which means some like the taste but none hate the taste—this can rarely be said of any variety. This is the tomato variety of choice for organic growers because of its crack-resistance fruit, its reliable productivity in cool and hot growing conditions, its storage ability and its superb flavor when grown on plants fertilized with copious amount of manure."—Jerry Parsons, Area Vegetable Specialist, San Antonio

VEGETABLES FOR THE HIGH PLAINS

The successful High Plains gardeners are the mulchers, drip irrigators, windbreak makers, and eternal optimists," explains Roland Roberts, a Texas A&M vegetable specialist in Lubbock and one of the many hardworking Extension professionals in Texas. He conducts extensive variety trials, lectures to a wide variety of audiences from commercial vegetable growers to Master Gardeners, and answers millions (well, almost) of phone calls. Rollie knows a lot about growing vegetables on the High Plains of Texas: "The unique climate and topography of the Texas High Plains present exciting challenges and great opportunities to vegetable gardeners. Most vegetables grow very well in their season here, as long as they are protected from 15 to 30 miles-per-hour gusty winds, especially in spring. Here we have a high elevation of 3,000 to 5,000 feet, intense sunlight (the result of clear, cloudless skies), and a low relative humidity. Most well water is high quality, though many towns use water from Lake Meredith, which has elevated soluble salts. Thirty-degree swings between day and night temperatures make for warm to hot days and cool nights all through the growing season of over 200 days."

Additional problems for the High Plains are drying winds and temperatures reaching mid to high 80s in April and May. Rollie says because of these conditions, the survival of newly transplanted vegetables and successful greens growers is heavily dependent on windbreaks. "Winds moderate during the summer, and our fall days are relatively calm and very sunny. It has been said that fall seems to just go on forever here."

LEAF LETTUCE

Most of the varieties in the following list will work anywhere in Texas if you situate your garden in a suitable location with plenty of sun, prepare a good soil environment rich in organic matter, provide adequate water, control pests, and in general, work your blankity, blankity off.

Asparagus	Jersey Giant, UC 157
Black Turtle Bean	Black Turtle T39, Midnight
Cranberry Bean	Dwarf Horticultural Green Pod
Pinto Bean	Arapaho, Othello, Pinray, Fiesta, #84350, Olathe
White Bean	Great Northern, Navy
Horticultural Bean	French Horticultural, Dwarf Horticultural Green Pod
Bush Lima Bean	Dixie Speckled, Dixie White, Henderson Bush, Baby Fordhook
Pole Lima Bean	Florida Speckled, Sieva, King of Garden
Mung Bean	TexSprout, Berkin
Flat-Pod Snap Bean	Greencrop Bush, Jumbo, Romano, Roma II
Oval-Pod Snap Bean	Bush Blue Lake 274, Contender, Tenderpod, Earliserve
Yellow Snap Bean	Slenderwax, Goldkist, Dorabel
Pole Snap Bean	Blue Lake Pole, Kentucky Blue, Romano Italian Pole
Beet Greens	Crosby Green Top, Avenger F1, Lutz Green Leaf
Beet Roots	Pacemaker III, Avenger, Cylindra, Lutz Green Leaf
Broccoli	Green Comet, Mariner, Packman
Brussels Sprouts	Prince Marvel, Jade Cross

Chinese Heading Cabbage	Jade Pagoda, China Express
Lei Choi Cabbage	Joy Choi
Green Heading Cabbage	Early Jersey Wakefield, Market Prize, Blue Dynasty
Red Heading Cabbage	Cardinal, Red Rock, Red Dynasty
Savoy Cabbage	Savoy Ace, Savoy King
Cantaloupe, Muskmelon	Ambrosia, Israeli (Ogen), TAM Uvalde, Rocky Sweet, Don Carlos
Carrot	Gold King, Texas Gold Spike, BetaSweet, Scarlet Nantes, Snakpak
Cauliflower	Snow Crown, Stardust
Celeriac	Large Smooth Prague, Marble Ball
Celery	Florida 683
Collards	Blue Max, Georgia Southern, Vates
Ornamental Corn	Indian, Rainbow, Seedway Elite, Strawberry
Popping Corn	Robust 21-82W (replaces White Cloud), Japanese Hulless, Yellow
Early Sweet Corn	Early Sunglow, Seneca Daybreak, Seneca Arrowhead, Spring Snow
Mid-Season Sweet Corn	Bodacious, Terrific, Brilliance
Late Sweet Corn	Merit, Seneca Dancer, Argent
Greenhouse Cucumber	Bruneve, Brunex, Vetomil
Pickling Cucumber	Calypso, Carolina
Slicing Cucumber	Burpless, Dasher II, Sweet Slice, Sweet Success
Dill	Bouquet, Long Island Mammoth
Eggplant	Black Magic, Classic, Black Bell
Oriental Eggplant	Millionaire, Ichibon, Tycoon
Endive	Florida Deep Heart, Green Curled, Salad King
Garlic	California Early, Elephant, French Mild, Mexican Pink, Texas White
Honeydew Melon	TAM Dew
Horseradish	Maliner Kren
Jicama	de Agua
Kale	Dwarf Scotch
Kohlrabi	Early White Vienna, Grand Duke
Leek	American Flag, Electra, Titan
Butterhead Lettuce	Buttercrunch, Salad Bibb
Head Lettuce	Great Lakes 659 MT, Summertime MTO
Leaf Lettuce	Salad Bowl, Raisa (red), Black Seeded Simpson, Green Ice
Mustard	Southern Giant Curled, Tendergreen
Okra	Annie Oakley, Emerald
Short-Day Onion	Texas Grano 1015Y, Red Burgundy, White Granex
Intermediate Onion	Texas Grano 438, Cimarron, Riviera, Yula, Calred, Alabaster
Long-Day Onion	Candy, Yellow Sweet Spanish, Vega, Carmen, White Sweet Spanish, Sterling
Parsley	Plain Italian, Moss Curled, Banquet
Parsnip	Harris Model, Large Hollow Crown
Pea	Little Marvel, Wando, Knight
Edible-Pod Snowpea	Mammoth Melting Sugar, Oregon Sugar Pod #2
Edible-Pod Snap Pea	Early Snap, Sugar Ann, Super Sugar Snap
Southern Pea	Texas Pinkeye, Early Scarlet, California Blackeye #5, Arkansas #1, Zipper Cream, Cream 40
Bell Pepper	TAMBELL-2, Commandant, King Arthur, Admiral, Yellow Bell, Golden Bell
Chile Pepper	TAMU Hidalgo (serrano), TAMU Mild Chile-2 and TAMU Sweet Chile (mild, sweet long chile), Big Jim (long chile), TAMU Mild Jalapeño II, Firenza (hot jalapeño), Tula (medium hot, jumbo jalapeño), Pecos (medium hot, jumbo jalapeño), Delicias (medium hot jalapeño), Dulce (sweet jalapeño), TAMU Veracruz (hot jalapeño)
Potato	Texas Russet Norkotah 278, Atlantic, Yukon Gold, Red LaSoda
Pumpkin	Magic Lantern, Merlin, Fairytale, Prizewinner, Munchkin, Mystic, Oz, Snackjack

Radish	Champion, Cheriette, White Icicle
Rhubarb	Texas High Plains Green, Valentine
Rutabaga	American Purple Top
Salsify	Mammoth Sandwich Island
Spinach	Melody, Fall Green, Ozarka II
Squash	Sweet Meat, Waltham Butternut, Vegetable Spaghetti, Buttercup Burgess, Carnival, Ambercup, Table Ace
Summer Squash	Dixie, Supersett, Multipik, Superpik, Zucchini Elite, Seneca Zucchini, Gold Rush, Eight Ball
Sweet Potato	Hernandez, Vardaman
Swiss Chard	Large White Rib, Rhubarb Chard, Bright Lights, Silverado
Tomato	Carnival, Celebrity, Santiago, Sunmaster, Cherry Grande, Spitfire
Tomatillo	Toma Verde
Turnip	Just Right, Purple Top White Globe, Shogoin
Turnip Greens	Seven Top, Tyfon
Seeded Watermelon	Stars & Stripes, Big Stripe, Pinata, Super Gold, Summer Gold
Seedless Watermelon	Tri-X-Carousel, CS 4830, Gem Dandy, Triple Sweet, SummerSweet 5244

Roland Roberts, a Lubbock area vegetable specialist, advises that when growing tomatoes, foliage cover can be important. "It is very necessary to shade the fruit from intense High Plains sunlight." He recommends Santiago for excellent foliage cover over the fruit and good heat-setting ability, and he notes that SunMaster sets many fruit at high temperatures but must have very fertile soil and frequent irrigation to keep the foliage growing ahead of the fruit during hot weather.

Willie's Salsa

One day during tomato season (the plump, juicy, red things were lying all over the counter), I decided it was time to create my own version of the fresh salsas I had enjoyed at Tex-Mex restaurants. I started chopping tomatoes, onions, jalapeños, cilantro, and garlic. I'd chop, then add a dash of Creole seasoned salt, chop some more, more seasoned salt and some black pepper, then some fresh lime juice. Before I knew it, the stuff started to taste pretty good. After a few hours in the fridge, it was even better. The garlic sorta knocked your head off, but as long as everyone ate some, no one seemed to mind.

4 to 6 regular tomatoes, or 6 to 8 Roma type
½ to 1 Texas Supersweet or 1015 onion
Juice of one lime
1 T. Creole seasoning salt
1 tsp. coarsely ground black pepper
1 to 2 jalapeños (serranos or similar hot peppers)
1 to 2 cloves of fresh garlic (do not substitute)
1 to 2 fistfuls of fresh cilantro (do not substitute or omit)

Chop the tomatoes into fine pieces. Do the same with the onion or use your vegematic. Combine tomatoes and onions in a bowl, squeeze the lime juice over both, and add the seasoning salt and pepper. Mince the peppers and garlic or chop in a small food processor. Stir all of this together.

Wash the cilantro thoroughly and chop into fine pieces; this is the most tedious part of the job, but it is essential. Add to the mixture, stir, and put in the refrigerator to allow the flavors to blend. Tomatoes taste best at room temperature but don't get careless—even though this salsa has a lot of acidity, it shouldn't be left out of the refrigerator for more than a few hours, or one football game or ice-skating championship.

For a little variety, add ¼ to ½ tsp. chipotle powder or cinnamon.

LOW-CHILL FRUITS FOR TEXAS

Texans gardening along the Upper Gulf Coast and farther south will find that most of the standard fruit varieties don't grow well. They need more chilling hours in the winter to break dormancy. These hours basically occur below 45 degrees F and above 32 degrees F. Gardeners in Houston usually get 400 to 500 chilling hours, while in the Rio Grande Valley they may be lucky to get 150. In the Hill Country, 800 to 1000 chill hours are expected. At best, it's an imperfect system. In the fall while trees still have their leaves, chill hours don't count as much. January chill hours seem to be most critical in these marginal areas, and hot days may erase some of the accumulated hours. Biological processes just don't fit well in mathematical systems.

Apples
Anna   Yellow Delicious type; needs Dorsett Golden for pollination
Dorsett Golden   Yellow Delicious type; needs Anna for pollination

Pears
Hosui   russeted, Asian type
Kieffer   hard, canning type
Pineapple   prolific, canning type
Southern Queen   desert pear quality
Tenn (Tennessee)   crisp, tart yet sweet, bell shaped

Peaches
Earlitreat   yellow fleshed, ripens early May
Eva's Pride   yellow freestone, ripens late May
Florida Belle   yellow fleshed, very low chill
Red Baron   beautiful flowers, upper Gulf/Central
TexRoyal   high quality yellow, upper Gulf/Central
Tropic Snow   white fleshed, semi-freestone, early
Tropic Sweet   yellow fleshed, very low chill

Nectarines
Artic Glo   ripens over extended period
Artic Star   white fleshed, ripens mid June
Desert Dawn   yellow, semi-freestone, ripens late May
Karla Rose   good quality, needs thinning
Mayglo   good quality, dark red
Sunmist   high quality, white fleshed

Plums
Methley   small, soft, very tasty
Santa Rosa and other Calif. hybs. high quality but susceptible to Bacterial Canker
Wade   dark red flesh, larger than Methley

Blackberries
Arapaho   delicious large berries, upright thornless, for Gulf, C, N
Brazos   large berries, large seeds
Brison   large berries, semi-large seeds
Navaho   delicious large berries, upright thornless, for Gulf, C, N
Rosborough   large berries, semi-large seeds

Strawberries
Chandler   main commercial variety
Florida 90   old variety but still good
Sequoia   large, soft California variety

CHILL HOURS

Fruit trees are often referred to by their chill-hour requirements—the hours of temperature below 45 degrees F but above freezing. It's really much more complicated, but the system can still be used as a guideline. Hot weather can wipe out chill hours. Chill hours are more effective in the last months of the winter, and there are many other factors that have been proposed for this equation. Most years a 500-chill-hour peach will break dormancy in Houston and an 800-chill-hour peach will burst forth and grow normally in the Texas Hill Country. In the meantime, pomologists will continue to debate the merits of the chill-hour rating system and propose new rating methods.

BLUEBERRIES FOR EAST TEXAS

Blueberries are pretty easy to grow, but they do require some planning. The southern highbush hybrids need cross-pollination, and southern rabbiteye blueberries benefit from it, too. Blueberries demand acid soils and good drainage, and there are also various chilling requirements to consider.

One thing you don't want to do is to plunk them into a heavy clay soil with an alkaline pH. You also shouldn't plant them anywhere in West Texas. The bottom line is that blueberries thrive in acid (below pH 5.5), sandy soils and nowhere else. The occasional zealot will build a raised bed, fill it with a mix of sand and peat moss, and grow them where they aren't adapted. If alkaline water is an additional problem, even this extreme effort may not suffice. If your soil is okay but marginal, expect to use lots of iron chelate for soil or foliar treatments.

Rabbiteye Varieties

Baldwin — vigorous, upright plant; medium berries ripen mid to late season
Brightwell — vigorous, upright plant; medium berries, early
Briteblue — moderately vigorous and spreading; large early to mid-season berries
Climax — upright and spreading; medium berries, very early
Delite — vigorous, upright, but thin leaf canopy; early sugar development
Premier — moderately vigorous; large berries, early
Southland — moderately vigorous, mounding, with dense foliage; medium berries, mid season
Tifblue — vigorous, upright; medium to large berries, mid season
Woodard — medium-size, high yielding; large berries, early

Southern Highbush Hybrids

Avonblue — small, spreading plant with tendency to overbear; ripens early June
O'Neal — vigorous, semi-upright; large berries
Sharp Blue — small, self-pollinated; may be knocked out by late spring freezes; early
Southmoon — medium-chill requirement but tolerate low-chill years; large berries; cross-pollinate with Star
Star — blooms later so can miss late freezes; cross-pollinate with Southmoon

"Even if you have sandy, acid soil," advises Thomas R. LeRoy, a Montgomery County Extension agent in Conroe, "it pays to work lots of organic matter, preferably compost, with the soil before planting blueberries. They also like a heavy mulch, and you want to avoid using animal manure. Since blueberries need cross-pollination, it's best to plant at least three varieties for good fruit set."

FRUIT VARIETIES FOR CENTRAL AND NORTH TEXAS

The fruit varieties on this list generally fall in the 700 to 1,000 chill-hour range. Be sure to check with your local nursery and County Extension office for exact recommendations. Many of the low-chill varieties will grow in Central and North Texas, but they may have the flowers or fruit frozen out in a late spring freeze.

Apples
Braeburn
Fuji
Gala
Granny Smith
Holland
Jerseymac
McLemore
Mollies Delicious
Prime Gold
Red Chief
Smoothee
Starkrimson Golden Delicious
Starkrimson Red Delicious
Top Red

Apricots
Duecker
Hungarian
Moorpark
Peggy
Tisdale

Peaches
Bicentennial
Contender
Denman
Dixieland
Dixiered
Fireprince
Flameprince
Flavorcrest
Frank
Gala
Harvester
Hawthorne
Indian Cling
Jefferson
Loring
Majestic
Melba
Monroe
Parade
Quachita Gold
Ranger
Redglobe
Redhaven

Redskin
Rustin Red
Sentinel
Veteran

Pears
Hosui (Asian pear)
Magness
Moonglow
Twentieth Century (Asian pear)
Warren

Plums
Morris
Ozark Premier

Blackberries
Apache
Arapaho
Cheyenne
Kiowa
Navaho
Shawnee

BUNCH GRAPES FOR EAST TEXAS

GRAPES

Bunch grapes in East Texas have to be able to survive Pierce's Disease, which plugs up the vascular tissue, eventually killing the vines. Fortunately a few bunch grapes, mostly American hybrids, are resistant to the disease. Most aren't very good (wild mustang grapes make better jam), they aren't very productive, and they have other disease problems. A valid question is, "When you can grow muscadines, why bother?" Some people just like their grapes in bunches. If you must have bunch grapes, the following are resistant to Pierce's Disease.

Blanc duBois	white wine grape, hyper-susceptible to Anthracnose fungus
Champanel	makes excellent jams and jellies, great for an arbor
Lake Emerald	green, used for white wine, less susceptible to anthracnose
Le Noir (Black Spanish)	Port type wine, also good for jams, jellies, and juice
Orlando Seedless	white grape, very small berries, only good for attracting wildlife
Stover	white wine grape, doesn't come up to commercial production standards

Other varieties worth trying that are also resistant to Pierce's Disease:

Muench (Munson Var.)	Mid South	Miss Blanc
Carman (Munson Var.)	Miss Blue	Herbemont

MUSCADINE GRAPES

Muscadines don't produce large bunches of grapes, but they produce lots of clusters. In fact, they are typically more productive per acre than bunch grapes. Muscadines offer the best potential for East Texas. They are generally resistant to Pierce's Disease (the single, most limiting factor in the production of grapes in Texas), though growers have found some infection of muscadines in heavily planted areas.

Wine made from muscadines can be quite good, but so far they have been more popular for fresh juice, jams, jellies, and of course for fresh use. You might say they taste like "cheap perfume" because of the esters and strong flavors, but that is being a little unfair. There aren't any good seedless varieties yet, and the skins can be a little tough, but once you've tried a flavorful muscadine, the so-called "table grapes" like Thompson Seedless will seem pale by comparison.

Muscadines also have beautiful, glossy-green leaves that turn bright yellow in the fall. They would make spectacular arbor plants even if they didn't produce fruit. To insure good production, some pruning is in order. You don't have to plan for renewal canes when you prune. The main fruiting arms are left indefinitely. Smaller twigs are pruned back to 2 to 3 bud spurs (small one-year shoots). There are lots of them, however—muscadines can cover your house in a couple of years. Muscadines are a bit puny the first year, but after that, look out—they grow like crazy.

Muscadines are typically spaced 10 to 20 feet, though 20 feet in the row may be advisable with the more vigorous varieties. If female varieties are planted, they should have at least two self-fertile varieties within 50 feet (at least one in each direction at 25 feet or less). Home gardeners will do better if they stick to the self-fertile varieties. Slow-release fertilizer tablets are good to use the first year: two to three 20-gram pellets per plant. In succeeding years, using enough fertilizer to insure 3 to 4 feet of growth should be adequate.

The berries of the listed varieties will ripen late July to September.

Carlos	light bronze fruit, self-fertile
Cowart	dark fruit, self-fertile, good for wine, jelly, or fresh consumption
Darlene	bronze, female, large berry, high sugar content
Fry	bronze, female, high quality, very productive
Higgins	black to reddish bronze, female, high quality with low acidity
Hunt	black, female, high quality, good wine grape
Ison	black, self-fertile, good for wine, juice or jelly
Janebell	bronze, self-fertile, very large, high sugar content
Magnolia	bronze, self-fertile, one of the best for wine production
Noble	dark red, self-fertile, even ripening, good for wine production
Pam	bronze, female, extra large, high sugar content
Scuppernong	bronze, female, small but highly flavored
Summit	bronze, female, excellent overall variety, thin-skinned
Sweet Jenny	bronze, female, huge berries, very high sugar content
Triumph	bronze, self-fertile, thin-skinned, in large clusters

"If you decide to grow muscadines, forget everything you've ever learned about growing bunch grapes. Make sure you have good drainage and train the vines so they don't grow higher than 54 inches. Otherwise you'll wear out trying to prune them. Pruning muscadines is laborious because they are so vigorous. The best varieties for wine are Magnolia, Carlos, Noble, and Cowart. They have a concentrated fruit set, so you can harvest a uniform product, and the berries have a high sugar content."
—Alfred Flies, Piney Woods Country Wine, Orange

VIRUS-FREE CITRUS

Mani Skaria, a professor at Texas A&M University's Kingsville Citrus Center in Weslaco, introduced the virus-free program in Texas and developed the virus-free production techniques that have made it possible. He explains that citrus species are susceptible to a number of virus diseases that are transmitted during propagation by buds, grafting, or by rooted cuttings. Some viruses are transmitted by insects like the brown citrus aphid. "Regardless of the source of infection, citrus with these diseases decline in productivity and often die. Unfortunately the trees may appear perfectly healthy for several years before symptoms begin to show up. This makes it especially important to buy trees that are certified virus free, since you could waste several years with newly planted virus-infected stock and then have them die. During the same period they may also have served as inoculum sites to infect other healthy trees."

The virus free program is just beginning, so currently few citrus trees are available to the homeowner that can be certified virus free. Even if nurseries are required to grow certified virus-free citrus trees, amateur propagators may still be spreading diseases such as citrus tristeza virus and exocortis viroid. In 1997 the Texas Legislature passed House Bill 2807, which applies to all nurseries that maintain their own citrus propagation stock (trees for budwood). When an adequate supply of a given cultivar, for example, Rio Red grapefruit, is available, the commissioner of agriculture can adopt a rule saying that citrus rootstocks cannot be budded with Rio Red unless the budwood is virus free. For more information, visit *http://primera.tamu.edu/kcchome/depts/texas_citrus_budwood.htm.*

The following are a few of the currently available citrus cultivars.

Oranges	Mandarins	Tangelos/Tangors	Limes/Lemons
Marrs early	Owari	Orlando	Mexican lime
N-33 navel	Dobashi Beni		Improved Meyer lemon
Everhard navel	Clementine	**Grapefruit/Pummelo**	Frost Eureka
Pineapple	Honey	Rio Red	Ponderosa
Olinda Valencia	Nova	Star Ruby	
Midknight Valencia	Fairchild	Henderson	**Other Cultivars**
Campbell Valencia	Kinnow	Sarawak	Meiwa kumquat
Hamlin	Okitsu	Chandler	Calamondin
Cara Cara	Sunburst		
Fukumoto	Kishu		
Lana late navel			

"Most citrus production is located in the Lower Rio Grande Valley along the Mexican border," explains Mani Skaria, a Texas A&M professor at the Kingsville Citrus Center in Weslaco. "It includes over 33,000 acres with approximately 70 percent of the acreage in grapefruit, 25 percent in oranges, and the rest in tangerines, Meyer lemon, and others. The total economic impact of the Texas citrus industry is about $150 million, involving more than 5,000 employees."

Several exotic diseases of citrus and other fruit trees are present throughout the world, Mani points out, and could seriously impact the U.S. fruit tree industry if introduced. Most of the economically important diseases can be transmitted through the buds taken from an infected tree for plant propagation. "This situation is common because an infected tree may be symptomless for some time. Production and the distribution of pathogen-free fruit trees with superior horticultural qualities can be achieved through proper planning and implementation."

CITRUS VARIETIES FOR SOUTH TEXAS

The upper Gulf Coast region and the Rio Grande Valley of Texas are good locations for homeowners to try their luck with citrus. There's considerable production of citrus in south Texas, mostly grapefruits, and there's production of Bower tangerines around Carrizo Springs, satsumas at Pearsall, and Hamlin oranges at Santa Catarina.

It's a lot easier to save one or two trees planted on the south side of the house than it is to save forty acres when temperatures are predicted to drop into the mid 20s or lower. Even low temperatures may not be the barrier that most people perceive. New technology using mist sprinklers in the tree canopy can help to reduce freeze damage. Louis Walden, a member of the Galveston County Extension Fruit and Pecan Committee, recommends you consider these factors: (1) Select varieties with cold hardiness. (2) Plant virus-free trees. (3) Select varieties with good-quality, early ripening fruit. (4) Select the proper rootstock for your area.

Because of the fear that we might introduce insect pests and diseases, it is very difficult to bring citrus plants or even budwood into the state. Along the upper Gulf Coast, most citrus does best when grafted on trifoliate orange or a hybrid like Thomasville citrangequat. In the Valley, because of alkaline, salty soils, sour orange is preferred. The Texas A&M research center in Weslaco is currently making available virus-free citrus budwood of a number of varieties (see the "Virus-Free Citrus" list), and eventually this should improve the quality of Texas-grown citrus trees. Most hobbyists just pass budwood around, which can spread diseases. Tristeza virus is especially worrisome since it is easy to spread.

Oranges	Cold Hardiness
Tomango	Good
Louisiana Sweet	Good
Naval	Good
Marrs	Fair
Pineapple	Fair
Hamlin	Fair
Republic of Texas	Good

Grapefruit	
Bloom Sweet	Fair
Marsh	Fair
Ruby Red	Fair
Henderson	Fair
Rio Red	Fair
Star Ruby	Fair
Golden	Fair

Mandarins/Tangelos	
Satsuma (Big Early, Armstrong, and Okitsu)	Very good
Clementine Tangerine (Monreal)	Very good
Fairchild Tangerine	Good
Changsha Tangerine	Very good
Orlando Tangelo	Good

Kumquats	
Nagami Kumquat	Very good
Meiwa Kumquat (seedless)	Very good
Chang Chou	Very good

Acid Citrus	
Calamondin	Good
Thomasville Citrangequat	Very good
Meyer Lemon	Fair
Ponderosa Lemon	Poor
Eureka Lemon	Poor
Mexican Lime	Poor
Eustis Limequat	Good
Sunquat	Good
Yuzuquat	Good

> "My own citrus trees are grown between pecan trees, with evergreens and timber bamboo to the north. Pecan trees are deciduous in the winter, allowing sun to penetrate for the citrus, and in the summer the pecan canopy keeps the average air temperature around 85 degrees F, the growing range for citrus. I use the mulch from tree and bamboo prunings to reduce the need for irrigation."
> —Louis Walden, Galveston County Extension Fruit and Pecan Committee

FIGS

Figs are among the easiest fruits to grow in Texas gardens, but they do have a few quirks. They don't like dry, hot summers. Some varieties, like Celeste or Blue Sugar, are notorious for producing leathery fruits that never become palatable under these conditions. Celeste is one of the figs that produces best on one-year-old wood. If it freezes back severely or is pruned too hard, leaving none of last year's growth, it doesn't produce the early crop of fruit that it is famous for. Figs that develop on the current season's growth late in the season rarely mature.

Use a strawy manure mulch; it provides a weak fertilizer and helps to keep the soil cool and conserve moisture. Too much fertilizer and the tree produces lots of vegetative growth that it may not be able to support under stress from heat, drought, and nematodes. During dry spells, water thoroughly by letting the hose run at a trickle in three to four spots around the drip line, for several days if necessary, to soak the soil 8 to 12 inches deep.

FIG

Another factor makes it even more important not to stress figs. The fruit isn't pollinated, so the seeds aren't viable. This means that there is a low hormone concentration in the fruit (the tree doesn't have much to gain from a survival standpoint by maturing the fruit), and under stress the trees will drop or shrivel fruit first.

Generally, varieties with a closed eye or a drop of honey-like substance in the eye are best, since they discourage beetles from entering the fruit and causing it to sour.

Alma	Kadota type fig with drop of honey in the eye
Banana	Kadota type with a long production season and high-quality fruit
Black Jack	best in warmer areas, large brown fruit
Black Negronne (Violette de Bordeaux)	high-quality, purplish-black fruit
Brown Turkey (Texas Everbearing)	medium-brown fig, open eye
Celeste (Blue Sugar)	top quality, bears on last year's wood, closed eye
Excel	Kadota type, best in high-rainfall areas
Ischia (Green)	medium size, red flesh, low production, high quality
LSU purple	similar to Celeste, bears on new growth, prolific
Magnolia	canning variety, large open eye
Petite Negri	bush type, tasty rich flavor
San Piero (CA Brown Turkey)	large, open eye

ASIAN PERSIMMONS

You never forget biting into an astringent persimmon. Puckering is one response; then there's that feeling that you have gloves on your teeth—and it takes a long time to go away. You may decide never to try another persimmon. Take heart: While all of the native persimmons (*Diospyros virginiana*) remain astringent until jelly ripe, some of the Asian persimmons (*Diospyros kaki*) are nonastringent and can be eaten while still crisp. They tend to be at their best when they develop full color, but they don't have to be soft and mushy.

Even the astringent varieties like Saijo and Hachiya are good once they take on that translucent look and get jelly-like inside. They actually have more complex flavors than the nonastringent varieties develop, but the texture takes some getting used to.

The following Asian persimmons are nonastringent varieties.

Fuyu	excellent variety with many variations (Giant Fuyu or Hana Fuyu, Matsumoto Wase Fuyu, Fuyugaki); not many seeds
Hanagosho	large, round, conical-shaped fruit; matures late November so may not ripen before the first hard freeze
Ichikikei Jiro	large, flat fruit on a relatively dwarf tree
Izu	medium-sized, very early fruit, often ripe in September
Suruga	ripens large fruit in November/December

HARDY BANANAS

A number of years ago, one of the authors of this book was asked by a gentleman about growing bananas in Houston and answered him, chuckling, "Bananas grow well in Panama. Why don't you move to Panama and take your banana with you?" He failed to share the humor. We've eaten a bunch (pun intended) of tasty, locally grown bananas since then. As long as we're having mild winters, there's a good chance folks will harvest bananas in the fall.

The trick is to get the large fruiting trunks through the winter unharmed. Some people wrap them with layers of newspaper, then white paper and red ribbons for Christmas decorations. Others use aluminum-coated insulation normally reserved for duct work, making them look like alien rocketships. Mulching will help, and planting on the south side of the house isn't a bad idea either. If all goes well, the next fall, watch the bananas to see when the ridges on the fruit begin to round off. They can be harvested at this stage and allowed to ripen in the garage. But as long as temperatures stay above freezing, leave them on the plant. If they stay on until they develop yellow color, you can expect a real taste treat.

Hardy is a relative term. The varieties in this list may survive the mild winters along the upper Gulf Coast and farther south, but they don't survive a Winter of '83 with a week of freezing temperatures. In the Rio Grande Valley they have a better chance, but no one is likely to grow them commercially.

Gran Nain	comparatively dwarf with large fruit clusters
Pysang Raja	tall and hardy with delicious pinkish fruit
Rajapuri	tough and hardy with medium-size fruit

EXOTIC FRUITS

The quest for exotic fruit makes normally sane gardeners plant some really bizarre plants. Then they use extreme methods just to prove they can succeed at something they should never have tried. Usually these gardeners have scored with petunias, tomatoes, and fruits like pears. They need a challenge, a mountain to climb. Sometimes they are just stubborn. Most are running on a full tank of ignorance—at least at the start. Many succeed. The quest might be as simple as planting an avocado seed from the grocery store, or as complicated as plant exploration in another country. You can never underestimate their sincerity.

Avocados

Avocados are rarely successful even in the Rio Grande Valley, but if you want to try them, look for Mexican avocados. Most commercial varieties are West Indian (the giant ones from Florida), Guatemalan, or hybrids of Mexican and Guatemalan types. The Mexican types have fruit with a thin skin and a large seed in relation to the fruit size. The foliage has an anise fragrance when crushed. Adding to the confusion, avocados are classified as type A or type B. One sheds pollen in the morning but is receptive the next afternoon, and vice versa. One of the most successful home plantings was in South Houston, where a lady had planted six seeds in one spot in the backyard. She had purchased the fruit at a stand in the Valley, and the trees grew up together as one plant. They were apparently Mexican avocados, and the six plants together must have solved the pollination problem.

Loquats

The loquat (*Eriobotrya japonica*) seems a bit confused. It blooms in the fall, and the tiny fruits have to survive the winter before they can mature. In gardens from Houston south, they often do mature, but the plants will survive a hundred miles or so north of this area. Loquats should be looked on as one of those gifts nature occasionally bestows on us following a mild winter. They ripen about the same time as strawberries, and the two combined make a wonderful jam. The loquat fruit is too tart to eat fresh until it begins to turn orange-ripe, and even then they contain a lot of large seeds.

Pawpaws

The pawpaw (*Asimina triloba*) has a wonderful name, and the fruit isn't bad either, though it does contain a number of large seeds. The basic flavor impression is of vanilla custard, but some fruits finish with a hint of kerosene. Even if you don't like the fruit, the trees are pretty. Pawpaws have large tropical-looking leaves, and they grow in a pyramidal shape up to 25 feet. They are typically understory trees, preferring a slightly acid, deep loam soil. Good drainage is essential, but they won't stand drought conditions without watering. For a plant that grows from Michigan to Florida, they aren't readily available in nurseries. Try nurseries that specialize in native plants, and ask for pawpaws grown from seed that originated in a similar climate. Michigan pawpaws wouldn't be at home in Texas.

Gumi Fruit

Gumi fruit (*Elaeagnus multiflora*) develops on a small, deciduous relative of the silverberry (*Elaeagnus pungens*), a common shrub in Texas landscapes. The gumi usually grows as a small tree with bright red, metallic berries. It prefers the higher rainfall and soil acidity of East Texas gardens, and it is nowhere common. Gardeners in Louisiana have a slightly better appreciation for this native of China. In fact, Louisiana Nursery in Opelousas, Louisiana, is one of the few mail-order sources for this plant. Jelly made with the berries has a nice red color but no discernable flavor. The birds like them, though.

Other Exotic Fruits

Exotic fruits like star fruit (*Averrhoa carambola*), lychee (*Litchi chinensis*), and mango (*Mangifera indica*) will require that you first build a conservatory, though star fruits have been grown as backyard trees in the Rio Grande Valley.

MAYHAWS

It's quite common in April and May to see signs for mayhaws and mayhaw jelly when driving along an East Texas highway. Mayhaws are the fruit of three hawthorn species that grow from East Texas to Virginia and Florida. *Crataegus opaca* is the one most commonly found in Texas, while *C. aestivalis* and *C. rufula* occur to our east. They typically grow in swampy areas and acid soils, but they also flourish in upland orchards with irrigation and the same good management one would give any fruit crop. They are equally successful when used in the landscape as small to medium-sized flowering trees.

Early settlers soon realized mayhaws could be used to make great jellies, syrups, pies, and even wine. "In the 1800s and early 1900s, southern folks used native fruits that were growing close by and that were in season," says Marty Baker, a horticulturist at the Research and Extension Center in Overton. "The mayhaw was the first tree to flower in the winter and the first to fruit in early spring." Unfortunately, mayhaws are too tart to be eaten fresh, and a bit small, too. Most mayhaws run five-eighths to three-quarters of an inch in diameter, with some selected varieties up to an inch in diameter.

"Few people today actually know what a mayhaw is," Marty observes. "At some point in the last forty years, the mayhaw seemingly dropped out of sight. Southerners moved into town and lost touch with nature. Much of the mayhaw's habitat also has been destroyed, so it's harder for a person to go out and find mayhaws now." Mayhaw trees are not commonly available in nurseries, and the named varieties are even harder to find. You may have to learn how to graft or bud your own trees, but the effort is worth it. The following varieties are recommended by Marty, whose favorite is Texas Star.

Angelina	Heavy	Super Spur
Big Mama	Highway Red	T. O. Warren Superberry
Big Red	Highway Yellow	Temple
Big V	Leaning	Texas
Cajun	Lindsey	Texas Producer
Capps	Loir	Texas Star
F1	Mason Superberry	Warren Opaca
Hanky	Pinder	Winnie (several)
Harrison No. 1 Pink	Rose Apple	Winnie yellow
Harrison No. 2 Pink	Stark LA No. 1	

MAYHAW JELLY
Combine a gallon container of mayhaws with one gallon of water. Cook until tender. Strain through cheese-cloth, making sure to get every last drop of juice. This should yield about 10 cups of juice. If not, add enough water to make 10 cups.
   To make the jelly, combine 5 cups of juice with 7 cups of sugar, and use with 1 box of Sure-Jell as directed (apple or crabapple jelly would be similar).

JUJUBES

Jujubes can be grown virtually anywhere in Texas. Birds and two-legged varmints do seem to find them some years, but otherwise they seem to be a fruit you really can grow organically. If they're this easy, then there must be something wrong with them, right? The early varieties introduced into this country a hundred years ago tended to be very thorny with small, sour fruits. Newer varieties are sweet as candy with a nice blend of tartness. They can be as large as a plum. The skins are still a bit tough but not objectionable, and they ripen late in the season—July to September—when fresh fruit is scarce. Think of jujubes as small apples that are very good for you. In fact, jujubes are elements in a number of Asian medicinal products, such as jujube tea. They can also be candied to make an excellent date substitute; this product is often available in Asian grocery stores as Chinese or red dates.

Jujube trees grow 25 to 30 feet tall (15 to 20 feet with pruning) and tend to spread by underground suckers. It's hard to find named variety jujube trees—Li and Lang are the most common. If you do find them, they are probably grafted. This means the suckers that pop up will be rootstock with small, sour fruits. The Meyer Nursery in California (see the "Resources" section of this book) is a major source for new varieties. Most varieties have thorns, but a few are relatively thornless. The foliage is a beautiful glossy green, and the tiny yellow flowers are very fragrant. Jujubes should be easy to blend into the landscape without establishing a separate fruit orchard.

Li	large round fruit, best when yellow green, mid August
Lang	large pear-shaped fruit, best half brown, late; use for dehydration or jujube butter
Sugar Cane	small to medium size, very sweet, crunchy, August
So	round, sweet, August; tree has zigzag growth habit
GA 866	large elongated fruit, August; sugars near 45 percent; poor production
Tsao	fruit pointed at both ends, sweet, early August
GI 7-62	round, flattened fruit, very sweet, August
Sweet Meaty	sweet, tart, marble-size fruit; extremely vigorous, thorny, and productive

Other Promising Varieties
Si Hong, September Late, and Ant Admire

"Jujubes grow in almost any soil that does not have standing water. The first year after transplanting, the trees may need some watering; after that, they can be ignored. A little watering may be needed, however, during long dry spells and to crisp up the fruit as it starts to ripen. For maximum crispness and flavor, the fruit should be picked early in the morning before the dew evaporates."
—Sam Powers, fruit enthusiast, Santa Fe, Texas

PECANS FOR THE HOME LANDSCAPE

Pecans really aren't good trees for most home landscapes. They often grow too large. They usually need a few pesticide sprays if one expects regular crops, and pumping chemicals 60 feet into the neighbor's airspace isn't popular these days. Why bother with a list? Pecans are a southern tradition, they're the State Tree of Texas, and they make wonderful pies. There are also a lot of Texas landscapes large enough for a pecan tree or two, and disease-resistant varieties make the spray problem less severe.

Big "papershell" varieties are the ones most people ask for, but to be honest, small to medium-size pecans with good disease resistance and beautiful kernels are a better choice. Unless you just have to have big nuts to put in a bowl and impress the neighbors, the medium ones can be cracked by a custom sheller (there's usually one at the local farmer's market). Then all you have to do is remove the shells and freeze the kernels. This is, after all, what you planted the pecan tree for. This is assuming you have enough to shell after the squirrels, bluejays, and crows finish feasting.

If you just want the tree for shade, then forget the spraying, save your money, and buy the pecans at the farmer's market. The shade is great, and with a nontoxic spray of zinc sulfate or one of the zinc/nitrogen products in the early spring (about the time when the new leaves have just matured), you will have the darkest green leaves in the neighborhood.

Most people only have room for one pecan in the landscape, but pecans need cross-pollination. You may still be all right because the pollen can carry for a mile in the wind and someone, upwind, probably has a complementing variety. Protandrus varieties shed pollen early in the season, and the female nutlets are receptive later. Protogynous varieties do just the opposite. This is nature's way of insuring cross-pollination.

Many of the eastern varieties listed below can be grown in the west, too, and have better scab resistance than the western varieties. Some of the western varieties, such as Western and Wichita, have very high-quality kernels when grown in a dry climate. Larry Womack, of Womack's Nursery in DeLeon, suggests drawing a line through San Antonio and Fort Worth. The western varieties should be grown west of this line.

In the following lists of pecans, the number of nuts per pound is a measure of their size. Fifty to sixty per pound is medium size. Kernel percentage is a measure of shell thickness and how much you have left to eat. The varieties with 55 percent or more kernel have acceptably thin shells.

Disease-Resistant Pecans for East Texas

Variety	Pollen	Nuts/lb.	Kernel
Caddo	early	60 to 70	50%
Candy	late	60 to 70	48%
Cape Fear	early	50 to 55	53%
Choctaw	late	35 to 40	55%
Desirable	early	40	55%
Elliot	late	75 to 80	50%
Forkert	late	50	60%
Gloria Grande	late	50	47%
Houma	early	40	55%
Jackson	early	42	60%
Jubilee	late	40 to 50	51%
Kanza	late	72	55%
Kernodle	late	60	60%
Oconee	early	48	54%
Pointe Coupee	late	69	53%
Prilop of Lavaca	undetermined	78	57%
Shawnee	late	55	60%
Sumner	late	55 to 60	55%
Surprise	early	40 to 45	49%

Western Pecan Varieties

Apache	late	50	60%
Kiowa	late	40 to 50	60%
Pawnee	early	55 to 60	60%
Western	early	55	60%
Wichita	late	60	60%

Pecan trees can be difficult to transplant. Larry Womack, of the Womack Nursery in DeLeon, advises: "First be sure that you have a good site for a pecan tree. It's best to have a deep loamy soil, and you need full sun and plenty of room. In the orchard, pecans are planted 50 to 75 feet apart. Make sure that the roots stay moist while you're digging the hole." Larry recommends planting the tree at the same level as it grew in the nursery. "In western areas it can be a half inch deeper, while in high-rainfall areas it is best left an inch or so high with soil or mulch pulled up to cover the roots. If the hole cannot be dug as deep as the length of the taproot, cut off the bottom of the taproot so that the tree can be planted at the proper depth." Larry warns against putting organic matter in the bottom of the hole because it can sour and kill the tree. Trees should be cut back one-half to one-third to compensate for the loss of roots during digging and transplanting. "Keep in mind that the wide-angle branches are the strongest. Limbs which form a narrow crotch are weak and will usually split at the crotch."

HERBS YOU WILL REALLY USE

The kitchen garden would be bland indeed without a few herbs. Until you decide to make herbs your life, it's best to plant the ones you will really use. You won't even need a special herb garden; you can plant them in pots or hanging baskets. Put a few in the flowerbed—some of them are very pretty. If you have a kitchen garden, reserve a row for herbs or tuck them in and around the vegetables and fruit trees. They may even repel a few pests.

Most herbs need good drainage, but mints do quite well under a leaky faucet. Herbs are generally pest free except for the occasional spider mite on rosemary, or thrips on garlic. If you have to spray, use low-toxic alternatives like wettable sulfur, biologicals, or botanicals.

The herbs listed here are all really useful. The leaves of cilantro or coriander, for example, are indispensable in Mexican dishes. This herb is also popular in Asian food, and the seeds are used for their spicy, very different flavor with fruits, desserts, and pastries. Cilantro likes cool growing conditions, and so does dill. Don't just use dill in pickles, though. Try some chopped up in mashed potatoes with lots of real butter and sour cream. Mexican mint marigold can be used as a substitute for tarragon in teas or in salads. Oregano provides the fragrance and flavor most of us associate with pizza, and try using a sprig of fresh rosemary to mop chicken with Bar-B-Q sauce. Winter and summer savory are both great with beans and other vegetables, and you can make a stew without it, but it's not advisable. Several varieties of thyme are widely used in the kitchen for seasoning meats and bean and vegetable dishes. Arugula, which is a spicy addition to salad mixes like mesclun, grows like a weed in fall and winter. Since it easily reseeds, arugula may become one of your favorite weeds.

Arugula	likes cool growing conditions in fall/winter; reseeds
Basil	loves Texas summers; in winter needs a greenhouse
Chives	garlic chives (flat leaf) are year round; delicately flavored onion chives survive summer with enough water and a bit of shade
Cilantro, Coriander	easy to grow in fall; bolts to seed in early spring
Dill	likes cool growing conditions in fall/winter; survives to early summer for the pickle crop if planted in late winter/early spring
Garlic	set the cloves about an inch deep in the fall; harvest new bulbs in late spring
Mexican Mint Marigold	mild, tarragon-like flavor; different species from flower type
Mints	peppermint, spearmint, orange mint, and apple mint are weed-like in their vigor
Oregano	easy to grow; looks great trailing over a wall or in a hanging basket
Parsley	easy to grow in fall; curly-leaf forms last into the summer
Rosemary	not hardy north of Houston; treat as an annual
Savory	winter (perennial) or summer (annual) savory thrive in cool weather; survive summer with lots of water
Thyme	many varieties: lemon, creeping, French, woolly, caraway, nutmeg, coconut, and common thyme

MEXICAN HERBS

This list comes from Lucinda Hutson in Austin, who wrote *The Herb Garden Cookbook.* "I am delighted that many of my favorite Mexican herbs are also at home in Texas gardens," she says. "Most are perennials. In fact, in mild winters they do not even freeze back—and most are more tolerant of drought than other plants." These versatile herbs delight garden guests, offering both ornamental and culinary virtue with their lively aromas, colors, textures, and flavors. Many are herbaceous shrubs that add form and texture to the garden and explode into a colorful array of flowers in the fall. The increasing popularity of these Mexican herbs makes them easily available at many local nurseries or by mail order.

Chile Petin, Pequin (*Capsicum* spp.), CS, V, Annual

Epazote, Wormwood, Goosefoot (*Chenopodium ambrosioides*), Annual

Chaya, medicinal (*Cnidoscolus chayamansa*), V

Cilantro, Coriander (*Coriandrum sativum*), Cool season annual

Jamaica, Tea Hibiscus (*Hibiscus sabdariffa*), Tropical, Annual

Mexican Oregano (*Lippia graveolens*), CS, V, Annual

Yerba Buena (*Satureja douglasii*), CS, V

Albacar, Mexican Spice Basil (*Ocimum basilicum* 'Mexican Spice'), Annual

Aztec Sweet Herb (*Phyla scaberrima* [*Lippia dulcis*]), CSs, V

Hoja Santa, Root-Beer Plant (*Piper auritum*), CSs, V

Mexican Oregano (*Poliomintha longiflora*), CSs, V, Annual

Papaloquelite (*Porophyllum ruderale*), CS, V

Pineapple Sage (*Salvia elegans*), C, CS, V

Yerbanis, Mexican Mint Marigold (*Tagetes lucida*), CSs, V, Annual

YERBA BUENA

Adding a few ornamentals will increase the Mexican ambience of your garden. Datura (*Brugmansia*), also known as angels' trumpets because of the flower shape, is common in Texas, and this shrub often finds its way into ornamental plantings. All parts of datura, however, are toxic. If you plant it, don't eat it.

Two other ornamentals for a Mexican garden are Mexican bush sage (*Salvia leucantha*), which has long racemes of white or purple flowers, and Copper Canyon daisy (*Tagetes lemmonii*), which has very aromatic foliage, bright orange flowers, and tolerates arid conditions.

HERBS COMMONLY FOUND IN ASIAN CUISINE

Mary Versfelt, a Harris County Master Gardener, prepared this list of herbs commonly found in Asian Cuisine. "The semi-tropical conditions of heat, humidity, high rainfall, and mild winters could be reason enough to call Houston 'Saigon, Texas.' Many of the herbs that are very familiar to us are commonly used in the various Asian cuisines. Due to a large Asian population here, we benefit by the variety of Asian owned nurseries, grocery markets, and restaurants. All of these can be sources of knowledge, techniques, seeds, and plants. These flavorful additions to our diets can be used to reduce excess fat and sodium."

Garlic (*Allium sativum*)	plant in late fall, harvest in June
Garlic Chives (*Allium tuberosum*)	pretty in the landscape and in Asian dishes; easy to grow
Lemon Verbena (*Aloysia triphylla*)	needs winter protection when temperatures drop below freezing
Chiles (*Capsicum annuum*)	grow quickly and well in containers or ground; brighten summer and fall landscape
Cilantro (*Coriandrum sativum*)	plant in late fall and eat all winter; in summer let plants go to seed and dry them
Turmeric (*Curcuma domestica*)	plant fresh rhizomes very shallow; showy large-leafed plant for garden or container
Lemon Grass (*Cymbogon citratus*)	may freeze down; if well mulched, spring will bring fresh new growth
Rau Kinh Giôi (*Elsholtzia ciliata*)	Vietnamese lemon balm
Ngò Gai (*Eryngium foetidum*)	"thorny coriander"; substitute for coriander
Giáp Câ (*Houttuynia cordata*)	pretty ground cover; can be invasive; fishy taste is heavenly in a spring roll
Mint (*Mentha* spp.)	spearmint, red-stem applemint grow easily here
Basils (*Ocimum basilicum*)	sweet, cinnamon, licorice, lemon, and holy basil; lemon most often used, Siam Queen available in most nurseries
Perilla (*Perilla frutescens*)	purple-leaved salad herb or for beans; considered a weed here
Rau Ram (*Polygonum odoratum*)	Vietnamese coriander; scent of coriander with hint of lemon
Ginger (*Zingiber officinalis*)	showy in a container; plant very shallow, barely covered with soil

"The fusion of Asian plants into our gardens adds a new dimension in design as well as new tastes for your table. Texas gardeners are always willing to try something new, and Asian herbs, especially the lesser known ones, should be tried in your favorite recipes."
—Mary Versfelt, Harris County Master Gardener, Houston

HERB GARDEN COMBINATIONS

Combining plants is a real art form. Ellen Barner, a Harris County Master Gardener, contributed this assortment of combinations to use in gardens and containers. Nel maintains (with a lot of help from Master Gardener volunteers) the herb garden at the Extension Center in Bear Creek Park, Houston. "Herbs are interesting for a number of reasons. Some are edible and/or medicinal. Others feel or smell wonderful. Planted together in containers, in gardens, or cut for arrangements, they give the eye a textural treat." The following herbs and other plants are some Nel likes to put together.

Plant in Spring (All Zones)

Lavender (*Lavandula* spp.) or curry plant (*Helichrysum angustifolium*)
Onion Chives (*Allium schoenoprasum*)
Purple Sage (*Salvia officinalis 'purpurea'*)
Tricolor Sage (*Salvia officinalis 'tricolor'*)
'Hopley's Purple' Oregano (*Origanum laevigatum*)

Pinks (*Dianthus* spp.)
Heliotrope (*Heliotrophium arborescens*)
Violas (*Viola cornuta*)
'Helene von Stein' Lamb's-Ears (*Stachys byzantina*)
Yarrow (*Achillea millefolium*)

Love-in-a-Mist (*Nigella damascena*)
'Helene von Stein' Lamb's-Ears (*Stachys byzantina*)
Yellow Yarrow (*Achillea filipendulina* x 'Coronation Gold')

Plant in Spring (N, C) or Fall (CS, V)

Variegated Thymes (*Thymus vulgaris*)
Oregano (*Origanum vulgare*)
Marjoram (*Origanum majorana*)
Chives (*Allium schoenoprasum*)
Vietnamese Coriander (*Polygonum odoratum*)

Dill (*Anethum graveolens*)
Bronze Fennel (*Foeniculum vulgare 'rubrum'*)
Green Fennel (*Foeniculum vulgare*)
Winter Savory (*Satureja montana*) or Germander (*Teucrium chamaedrys*)
Curly Parsley (*Petroselinum crispum*)
Golden Culinary Sage (*Salvia officinalis 'aurea'*)
White Violas (*Viola cornuta*)
Heliotrope (*Heliotropium arborescens*)

Nasturtiums (*Tropaeolum majus*)
Salad Burnet (*Poterium sanguisorba*)
Curly Parsley (*Petroselinum crispum*)
Calendula (*Calendula officinalis*)
Bronze Fennel (*Foeniculum vulgare 'rubrum'*)
Culinary Sages (*Salvia officinalis*) other than 'Tricolor'

Plant in Summer (All Zones)

Silver King Artemisia (*Artemisia ludoviciana 'albula'*)
'Powis Castle' Artemisia (*Artemisia*)
Opal Basil (*Ocimum purpurem*)
Mrs. B. R. Cant or other medium-pink rose (*Rosa* spp.)
Pink Salvia (*Salvia coccinea* 'Coral Nymph')
White Salvia (*Salvia coccinea*)

Opal Basil (*Ocimum purpurem*)
Horehound (*Marrubium vulgare*)
Purple Coneflower (*Echinacea purpurea*)
Pinks (*Dianthus* spp.)

Plant in Late Summer/Fall (CS, V)

Magenta Salvia (*Salvia involucrata*)
Mexican Sage (*Salvia leucantha*)
Radiance, Souvenir de la Malmaison, Old Blush, or other light-pink rose (*Rosa* spp.)
Globe Amaranth, light-pink variety (*Gomphrena globosa*)
Pinks (*Dianthus* spp.)

Plant in Fall (CS, V)

Lion's-Ear (*Leonotis leonurus*)
Mexican Marigold Mint (*Tagetes lucida*)
White Salvia (*Salvia coccinea*)
Turk's-Cap (*Malvaviscus arboreus*)
'Lady in Red' Salvia (*Salvia coccinea*)
Chile Pequin (*Capsicum annuum*) or Opal Basil (*Ocimum purpurem*)
Forsythia Sage (*Salvia madrensis*) for background

Plant in Fall (Cool-Season Annuals for Shade)

Pennyroyal (*Mentha pulegium*)
Columbine (*Aquilegia* spp.)
Violets (*Viola odorata*)
Southernwood (*Artemisia abrotanum*)
Lemon Balm (*Melissa officinalis*)
Borage (*Borago officinalis*) or Comfrey (*Symphytum officinale*) for landscape use only

ROSES

There's no more romantic plant than the rose. This year for Valentine's Day, instead of a "dozen reds," why not give a dozen rose bushes? Even one rose bush will produce dozens of flowers in a single season.

Some gardeners shy away from roses because they have a reputation for requiring a lot of care—spraying, pruning, etc. That's one reason the old-fashioned roses are so popular. Many are resistant to black spot and other pests. Not all are, though, and it pays to investigate, especially if you live along the humid Gulf Coast. Even hybrid teas aren't necessarily the pest magnets we tend to picture them as. Plant breeders look for disease resistance in every seedling row.

There is also an exciting trend toward breeding good landscape roses. Landscape roses, also referred to as shrub roses, tend to be more bush-like. They require less pruning and have excellent disease resistance. This makes them very easy to maintain when compared to the upright, leggy hybrid tea roses that are so valued for their spectacular blooms.

Before you build your first rose bed, test the existing soil (see the Resources section). Even if you plan to build raised beds, it's good to know what the native soil is like. Whatever formula you use to fill the beds, make sure it includes lots of organic matter. One old rosarian used to fill beds with nothing more than rotted stable litter. She grew magnificent roses. Also check with local "dirt yards" (where you can buy soil mixes in bulk quantities); they probably have a rose soil mix ready to deliver.

Don't forget to water your roses in the winter. The roots are still growing, and the damage from freezing amounts to desiccation. Rose beds with adequate moisture will survive better.

Contributor Clyde Cannon, who is responsible for many of the lists in this chapter, says that after roses have finished a heavy bloom, give them an Epsom salts (hydrated magnesium sulfate) cocktail. Mix three tablespoons per gallon of water, and pour a gallon of the solution around each bush.

Rose Types

The lists that follow identify roses as belonging to a certain group or class. All roses generally fall into one of three categories: modern roses (varieties developed after 1867), old garden or old-fashioned roses, and antique roses. Technically, antique roses are specific varieties introduced before 1867, as well as all species roses. Old garden roses are varieties that belong to a class that existed before 1867 but the individual variety may be more modern. To make things more confusing, new hybrids whose parents are old garden roses are also called old garden roses, even though they are new! The term heirloom rose is used synonymously with the terms old garden rose and old-fashioned rose.

Classes of Modern Roses

Modern roses include hybrid teas and floribunda, grandiflora, polyantha, and David Austin roses.

- **Hybrid tea roses** originated in 1867 when a tea rose was crossed with a hybrid perpetual to create 'La France.' It and such subsequent crosses became known as hybrid teas. Hybrid teas produce one exquisite rose per stem and are popular for cutting. This is the rose you see exhibited at rose shows.
- **Floribundas** were introduced in 1930. They are relatively compact bushes with clusters of small blooms. Many are respectable as landscape or shrub roses.

- *Grandifloras* originated in 1954 as new hybrids that were crosses between hybrid teas and floribundas. They have one or two blooms per straight, long stem and they bloom continuously. 'Queen Elizabeth' is the classic grandiflora.
- *Polyanthas* produce large clusters of small roses. They contribute a great deal of color to the landscape.
- *David Austin roses* are modern landscape or shrub roses.

Classes of Antique and Old Garden Roses

A specific variety of rose that existed before 1867 is known as an antique rose. Varieties referred to as "found" have been collected from old gardens and are awaiting final classification. Antiques and old garden roses have stood the test of time and are generally more carefree than modern roses. They don't take nearly as much water; nor do they need to be fertilized as often. Generally they can be grown without pesticide sprays. Most will get some black spot, but they usually live with it. A few are best in the dryer regions of the state. Not only may disease be a problem, but some varieties with high petal counts (80+) can't seem to open their flowers in high-humidity areas.

Most of the antiques and old garden roses are landscape roses. They generally make much fuller plants than modern roses. However, they vary greatly in habit from shrubby to climbing, so you need to learn more about each rose variety listed here before buying it. The blossoms of some antique and old garden roses look great in Victorian-style arrangements, but most shatter easily.

Most antique roses are grown on their own roots. This means they make great "pass along" plants because you can root cuttings for friends. Also, antique roses on their own roots will come back true to variety if they freeze back. You won't end up with a wild and rank multiflora rootstock.

The following are the major classes of antique and old garden roses.

- **Bourbons** have large flowers, a rich scent, and repeat bloom. They make good landscape or shrub roses with dense foliage.
- **Chinas** match the floral display of azaleas in spring and will rebloom until frost. They are generally disease resistant.
- **Hybrid musks** are useful landscape roses that tolerate some shade, have good disease resistance, and are very fragrant. They bloom best in spring, and some have a strong fall repeat. These flowers are produced on large bushes with long canes—great to train on a fence.
- **Hybrid perpetuals** are the forerunners of hybrid teas. Some repeat bloom in the fall.
- **Noisettes** are hybrids of chinas and musk roses. They produce loose, mounding bushes that can be trained to a pillar or fence; they have fragrant blooms mostly in spring and fall.
- **Polyanthas** are a cross of chinas with rambling Japanese multiflora roses. They grow compact, bushy, and 2 to 5 feet tall, with small flowers in large clusters. They offer excellent repeat bloom from spring to frost. Some are fragrant; some are not.
- **Rugosa** roses are native to Japanese and Siberian coastal areas and are salt-spray tolerant. Most rugosas found in nurseries are hybrids of the species *Rosa rugosa*. They are very hardy. Rugosas need relatively little care and will grow well throughout Texas.
- **Species** roses are roses that have essentially been untouched by human hand. Some, like Lady Banks, don't seem to be capable of setting seed, or no doubt they would have been included in the parentage of many old rose varieties.

MINIMUM-CARE OLD GARDEN ROSES

It is a mistake to believe that all old garden roses require little or no care and are not susceptible to the ravages of insect pests and fungal diseases" says Field Roebuck, the Dallas rosarian who contributed this list and several others in this chapter. Field reminds us that very few old garden roses are immune to black spot and powdery mildew, and all of them are attacked by insects and spider mites. "However, these tough old roses have survived for a very long time, and many varieties require very little care beyond the normal fertilizing and watering. When attacked by pests or fungal diseases, they simply pause, shrug off a few leaflets, and then go back to their business of producing colorful flowers and hips."

The following are Field's recommendations for old garden roses that require a minimum of care. The list includes bloom color.

Bourbons
Grüss an Teplitz, red
Kronprinzessin Victoria, white
Maggie, red
Souvenir de la Malmaison, pink
Zéphirine Drouhin, cerise-pink

Chinas
Green Rose (*Rosa chinensis viridiflora*), green
Martha Gonzales, red
Mutabilis, yellow blend
Old Blush, pink
Sanguinea, red

Noisettes
Blush Noisette, pink
Lamarque, white
Maréchal Niel, yellow
Mme. Alfred Carrière, lavender pink fading to white

Ramblers
Albéric Barbier, pale yellow
Cherokee (*Rosa laevigata*), white
Mermaid, yellow
Memorial Rose (*Rosa wichuraiana*), white
Silver Moon, white
Yellow Lady Banks (*Rosa banksiae 'lutea'*), yellow

Teas
Baronne Henriette de Snoy, pink blend
Duchesse de Brabant, pink
Mme. Joseph Schwartz, white
Mme. Lombard, pink blend
Monsieur Tillier, cherry red
Mrs. B. R. Cant, pink
Mrs. Dudley Cross, yellow blend
Sombreuil, cream

 Lady Banks was the wife of botanist/explorer Sir Joseph Banks, who introduced *Rosa banksiae* to the West in 1807. It is one of the most vigorous roses known, often forming trunk-like canes. *Rosa banksiae* is thornless and evergreen in South Texas. The yellow form is more striking, but the white form has fragrance.

DISEASE-RESISTANT MODERN ROSES

This list of modern roses is from rosarian Field Roebuck, who notes, "Many modern roses show considerable resistance to or tolerance of pests and diseases. Happily, growers are once again breeding roses for this desirable quality. This effort is most notable with the many newer varieties of landscape or shrub roses, but most of them haven't been available long enough for the jury to render an educated verdict. On the other hand, some modern roses have been grown long enough to have demonstrated their toughness and reliability for Texas gardens."

Climbers
Altissimo, scarlet
America, coral-salmon
Cécile Brunner Climber, pink-cream
Climbing Iceberg, white
Don Juan, red
Dr. W. Van Fleet, blush-pink to white
New Dawn, pink

Floribundas
Class Act, white
Europeana, red
French Lace, white
Gene Boerner, pink
Gypsy Dancer, yellow blend
Iceberg, white
Ivory Fashion, white
Playboy, red blend
Showbiz, red

Spartan, red
Sunsprite, yellow

Grandifloras
Aquarius, pink blend
Caribbean, apricot blend
Pink Parfait, pink blend
Queen Elizabeth, pink
Shreveport, orange blend
Tournament of Roses, pink

Hybrid Musks
Buff Beauty, apricot
Cornelia, pink
Felicia, pink-cream
Lavender Lassie, lilac
Penelope, pink
Prosperity, white
Skyrocket (Wilhelm), red

Hybrid Teas
Crystalline, white
Double Delight, red blend
First Prize, pink blend
Fragrant Cloud, orange-red
Oklahoma, red
Peace, yellow blend
Pristine, white
Radiance, pink
Red Radiance, red
Rio Samba, yellow blend
Tropicana, brilliant red-orange
Uncle Joe (Toro), red

Polyanthas
Caldwell Pink, pink
Cécile Brunner, pink-cream

La Marne, pink
Marie Pavié, pale pink
Perle d'Or, yellow blend
The Fairy, pink

Shrub Roses
Belinda's Dream, pink
Bonica, pink
Carefree Beauty, pink
Carefree Delight, pink
Carefree Wonder, pink
Earth Song, pink
Fair Bianca, white
Heritage, pink
Lady of the Dawn, pink
Mary Rose, pink
Sally Holmes, white

"In most respects, the requirements for growing roses in Texas are the same as for anywhere else. All roses, no matter their location, need plenty of water and sunshine, and they need an organically rich, well-drained soil. But the secret to successful rose gardening in Texas—at least for the beginner—is to choose appropriate varieties of the proper types or classes."
—Field Roebuck, rosarian, Dallas

LANDSCAPE ROSES

Landscape roses, or shrub roses, are generally found in foundation plantings around a house or along the backyard fence. But relegating these roses to just foundations and fences wouldn't be fair. They're actually best used as background plants in a flower border. These groupings of large, medium, and small landscape roses come from Clyde Cannon, a Master Gardener in Houston who contributed several of the lists in this chapter. "The importance of allotting space to these roses cannot be overstressed," Clyde says. "Although pruning can control the height and width of rose bushes, it's better to limit pruning to light trimming. Research the growth habit of each rose. When you plant it, leave enough room for it to fill the desired area with a minimum amount of trimming."

Roses marked (R) are repeat bloomers. An asterisk (*) indicates a found rose whose class is questionable.

Large (6 feet by 6 feet, or more)

	Class	Color
Alchymist	shrub	pink
Applejack (R)	shrub	pink
Bailey's Red (R)	hybrid tea*	red
Banshee	shrub	pink
Baty's Pink Pillar (R)	hybrid perpetual*	pink
Basye's Blueberry (R)	Robert E. Basye	pink
Belinda (R)	hybrid musk	pink
Bishop Darlington (R)	hybrid musk	apricot
Bubble Bath (R)	hybrid musk	pink
Cherokee Rose (*Rosa laevigata*)	species	white
Chestnut Rose (*Rosa roxburghii*)	species	pink
Cramoisi des Alpes	gallica	reddish-purple
Duchesse de Brabant (R)	tea	pink
Francois Juranville	wichuraiana	pink

	Class	Color
Frau Karl Druschki (R)	hybrid perpetual	white
Gloire de Ducher (R)	hybrid perpetual	maroon
Hansa (R)	rugosa	pink
Hanseat (R)	shrub	pink
Lady Banks (*Rosa banksiae 'alba plena'*)	species	white
Lavender Lassie (R)	hybrid musk	lilac
Maggie (R)	bourbon	mauve-cerise
McClinton Tea (R)	unknown	pink
Mme. Isaac Pereire (R)	bourbon	pink-rose
Mme. Joseph Schwartz (R)	tea	cream-pink
Monsiur Tillier (R)	tea	rose-salmon
Moonlight (R)	hybrid musk	yellow-white
Mrs. B. R. Cant (R)	tea	pink
Mrs. Dudley Cross (R)	tea	pink-cream
Mutabilis (R)	china	multicolor
Portland from Glendora (R)	portland	pink
Russelliana or Russell's Cottage Rose	hybrid multiflora	crimson-lilac
Sea Foam (R)	shrub	white
Seven Sisters (*Rosa multiflora platyphylla*)	hybrid multiflora	multicolor
Swamp Rose (*Rosa palustris scandens*)	species	pink
Sweet Briar Rose (*Rosa eglanteria*)	sweet briar	pink
Will Scarlet (R)	hybrid musk	scarlet
Yellow Lady Banks (*Rosa banksiae 'lutea'*)	species	yellow
York and Lancaster	damask	red and white

Medium (3 to 6 feet)

	Class	Color
Archduke Charles (R)	china	crimson
Blush Noisette (R)	noisette	pink
Bon Silene (R)	tea	pink-rose
Champney's Pink Cluster (R)	noisette	pink
Coquette des Alpes (R)	bourbon	white
Cramoisi Supérieur (R)	china	crimson
Ducher (R)	china	white
Duchesse de Brabant (R)	tea	pink
Gipsy Boy (R)	bourbon	red
Gloire de Rosomanes (R)	china	crimson
Great Western (R)	bourbon	lilac-purple
Green Rose (*Rosa chinensis viridiflora*) (R)	china	green
Hermosa (R)	china	pink-lilac
Homere (R)	tea	cream-pink
Honorine de Brabant (R)	bourbon	pink-violet
Isabelle Sprunt (R)	tea	yellow
Jean Bach Sisley (R)	china	pink
Kronprincessin Viktoria (R)	bourbon	white
La Biche (R)	noisette	cream
Lady Hillingdon (R)	tea	apricot-yellow
Le Vésuve (R)	china	pink
Louis Odier (R)	bourbon	rose-pink
Louis Philippe (R)	china	crimson
Malton (R)	hybrid china	crimson
Martha Gonzales (R)	china	scarlet
Mme. Joseph Schwartz (R)	tea	white-pink
Mme. Laurette Messimy (R)	china	salmon-pink

SWEET BRIAR
ROSE

Monsieur Tillier (R)	tea	salmon-pink
Mrs. Bosanquet (R)	bourbon	pink
Mutabilis (R)	china	multicolor
Nastarama (R)	noisette	white
Old Blush (R)	china	pink
Papa Hémeray (R)	china	red
Rival de Paestum (R)	tea	cream
Safrano (R)	tea	apricot-yellow
Slaters Crimson China (R)	china	crimson
Souvenir de la Malmaison (R)	bourbon	pink
Souvenir de St. Anne's (R)	bourbon	pink

Small (3 feet or less)

	Class	Color
Baby Faurax (R)	polyantha	violet
Catherine Mermet (R)	tea	pink
Cécile Brunner (R)	polyantha	pink
Clotilde Soupert (R)	polyantha	cream
Enfant de France (R)	hybrid perpetual	pink
Excellenz vonShubert (R)	polyantha	carmine
Frau Dagmar Hartopp (R)	rugosa	pink
Gabrielle Privat (R)	polyantha	carmine-pink
Grüss an Aachen (R)	polyantha	pink-cream
Hermosa (R)	china	pink-lilac
Highway 290 Pink Buttons (R)	china miniature*	pink-lilac
Huilito (R)	china*	pink-purple
Jean Mermoz (R)	polyantha	pink
Kronprincessin Viktoria (R)	bourbon	white
Lavender Pink Parfait (R)	miniature*	pink-white
Lichterloh (R)	polyantha	red
Lindee (R)	polyantha*	white
Maman Cochet (R)	tea	pink-cream
Marie Pavié (R)	polyantha	pink
Martha Gonzales (R)	china	red
Mevrouw Nathalie Nypels (R)	polyantha	pink
Miss Edith Cavell (R)	polyantha	scarlet
Mrs. Oakley Fisher (R)	hybrid tea	yellow-orange
Mrs. R. M. Finch (R)	polyantha	pink
Nastarana (R)	noisette	pink-cream
Nearly Wild (R)	polyantha	pink
Perle d'Or (R)	polyantha	salmon-yellow
Petite Pink Scotch	wichuraiana*	pink
Pink Rosette (R)	polyantha	pink
Pinkie (R)	polyantha	pink
Rosette Delizy (R)	tea	carmine-yellow
Rouletii (R)	china	pink
Souvenir de St. Anne's (R)	bourbon	pink
The Fairy (R)	polyantha	pink
Valentine (R)	polyantha	scarlet
Vincent Godsif (R)	china*	pink
White Pet (R)	polyantha	white

In some of the lists in this chapter, a rose may be classified as a Robert E. Basye type. Basye is not technically a class in and of itself, but it is a valid descriptive term. The late Dr. Robert Basye was a Texas A&M University professor and an amateur rose breeder. He concentrated on thornless, disease-resistant shrub roses for Texas. Some of his best-known varieties include Basye's Blueberry, Belinda's Dream, and Basye's Purple Rose.

MINIATURE ROSES THAT THRIVE IN CONTAINERS AND LANDSCAPES

Field Roebuck, the Dallas rosarian who contributed this list, observes that miniature roses are ideal for borders or as edging shrubs, "as long as they are true miniatures; that is, they are actually miniature plants and not full-sized shrubs with diminutive flowers, as some are." Field says that miniatures can be grown in containers placed in just about any sunny spot, but he cautions: "Don't try to grow them inside the house—they will soon begin to drop leaves and look sick without enough sunlight." Most miniature varieties are rated good to excellent. This list is Field's representative sampling of the superb miniature rose varieties that are awarded consistently high marks from Texas rose gardeners. 'Jeanne Lajoie' and 'Red Cascade' are climbers.

Black Jade, red
Cinderella, pink
Gourmet Popcorn, white
Hurdy Gurdy, red blend
Jean Kenneally, apricot blend
Jeanne Lajoie, pink
Loving Touch, apricot blend
Magic Carrousel, red blend

Over the Rainbow, red blend
Peaches 'n Cream, pink blend
Rainbow's End, yellow blend
Red Cascade, red
Rise 'n Shine, yellow
Snow Bride, white
Starina, orange-red

MINIATURE ROSE

ROSES WITH OUTSTANDING FRAGRANCE

Flower fragrance is a very personal and subjective quality," says rosarian Field Roebuck. "Its perception is a subtle combination of taste and smell, coupled with subconscious memories of past places and events. An aroma that enthralls one person may not appeal to another, and the fragrance may not even be detected by a third. But most people will be delighted by the scent of the roses on this list, and almost everyone will admit that each of these roses has a strong and distinctive aroma."

Autumn Damask (Quatre Saisons)	ancient rose	pink
Chrysler Imperial	hybrid tea	rich crimson
Fair Bianca	David Austin shrub	white
Fragrant Cloud	hybrid tea	orange-red
Granada	hybrid tea	red and yellow blend
Heritage	David Austin shrub	pink
Ispahan	damask	pink
Maggie	bourbon	red
Margaret Merril	floribunda	white
Mister Lincoln	hybrid tea	red
Mme. Isaac Pereire	bourbon	pink
Perfume Delight	hybrid tea	deep pink
Rose de Rescht	damask	pink
Rose du Roi	portland/china	red
Sunsprite	floribunda	yellow

"I have always been struck by the intense beauty that antique roses bring to our gardens," says G. Michael Shoup, owner of the Antique Rose Emporium in Brenham, "but even greater joy comes from the satisfaction expressed from neighbors and visitors as they languidly stroll through the grounds. It is conversation depicting past memories, possibly evoked by the fragrance of nearby honeysuckle or roses. It is conversation that speaks of contentment, of family or of newfound goals. It makes the garden a place certainly more grand than the collection of plants comprised within it."

David Austin is an English rose breeder, but some of his varieties work well in Texas. He has been most successful in developing shrub or landscape roses with an old-fashioned look that have been dubbed the "English Rose" class. They combine the nostalgic charm of old-fashioned roses with the constant bloom of modern hybrids. David Austin roses are extremely fragrant. Their flower shapes vary in form from deep cups to flat rosettes. Singles and semidoubles are also available. English Rose plants range in size from dwarf to large background types.

ROSES WITH SHOW-WINNING FLOWERS

When he sent us this list, rosarian Field Roebuck pointed out: "It has been said that 'beauty lies in the eye of the beholder.' But in this case, the beholder is the rose show judge, and for the past several decades 'beauty' has meant, for modern roses, large flowers with twenty-five to forty petals and high-centered buds. For antique roses, the standard has been the very double, flat, quartered flowers of 'Souvenir de la Malmaison.' So any list of roses with show-winning flowers would be expected to include mostly varieties with these attributes." Here is Field's list of such prize-winning roses.

Old Garden Roses

Duchesse de Brabant	tea	pink
Mme. Isaac Pereire	bourbon	pink
Mme. Lombard	tea	rosy-salmon
Monsieur Tillier	tea	cherry-red
Mrs. B. R. Cant	tea	pink
Sombreuil	tea	cream
Souvenir de la Malmaison	bourbon	pink

Modern Roses

Brigadoon	hybrid tea	pink blend
Crystalline	hybrid tea	white
Double Delight	hybrid tea	red blend
Elizabeth Taylor	hybrid tea	pink
First Prize	hybrid tea	pink
Just Joey	hybrid tea	orange blend
Olympiad	hybrid tea	red
Royal Highness	hybrid tea	light pink
Saint Patrick	hybrid tea	yellow-green blend
Sheer Elegance	hybrid tea	orange blend
Touch of Class	hybrid tea	pink-cream-coral blend
Uncle Joe (Toro)	hybrid tea	red

ROSES FOR PILLARS, ARCHES, AND PERGOLAS

For this list of roses that can be trained against supporting structures, we combined the recommendations of Houston gardener Clyde Cannon and Dallas gardener Field Roebuck. "The use of these roses in the southern garden," Clyde says, "is limited only by your imagination. Pillars as a stand-alone feature or connected by two- to three-inch ship's hawsers decked out with 'Red Cascade' or 'Dortmund' are outstanding. The once-blooming *Rosa multiflora carnea* draped over a pergola is a blanket of pink."

No matter what type of structure you choose, "it is essential that it is strong, weather resistant, and termite proof," Clyde stresses. "If wood is used, it should be treated for ground contact and should be well braced. Pillars should not be smaller than a 6-by-6 and sunk a minimum of 2 feet into the ground, with the same dirt tamped back into the hole. Do not use concrete because it retains water around the base, causing a more rapid deterioration of the wood." Secure the rose canes to the structure with pliable plastic ties or strips of pantyhose loosely tied to allow for growth.

Roses in this list marked (R) are rebloomers.

	Class	Color
Albéric Barbier	hybrid wichuraiana	pale yellow
Alister Stella Gray (R)	noisette	cream-yellow
America (R)	climber	coral-salmon
American Beauty Climber	hybrid perpetual	pink
Baltimore Belle	rambler	pink-white
Belle Portugaise	rambler	pink
Blairii No. 2 (R)	bourbon	pink
Blush Noisette (R)	noisette	pink
Bouquet d'Or (R)	noisette	golden
Buff Beauty (R)	hybrid musk	apricot
Cécile Brunner Climber (R)	polyantha	pink
Céline Forestier (R)	noisette	yellow
Cherokee (*Rosa laevigata*)	species	white
Claire Jacquier	noisette	yellow
Climbing Iceberg (R)	floribunda	white
Climbing Old Blush (R)	china hybrid	pink
Climbing Pinkie (R)	polyantha	pink
Clytemnestra (R)	hybrid musk	salmon
Conrad Ferdinand Meyer (R)	rugosa	pink
Dorothy Perkins	wichuraiana	pink
Dortmund (R)	rambler	scarlet
Dr. W. Van Fleet	wichuraiana	pink
Francois Juranville	wichuraiana	pink
Graham Thomas (R)	David Austin	yellow
Ivy Alice	rambler	pink
Jaune Deprez (R)	noisette	apricot
Jeanne d'Arc (R)	noisette	white
Kennedy Yellow (R)	unknown	yellow
Lady Waterlow (R)	hybrid tea	salmon-pink
Lamarque (R)	noisette	white
Leverkusen (R)	kordes rambler	yellow
Memorial Rose	wichuraiana	white
Mermaid (R)	hybrid bracteata	yellow
Mme. Alfred Carrière (R)	noisette	pink
New Dawn (R)	rambler	pink
Paul's Lemon Pillar	hybrid tea	yellow
Rambling Rector	rambler	cream
Red Cascade (R)	miniature	red

Reve d'Or (R)	noisette	golden
Rosa multiflora carnea	rambler	pink
Silver Moon	hybrid wichuraiana	white
Sombreuil (R)	tea	cream
Souvenir de la Malmaison Climber (R)	bourbon	pink
Souvenir de Mme. Leonie Viennot (R)	tea	pink
Tausendschöon	hybrid multiflora	pink
Veilchenblau	hybrid multiflora	lavender-purple
Will Scarlet (R)	hybrid musk	scarlet
William Loeb	moss	purple
Yellow Lady Banks (*Rosa banksiae 'lutea'*)	species	yellow
Zéphirine Drouhin (R)	bourbon	cerise-pink

 If you haven't had much luck with rooting rose cuttings, try layering. In early spring (February or March), strip one-half to 1 inch of the bark off a limber cane, about two-thirds of the way up from the ground. Lay the cane down so that the stripped part is in contact with the soil. Pin the cane down with a U-shaped piece of coat hanger, or weight it down with a brick to maintain soil contact, and cover the wounded section with soil. By fall, the stem should be rooted and you can sever the new plant from the mother plant.

HEDGE ROSES

Hedges can be created from most of the rambling or arching-cane roses and can form a dense high or low wall," notes Clyde Cannon, who gardens in Houston. "Not only are rose walls or fences more attractive than a wooden fence, but they also provide a habitat for birds. The height of the hedge is easy to control by choosing roses with the proper growth habit; then only a light trim will be necessary." Clyde contributed this list of roses appropriate for such treatment. He advises that the low-growing and border roses should be planted about 12 to 18 inches apart, depending on the mature rose height. Most of the roses in the tall group, however, will send out 10- to 20-foot canes and will need a sturdy structure for support.

"To construct a 5-foot wall of roses," Clyde says, "sink 5-foot posts 2 feet into the ground, leaving 3 feet of post above the prepared rose bed. Space the posts 6 feet apart. Re-bar (reinforcing bar) or cattle panels (heavy wire fencing used to create cattle pens) should be secured to the top of the posts and also halfway down on the sides to give ample support for a 2-foot buildup of canes. This structure will serve equally well as a tank trap should there be a failure of World Peace."

All of the roses listed here are repeat bloomers except for the Swamp Rose and 'Mme. Plantier.'

Tall Hedge Roses

	Class	Color
Ballerina	hybrid musk	pink
Basye's Purple Rose	Robert E. Basye	purple
Belinda	hybrid musk	pink
Blanc Doublet de Coubert	rugosa	white
Calocarpa	rugosa	pink
Cécile Brunner Climber	polyantha	pink-cream
Climbing Pinkie	polyantha	pink
Cornelia	hybrid perpetual	pink
Crépuscule	noisette	apricot-yellow
Danae	hybrid musk	cream
Dr. Eckner	rugosa	yellow-pink
Felicia	hybrid musk	pink-cream
Hanseat	shrub	pink-coral
Lafter	hybrid tea	salmon/pink
Lavender Lassie	hybrid musk	lilac

Mermaid	rambler	cream
Mme. Plantier	alba	white
Monsieur Tillier	tea	rose-salmon
Mrs. Dudley Cross	tea	pink-cream
Mutabilis	china	multicolor
Penelope	hybrid musk	pink
Rosa rugosa rubra	rugosa	purple
Swamp Rose (*Rosa palustris scandens*)	species	pink
Thérèse Bugnet	rugosa	red
Zéphirine Drouhin	bourbon	cerise-pink

Low-Growing Hedge and Border Roses

	Class	Color
Dwarf King	miniature	carmine
Highway 290 Pink Buttons	china mini	pink
June Time	miniature	pink
Lavender Pink Parfait	miniature	pink
Lemon Delight	miniature	yellow
Lindee	polyantha	white
My Valentine	miniature	red
New Penny	miniature	orange-pink
Pandora	miniature	yellow-white
Peachy White	miniature	peach
Perla de Montserrat	miniature	pink
Pixie Rose	miniature	pink
Pour Toi	miniature	white
Red Ace	miniature	red
Rosa wichuraiana poteriifolia	wichuraiana	white
Rouletii	china	pink
Scarlet Pimpernel	miniature	scarlet
Snookie	miniature	orange-red
Starina	miniature	orange-scarlet
Sweet Fairy	miniature	pink
Titania	miniature	carmine
Tom Thumb	miniature	red
White Pet	polyantha	white
Yellow Sweet Heart	miniature	yellow

"I look at an antique rose as a trip back in time, because each cutting is a clone or a piece of that first bush. In some cases you are holding a piece of the same wood that some rose lover held over a thousand years ago. What would the cutting tell you if it could have kept a diary or, better yet, a video of its travels forward in time, revealing the sights of each garden home and the individual who cared for it? Imagine."
—Clyde Cannon, Harris County Master Gardener, Houston

ROSES THAT MAKE GOOD GROUND COVERS

This list of ground-cover or procumbent roses is from Master Gardener Clyde Cannon, who points out that, in many cases, these roses have the species rose *Rosa wichuraiana* in their heritage. These roses put out roots along their canes where the canes touch the ground, and they can form a dense mat. "They are an excellent choice for erosion control, area fill, or just tumbling over walls. Once these roses are established, they are practically weed and pruning free except for edge containment."

All of the roses in this list are repeat bloomers except for 'Raubritter,' 'Red Bells,' 'Repen Meidiland,' and 'Rosy Carpet.' One of the roses, 'Red Cascade,' is a miniature.

Caterpillar, pink

Fiona, red

Laura Ashley, lilac

Nozomi, pink

Pearl Drift, pink

Pink Chimo, pink

Pink Meidiland, pink

Pink Wave, pink

Raubritter, pink

Red Bells, red

Red Blanket, cerise

Red Cascade, red

Red Max Graf, scarlet

Repen Meidiland, white

Rosa wichuraiana, white

Rosa wichuraiana poteriifolia, white

Rosy Carpet, pink

Scarlet Meidiland, red

Simon Robinson, pink

Swany, white

Tall Story, yellow

Warwickshire, red

White Max Graf, white

White Meidiland, white

 Meidiland roses are bred in France by the Meidiland family nursery. This breeder concentrates on disease-resistant and shrub-type roses. Some of their outstanding cultivars for Texas gardens include Carefree Delight, Carefree Wonder, Scarlet Meidiland, and White Meidiland.

A COLOR SAMPLER OF ROSES FOR TEXAS GARDENS

Dallas rosarian Field Roebuck put together this color sampler of roses. He points out, "Flower colors are often combinations of subtle shades and blends, and this is never so true as when applied to the colors of roses. What is a red rose to one eye or in one location may be a dark pink or even a coral flower to another eye or in another garden. Roses that are white at one time of year may be blush pink at another. Some may see a rose as a yellow blend; others may consider it a pink blend. So many subtle shades exist that there will never be complete agreement about the proper color classification for some roses. Nevertheless, these are the assigned colors for the following rose varieties.

Red

Altissimo

Chrysler Imperial

Don Juan

Dortmund

Europeana

Grüss an Teplitz

Maggie

Martha Gonzales

Mister Lincoln

Oklahoma

Olympiad

Red Radiance

Rose du Roi

Sanguinea

Showbiz

Skyrocket (Wilhelm)

Spartan

Uncle Joe (Toro)

Coral, Orange

America

Fragrant Cloud

Touch of Class

Tropicana

Pink

Autumn Damask (Quatre Saisons)

Aloha

Blush Noisette

Bonica

Caldwell Pink

Carefree Beauty

Carefree Wonder

Cécile Brunner

Cécile Brunner Climber

Cornelia

Dr. W. Van Fleet

Duchesse de Brabant

Earth Song

Elizabeth Taylor

Gene Boerner

Heritage

Ispahan

Lady of the Dawn

La Marne

Mary Rose

Mme. Isaac Pereire

Mrs. B. R. Cant

New Dawn

Old Blush

Penelope

Perfume Delight

Queen Elizabeth

Radiance

Rose de Rescht

Royal Highness

Souvenir de la Malmaison
The Fairy
Tournament of Roses
Zéphirine Drouhin

White
Albéric Barbier
Cherokee (*Rosa laevigata*)
Class Act
Climbing Iceberg
Crystalline
Fair Bianca
French Lace
Iceberg
Ivory Fashion
Kronprinzessin Victoria
Lamarque
Margaret Merril
Memorial Rose (*Rosa wichuraiana*)
Mme. Alfred Carrière
Mme. Joseph Schwartz
Pristine
Prosperity
Sally Holmes
Silver Moon
Sombreuil

Yellow
Graham Thomas
Maréchal Niel
Mermaid
Sunsprite
Yellow Lady Banks (*Rosa banksiae 'lutea'*)

Green
Green Rose (*Rosa chinensis viridiflora*)

Blends
Aquarius, pink blend
Baronne Henriette de Snoy, pink blend
Brigadoon, pink blend
Buff Beauty, apricot blend
Caribbean, apricot blend
Double Delight, red blend
First Prize, pink blend
Felicia, pink blend
Granada, red blend
Gypsy Dancer, yellow blend
Just Joey, orange blend
Mme. Lombard, pink blend
Monsieur Tillier, pink blend

Mrs. Dudley Cross, yellow blend
Mutabilis, yellow blend
Peace, yellow blend
Perle d'Or, yellow blend
Pink Parfait, pink blend
Playboy, red blend
Rio Samba, yellow blend
Saint Patrick, yellow blend
Sheer Elegance, orange blend
Shreveport, orange blend

YELLOW LADY
BANKS

TROPICALS, SUCCULENTS, AND EXOTICS

Many of the plants in this chapter are for the overachieving gardener, but some are very easy to grow if you meet their special requirements. For example, water lilies don't require much attention after being properly planted. Tropical hibiscus are easy to care for during the summer months, but protecting them through the winter can be a challenge.

Tropicals are those plants that have been imported from tropical rain forests or other tropical regions around the world. Texas has no real tropic zone; even the Rio Grande Valley suffers a hard freeze several times per decade. Tropicals can be used as summer annuals in all areas of the state, or if left outside in South Texas, they may have to be replaced every few years after a freeze.

Most tropicals become stressed even when temperatures begin to creep down into the 40s F. Before the first hard freeze hits, they will need to be brought into a greenhouse or other protected location, like the garage. Often they are grown in porous clay pots, which can be sunk into the garden bed through the summer. This makes it easy to pull them up for the winter with a minimum of damage to the root system. Plumerias can be bare-rooted and stored dry until spring in the garage, attic, or anyplace where it doesn't freeze. Some tropical plants like pentas and even some tropical hibiscus are so inexpensive and readily available that we can let them freeze and buy new ones next year.

All cacti are succulents, but not all succulents are cacti. The term succulent is a broader term that includes a wide variety of fleshy-leafed plants such as *Euphorbias* and *Echeverias* (hen-and-chicks). Cacti and succulents always require good drainage. Some gardeners go to the extreme of building up raised beds filled with gravel. This can be a vital feature if you are trying to grow these plants in high-rainfall areas like Houston. Some of the cacti and succulents are so finicky, they may only survive in a greenhouse where the cover allows you to apply precise and limited amounts of water.

Exotics, from orchids to insectivorous plants, are so different in their requirements that it's difficult to make a general statement about their needs. Most of the plants in this chapter, however, have the same basic needs as plants in the other categories. They need rich organic soil, and it's always best to have your soil tested before you plant.

This book is designed to be a launching pad, and additional research is advised for most of the plants in these lists. Call your County Extension agent, visit your local library or nursery, and surf the web for more specific details.

CACTI AND SUCCULENTS

Cacti and succulents in your landscape just say TEXAS!" says Larry Fagarason, president of the Texas Cactus and Succulent Society. "Texas has over 300 species of cacti, and about 80 percent of them occur west of the Balcones Fault, about 50 percent of them in Far West Texas. Most need dry and hot conditions, and the majority would not do well in East Texas and Valley areas without lots of extra vigilance." Nevertheless, he adds that species of cacti and succulents are available for all regions of Texas and are relatively carefree if you provide the basic conditions they need. "The use of these plants is increasing yearly due to their ease of maintenance as well as their beauty," Larry points out. "The majestic presence of a large agave, the flowerful beauty of cacti in spring, and the varied hues of ground succulents are all possible for every xeric gardener."

Cacti and succulents demand several basics. "Because cacti and most succulents do poorly or die in soggy soil, rapidly draining soil mix is important," Larry stresses. "All soils should be at least half made up of drainage-enhancing coarse sand and crushed limestone. A successful mix for outdoor raised beds is one part each of top-soil, coarse builder's sand, and unwashed crushed limestone (road base). The raised beds should be formed from rocks, with no mortar or timbers." The idea is to avoid a bathtub effect. The bed should drain readily. Larry also suggests planting cacti and succulents in the crevices of a rock pile, after adding enough soil mix for the plants to root. "This lends a more natural appearance not realized with a geo-metrical bed."

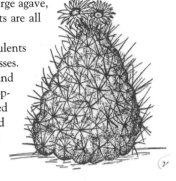

SPINY STAR CACTUS

Cacti and succulents can also be grown in containers. "The pot mix should be of equal parts sand, potting soil, decayed granite, and Sunshine Mix," Larry points out. "This variation recog-nizes the root restriction of potted plants and the propensity of the soil to harden with successive watering."

If you have planted cacti that come from Far West Texas or other arid areas, you should cover them dur-ing a prolonged rain. They can only tolerate a brief period of rainfall. In general, succulents other than cacti can tolerate more rain.

Fertilize cacti and succulents with half-strength Miracle Grow or a similar soluble fertilizer, applied at the first signs of new growth in the early spring, and at bud-set several weeks later, Larry recommends. "These times will vary by species, but the first must be when danger of freeze is past."

The cacti and succulents in these lists from Larry are native unless marked with an asterisk (*). "All are available, some not readily, through nurseries specializing in cacti and succulents."

Cacti

Night Blooming Cereus (*Acanthocereus pentagonus*), CSw, V

Living Rock Cactus (*Ariocarpus fissuratus*), N, Cw, CSw

Silver Cob Cactus (*Coryphantha albicolumnaria*), N, Cw

Mountain Cob Cactus (*Coryphantha dasyacantha*), N, Cw

Duncan Cory Cactus (*Coryphantha duncanii*), N, Cw, CSw

Sea Urchin Cactus (*Coryphantha echinus*), N, Cw, CSw

Long Mamma (*Coryphantha macromeris*), N, Cw, CSw

Big Bend Cory Cactus (*Coryphantha ramillosa*), N, Cw, CSw

Nipple Cactus (*Coryphantha sulcata*), N, Cw, CSe, CSw

Spiny Star Cactus (*Coryphantha vivipara*), N, Cw, CSnw

Sea Urchin Cactus (*Echinocactus asterias*), V

Turk's-Head, Eagle Claw (*Echinocactus horizonthalo-nius*), N, Cw, CSw

Twist Rib Hedgehog (*Echinocactus setispinus*), N, Cw, CSe, CSw

Horse Crippler (*Echinocactus texansis*), N, Cw, CSw

Brown-Flowered Hedgehog (*Echinocactus uncinatus*), N, Cw, CSnw

Devil's-Claw Barrel Cactus (*Echinocactus whipplei*), N, Cw, CSw

White Lace Cactus (*Echinocereus caespitosis*), N, Cw, CSw

Chisos Mountain Hedgehog (*Echinocereus chisoen-sis*), N, Cw, CSnw

Green-Flowered Torch Cactus (*Echinocereus chloran-thus*), N, Cw, CSnw

Brown-Flowered Pitaya (*Echinocereus chloranthus 'neocapillus'*), N, Cw, CSnw

Texas Rainbow Cactus (*Echinocereus dasyacanthus*), N, Cw, CSnw

Strawberry Pitaya (*Echinocereus dubius*), N, Cw, CSnw

Strawberry Hedgehog Cactus (*Echinocereus ennea-canthus*), N, Cw, CSnw

Strawberry Pitaya (*Echinocereus enneacanthus 'carnosus'*), N, Cw, CSnw

Lady-Finger Cactus (*Echinocereus pentalophus*), Csw, CSw, V

Orange-Flowered Pitaya (*Echinocereus russanthus*), N, Cw, CSnw

Strawberry Cactus (*Echinocereus straminius*), N, Cw, CSnw

Claret-Cup Hedgehog Cactus (*Echinocereus triglochidiatus*), N, Cw, CSw, Vn

Green-Flowered Pitaya (*Echinocereus viridifloris*), N, Cw, CSnw

Chihuahua Pineapple Cactus (*Echinomastus*

intertextus), N, Cw, CSnw

Mariposa Cactus (*Echinomastus mariposensis*), N, Cw, CSnw

Warnock Cactus (*Echinomastus warnockii*), N, Cw, CSnw

Boke Button Cactus (*Epithelantha bokei*), N, Cw, CSnw

Common Button Cactus (*Epithelantha micromeris*), N, Cw, CSnw

Texas Red Barrel Cactus (*Ferocactus hamatacanthus*), N, Cw, CSnw

Barrel Cactus, Candy Barrel (*Ferocactus wislizenii*), N, Cw, CSw

Heyder Pincushion Cactus (*Mammillaria heyderi*), N, Cw, CSnw

Flat Pincushion Cactus (*Mammillaria heyderi 'applanata'*), N, Cw, CSnw

Mammillaria lasiacantha, N, Cw, CSnw

Fish-Hook Cactus (*Mammillaria microcarpa*), N, Cw, CSnw

Grape Cactus (*Mammillaria multiceps*), N, Cw, CSnw

Mammillaria pottsii, N, Cw, CSnw

Mammillaria wrightii, N, Cw, CSw

White-Flowered Visnagita (*Neolloydia conoideus*), N (very dry), Cw

Green-Flowered Visnagita (*Neolloydia mariposensis*), N (very dry), Cw

Spineless Prickly Pear (*Opuntia engelmannii*), All

Red-Flowered Prickly Pear (*Opuntia engelmannii 'alta'*), N, Cw, CSw

Opuntia engelmannii 'engelmannii', All

Yellow-Spined Prickly Pear (*Opuntia engelmannii 'texana'*), All

Green-Flowered Cholla (*Opuntia davisii*), N (dry), Cw, CSw

Prostrate Prickly Pear (*Opuntia humifusa*), N, Cw, CSw

Tree Cactus (*Opuntia imbricata*), All

Candle Cholla (*Opuntia kleiniae*), All

Tasajillo, Christmas Cactus (*Opuntia leptocaulis*), All

Cow's-Tongue Prickly Pear (*Opuntia lindheimeri*), All

Purple Prickly Pear (*Opuntia macrocentra*), N, Cw, CSnw

Blind Pear (*Opuntia rufida*), N, Cw, CSw

'Santa Rita' Prickly Pear (*Opuntia violacea*), N (dry), Cw, CSw

Cane Cholla (*Opuntia spinosior*), All

Texas Night-Blooming Cereus (*Peniocereus greggii*), Cw, CSnw

Star Flower Cactus (*Thelocactus bicolor 'flavidispinus'*), N, Cw

Glory-of-Texas (*Thelocactus bicolor 'schottii'*), Cw, CSnw

Dahlia, Pencil Cactus (*Wilcoxia poselgeri*), N (dry), Cw, CSnw

Succulents

Maguey Century Plant (*Agave americana 'americana'*), All

Striped Agave (*Agave americana 'variegata'*)*, CS, V

Chisos Agave (*Agave glomeruliflora*), Ns, Cw, Csw, V

Slim Foot Agave (*Agave gracilipes*), Cw, CSnw (dry)

Havard Agave (*Agave havardiana*), Cw, CSnw

Shin Sabre (*Agave lechuguilla*), N, Cw, CSw

Thorn-Crested Agave (*Agave lophantha*), All

New Mexico Agave (*Agave neomexicana*), N (dry), Cw, CSw

Agave scabra, Csw, CSw, V

Maguey Liso Agave (*Agave weberi*)*, Csw, CSw, V

Medicine Aloe (*Aloe barbadensis*)*, Cse, CSw, V

Aloe mitriformis, Cse, CSw, V

Royal Aloe (*Aloe nobilis*), Cse, CSw, V

Speckled Aloe (*Aloe saponaria*)*, Cse, CSw, V

Smooth Sotol (*Dasylirion leiophyllum*), Ns, Cw, CSw, V

Texas Sotol (*Dasylirion texanum*), All

Wheeler's Sotol (*Dasylirion wheeleri*), All

White Margin Euphorbia (*Euphorbia albomarginata*), All

Candililla (*Euphorbia antisyphlitica*), N (dry), Cw, CSnw

Toothed Spurge, Mexican Poinsettia (*Euphorbia dentata*), All

Snow-on-the-Mountain (*Euphorbia marginata*), N, Cw, CSw

Trailing Spurge (*Euphorbia myrsinites*)*, Cw, CS

Coachwhip, Ocotillo (*Fouqueria splendens*), Ns, Cw, CSw, Vn

Ghost Plant (*Graptopetalum paraguensis*)*, All

False Agave (*Hechtia glomerata*), CSw, V

False Agave (*Hechtia texensis*), Cw, CSw

Hesperaloe funifera, Cw, CSw

Hesperaloe loweryii, Cw, CSw

Red Yucca (*Hesperaloe parviflora*), All

Yellow Red Yucca (*Hesperaloe parviflora 'flavum'*), All

Nettle Spurge, Jicamilla (*Jatropha cathartica*), CSe, V

Sangre-de-Drago (*Jatropha dioica 'dioica'*), Cw, CS

Bigroot Nettle (*Jatropha macrohiza*), Cw, CSnw

Havard's Sedum (*Sedum havardii*), Ns, Cw, CSw

Yellow Sedum (*Sedum nuttallianum*), C, CS

Pork-and-Beans Sedum (*Sedum rubrotinctum*)*, Cw, CS

Common Sedum (*Sedum spectabile*), All

Hen-and-Chicks (*Sempervivum tectorum*)*, All

Arkansas Yucca (*Yucca arkansana*), All

Datil Yucca, Blue Yucca (*Yucca baccata*), All

Plains Yucca (*Yucca compestris*), All

Buckley Yucca (*Yucca constricta*), All

Soaptree Yucca (*Yucca elata*), N, Cw, CSw, V

Spanish Dagger, Carneros Yucca (*Yucca faxonia*), N, Cw, CSw, V

Weakleaf, Flaccid Yucca (*Yucca filamentoia*)*, Ce, CS, V

Narrowleaf Yucca (*Yucca glauca*), N, Cw, CSw

Shinner's Yucca (*Yucca louisianensis*), Ce, CS, V

Yucca necopina, C, CSw

Pale Yucca (*Yucca pallida*), C, CSw, V

Plateau Yucca (*Yucca reverchonii*), Ce, CSw, V

Beaked Yucca (*Yucca rostrata*), Cw, CSw

Twist-Leaf Yucca (*Yucca rupicola*), Ce, CSw

Whiterim Yucca (*Yucca tenuistyla*), Ce, CSw

Torrey Yucca, Spanish Dagger (*Yucca torreyi*), CSw, V

Trecul Yucca, Palma Pita, Spanish Dagger (*Yucca treculeana*), Ns, Cw, CSnw, V

Larry Fagarason, in Kerrville, is president of the Texas Cactus and Succulent Society. He suggests combining cacti, succulents, and native perennials for pleasing garden displays. "The intermix of native woody perennials imitates the desert setting where the minority of plants are cacti and succulents and provides lasting colorful blooms," Larry says. When cacti and succulents are combined with flowering native perennials, the varied forms, textures, and colors are "irresistible for those of us who take our landscaping cues from our Texas surroundings."

A SELECTION OF PALMS

Palms lend a tropical feeling to the landscape. They also contribute to a mood of relaxation. It's almost impossible to look at a palm and not have your mind drift off to a warm beach and tropical isle.

It's best to plant palms when the soil is warm, so it is quite acceptable to plant them in midsummer when you might be hesitant to plant other trees. Grant Stephenson, owner of Horticultural Consultants, a wholesale nursery in Houston that specializes in cold-hardy palms and cycads, cautions that they shouldn't be planted when they are making growth spurts. They particularly need good drainage, so plant them 6 to 8 inches higher than the existing soil. Use a loose, organic topsoil for backfilling the hole.

To achieve maximum hardiness, protect palms for the first two years and especially during very long periods of extreme temperatures. The temperatures indicated in this list from Grant are not guarantees, but they are the coldest temperatures that these plants have been documented to survive. The plants are arranged in the order of their cold hardiness, from most to least cold hardy.

	Min Temp (°F)	
Mazari Palm (*Nannorrhops richiana*)	-15	CS, V
Needle Palm (*Rhapidophyllum hystrix*)	-15	CS, V
Dwarf Palmetto (*Sabal minor*)	-5	CS, V
Silver-Back Fan Palm (*Guihaia argyrata*)	-5	CS, V
Narrowleaf Silver-Back Fan Palm (*Guihaia grossefibrosa*)	-5	CS, V
Trunking Palmetto (*Sabal* x *texensis*)	0	CS, V
Windmill Palm (*Trachycarpus fortunei*)	0	CS, V
Himalayan Windmill (*Trachycarpus wagnerianus*)	5	CS, V
Dwarf Himalayan Windmill Palm (*Trachycarpus takil*)	5	CS, V
Scrub Palmetto (*Sabal etonia*)	5	CS, V
Silver Sabal (*Sabal urseana*)	6	CS, V
North Florida Fan Palm (*Sabal palmetto* spp.)	8	CS, V
Rusty Fiber Sabal (*Sabal blackburnianum*)	8	CS, V
Texas Sabal (*Sabal texana*)	8	CS, V
Guadamalan Sabal (*Sabal guadamaliensis*)	8	CS, V
Mexican Sabal (*Sabal mexicana*)	8	CS, V
Dwarf Spiny Fiber Palm (*Trithrinax campestris*)	10	CS, V
Dwarf-Frond Mediterranean Fan Palm (*Chamaerops humilis*)	10	CS, V
Pindo Palm (*Butia capitata*)	10	CS, V
Wooly Butia (*Butia eriospatha*)	10	CS, V
Mexican Blue Fan or Hesper Palm (*Brahea armata* [*Erythea armata*])	12	CSs, V

Canary Island Date Palm (*Phoenix canariensis*)	12	CSs, V
Chilean Wine Palm (*Jubaea chilensis*)	12	CSs, V
Butia X Queen Palm (*Butia capitata* X *stagrys*)	12	CSs, V
California Fan Palm (*Washingtonia filifera*)	12	CSs, V
Wild Date Palm (*Phoenix sylvestris*)	14	CSs, V
Cretan Date Palm (*Phoenix theofrasty*)	14	CSs, V
Silver-Frond Mediterranean Fan Palm (*Chamaerops humilis* 'cerifera')	14	CSs, V
Saw Palmetto (*Serenoa repens*)	14	CSs, V
Trithrinax acanthocoma	14	CSs, V
Sea Shore Palm (*Allagoptera arenaria*)	14	CSs, V
'Medjool' Date Palm (*Phoenix dactylifera*)	15	V
'Zahedii' Date Palm (*Phoenix dactylifera*)	15	V
Caranday Palm (*Copernicia alba*)	16	V
Sonoran Hesper Palm (*Brahea clara*)	16	V
Mexican Fan Palm hybrid (*Washingtonia robusta* X *filifera*)	17	V
Hardy Bamboo Palm (*Chamaedorea microspadix*)	18	V
Hardy Bamboo Palm (*Chamaedorea radicalis*)	18	V
Ribbon Fan Palm (*Livistona decipiens*)	18	V
Queen Palm (*Syagrus romanzoffiana*)	18	V
Dypsis decipiens	20	V
Sugar Palm (*Arenga engleri*)	20	V
Mexican Fan Palm (*Washingtonia robusta*)	20	V
Ravenea xerophyla	22	V
Licury Palm (*Syagrus coronata*)	22	V
Finger Palm (*Rhapis multifida*)	22	V
Taraw Palm (*Livistona saribus*)	22	V
Wallichia disticha	24	V
Paurotis Palm, Everglades Palm (*Acoelorraphe wrightii*)	26	V
Cat Palm (*Chamaedorea cataractarum*)	26	V
Senegal Date Palm (*Phoenix reclinata*)	26	V
Cherry Palm (*Pseudophoenix sargentii*)	26	V
Cairns Dwarf Fan Palm (*Livistona muellerii*)	26	V

"Palms are not only beautiful; they add a certain ambiance, an allure of the exotic. Few other symbols so readily conjure up such magic as the instantly recognizable silhouette of a palm. Texas has three native palms and forty-five plus others that flourish here, adding a touch of the tropics."
—Grant Stephenson, Horticultural Consultants, Houston

CYCADS FOR TEXAS GARDENS

Cycads have been described as living fossils and the ancient ancestors of the plant world. They have also been linked to dinosaurs, for their history can be traced back to the time when those extraordinary creatures roamed the earth. However, unlike the dinosaurs, the cycads have direct living remnants that still cling to life today. Cycads reached their peak in the Jurassic and early Cretaceous periods, dominating the plant life of that day. The living species share many characteristics with these early plants, which is obvious from an examination of fossils. It is easy to believe these plants have survived more than 200 million years with very little change.

SAGO
PALM

Cycads typically are less hardy than palms. In Texas, most do better from Corpus Christi south, but some, like the sago palm (*Cycas revoluta*), are common in Houston-area landscapes. Almost all of the cycads in this list, which comes from

Grant Stephenson, owner of Horticultural Consultants in Houston, are good candidates for the protected microclimate of the atrium or a similarly protected landscape setting. The temperatures indicate their relative cold hardiness. The plants are listed in the order of most to least cold hardy.

Min Temp (°F)

'Edule' Mexican Fern Palm (*Dioon edule*)	12	*Macrozamia johnsonii*	22
Sago Palm (*Cycas revoluta*)	16	*Cycas media*	24
Macrozamia communis	16	*Zamia fischeri*	24
Ceratozamia hildae	18	*Encephalartos ferox*	24
Ceratozamia kuesteriana	18	*Zamia roezlii*	26
Macrozamia moorei	18	*Encephalartos gratus*	26
Coontie Palm (*Zamia integrifolia*)	18	*Encephalartos hildebrandtii*	26
Zamia amblyphyllidia	20	*Encephalartos horridus*	26
Cardboard Palm (*Zamia furfuracea*)	20	*Lepidozamia peroffskyana*	26
Zamia pumila	20	*Dioon spinulosum*	28
Encephalartos lehmannii	22		

ROOT-HARDY TROPICAL PERENNIALS FOR SUN

Plants in this list from Linda Gay, chief horticulturist at the Mercer Arboretum in Humble, have tropical-looking foliage, exotic flowers, or summer fragrance. Peak season for this group of plants is midsummer, when everything else is floundering in the garden. Most of these plants, like the gardeners that care for them, will appreciate a little shade in the summer.

	Flowers	
Achimenes (*Achimenes* spp.)	petunia-like	CSs, V
'Peter Pan' Dwarf Lily-of-the-Nile (*Agapanthus*)	small, blue	C, CS, V
Lily-of-the-Nile (*Agapanthus africanus*)	blue	CS, V
Shell Ginger (*Alpinia zerumbet*)	white pearly shells	CS, V
Red Bauhinia (*Bauhinia punctata*)	orange	CSs, V
Angel Trumpet (*Brugmansia* [*Datura*] hyb.)	fragrant, various colors	CS, V
Canna (*Canna* x *generalis*)	many colors	All
Flowering Senna (*Cassia corymbosa*)	yellow clusters	CS, V
Shower Tree (*Cassia splendida*)	yellow	CS, V
Turk's Turban (*Clerodendrum indicum*)	white; red fruit	CS, V
Pagoda Flower (*Clerodendrum paniculatum*)	orange panicles	CS, V
Glory Bower (*Clerodendrum speciossimum*)	round orange clusters	CS, V
Tree Glory Bower (*Clerodendrum trichotomum*)	fragrant white; red/blue fruit	V
Blue Butterflies (*Clerodendrum ugandense*)	blue with long stamens	CS, V
Milk-and-Wine Lily (*Crinum amabile*)	white/red striped	CS, V
Crinum (*Crinum asiaticum*)	fragrant white	CS, V
Hidden Ginger (*Curcuma* spp.)	yellow/pink bracts	CSs, V
Blue Ginger (*Dichorisandra thyrsiflora*)	blue	Cs, CS, V
Hummingbird Plant (*Hamelia patens*)	red tubular	CSs, V, Annual
Butterfly Gingers (*Hedychium* spp.)	white/yellow/coral	Cs, CS, V
Mexican Morning Glory (*Ipomoea fistulosa*)	pink or white	CSs, V
Oxypetalum (*Oxypetalum caeruleum*)	pale blue	CSs, V
Rice-Paper Plant (*Tetrapanax papyriferus*)	white panicles	Cs, CS, V

Grown for Their Foliage or Form

'Variegatus' Spiral Ginger (*Costus speciosus*)	green/white varied foliage	CS, V
Blue Ginger (*Dichorisandra thyrsiflora*)	silver/green foliage	Cs, CS, V

Rojo Banana (*Musa zebrina*)	good foliage and form	CS, V
Burgundy Tropical Giant (*Pennisetum* hyb.)	wide burgundy foliage/plumes	CS, V
Palm Grass (*Setaria palmifolia*)	weeping foliage, spines	V, Annual
Rice-Paper Plant (*Tetrapanax papyriferus*)	bold textured leaves	Cs, CS, V

TENDER BUT WORTH PROTECTING

Most gardeners are willing to take a chance on tender plants even if one year out of ten they get frozen to the ground. Some are so tender, we plant them as annuals, or we expect to pot them up in the fall and put them in a protected place. Many of the plants in this list can be grown in a porous clay pot that is sunk into the soil (leaving the rim exposed). Set the pot out each year after the danger of frost is past. Before cold weather hits in the fall, pull up the pot and move the plant into the greenhouse. These tender plants will not withstand temperatures below 25 degrees F.

Philippine Violet (*Barleria cristata*)
Variegated Orchid Tree (*Bauhinia variegata*)
'Candida' Variegated Orchid Tree (*Bauhinia variegata*)
Pride-of-Barbados (*Caesalpinia pulcherrima*)
Powderpuff Plant (*Calliandra emarginata*)
Flowery Senna (*Cassia splendida*)
Pagoda Flower (*Clerodendrum paniculatum*)

Australian Tree Fern (*Cyathea cooperi*)
Abyssinian Banana, Black Banana (*Ensete ventricosum*)
Yellow Jacobinia (*Justicia aurea*)
Mexican Breadfruit (*Monstera deliciosa*)
Variegated Moses-in-a-Boat (*Rhoeo spathacea* 'variegata')
Yellow Bells (*Tecoma stans* 'angustata')

TENDER PLANTS THAT SURVIVE FREEZING BACK

Gardeners from the Gulf Coast south (CSs, V) will find that growing the plants on this list is well worth the effort. They usually survive a freeze back. Some will do just fine with little protection, coming back strong in the spring. Others will need 6 to 8 inches of mulch to insure survival.

Allamanda (*Allamanda cathartica*)
Shell Ginger (*Alpinia sanderae*)
Variegated Shell Ginger (*Alpinia zerumbet* 'variegata')
Wood Rose (*Argyreia nervosa*)
Calico Flower (*Aristolochia littoralis* [*elegans*])
'Aaron' Caladium (*Caladium*)
Powderpuff Plant (*Calliandra emarginata*)
Candlestick Plant (*Cassia alata*)
Black Taro (*Colocasia antiquorum*)
Spiral Ginger (*Costus speciosus*)
Air Potato Vine (*Dioscorea bulbifera*)
Council Fig (*Ficus altissima*)
Parrot-Beak (*Heliconia schiedeana*)

Variegated Tapioca (*Manihot esculenta* 'variegata')
Pink Banana (*Musa velutina*)
Crimson Passion Vine (*Passiflora vitifolia*)
Sandpaper Vine (*Petrea volubilis*)
Root-Beer Plant (*Piper auritum*)
Chocolate Plant (*Pseuderanthemum alatum*)
Garlic Vine (*Pseudocalymma alliacea*)
Rangoon Creeper (*Quisqualis indica*)
Castor Bean (*Ricinus communis*)
Sanchezia (*Sanchezia speciosa* [*nobilis*])
Chalice Vine (*Solandra maxima*)
Butterfly Vine (*Stigmaphyllon ciliatum*)
Rice-Paper Plant (*Tetrapanax papyriferus*)
Blue Trumpet Vine (*Thunbergia grandiflora*)

PLUMERIAS

Plumerias are tropical shrubs that come in all colors, including stripes and multicolor blends. They're very fragrant—some even smell like peaches, pineapple, or coconut. Fertilizing with a high middle number (phosphorous) fertilizer, such as Super Bloom, is the secret to getting them to bloom better. They should be fertilized monthly when they leaf out in the spring, or weekly to force bloom on older plants.

To propagate new plants or to shape up plants, take cuttings in the spring. Only cut every other branch so as not to cut off all the bloom-tip ends. The cuttings can be rooted to produce more plants identical to the parent plant. Let the cut end dry for at least three days, apply rooting hormone, place in a pot, and keep the soil moist but not wet. Rooting should take place in six to eight weeks.

New varieties of plumerias are derived from seed. However, it may take five to ten years to get a seedling to bloom, although some varieties may bloom in as little as two years. There are currently almost a hundred registered and named varieties of plumerias. Lee Jacobs rates the following registered varieties as the best.

Aztec Gold	yellow and pink, very fragrant, large flowers
Celadine	yellow flowers, lemon fragrance; good keeping
Puu Kahea	large yellow flowers with red bands
Cerise	large clusters of bright-red, star-shaped flowers
Hilo Beauty	very dark, velvety red, star-shaped blossoms
Japanese Lantern	rose-red, pendulous clusters hang like a basket
Rose Red	very fragrant, continuous bloomer
Espinda	soft pastel-pink, overlapping petals, large clusters
Tomlinson	pink petals with white radiating lines; great bloomer
Dean Conklin	large, salmon-pink blooms
Kimo	apricot-orange, fragrant flowers
Madame Poni	curled petals show red back edge on white
Daisy Wilcox	very large white flowers, pink edge, large clusters
Samoan Fluff	large white flowers, overlapping petals
Jean Moragne	large orange-pink flowers
Dwarf Pink Singapore	small pale-pink flowers; very small evergreen plant
Dwarf Deciduous Singapore	large white flowers, small plant; dormant in winter

"Plumerias are currently the most popular of tropical plants," notes Lee Jacobs of the International Plumeria Society. **"People all over the world are growing them even though they are tropical. Fortunately they can be grown anywhere because, even in cold climates, they can be container grown and protected in winter. Allowing them to go dormant is the key, and storing them in a protected place that does not freeze. Not only should they not freeze, but frost on the tips of branches where the bloom stem comes out can eliminate blooming the next year."**

TROPICAL HIBISCUS

Few plants have the power to inspire a tropical impression like the Chinese hibiscus (*Hibiscus rosa-sinensis*). Toss in a few palm trees and it's easy to pretend you're on a tropical isle even if you're just in a backyard in Houston. Chinese hibiscus are pretty tender, however, so even Houston enthusiasts keep most of their prized varieties in large containers and bring them indoors for the winter.

Hibiscus are relatively easy to grow, but they have a few special requirements. Don't use too much phosphorous (the middle number on a bag of fertilizer). Don't let them dry out to the point of wilting. And if you plant them in the flower bed, don't be surprised if they don't bloom much the next year. This latter point can seem puzzling, but what happens is really very simple. The plants are often damaged by winter freezes; they survive, but often they come back so vegetative and vigorous that they don't slow down to bloom until late in the season.

Exotic Hybrid Hibiscus, Best When Grafted	Flower diameter and type	Flower color
Al Schlueter	7" single	pinkish brown
Amber Suzanne	8" double	pink and white
Antique Rose	7" single	medium rose/purple
Burnished Gold	7" single	bright orange, darker center, gold/yellow edge
Chocolate Mousse	6" single	brown with red center
Copper Moon	7" double	bronze with yellow freckles
Corona	5" single	yellow/orange blend
Dorothy Wolfe	7" double	butterscotch gold

Double Date	6" double	hot pink
Dusk	7" double	dark rosy purple
Elaine's Delight	6" single	pink and white
Erma K	7" double	pale yellow
Fantasy Charm	9" single	medium pink with a white edge
5th Dimension	7" single	steel gray and lavender with orange edge
Fran G	7" single	light orange with yellow edge
Georgia's Pearl	9" single	orange/yellow blend
Guy Mitchell	7" double	medium orange with a dark orange edge
Harvest Sunset	8" single	bright yellow with maroon sunburst center
High Voltage	8" single	white with a deep maroon center
Jason Blue	6" single	yellow with blue center
Kirk's Purple	5" single	medium purple with a pink center
Lavender Pearl	6" single	pale lavender with pink and white center
Lora	7" single	lavender with pink center
Melissa Morrison	7" single	ivory with light yellow edge and pink center
Miss Liberty	8" single	dark pink with white splotches
Occam's Razor	8" single	light orange
Orville Davis	6" single	orange/brown with medium pink center
Peggy's Pride	7" single	pink with yellow and white bands
Pompano Pink	8" single	pink with white edge
Raspberry Swirl	7" single	raspberry red with rosy pink edge
Razzle Dazzle	7" single	bright orange/yellow blend, white freckles
Red Snapper	8" double	red with white splotches
Samuel Dubin	8" single	dark orange with yellow veins
Sassi	8" single	dark red with darker center
Show Girl	8" double	medium red with dark-red center
Spring Break	7" single	creamy white with maroon center
Sun Shower	7" single	orange/red with white and yellow splotches
Sunny Moon	9" single	brown with yellow edge, white frosting
Tamibon	7" single	pink with yellow edge
Terrence Watson	7" single	golden yellow with deep rust center
Top Knot	6" double	orange/red
Tubize	8" double	pale pink with darker center

Garden Variety Cultivars That Grow on Their Own Roots

Own Roots	Flower diameter and type	Flower color
Albo Lacinatus	4" single	light pink with darker veins
Aldalarian, Lipstick	6" single	hot pink
Amour	6" single	light pink with white frosting
Bride	7" single	white with slight pink blush
Brilliant	6" single	red with darker center
Butterfly, Delight	6" single	medium yellow
Cooperii	3" single	red; variegated foliage
Crown of Bohemia	6" double	golden yellow
Dainty Pink	3" single	light pink
Dainty White	3" single	white
Double Psyche	4" double	deep velvety red
El Capitolio	4" crested single	red with white
Florida Sunset	5" single	orange-red with buff edge
Grandaflora	6" single	rose with darker center
Hawaiian Salmon	3" single	salmon with pink fringed edge
Indian Princess	6" single	hot pink with darker center and veins

Lutea	5" single	buff with deep rust center
Mary Morgan	6" double	medium pink
Orange Key	6" double	light orange with darker center
Powder Puff, White Kalakua	6" double	creamy white
President	6" single	orange/red
Pride of Hankins	4" double	hot pink
Psyche	4" single	deep velvety red
Red Dragon	6" double	medium red
Ross Estey	6" single	rosy coral
Rowena Wedding	5" single	buff pink with deep rose center and veins
Schizopetalus	3" single	medium-orange, pendulous fringed petals
Seminole Pink	6" single	medium pink with darker center
Silver Queen	3" single	red; variegated foliage
Sprinkle Rain	4" single	light orange with red-orange center
Sweet Violet	4" single	violet with darker center
Sylvia Goodman	4" single	buff-yellow and white with deep red center
Yellow Lagos	5" single	golden yellow with white and rust center

Pat and Roswell Merritt are hibiscus enthusiasts. "We now grow more than 1,000 cultivars," they point out, and many of them are Roz's seedlings. One Roz Merritt creation, 'Copper Moon,' is in the final four competing for the Hibiscus of the Year Award. Pat and Roz, who contributed the "Tropical Hibiscus" list, belong to the Lone Star Chapter of the American Hibiscus Society. This 400-member chapter, which is the largest in the country, meets monthly from March through October at the Houston Garden Center in Hermann Park. According to the Merritts, "Gardeners can view more than 1,500 hibiscus photographs found on the Lone Star Hibiscus Chapter's website, http://www.lonestarahs.org."

If you're online, you can visit several other hibiscus websites for more information, including http://americanhibiscus.org, and http://trop-hibiscus.com.

ORCHIDS FOR TEXAS

Orchids, the aristocrats of the plant world, are rapidly increasing in popularity as a plant hobby. No longer are orchids rare and difficult to find," says Dotty Woodson, a horticultural County Extension agent in Fort Worth. "Increased knowledge of orchid propagation and culture have made them available at floral shops, local garden centers, and grocery stores at a price reasonable enough for most budgets."

ONCIDIUM

Dotty points out that the *Cymbidium* orchid was cultivated by the Chinese more than 2,500 years ago, and the ancient Greeks used the tubers of a European terrestrial orchid as an aphrodisiac. "Yet orchids did not become popular as a flower and plant hobby until the discovery of the large, colorful orchid flowers from the tropical New World. During the latter half of the nineteenth century, orchid growing became a mania. Their popularity demanded high prices and encouraged new discoveries. Wealthy plant collectors sent plant explorers to many exotic regions to bring back these jewels of the jungles."

Orchids range in size from the tiny *Bulbophyllum minutissimum* to the massive *Grammatophyllum speciosum*—a 5- to 10-foot plant with a 10-foot bloom. According to Dotty, "The *Orchidaceae* is the largest plant family in the world, with 600 genera and 30,000 species. The diversity of orchids and their habitats makes growing orchids an exciting, never-ending challenge. Orchids grow from the edge of the Arctic Circle to the islands that rim the Antarctic. In the temperate regions, orchids are terrestrial. In the tropics, orchids are epiphytes, growing on trees or rocks, or in leaf litter."

Whatever your growing conditions, you can find an orchid to thrive. "Light, temperature, humidity, water, fertilizer, and growing media all influence the selection and culture of orchids. To select your first orchids, identify your growing conditions, like low light from a window or high light in a greenhouse. Light is the most limiting factor involved. Purchase orchids that grow in your existing conditions. General requirements for all tropical orchids are 50 to 80 percent humidity, loose, fast-draining potting media, good air circulation, and water with neutral or slightly acid pH and little or no sodium. Light and temperature requirements vary greatly, depending on the natural growing conditions of the orchid. If you are growing them indoors, select orchids that require low light." Dotty says that you can grow both high-light and low-light varieties in a greenhouse if you shade one end of the greenhouse for the low-light orchids. The second most important factor is temperature. "Orchids that grow high in the mountains require low night temperatures. During the summer, low night temperature is not possible to provide in all greenhouses or homes."

Before purchasing an orchid, Dotty says, explain to the salesperson what your growing conditions are and ask for advice about what to purchase. "*Cymbidium, Dendrobium, Oncidium,* and *Phalaenopsis* are the four genera of orchids commonly sold by garden centers and florists because their flowers last a long time and they are easy to grow. Other genera less readily available but easy to grow include *Cattleya* (which includes the traditional purple orchid), Lady's Slipper (several genera), and *Vanda.*"

There are about 3 million orchid hybrids. "Botanically most plants in different genera won't cross. Orchids, however, are a glaring exception, as many genera can be crossed. To group these genera that will interbreed (producing intergeneric hybrids), orchid botanists have placed them in tribes or *alliances.*"

The following is Dotty's list of orchid hybrids and species within several of the major orchid alliances that are easy to grow in Texas—indoors on a windowsill during the winter and outdoors during the summer, or in a greenhouse year round. "Many more orchids will grow in Texas. If you catch the orchid bug, consult any of the many orchid books available at the bookstore and library." Local orchid societies are another good source of information. Contact the American Orchid Society, 6000 South Olive Avenue, West Palm Beach, FL 33405-9974, or call 561-585-8666 for information about an orchid society near you.

Cymbidiums
Most Cymbidiums require night temperatures of 50 to 55 degrees F in August and September to flower, so not many are recommended for Texas. The best way to find a Cymbidium that flowers in the Texas heat is to find a division from another orchid grower near you. Better yet, concentrate on orchid varieties better adapted to Texas.

Phalaenopsis Alliance

HYBRIDS	FLOWER COLOR	BLOOM PERIOD
Phalaenopsis Florida Snow	white	spring
Phalaenopsis Frank Gottberg	white	spring
Phalaenopsis Tyler Rose	pink	spring
Phalaenopsis Abendrot	pink	spring
Phalaenopsis Maraldee Brecto-Tiger	yellow	spring
Phalaenopsis Taida Lawrence	yellow	spring
Phalaenopsis Spirit House	red	spring
Phalaenopsis Franz Lizst	red	spring
Phalaenopsis Dotty Woodson	red	spring
Hale Be Glad	multiflora pink	spring

SPECIES		
Phalaenopsis equestris	lavender	spring/summer/fall
Phalaenopsis violacea	green/white/magenta	summer
Doritis pulcherrima	pink or white	summer

Oncidium Alliance

HYBRIDS		
Oncidium Sharry Baby	lavender	summer/fall
Oncidium Grower Ramsey	yellow	summer/fall

SPECIES

Oncidium sphacelatum	yellow	summer/fall
Oncidium ampliatum	yellow	summer/fall
Oncidium papilio (Butterfly Orchid)	yellow-brown	summer/fall

Cattleya Alliance
HYBRIDS

Laeliocattleya Bonanza	purple	summer/fall
Sophrolaeliocattleya Anzac	red	summer/fall
Sophrolaeliocattleya Jewel Box	red	summer/fall
Cattleya Bow Bells	white	summer/fall
Sophrolaeliocattleya Hazel Boyd	red or orange	summer/fall
Laeliocattleya Dorset Gold	yellow with red lip	summer/fall
Brassolaiocattleya Memoria Helen Brown	green with purple lip	summer/fall
Laeliocattleya Persepolis	white with red lip	summer/fall

SPECIES

Brassovola nodosa	white	summer
Cattleya amethystoglossa	purple	summer/fall
Cattleya dowiana	yellow with purple lip	summer/fall

Lady's Slipper Alliance
HYBRIDS

Paphiopedilum St. Swithin	dark purple	winter
Paphiopedilum Key Lime	green	winter
Paphiopedilum F. C. Puddle	white	winter
Paphiopedilum Maudiae	green/white	winter
Phragmipedium Eric Young	orange	winter

SPECIES

Paphiopedilum hirsutissimum	green/red	winter
Paphiopedilum venustum	green/red	winter
Paphiopedilum delenatii	pink	winter
Paphiopedilum micranthum	pink	winter
Paphiopedilum collosum	purple	winter
Paphiopedilum armeniacum	pink	winter
Phragmipedium besseae	pink	winter

Vanda Alliance
HYBRIDS

Vanda Southwest Beauty	yellow	summer/fall
Vanda Fuch's Blue	blue	summer/fall
Vanda Kasem's Delight	purple	summer/fall
Vanda Fuch's Beauty	magenta	summer/fall
Ascocenda Su-Fun Beauty	orange	summer/fall
Ascocenda Mickey Nax	yellow	summer/fall

SPECIES

Vanda sanderiana	green/white	summer/fall
Vanda coerulea	blue	summer/fall

Angraecum Alliance

Angraecum sesquipedal	white	winter

Dendrobiums

HYBRIDS

Dendrobium Dawn Maree	white with red lip	summer/fall
Dendrobium Suzanne Neil	purple	summer/fall
Dendrobium Palolo Sunshine	yellow	summer/fall

SPECIES

Dendrobium callipes	yellow	summer/fall
Dendrobium phalaenopsis	white and purple	summer/fall

Jewel Orchid

Ludisia discolor	white	winter/spring

> "Orchid seeds are tiny, dust-like embryos with no food source like regular seeds. To germinate in nature, an orchid seed needs the presence of a mycorrhiza fungus to provide food. In 1899, French biologist Noel Bernard discovered that mycorrhiza fungus was necessary for germination. In 1904, German botanist Hans Burgeff discovered orchid seeds would grow in agar-filled test tubes inoculated with mycorrhiza fungus. In 1922, Lewis Knudson, a plant physiologist from Cornell University, discovered a way to germinate orchid seeds on an artificial medium without the use of mycorrhiza. These discoveries increased orchid hybridization. Improved hybrids made orchids even more popular."
> —Dotty Woodson, County Extension horticulturist, Fort Worth

INSECTIVOROUS PLANTS

Insectivorous plants—or carnivorous plants, as some prefer to call them—are fascinating members of the botanical world. "They have developed methods of capturing and digesting insects to supplement the lack of nutrition in their native soils," explains Greg Harmison, a horticulturist with the Mercer Arboretum and Botanic Gardens in Humble. Greg says that insectivorous plants, which range in form from tiny rosettes to rambling vines, can be found worldwide, in semi-deserts, swamps, rain forests, and tundra.

All of the plants in Greg's list are native to the United States and some are native to Texas. "Many non-native species may do well here, but trial and error tests would need to be done, based on native climates." Greg advises that insectivorous plants requiring a winter dormancy are better suited to the northern part of Texas.

Pitcher Plants

The *Sarracenia*, or pitcher plants, are native from Texas to New England and are well adapted to the humid climate of East Texas and the Gulf Coast. Their trumpet-shaped leaves, many around 2-feet tall, act as pitfall traps for insects. All need winter dormancy for about three months.

Sarracenia purpurea	A small species with a curved pitcher; often turns red to maroon in full sun.
Sarracenia flava	The Yellow Trumpet; yellow pitchers with red or chartreuse veins.
Sarracenia alata	A Texas native found in the Big Thicket area; does well on the Gulf Coast.
Sarracenia minor	Large pitchers to almost 3 feet; very pronounced hood over the top of the pitcher.
Sarracenia psittacina	The Parrot Pitcher; pitchers lay on the ground and have an almost entirely enclosed hood.
Sarracenia leucophylla	Very striking pitcher; a white top with green or red veins.
Sarracenia rubra	The Red Pitcher.

Venus Flytraps

The Venus flytrap, *Dionaea muscipula*, is the quintessential bug eater. The traplike jaw snaps shut around its helpless prey. They are native to a small area in North Carolina but have been in the nursery trade for years. They require a winter dormancy to thrive and may need some protection from our hot Texas sun. Keep them moist but not soggy.

Sundews

The leaves of the *Drosera*, or sundews, are covered in sticky hairs that snare small insects. A dewy glue at the end of the hairs makes the plants sparkle like jewels. Many of these plants are small rosettes, but some of the tropical species are like small shrubs. The natural range of the sundews listed here extends to the southern United States, but many northern species may adapt with some summer protection.

Drosera intermedia	Small plant with the trapping area at the end of the leaf.
Drosera filiformis	Tall, threadlike leaves with hairs running the length.
Drosera capillaris	Spatula-shaped trapping leaves; pink flowers.
Drosera brevifolia	A small Texas native; plant is about an inch across.

Butterworts

Butterworts, *Pinguicula*, are small rosettes with sticky, fleshy leaves that act like flypaper. They often have pretty, violet-like flowers ranging from pink to yellow. They are generally delicate and may require extra care. The ones that would take our Texas heat may need some protection from our cold.

Pinguicula pumila	Texas native with small rosettes barely an inch across.
Pinguicula lutea	Beautiful yellow flower.
Pinguicula caerulea	Pink flower with dark purple veins.
Pinguicula plainifolia	Pale purple flower.
Pinguicula primuliflora	Often forms new plantlets from the leaf tips.

Bladderworts

Utricularia, or bladderworts, are small and mostly aquatic, with some terrestrial or epiphytic species. Small bladders suck in their prey, and they have small, orchid-like flowers. They may be grown in ponds and wet areas of bogs.

Utricularia olivacea	White flowers.
Utricularia purpurea	Purple flowers.
Utricularia subulata	Terrestrial plants with yellow flowers.
Utricularia cornuta	An aquatic, yellow-flowered, Texas native.
Utricularia inflata, U. radiata	Spokelike floats support the yellow-flowered plants.
Utricularia gibba, U. biflora	Tangled mats of thread-like stems; yellow flowers.

"Insectivorous plants are relatively easy to grow as long as certain basic (and a few specific) requirements are met. They typically need a constantly moist, peat-based, acidic soil," says Greg Harmison, a horticulturist with the Mercer Arboretum and Botanic Gardens in Humble. "They need pure water (rainwater is excellent), as they are not adapted to water with a high mineral content, and they (with few exceptions) should never be fertilized. The plants that adapt well to our area can be grown in an outdoor bog. The bog may be the size of a large pot or as big as a small pond. It should be placed where it gets sun most of the day, with some shade in the hottest part of the afternoon. The soil should be one part peat and one part sand, and the container should hold some water so the soil stays moist."

WATER LILIES AND LOTUS

Water gardens, especially when they include the spectacular blooms of water lilies and lotus, are the most tranquil areas of the landscape. They beckon one to sit down, relax, and forget the tensions of the day. Most gardeners, however, find them a bit scary. It's hard enough to grow petunias and a decent lawn—why take on anything as mysterious as a pond with plants? It's really quite easy these days, however, with flexible pond liners and a number of water garden nurseries (see the "Resources" section in this book).

Water lilies are usually planted in containers with a heavy garden soil topped with gravel. Don't add materials such as peat moss or humus, though, because these elements can cloud the water. The pots are then positioned on rocks or gravel in the water so that the leaves float on the surface. These plants are heavy feeders, so be sure to purchase some fertilizer pellets from the nursery. Add a few fish and you have a complete water environment. Be careful, though, because large koi can dig up water lilies.

Lotus can be planted deeper than water lilies, but the potting information is essentially the same. The only similarity, however, between lotus and water lilies is that they both grow in water. Lotus are not necessarily tropical; they grow anywhere that the water doesn't freeze to the root stocks—so all of Texas would be a possibility.

Kirk Strawn, a retired wildlife and fisheries science professor from Texas A&M, provided this list of water lilies and lotus. He started growing water lilies as a hobby in 1975 and in 1981 opened the Strawn Water Gardens, a wholesale nursery in College Station. Kirk has developed more than forty-three varieties of water lilies and lotus. Plants in his list that are marked with an asterisk (*) are hybrids developed by Kirk.

The hardy water lilies listed here are hardy throughout Texas. The tropical water lilies have to be stored in a frost-free location during the winter in areas north of the lower Coastal South (CSs) region.

YELLOW
WATER LOTUS

Hardy Pink Water Lilies
Amabilis, large, pink, star-shaped flower
Anna Epple, large pink from Germany
Arc-En-Ciel, light-pink flower, unique variable
  leaves
Colorado,* salmon
Dallas,* pink, very free blooming
Fabiola, reddish pink, large flower
Helen Hariot,* opens light pink, ages to red
Hollandia, double pink
Louise Villemarette,* large pink
Marliacea Rosea, pink
Martha,* large pink
Masaniello, spotted rose-pink petals with white
  sepals
Mayla,* large, vivid fuschia; likes some shade in hot
  climates
Patio Joe,* cool pink with apricot overtones
Pink Beauty, Fabiola, yellow stamens
Pink Opal, small; does well in gallon pot
Pink Pumpkin,* huge medium-pink flower, petals
  curve inward
Pink Sensation, pink
Pink Sparkle,* pink with deeper color on center
  petals
Rosy Morn, pink
Somptuosa, rosy pink deepening toward center
Starburst,* pink with brown and green leaves
Sunny Pink,* large pink
Yuh-Ling,* deep pink, cup shaped

Hardy Red Water Lilies
Attraction, No. 1–4, red
Burgundy Princess,* small, deep red; can wilt from
  heat
Charlie's Choice,* small, red center, white on outer-
  most petals
Conqueror, red
Ellisiana, small to medium red
Gloriosa, red
Gypsy,* first-day rose tones, third-day
  white/mauve/pink
James Brydon, red
Laydekeri Fulgens, deep red
Liou,* small deep red
Mary,* deep-rose center softening to light pink
Perry's Baby Red, dark red; stays open late
Red Spider,* narrow-petals, red
Reflected Flame,* red flame
Rembrandt, red
Rene Gerard, red
Sultan, red

Hardy White Water Lilies
Chubby,* perfect waxy cream flowers
Colossea, pale peach, turning white
Denver,* double white with hint of peach
Gladstone, English white
Hermine, small white
Highlight,* cream with peach overtones
Marliac White, white

Marliacea Albida, white
Marliacea Carnea, blush of peach graduating to
    white
Nymphaea candida, small white
Queen of Whites, white
Starbright,* white with pink tint, dark-brown leaves
Virginalis, white
Virginia, large white
Walter Pagels,* small cream-white
White Sultan,* white

Hardy Yellow Water Lilies
Berit Strawn,* small orange-yellow
Charlene Strawn,* yellow; can take some shade
Chromatella, yellow
Helvola, miniature yellow
Inner Light,* yellow with bright yellow center
Joey Tomocik,* vivid yellow; good cut flower
Lemon Chiffon,* double yellow
Lemon Mist,* double soft yellow
Mexicana, yellow
Moorei, yellow
Sulphurea, yellow
Sunrise, yellow
Texas Dawn, yellow

Hardy Changeable/Peach Water Lilies
Barbara Dobbins,* peach
Chrysantha, small yellow-vermilion
Georgia Peach,* peach
Graziella, small yellow-vermilion
Indiana, small yellow-orange, changes to red; stays
    open
J.C.N. Forestier, bright copper-red, matures to deep
    red
Little Sue,* light lemon pastel streaked with mauve
Peach Lily,* large light yellow/peach
Peach Glow,* light peach, lightly mottled green
Sioux, yellow shaded with copper
Thomas O'Brien,* light peach

Tropical Blue Water Lilies
Bagdad, blue with mottled leaf
Blue Beauty, blue
Blue Star, blue
Bob Trickett, blue
Colorata, small blue
Dauben, light blue
Electra, blue
Green Smoke, blue-green
Judge Hitchcock, dark blue, purple
Margaret Randig, blue
Marmorata, blue
Midnight , blue

Nymphaea coerulea, blue
Nymphaea elegans, lavender
Nymphaea gigantica, medium blue
Pamela, blue
Robert Strawn,* tall lavender
Wood's Blue Goddess, blue

Tropical Pink Water Lilies
Castaliflora, pink
Evelyn Randig, dark pink with mottled leaf
Mrs. C. W. Ward, pink
Persian Lilac, pink
Pink Pearl, gentle pink
Pink Platter, medium pink
Pink Star, pink

Tropical Red Water Lilies
Mr. Martin E. Randig, reddish
Jack Wood, reddish

Tropical White Water Lilies
Alice Tricker, white
Hudsonia, blush white
Marian Strawn,* white

Tropical Yellow Water Lilies
Afterglow, shades of yellow, pink, orange
Albert Greenberg, yellow, pink, orange
Aviator Pring, yellow
St. Louis, light-yellow

Tropical Night-Blooming Water Lilies
Brazos White,* large center; early bloomer
Mrs. Emily Grant Hutchins, pink; no tubers
Red Cup,* deep red; good cup shape
Red Flare, flat, deep-red flower, red leaves
Sturtevantii, cup-shaped, pink flower
Texas Shell Pink, pink
Trudy Slocum, white
Wood's White Knight, white
White Night Bloomer, white
Pink Night Bloomer, pink
Red Night Bloomer, red
Light Red Night Bloomer, light red

Lotus
Double Rose, double pink
Momo Botan, small, double pink; will bloom in
    gallon pot
Mrs. Perry D. Slocum, deep pink to creamy yellow
Nelumbo lutea, yellow
Perry's Giant Sunburst, yellow
Ruby Gardener, pink
Tulip Lotus, white

"The combination of a water feature and the spectacular blossoms of water lilies, lotus, and other water garden plants bring magic, serenity, and exquisite beauty to the landscape. Nothing surpasses water gardening for enjoyment."
—Kirk Strawn, Strawn Water Gardens, College Station

HIDDEN GINGERS—CURCUMAS

Linda Gay, chief horticulturist of the Mercer Arboretum in Humble, provided this list of curcumas, or hidden gingers. Curcumas have foliage that resembles banana plants, some producing basal flowers from the ground, with others flowering out of the top of the plant. Spring blooming curcumas are very beautiful, for they flower before their foliage has a chance to come up and hide them—hence the name hidden ginger. Curcumas have no fragrance, but the bloom is very exotic and reminiscent of Hawaii. Curcumas that bloom out of the top are being used extensively in the cut flower industry.

The plants on this list do well in the Houston area. Plant them with protection from the hot, afternoon summer sun. They go dormant with a week of consistent night temperature of 40 degrees. You will know this when the plant turns bright yellow in fall/winter.

'Khymer' (*Curcuma*)	burnt orange with yellow flowers
'Rainbow' (*Curcuma aurantiaca*)	many flower colors, waffled leaves
Siam Tulip (*Curcuma alismatifolia*)	narrow strap leaves
Curcuma australasica	hot pink flowers on long stems
Pink Roscoeana (*Curcuma* spp. *affinis cordata*)	exotic waxy bloom
Giant Plume (*Curcuma elata*)	dark pink bracts, yellow flowers
'Emperor' (*Curcuma*)	green leaves with white margins, blush pink flowers
'Fire' (*Curcuma flaviflora*)	red bracts and orange flowers
Curcuma ornata	red stems, white flowers, fuchsia-tipped bracts
'White Angel' (*Curcuma parviflora*)	white flowers
'Pride of Burma' (*Curcuma roscoeana*)	orange inflorescence, yellow flowers
'Olena' (*Curcuma sumatrana*)	glossy green foliage, fuchsia flower
Curcuma zeodaria/inodora	fuchsia flowers, maroon midrib on foliage

SHRUBS

Shrubs occupy the mid-range of the landscape. They soften the gap between tree canopy and foundation. But shrubs aren't just for foundation planting anymore. In fact, ugly foundations or concrete blocks are rarely a problem these days. Use shrubs as background plants in a flower border, or to hide an unsightly view. Shrubs can even be put to use as ground covers.

Many shrubs bloom or produce berries. This chapter includes various lists of flowering shrubs and a list of shrubs with ornamental fruit or berries. You will also find lists of shrubs with interesting foliage. Moreover, shrubs often make good specimen trees. As they become mature, trim lower twigs and leaves from the woody stems to create a small single or multi-trunk tree. You'll find a list of good candidates in this chapter.

Basic Cultural Requirements

- Good soil preparation is basic to success with shrubs. The more organic matter you can add to the soil, the better. Filling raised beds with a soil mix from the local dirt yard (where you can buy soil mixes in bulk quantities) is usually a good idea, even if the stuff seems to be planted with nutgrass (nutsedge). Soil tests of the native soil and of any soil mixes you might add to raised beds are recommended. See the "Resources" section of this book for soil test information.
- If in doubt concerning drainage, plant 1 to 2 inches high. Especially in heavy clay soils, it is easy to drown plants. Save any organic matter for the last one-third of backfill to avoid anaerobic decomposition of these materials in the bottom of the planting hole.
- Cut the roots of plants grown in containers and spread them out before planting. This is a very critical requirement with plants that have roots massed in a circular growth pattern around the outside of the root ball. Cut an inch deep in three to four places around the root ball in a line from top to bottom, and then pull the bottom 1 to 2 inches out from the root ball. This gives the plant a chance to quickly develop new roots. Cutting the top back one-third to compensate for the root damage also helps. Otherwise, plants may survive but won't thrive; after several years, weak and spindly, they can be pulled out with the roots still in the same cylindrical shape they were in when planted.
- Balled and burlapped plants should have the burlap removed, if possible. Any twine or wire in the stem area should be cut or removed to prevent girdling as the plant grows.
- Always water plants after they are set out. Even if the soil is wet from recent rains, more water is needed to settle the soil around the root system and eliminate air pockets.

SHRUBS WITH FRAGRANT BLOSSOMS

Fragrance is a subtle, sophisticated element in the landscape. It always seems a pleasant surprise—appreciated, but not expected. It usually sparks an intense interest in the landscape, and visitors will ask, "Where is that fragrance coming from?"

Sweet Shrub (*Calycanthus floridus*), Ce, CSe

Night-Blooming Jasmine (*Cestrum nocturnum*), CSs, V

Mexican Orange (*Choisya ternata*), CSsw, V

Thorny Elaeagnus (*Elaeagnus pungens*), All

Gardenia (*Gardenia jasminoides*), Ce, CSe

Dwarf Gardenia (*Gardenia jasminoides* 'radicans'), Ce, CSe

Loblolly Bay (*Gordonia lasianthus*), Ce, CSe

Spicebush (*Lindera benzoin*), C, CS

Winter Honeysuckle (*Lonicera fragrantissima*), N, C
Loropetalum (*Loropetalum chinense*), Ce, CSe
Banana Shrub (*Michelia figo*), CS, V
Fragrant Mimosa (*Mimosa borealis*), Cw, CSw, V
Devilwood (*Osmanthus americanus*), Ce, CSe
Sweet Olive (*Osmanthus fragrans*), CS, V
Holly-Leaf Osmanthus (*Osmanthus heterophyllus*),
    Ce, CSe
Mock Orange (*Philadelphus coronarius*), N, C, CS

Texas Mock Orange (*Philadelphus texensis*), Cs, CS
Pittosporum (*Pittosporum tobira*), CS, V
Yedda Hawthorn (*Rhaphiolepis umbellata*), C, CS, V
Native Azalea (*Rhododendron* spp.), Ce, CSe
Carolina Rose (*Rosa carolina*), All
Lilac (*Syringa vulgaris*), N, Cn
Arrowwood (*Viburnum dentatum*), Ce, CSe
Sweet Viburnum (*Viburnum odoratissimum*), C

SHRUBS THAT BLOOM FOUR WEEKS OR LONGER

A bloom period of four or more weeks is a lot to expect from a plant. Sometimes an unseasonable drought or heat wave will cut short the bloom period of the shrubs on this list, but most years these are the overachievers of the plant world.

Chinese Abelia (*Abelia chinensis*), C, CS
Glossy Abelia (*Abelia* x *grandiflora*), All
Narrow-Leafed Hummingbird Bush (*Anisacanthus
    linearis*), Csw, CSw, V
Yesterday-Today-&-Tomorrow (*Brunfelsia australis,
    B. pauciflora*), CSs, V
Butterfly Bush (*Buddleia davidii*), N, C, CS
Bottlebrush (*Callistemon rigidus*), CSs, V
Camellia (*Camellia japonica*), Ce, CSe
Sasanqua Camellia (*Camellia sasanqua*), Ce, CSe
Bluebeard (*Caryopteris* x *cladonensis*), N, C, CS
Tree Glory Bower (*Clerodendrum trichotomum*), V
Summersweet (*Clethra alnifolia*), Ce, CSe
Ti Ti, Leatherwood (*Cyrilla racemiflora*), Ce, CSe
Gardenia (*Gardenia jasminoides*), Ce, CSe
Tropical Hibiscus (*Hibiscus rosa-sinensis*), CSs, V,
    Annual
Althaea (*Hibiscus syriacus*), N, C, CS
French Hydrangea (*Hydrangea macrophylla*), N, C,
    CS
Lacecap Hydrangea (*Hydrangea macrophylla
    'mariesii'*), N, C, CS
Peegee Hydrangea (*Hydrangea paniculata*

'grandiflora'), N, C, CS
Oakleaf Hydrangea
    (*Hydrangea quercifolia*),
    Ce, CSe
Winter Jasmine (*Jasminum
    nudiflorum*), N, C, CS
Oleander (*Nerium
    oleander*), CSs, V
Sweet Olive (*Osmanthus
    fragrans*), CS, V
Mock Orange (*Philadelphus
    coronarius*), N, C, CS
Japanese Andromeda (*Pieris
    japonica*), Ce, CSe
Pomegranate (*Punica granatum*), C, CS, V
India Hawthorn (*Rhaphiolepis indica*), C, CS, V
Coral Fountain Plant (*Russelia equisetiformis*), CS, V
Lilac (*Syringa vulgaris*), N, Cn
Persian Lilac (*Syringa* x *persica*), N, Cn
Yellow Bells (*Tecoma stans 'angustata'*), CSs, V
Snowball (*Viburnum opulus*), N, C
Chaste Tree (*Vitex agnus-castus*), All
Weigela (*Weigela florida*), N, C

SASANQUA
CAMELLIA

EVERGREEN SHRUBS FOR BACKGROUND AND SCREENS

Trees and background shrubs define the boundaries of the landscape. They also screen unwanted views and prevent others from seeing in. The shrubs on this list may serve as the background for statuary or to delineate a rose garden, play area, or service area. They are typically big and green with an occasional splash of color, but some are just big and green.

Most of the plants on this list grow best in full sun. Indica hybrid azaleas do best in partial shade. Plants marked with an asterisk (*) are for shady areas.

American Boxwood (*Buxus sempervirens*), All
Bottlebrush (*Callistemon rigidus*), CSs, V
Camellia (*Camellia japonica*),* Ce, CSe
Sasanqua Camellia (*Camellia sasanqua*),* Ce, CSe
Evergreen Summersweet (*Clethra pringlei*), CSs, V

Evergreen Euonymus (*Euonymus japonica*), All
Pineapple Guava (*Feijoa sellowiana*), CS, V
Burford Holly (*Ilex cornuta 'burfordii'*), All
Yaupon (*Ilex vomitoria*),* All
Nellie Stevens Holly (*Ilex* x *hybrida*),* N, C, CS

Florida Anise (*Illicium floridanum*), Ce, CSe
Chinese Junipers cultivars (*Juniperus chinensis*), N, C
Bay Laurel (*Laurus nobilis*), CSs, V
Japanese Privet (*Ligustrum japonicum*), All
Wax-Leaf Privet (*Ligustrum lucidum*), C, CS, V
Banana Shrub (*Michelia figo*),* CS, V
Wax Myrtle (*Myrica cerifera*), Ce, CSe
Devilwood (*Osmanthus americanus*), Ce, CSe
Sweet Olive (*Osmanthus fragrans*), CS, V
Holly-Leaf Osmanthus (*Osmanthus heterophyllus*), Ce, CSe

Fortune's Sweet Olive (*Osmanthus x fortunei*), Ce, CSe
Pittosporum (*Pittosporum tobira*), CS, V
Japanese Yew (*Podocarpus* spp.), C, CS, V
Azalea, Indica hybrids (*Rhododendron*), Ce, CSe
Sweetleaf (*Symplocos tinctoria*), Ce, CSe
Spreading Yew (*Taxus densiformis*), N
Cleyera (*Ternstroemia gymnanthera*), Ce, CSe
Sandwanka Viburnum (*Viburnum suspensum*), CS, V
Laurustinus Viburnum (*Viburnum tinus*), Cs, CS, V
Shiny Xylosma (*Xylosma congestum*), CSs, V

Yaupon (*Ilex vomitoria*) and azaleas (*Rhododendron*) are shrubs that can be used as background elements in a garden or to provide screening. A great many yaupon cultivars are currently being propagated. These include Will Fleming, Saratoga Gold, US 69, Grey's Greenleaf, Goodyear Blimp, Pride of Houston, Lynn's Big Leaf, Sandy Hook, and Fencerow.

SHRUBS FOR DRY SITES

The plants on this list will be most appreciated during periods of water rationing. Tough as these shrubs may be, they still appreciate having organic matter worked into the soil, and a good mulch 2 to 4 inches thick can help to get them through dry spells.

There's also a big difference in plants for dry sites in El Paso vs. Nacogdoches. El Paso sites stay really dry, while dry sites in East Texas are more seasonal. Most of the plants in this list that are suitable for West Texas will include a "west" qualifier, indicating they would drop like flies during rainy weather in the eastern half of the state. Dry sites are usually alkaline sites, so check the list of "Shrubs for Alkaline Soil" for more plant choices.

Dry shade is one of the most challenging areas of the landscape because of the competition from trees. The plants on this list that are marked with an asterisk (*) will grow in partial shade.

Glossy Abelia (*Abelia x grandiflora*),* All
Blackbrush Acacia (*Acacia rigidula*), CSw, V
Hummingbird Trumpet (*Anisacanthus thurberi*), N, Cw
Pointleaf Manzanita (*Arctostaphylos pungens*), N, Cw
Chokeberry (*Aronia arbutifolia*), N, C
Silver Sagebrush (*Artemisia cana*), N, Cw
Sand Sagebrush (*Artemisia filifolia*), N, Cw, CSw
Prairie Sagebrush (*Artemisia ludoviciana*), N, Cw, CSw
Big Sagebrush (*Artemisia tridentata*), N, Cw, CSw
Four-Wing Saltbush (*Atriplex canescens*), N, Cw, CSw, V
Japanese Aucuba (*Aucuba japonica*),* C, CS, V
Desert Broom (*Baccharis sarothroides*), Cw, CSw
Fragrant Orchid Tree (*Bauhinia lunaroides*), CS, V
Barberry (*Berberis haematocarpa*), Cw, CSw
Mentor Barberry (*Berberis mentorensis*), Cw, CSw
Japanese Barberry (*Berberis thunbergii*), N, C
Agarita (*Berberis* [*Mahonia*] *trifoliolata*), C, CS, V

Lindley's Butterfly Bush (*Buddleia lindleyana*), N, C, CS
Yellow Bird-of-Paradise (*Caesalpinia gilliesii*), CSs, V
Red Bird-of-Paradise (*Caesalpinia pulcherrima*), CSs, V
Fairy Duster (*Calliandra eriophylla*), CSs, V
Beautyberry (*Callicarpa americana*), N, C, CS
Blue Mist Spiraea (*Caryopteris x clandonensis*), N, C, CS
Velvet-Leaf Senna (*Cassia lindheimeriana*), CSs, V
Shrubby Senna (*Cassia wislizenii*), CSsw
Ceanothus (*Ceanothus fendleri*), N, Cw
Desert Hackberry (*Celtis pallida*), N, Cw
Mountain Mahogany (*Cercocarpus montanus*), N, Cw
Yellow Cestrum (*Cestrum aurantiacum*), CSs, V
Flowering Quince (*Chaenomeles speciosa*), All
Fernbush (*Chamaebatiaria millefolium*), N, Cw, CSw
European Fan Palm (*Chamaerops humilis*), CS, V
Rubber Rabbitbrush (*Chrysothamnus nauseosus*), N, Cw, CSw

Cotoneasters (*Cotoneaster* spp.), N, Cw, CSw
Cliffrose (*Cowania mexicana*), N, Cw, CSw
Sago Palm (*Cycas revoluta*), CSs, V
Thorny Elaeagnus (*Elaeagnus pungens*),* All
Turpentine Bush (*Ericameria laricifolia*), N, Cw
Winterfat (*Eurotia lanata*), N, Cw, CSw
Texas Kidneywood (*Eysenhardtia texana*), CS, V
Apache Plume (*Fallugia paradoxa*), N, Cw, CSw
Fatsia (*Fatsia japonica*),* C, CS, V
Pineapple Guava (*Feijoa sellowiana*), CS, V
Cliff Fendlerbush (*Fendlera rupicola*), N, Cw
New Mexican Privet (*Forestiera neomexicana*), N,
   Cw, CSw
Forsythia (*Forsythia* x *intermedia*),* N, C
Wright's Silk Tassel (*Garrya wrightii*), N, Cw
Summer Broom (*Genista tinctoria*), N, Cw
Althaea, Rose-of-Sharon (*Hibiscus syriacus*), N, C,
   CS
Chinese Holly (*Ilex cornuta*), All
Dwarf Yaupon (*Ilex vomitoria*), All (N protected)
Winter Jasmine (*Jasminum nudiflorum*), N, C, CS
Juniper (*Juniperus* spp.), All
Beauty Bush (*Kolkwitzia amabilis*), N, Cnw
Creosote Bush (*Larrea tridentata*), Cw, CSw, V
Bay Laurel (*Laurus nobilis*), CSs, V
Silvercloud Cenizo (*Leucophyllum candidum*), C, CS,
   V
Texas Sage, Cenizo (*Leucophyllum frutescens*), C, CS,
   V
Chihuahuan Sage (*Leucophyllum laevigatum*), CSw,
   V
Winter Honeysuckle (*Lonicera fragrantissima*), N, C
Oregon Grape (*Mahonia aquifolium*), N, C

Nandina (*Nandina domestica*),* All
Oleander (*Nerium oleander*), CSs, V
Mock Orange (*Philadelphus* spp.), All
Chinese Photinia (*Photinia serrulata*), All
Pittosporum (*Pittosporum tobira*),* CS, V
Shrubby Cinquefoil (*Potentilla fruticosa*), N, C, CSn
Broom Dalea (*Psorothamnus scoparia*), N, Cw
Pomegranate (*Punica granatum*), C, CS, V
Antelope Bitterbush (*Purshia tridentata*), N
Firethorn (*Pyracantha coccinea*), All
India Hawthorn (*Rhaphiolepis indica*),* C, CS, V
Sumac (*Rhus* spp.), All
Copper Rose (*Rosa foetida*), All
Rugosa Rose (*Rosa rugosa*), All
Woods Rose (*Rosa woodsii*), N, Cw
Coral Fountain Plant (*Russelia equisetiformis*), CS, V
Desert Sage (*Salvia dorrii*), N
Autumn Sage (*Salvia greggii*), All
Lavender Cotton (*Santolina chamaecyparissus*), N,
   Cw, CSw
Green Santolina (*Santolina virens*), N, Cw, CSw
Silver Buffaloberry (*Shepherdia argentea*), N
Texas Mountain Laurel (*Sophora secundiflora*), C,
   CS, V
Spanish Broom (*Spartium junceum*), N, Cw, CSw
Spiraea (*Spiraea* spp.), N, C, CS
Snowberry (*Symphoricarpos albus*), N
Indiancurrant Coralberry (*Symphoricarpos
   orbiculatus*), N, C, CS
Lilac (*Syringa vulgaris*), N, Cn
Yellow Bells (*Tecoma stans 'angustata'*), CSs, V
Windmill Palm (*Trachycarpus fortunei*),* CS, V
Yucca (*Yucca* spp.), All

"El Paso has many complex gardening challenges," observes John White, formerly a County Extension horticulturist in El Paso and currently an Extension horticulturist in Las Cruces, New Mexico. "The soils are
alkaline (pH 7.2 to 8.8) and vary from sandy, alluvial soils in the valley areas to shallow, gravelly soils in the
mountainous regions. Some areas in the valley have heavy, clay soils, and in higher locations the soil may
have an impermeable caliche layer. Soils vary from 4 to 24 inches deep, and the organic-matter content is
typically less than 1 percent."

John notes that the climate is a challenge, too. "Humidity is very low, often less than 10 percent, especially during the spring and summer months. This means we have few disease problems, but there are plenty of insect pests to contend with. Rainfall averages 8.8 inches per year, and typically we have a very dry
spring. We receive some moisture in July and August, but not much else, except a little snow and rain in the
winter. Most winters will see a low of 10 degrees F, but we get to 110 degrees F in the summer." The El Paso
region is rated zone 8 by the USDA hardiness map, but John points out that many spots are closer to zone 7.
Much of the variation is due to elevation, which ranges from 3,200 feet in the valley to 5,200 feet in the
mountains. "In addition, there are microclimates all over town. You can find fruiting citrus, date palms, and
bougainvillea in some areas. The growing season includes approximately 225 frost-free days. The last average frost in the spring is March 21 and the first average freeze in the fall is November 10."

SHRUBS FOR WET SOIL

Usually we try to correct wet areas in the landscape. However, there are natural wet areas along streams, ponds, and natural bog areas where plants that will tolerate "wet feet" are needed.

Florida Leucothoe (*Agarista [Leucothoe] populifolia*), Ce, CSe

Chokeberry (*Aronia arbutifolia*), N, C

Sweet Shrub (*Calycanthus floridus*), Ce, CSe

Buttonbush (*Cephalanthus occidentalis*), Ce, CSe

Ninebark (*Clethra acuminata*), Ce, CSe

Summersweet (*Clethra alnifolia*), Ce, CSe

Ti Ti, Leatherwood (*Cyrilla racemiflora*), Ce, CSe

Florida Anise (*Illicium floridanum*), Ce, CSe

Ocala Anise (*Illicium parviflorum*), Ce, CSe

Virginia Sweetspire (*Itea virginica*), Ce, CSe

Coastal Leucothoe (*Leucothoe axillaris*), Ce, CSe

Spicebush (*Lindera benzoin*), C, CS

Tetterbush (*Lyonia lucida*), Ce, CSe

Leatherleaf Mahonia (*Mahonia bealei*), C, CS

Wax Myrtle (*Myrica cerifera*), Ce, CSe

Devilwood (*Osmanthus americanus*), Ce, CSe

Swamp Rose (*Rosa palustris scandens*), Ce, CSe

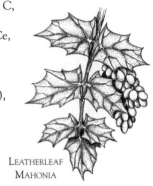

LEATHERLEAF
MAHONIA

 Virginia Sweetspire (*Itea virginica*) has become increasingly popular, and a number of cultivars have been propagated. They include Henry's Garnet, Merlot, Little Henry, Saturnalia, Long Spire, Sarah Eve, and Sabine. Another, Peach Creek, is evergreen in mild winters.

DWARF SHRUBS FOR THE COASTAL BAY AREA

Salt spray, constant winds, and heavy rains followed by long periods of drought are typical of the Coastal Bay area. It's no wonder a plant has to be tough to make this list of recommended plants by Mark D. Fox, owner of Fox Landscaping in Baycliff. These dwarf shrubs usually grow to a height of 3 feet or less. (For taller shrubs, see "Large Shrubs for the Coastal Bay Area.")

Don't overlook compost as a cure for some of the problems these plants will face. Microclimates created by windbreaks, shade structures, and intermittent fog sprays also can significantly increase your chance of having a beautiful garden.

Plants in this list marked with an asterisk (*) are tolerant of the especially severe conditions along the beachfront.

Century Plant (*Agave americana*)*

Hedgehog Agave (*Agave stricta*)*

Saltshrub (*Baccharis halimifolia*)

Chile Pequin (*Capsicum annuum*)

Natal Plum (*Carissa grandiflora*)*

Red Yucca (*Hesperaloe parviflora*)*

Carissa Holly (*Ilex cornuta 'carissa'*)

Dwarf Yaupon (*Ilex vomitoria 'nana'*)*

False Indigo (*Indigofera kirilowii*)

Texas Sage, Cenizo (*Leucophyllum frutescens*)

Dwarf Barbados Cherry (*Malpighia glabra*)*

Manfreda (*Manfreda* spp.)

Dwarf Wax Myrtle (*Myrica pusilla*)*

Dwarf Oleander (*Nerium oleander*)

Giant Liriope (*Ophiopogon jaburan*)*

Pavonia, Rock Rose (*Pavonia lasiopetala*)*

'Clara,' 'Snow' Dwarf White India Hawthorn (*Rhaphiolepis indica*)*

Roses (*Rosa* spp.)*

Rosemary (*Rosmarinus officinalis*)*

Dwarf Palmetto (*Sabal minor*)*

Autumn Sage (*Salvia greggii*)

Dwarf Skullcap (*Scutellaria suffrutescens*)

Coralberry (*Symphoricarpos orbiculatus*)

Soft Blue Yucca (*Yucca pallida*)*

LARGE SHRUBS FOR THE COASTAL BAY AREA

Coastal Bay areas are bombarded by constant winds and salt spray. Mark D. Fox, owner of Fox Landscaping in Baycliff, recommends these tough shrubs for their ability to withstand the winds and spray as well as the heavy rains that are so common in these areas. These large shrubs usually exceed a height of 3 feet. As mentioned in other lists for the Coastal Bay, microclimates created by windbreaks, shade structures, and intermittent fog sprays can be a significant aid in creating and maintaining your garden.

Those plants marked with an asterisk (*) are tolerant of bayside or beachfront plantings, where the extremes of wind and salt are especially severe.

Glossy Abelia (*Abelia* x *grandiflora*)
Adina (*Adina rubella*)
Florida Leucothoe (*Agarista* [*Leucothoe*] *populifolia*)
False Indigo (*Amorpha fruticosa*)
Desert Honeysuckle (*Anisacanthus* spp.)
Agarita (*Berberis* [*Mahonia*] *trifoliolata*])
Butterfly Bush (*Buddleia davidii*)
Mexican Beautyberry (*Callicarpa acuminata*)
American Beautyberry (*Callicarpa americana*)
Chinese Beautyberry (*Callicarpa dichotoma*)
Sasanqua Camellia (*Camellia sasanqua*)
Mediterranean Fan Palm (*Chamaerops humilis*)*
Sago Palm (*Cycas revoluta*)*
Ti Ti, Leatherwood (*Cyrilla racemiflora*)
Silverberry (*Elaeagnus pungens*)*
Strawberry Bush (*Euonymus americanus*)
Texas Kidneywood (*Eysenhardtia texana*)
Pineapple Guava (*Feijoa sellowiana*)*
Hydrangea (*Hydrangea macrophylla*)
White-Flowered Anise (*Illicium anisatum*)
Virginia Sweetspire (*Itea virginica*)

Texas Sage (*Leucophyllum frutescens*)*
Winter Honeysuckle (*Lonicera fragrantissima*)
'Plum Delight' Loropetalum (*Loropetalum chinense*)
'Burgundy' Loropetalum (*Loropetalum chinense*)
Nandina (*Nandina domestica*)
Oleander (*Nerium oleander*)
Spineless Prickly Pear (*Opuntia engelmannii*)*
Sweet Olive (*Osmanthus fragrans*)
Texas Pistache (*Pistacia texana*)
Pittosporum (*Pittosporum tobira*)
Carolina Buckthorn (*Rhamnus caroliniana*)
Upright India Hawthorn (*Rhaphiolepis umbellata*)*
Azalea (*Rhododendron* spp.)
Silverbush (*Sophora tomentosa*)*
Bridal-Wreath Spiraea (*Spiraea prunifolia*)
Cleyera (*Ternstroemia gymnanthera*)
Luzon Viburnum (*Viburnum luzonicum*)
Possumhaw Viburnum (*Viburnum nudum*)
Walter's Viburnum (*Viburnum obovatum*)
Arrowwood Viburnum (*Viburnum dentatum*)
Yucca (*Yucca* spp.)*

"Good compost is generally not cheap compost. Expect it to cost between $18 and $35 per cubic yard. It should smell clean and earthy, like a handful of soil from the forest floor. If it smells sour or stinky, beware. Why use compost? It provides primary nutrients as well as trace minerals, and it can help to unlock existing nutrients in the soil. It's also a wonderful source of beneficial microorganisms. Compost is the closest thing to magic we can use in the garden."
—John Ferguson, president, Nature's Way Resources, Conroe

OLEANDERS

OLEANDER

Oleanders (*Nerium oleander*) have been growing in Galveston since the mid-nineteenth century, so it is only fitting that the International Oleander Society should be located there. They have published a wonderful booklet on oleanders—how to grow them, their varieties, and other information, and if you log on to their website (http://www.oleander.org), you can find a lot of the same information plus color pictures of a number of varieties.

Unless you grow them in pots and protect them in the winter, oleanders are limited to the Upper Gulf Coast and farther south. Even in Galveston many varieties, especially the dwarfs, are damaged in a cold winter. There are lots of oleanders planted in Houston, but they seem to thrive best in full sun and sandy, well-drained soils. Oleanders are salt and drought tolerant, which makes them ideal coastal plants. The free-blooming varieties, listed below, bloom all summer and into the fall.

Algiers, pinkish red
Apple Blossom, light pink
Barbara Bush, pale pink
Casablanca, white
College Beauty, pink
Ed Barr, white
Hawaii, light pink

Kewpie, light pink
Magnolia Willis Sealy, white
Mrs. Burton, pale pink
Mrs. Isadore Dyer, medium pink
Mrs. Trueheart, pale pink
Mrs. Willard Cooke, white
Mrs. Moody, white

Petite Pink, pale pink
Petite Salmon, salmon
Pink Beauty, medium pink
Sorrento, white
Turner's Kim Bell, light yellow

SHRUBS THAT DO WELL IN DEEP SHADE

Areas of deep shade are hostile environments for most plants. If the light isn't adequate, more water or more fertilizer won't substitute for the deficiency. Plants have to be tough to make this list. Those marked with an asterisk (*) are special treasures because they will grow in dry shade.

Agarista, Florida Leucothoe (*Agarista* [*Leucothoe*] *populifolia*), Ce, CSe
Japanese Aucuba (*Aucuba japonica*),* C, CS, V
Fatshedera, Tree Ivy (*Fatshedera lizei* [*Fatsia* × *Hedera*]),* C, CS, V
Fatsia (*Fatsia japonica*),* C, CS, V
English Ivy, mature form (*Hedera helix*),* All
Nellie Stevens Holly (*Ilex* × *hybrida*), N, C

Coastal Leucothoe (*Leucothoe axillaris*), Ce, CSe
Leatherleaf Mahonia (*Mahonia bealei*),* C, CS
Nandina (*Nandina domestica*),* All
Needle Palm (*Rhapidophyllum hystrix*),* C, CS, V
Lady Palm (*Rhapis excelsa*),* V
Leatherleaf Viburnum (*Viburnum rhytidophyllum*),* Ce, CSe

SHRUBS YOU CAN TRAIN INTO SMALL TREES

Using shrubs as small trees isn't as uncommon as one might think. Most of the more vigorous shrubs make rather nice, usually multi-trunked, small trees. Particularly where you may have inherited overgrown shrubs in the landscape, this is a way to remove lower branches and thus better define the trunk structure of the plant. Old hollies and junipers often lend themselves to this treatment, but there are many others that benefit from this type of pruning.

If you're looking for a big shrub to train this way, either as an accent plant or for a plant that won't grow up into the power lines, or wondering what to do with the huge, overgrown shrubs you've inherited, check out the following list for some good candidates.

Ninebark (*Clethra acuminata*), Ce, CSe
Mexican Clethra (*Clethra pringlei*), CS, V
Ti Ti, Leatherwood (*Cyrilla racemiflora*), Ce, CSe
Pineapple Guava (*Feijoa sellowiana*), CS, V
Witch Hazel (*Hamamelis* spp.), Ce, CSe
Althaea (*Hibiscus syriacus*), N, C, CS
Burford Holly (*Ilex cornuta* 'burfordii'), All
Yaupon (*Ilex vomitoria*), All
Japanese Privet (*Ligustrum japonicum*), All
Wax-Leaf Privet (*Ligustrum lucidum*), C, CS, V
Spicebush (*Lindera benzoin*), C, CS
Loropetalum (*Loropetalum chinense*), Ce, CSe
Star Magnolia (*Magnolia stellata*), Ce, CSe
Banana Shrub (*Michelia figo*), CS, V
Wax Myrtle (*Myrica cerifera*), Ce, CSe
Devilwood (*Osmanthus americanus*), Ce, CSe
Sweet Olive (*Osmanthus fragrans*), CS, V

Pittosporum (*Pittosporum tobira*), CS, V
Pomegranate (*Punica granatum*), C, CS, V
Southern Indica Azalea (*Rhododendron indica*), Ce, CSe
Sumac (*Rhus* spp.), All
Evergreen Sumac (*Rhus virens*), Cw, CSw
Luzon Viburnum (*Viburnum luzonicum*), CSs, V
Walter's Viburnum (*Viburnum obovatum*), Ce, CSe
Double-File Viburnum (*Viburnum plicatum* 'tomentosum'), C
Leatherleaf Viburnum (*Viburnum rhytidophyllum*), Ce, CSe
Sandwanka Viburnum (*Viburnum suspensum*), CS, V
Chaste Tree (*Vitex agnus-castus*), All
Shiny Xylosma (*Xylosma congestum* [senticosa]), CSs, V

CAMELLIAS

Greg Davis of the Houston Camellia Society advises, "Camellias are evergreen shrubs for the acid soils of East Texas. Saying that, you can be sure that someone in Austin or San Antonio is growing a few. They may be planted in raised beds with a mix of peat moss and sand, pampered with iron chelates, and replaced occasionally, but they are there." Greg advises that even in most areas of Houston, raised beds are best for camellias. "If you have sandy, acid soil and you're east of a line from Dallas to Houston, then it's hard to imagine not having some camellias in the landscape."

The three main species of camellias are *Camellia japonica, Camellia sasanqua,* and *Camellia reticulata.* Sasanquas are considered the hardiest, though new hybrids have survived temperatures below zero. These include Betty Sette, Ice Follies, Snow Flurry, Spring Frill, Polar Ice. Also look for hybrids that have the word winter in their name, such as Winter's Hope, Winter's Charm, Winter's Rose, and Winter's Waterlily. Greg notes, "One more species worth mentioning for gardeners along the upper Gulf Coast is the tea plant, *Camellia sinensis.* You could grow your own tea! Well, maybe. Anyway it would be fun to try, and the foliage is nice even if the flowers are just single and white."

Many of the Japonica camellias offered in the nursery trade are grown from cuttings. "These plants have been watered and foliar fed each day, so they are in for a real culture shock when planted in a hot, dry Houston garden. Thus they are sometimes short-lived in Houston. The Houston Camellia Society recommends plants that have been grafted on sasanqua rootstock or have been field grown in Texas or Louisiana. It's also important to examine the plants for withered leaves and cankers, a sign they may be infected with the dieback fungus. Also check the underside of the leaves for tea-scale insects, one of the most common pests of these plants. Dormant oil sprayed on the underside of the foliage in late winter usually takes care of scale insects and it's relatively nontoxic. The oil also gives the leaves a nice shiny appearance."

Reticulatas are marginally hardy in Texas. They do best in areas with cool nights and no deep freezes. Regardless, the huge, spectacular blooms of some of the new reticulata hybrids are worth the risk for camellia enthusiasts.

Japonicas

Alba-plena	white, medium formal double
Betty Sheffield	white striped red and pink, medium to large semidouble
Debutante	light pink, medium full peony form
Don Mac	dark red, medium to large semidouble
Dr. Tinsley	very pale pink shading to flesh pink, medium semidouble
Drama Girl	deep salmon rose pink, very large semidouble
Elaine's Betty	pale peach pink, medium peony form with ruffled petals
Elegans	rose pink with center petaloids, large to very large
Flowerwood	fimbriated sport of Mathotiana Supreme
Guilio Nuccio	coral rose pink, large to very large semidouble with irregular petals
Julia France	light pink, large semidouble with fluted petals
Mary Alice Cox	white, medium to large formal double with slightly cupped petal ends
Mathotiana, Purple Dawn	crimson with purple cast, large rose form to formal double
Mathoiana Supreme	sport of Mathotiana, very large semidouble with loose, irregular petals
R.L. Wheeler	rose pink, very large semidouble to anemone form, solid circle of stamens
Rosea Superba	rose pink sport of Mathotiana, large to very large
Snowman	white, large semidouble with twisted inner petals

Sasanquas

Apple Blossom	white blushed pink, single
Bonanza	deep red, medium semipeony form
Cotton Candy	clear pink, medium semidouble with ruffled petals
Hana-Jiman	white-edged pink, medium semidouble
Leslie Ann	white tipped reddish lavender, small semidouble
Sparkling Burgundy	ruby rose overlaid with sheen of lavender, small to medium
Yuletide	orange red, small single with prominent yellow stamens

Reticulata Hybrids

Betty Ridley	pink, medium to large formal double
Black Lace	dark velvet red, medium rose form double with incurved petals
Dr. Clifford Parks	red with orange cast, very large semidouble to anemone form
Emma Gaeta	deep rose pink, very large semidouble with folded upright center petals
Francie L.	rose pink, very large semidouble with irregular upright petals
Frank Houser	red, very large semidouble to peony form
Valentine Day	salmon pink, large to very large formal double

Non-Reticulata Hybrids

Anticipation	deep rose, large peony form
Buttons 'n Bows	light pink with deeper shading at edges, small formal double
Charlean	pink with faint orchid overtone, large semidouble
Debbie	clear spinel pink, medium to large peony form
Elsie Jury	clear pink with shaded orchid undertone, large full peony form
Helen B.	bright pink, miniature formal double
Julia	lavender pink and white, medium to large rose form double
Julie	salmon pink to peach pink, medium to large peony to rose form double
Night Rider	very dark black red, miniature to small semidouble
Tom Perkins	rose red outer petals to blossom pink inter petals, formal double

"I would encourage everyone to try growing camellias in their garden or in containers on the back patio. They take more care than crape myrtles do, but the spectacular blooms in the late fall and winter make the extra effort well worthwhile. The major challenges to growing camellias in Houston are the mid-day summer sun, the tight clay soils, and the lack of rainfall in July and August. Any member of the Houston Camellia Society or the American Camellia Society will be more than willing to share their camellia-growing knowledge with gardeners new to camellias or with experienced growers who are having problems."

—Greg Davis, Houston Camellia Society

SHRUBS FOR SHOWY FOLIAGE IN THE SHADE

Foliage texture and color are the main elements in the shady portion of the garden. Flowers are typically few and far between in the shade, so for interest it's only natural to go for striking foliage. Be sure to check out the "Tropicals, Succulents, and Exotics" chapter for gingers and tender tropicals. Even where they are not hardy, it's worth planting them new each year or protecting them in the garage or greenhouse. Plants on this list that are marked with an asterisk (*) also do pretty well in dry soil.

Japanese Aucuba (*Aucuba japonica*),* C, CS, V
Sweet Shrub (*Calycanthus floridus*),* Ce, CSe
Camellia (*Camellia japonica*), Ce, CSe
Sasanqua Camellia (*Camellia sasanqua*), Ce, CSe
Fatsia (*Fatsia japonica*),* C, CS, V
Variegated French Hydrangea (*Hydrangea macrophylla* 'quadricolor'), N, C, CS
Oakleaf Hydrangea (*Hydrangea quercifolia*), Ce, CSe
Large-Leaf Holly (*Ilex latifolia*), Ce, CSe
Japanese Anise (*Illicium anisatum*), Ce, CSe
Florida Anise (*Illicium floridanum*), Ce, CSe
Ocala Anise (*Illicium parviflorum*), Ce, CSe
Coastal Leucothoe (*Leucothoe axillaris*), Ce, CSe

Drooping Leucothoe (*Leucothoe fontanesiana*), Ce, CSe
Variegated Privet (*Ligustrum sinense* 'variegatum'), All
Leatherleaf Mahonia (*Mahonia bealei*),* C, CS
Nandina (*Nandina domestica*),* All
Japanese Andromeda (*Pieris japonica*), Ce, CSe
Cherry Laurel (*Prunus caroliniana*), All
English Laurel (*Prunus laurocerasus*) , C, CS
Lady Palm (*Rhapis excelsa*),* V
Dwarf Palmetto (*Sabal minor*),* C, CS, V
Cleyera (*Ternstroemia gymnanthera*),* Ce, CSe
Leatherleaf Viburnum (*Viburnum rhytidophyllum*), Ce, CSe

EVERGREEN SHRUBS WITH HANDSOME WINTER FOLIAGE

To some extent, in the winter landscape, all we have is foliage. Flowers are scarce, depending on the severity of the winter. Berries help, and a greenhouse can be a gardener's heaven during the bleak days of winter. Most of us, though, turn to the evergreens for our inspiration. They help to lift the depression of winter.

Agarista (*Agarista* [*Leucothoe*] *populifolia*), Ce, CSe
Japanese Aucuba (*Aucuba japonica*), C, CS, V
Agarita (*Berberis* [*Mahonia*] *trifoliata*), C, CS, V
Littleleaf Boxwood (*Buxus microphylla*), All
American Boxwood (*Buxus sempervirens*), All
Camellia (*Camellia japonica*), Ce, CSe
Sasanqua Camellia (*Camellia sasanqua*), Ce, CSe
Clusterberry (*Cotoneaster lacteus*), N, Cw, CSw
Thorny Elaeagnus (*Elaeagnus pungens*), All
Japanese Holly (*Ilex crenata*), N, C, CS
Large-Leaf Holly (*Ilex latifolia*), Ce, CSe
Yaupon Holly (*Ilex vomitoria*), All
Chinese Juniper (*Juniperus chinensis* cvs.), N, C
Junipers (*Juniperus* spp.), N, C, CS
Coastal Leucothoe (*Leucothoe axillaris*), Ce, CSe
Japanese Privet (*Ligustrum japonicum*), All

Loropetalum (*Loropetalum chinense*), Ce, CSe
Tetterbush (*Lyonia lucida*), Ce, CSe
Oregon Grape (*Mahonia aquifolium*), N, C
Leatherleaf Mahonia (*Mahonia bealei*), C, CS
Chinese Mahonia (*Mahonia fortunei*), CSs, V
Burmese Mahonia (*Mahonia lomariifolia*), CSs, V
Southern Wax Myrtle (*Myrica cerifera*), Ce, CSe
Nandina (*Nandina domestica*), All
Osmanthus (*Osmanthus* spp.), CS, V
Japanese Andromeda (*Pieris japonica*), Ce, CSe
Japanese Yew (*Podocarpus* spp.), C, CS, V
Cherry Laurel (*Prunus caroliniana*), All
English Laurel (*Prunus laurocerasus*), C, CS
Firethorn (*Pyracantha* spp.), All
Yew (*Taxus* spp.), N
Cleyera (*Ternstroemia gymnanthera*), Ce, CSe

DECIDUOUS SHRUBS WITH GOOD FALL COLOR

Shrubs with fall color bring interest into the landscape at eye level. They can be used to contrast with evergreens and fall-planted annuals. If their statement in the landscape is reduced to twigs over the winter, that's forgivable considering the spectacular show they put on in the fall. The shrubs in this list are organized by fall foliage color.

Red to Purple or Maroon
Chokeberry (*Aronia arbutifolia*), N, C
Japanese Barberry cultivars (*Berberis thunbergii*), N, C
Cranberry Cotoneaster (*Cotoneaster apiculatus*), N, Cw, CSw
Rockspray Cotoneaster (*Cotoneaster horizontalis*), N, Cw, CSw
Winged Euonymus (*Euonymus alatus*), Ce, CSe
Dwarf Winged Euonymus (*Euonymus alatus* 'compacta'), Ce, CSe
Strawberry Bush (*Euonymus americana*), Ce, CSe
Oakleaf Hydrangea (*Hydrangea quercifolia*), Ce, CSe
'Henry's Garnet' Virginia Sweetspire (*Itea virginica*), Ce, CSe
Sumac (*Rhus* spp.), All
Rabbit-Eye Blueberry (*Vaccinium ashei*), Ce, CSe

Mapleleaf Viburnum (*Viburnum acerifolium*), Ce
Double-File Viburnum (*Viburnum plicatum* 'tomentosum'), C

Orange to Red
Baby's-Breath Spiraea (*Spiraea thunbergii*), N, C, CS
Blackhaw Viburnum (*Viburnum prunifolium*), Ce, CSe

Yellow
Japanese Barberry cultivars (*Berberis thunbergii*), N, C
Beautyberry (*Callicarpa americana*), N, C, CS
Chinese Beautyberry (*Callicarpa dichotoma*), C, CS
Ninebark (*Clethra acuminata*), Ce, CSe
Summersweet (*Clethra alnifolia*), Ce, CSe
Forsythia (*Forsythia* x *intermedia*), N, C

SHRUBS THAT MAKE GOOD GROUND COVERS

Shrubs have to be low-growing to make this list of good ground covers. It also helps if they have a trailing growth habit or if they're stoloniferous (spread by underground stems). See the "Ferns and Ground Covers" chapter for more plant ideas.

'Sherwoodii' Dwarf Abelia (*Abelia* x *grandiflora* '*prostrata*'), All

Crimson Pygmy Barberry (*Berberis thunbergii* '*atropurpurea*'), N, C

Prostrate Plum Yew (*Cephalotaxus* spp.), Ce, CSe

Rockspray Cotoneaster (*Cotoneaster horizontalis*), N, Cw, CSw

Willowleaf Cotoneaster (*Cotoneaster salicifolius* '*repens*'), Cw, CSw

'Elegans,' 'Nana' Dwarf Japanese Elegans Cedar (*Cryptomeria japonica*), Ce, CSe

'Globosa,' 'Nana' Dwarf Japanese Cedar (*Cryptomeria japonica*), Ce, CSe

Texas Wintercreeper (*Euonymus fortunei* '*coloratus*'), N, C

'Emerald Gaity' Euonymus (*Euonymus fortunei*), N

'Emerald 'n Gold' Euonymus (*Euonymus fortunei*), N

Dwarf Gardenia (*Gardenia jasminoides* '*radicans*'), Ce, CSe

Shrubby St. John's Wort (*Hypericum patulum*), Ce, CSe

Chinese Holly (*Ilex cornuta*) , All

Japanese Holly (*Ilex crenata*), N, C, CS

Dwarf Yaupon (*Ilex vomitoria*), All (N protected)

Showy Jasmine (*Jasminum floridum*), CS, V

Winter Jasmine (*Jasminum nudiflorum*), N, C, CS

Parson's Juniper (*Juniperus chinensis* '*parsonii*'), N, C

Shore Juniper cultivars (*Juniperus conferta*), N, C, CS

'Blue Rug' Creeping Juniper (*Juniperus horizontalis*), N, C

Coastal Leucothoe (*Leucothoe axillaris*), Ce, CSe

Dwarf Nandina (*Nandina domestica*), All

Formosa Firethorn (*Pyracantha koidzumii*), All

Dwarf India Hawthorn (*Rhaphiolepis indica* cvs.), C, CS, V

Azalea, low and spreading (*Rhododendron* hyb.), Ce, CSe

Butcher's Broom, Ruscus (*Ruscus hypoglossum*), Cs, CS, V

Coralberry, Snowberry (*Symphoricarpos orbiculatus*), N, C, CS

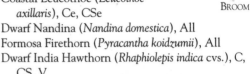

BUTCHER'S BROOM

SHRUBS THAT DESERVE WIDER USE

This can be a frustrating list. These plants have shown great promise but are sometimes hard to find. This doesn't make them any less meritorious, just challenging. Peter Loos, one of the best plantsmen in East Texas, votes for the ti ti, or leatherwood, as his favorite woody plant. "It tolerates poorly drained soils, it's semi-evergreen, has showy blooms, and it's a good honey plant."

Adina (*Adina rubella*), CS, V

Agarista, Florida Leucothoe (*Agarista* [*Leucothoe*] *populifolia*), Ce, CSe

Whitebrush (*Aloysia gratissima*), All

Anisacanthus (*Anisacanthus wrightii*), Cw, CSw, V

Sand Sagebrush (*Artemisia filifolia*), N, Cw, CSw

Aucuba (*Aucuba japonica*), C, CS, V

Baccharis (*Baccharis halimifolia*), C, CS

Agarita (*Berberis trifoliata*), C, CS, V

Copper False Chestnut (*Castanopsis cuspidata*), CS, V

Damianita (*Chrysactinia mexicana*), Cw, CSw, V

'Hummingbird' Summersweet (*Clethra alnifolia*), Ce, CSe

Japanese Clethra (*Clethra barbinervis*), Ce, CSe

Mexican Clethra (*Clethra pringlei*), CSs, V

Ti Ti, Leatherwood (*Cyrilla racemiflora*), Ce, CSe

Dalea (*Dalea* spp.), Cw, CSw, V

Winterfat (*Eurotia lanata*), N, Cw, CSw

'Blue Wave' Lacecap Hydrangea (*Hydrangea macrophylla* '*mariesii*'), C

Dahoon Holly (*Ilex cassine*), Ce, CSe

Deciduous Holly, Possumhaw (*Ilex decidua*), All

Ocala Anise (*Illicium parviflorum*), Ce, CSe

'Henry's Garnet' Virginia Sweetspire (*Itea virginica*)', Ce, CSe

White Honeysuckle Bush (*Lonicera albiflora*), All

Loropetalum (*Loropetalum chinense*), Ce, CSe

Pink Loropetalum (*Loropetalum chinense* '*rubrum*'), Ce, CSe

Barbados Cherry (*Malpighia glabra*), CSs,V

Dwarf Wax Myrtle (*Myrica pusilla*), Ce, CSe

Nandina (*Nandina domestica*), All

Devilwood (*Osmanthus americanus*), Ce, CSe

Japanese False Oak (*Pasania edulis*), CS, V

Texas Mock Orange (*Philadelphus texensis*), Cs, CS

Havard Oak (*Quercus havardii*), N, Cw, CS

Carolina Buckthorn (*Rhamnus caroliniana*), C, CS, V

Native Azaleas (*Rhododendron* spp.), Ce, CSe

Texas Mountain Laurel (*Sophora secundiflora*), C, CS, V

Arrowwood Viburnum (*Viburnum dentatum*), Ce, CSe

Luzon Viburnum (*Viburnum luzonicum*), CSs, V
Possumhaw Viburnum (*Viburnum nudum*), Ce, CSe
Walter's Viburnum (*Viburnum obovatum*), Ce, CSe

Tea Viburnum (*Viburnum setigerum*), C,CS
Shiny Xylosma (*Xylosma congestum* [*senticosum*]),
  CSs, V

AZALEAS

Gardeners in the eastern third to half of the state can grow spectacular azaleas. The reason for hedging on the zones is that there are some nice azaleas in Austin's Zilker Park, and no doubt there are a few in San Antonio, but it must be a challenge. Even Chinese tallow trees show iron chlorosis in these areas. Azaleas in the average garden, if it's much west of a line from Dallas through Houston, are going to need lots of acid organic matter and iron treatments. Even in Houston and Dallas, raised beds with lots of organic matter plus two pounds of sulfur per 100 square feet (mixed in) are required to get azaleas off to a good start. There are, of course, pockets of acid soil in these areas that don't require these extremes, but if in doubt, raised beds are usually best.

Carter Taylor, the owner of Condon Gardens in Houston, is a lifelong fan of azaleas. He uses thousands of them each year in landscapes, and the azaleas in the following list are his favorites. They are grouped according to bloom season. Early bloomers start about two weeks ahead of the midseason bloomers, and late bloomers extend about two weeks beyond the midseason bloomers. The multi-season bloomers begin to scatter a few blooms in the fall and continue this partial bloom with a full bloom in early to midseason. In Houston, azaleas begin to bloom in late March and continue through April most years, but recent mild winters have made it difficult to predict when they're going to bloom. In North Texas, the seasons can be pushed back about two weeks.

For more azaleas, see the "Native Azaleas" list in this chapter.

Early bloomers	Flower color	Growth habit
Betsy	white with pink fringe	upright
Canescens	light pink	tall, open
Christmas Cheer	brilliant opal red	dwarf, spreading
Coral Bells	coral pink	low, dwarf, spreading
Corsage	orchid-lavender	medium, spreading
Flame	brilliant orange red	tall, dwarf, upright
Gulf Pride	lavender	tall, upright
Hino Crimson	red	low, dwarf
Hinode-giri	red	low, dwarf
Judge Solomon	deep watermelon pink	tall, upright
Kate Arendall	white	tall, upright
King's White	white	medium
Mrs. G. G. Gerbing	white	medium, upright
Phoenicia	light purple	upright, large
Rebekah	soft pink	tall, upright
Snow	white	medium, dwarf

Early midseason bloomers		
Bessie A. Dodd	coral pink	low, dwarf, spreading
Daphne Salmon	salmon pink	medium, tall
Duc De Rohan	orange-red	medium
Gloria	pink/white	medium
Poukhanense	orchid	upright, vigorous
Poukhanense Compacta	orchid	medium, compact

Midseason bloomers		
Admiral Semmes	yellow	tall, upright
Arabeck	red	medium, upright

Austrinum	yellow	tall, upright
Blaauws Pink	salmon pink	medium
Brilliant	watermelon red	medium
Carror	deep pink	low, dwarf
China Seas	pink	medium, dense
Conversation Piece	white, light pink, dark pink	low
Delaware Valley White	pure white	tall
El Frida	pale lavender	semidwarf
Fielder's White	white with chartreuse	medium, spreading
Fisher's Pink	light pink	tall
Formosa	magenta with deep blotch	tall, upright
George L. Taber	white with magenta	medium, upright
Glory	peach pink	medium, spreading
Gwenda	white, light pink	medium
H. H. Hume	white	medium, erect
Hampton Beauty	light pink with dark blotch	medium, spreading
Hardy Gardenia	white	low
Herbert	vivid purple	medium
Hershey's Red	bright red	medium, spreading
Hexe	violet red	low, medium
Madame Pericat	pastel pink	medium
Massasoit	dark red	low, dwarf, thick
Moss Point Red	red	large
Mother's Day	red	dwarf, upright
Orange Cup	orange red	dwarf, upright
Pink Cascade	salmon pink	low
Pink Pearl	pearl pink	medium, dwarf
Pink Ruffles	strong pink	tall, upright, vigorous
President Claeys	brick red	tall, upright
Pride of Mobile	deep watermelon pink	tall, upright
Red Formosa	reddish purple	tall, upright
Red Ruffles, Red Wing	deep red	medium
Refrain	light pink	low
Rose Greeley	white with chartreuse	low, spreading, dense
Rosea	violet, orange pink	upright
Salmon Formosa	salmon red	tall, full
Salmon Solomon	salmon red	tall, upright
Sandra Ann	reddish purple	low, dwarf
Seikedera	white/pink	tall, upright
Sherwood Red	orange red	low, dwarf
Sir Robert	white/pink combo	medium
Southern Charm	watermelon red	tall, upright
Stewartstonian	clear red	tall, upright
Stonewall Jackson	orange	tall, upright
Sunglow	purple red	medium, upright
Tradition	pink	low-medium, compact
Treasure	white with pink margins	spreading, vigorous

Late midseason bloomers

Amy	soft pink	upright
Ben Morrison	red/white, variegated	tall
Copperman	orange red	medium, spreading
Glacier	white	vigorous, erect
L. J. Bobink	white orchid	medium
Martha Hitchcock	white with magenta margin	bush habit, spreading

Late bloomers

Amaghasa	vivid red	late
Flame Creeper	orange red	low, spreading
Gumpo	white with pink flakes	low, dwarf, spreading
Gumpo Light Pink	light pink	low, dwarf, spreading
Gumpo Pink	pink with deeper flakes	low, dwarf, spreading
Heiwasa	rose red	low, spreading
Hiawatha	dark red	medium
Kozan	orange	low, dwarf
Macrantha Orange	orange red	low, dwarf, compact
Macrantha Red	red	medium
Macrantha salmon	salmon red	medium
Margaret Douglas	white with salmon margin	short, broad
Marion Lee	pink with dark edges	medium low
Nancy	purple red	medium
Nancy of Robin Hill	light purple, pink	low
Okina-nishiki	orange red	low, dwarf
Peter Pooker	light pink-white	medium
Pink Pericat	pale pink	medium
Prunifolium	orange to deep red	tall, upright
Robin Dale	white	low
Roddy	white	medium
Sweetheart Supreme	pink	medium, spreading
Wakaebisu	medium pink	low, dwarf
Watchett	light pink with blush	low

Multi-season bloomers

Encore, Autumn Cheer	rose pink	medium
Encore, Autumn Coral	coral pink	medium
Encore, Autumn Royalty	rich purple	large
Encore, Autumn Embers	deep orange red	low, spreading
Fashion	red orange with blotch	medium, erect
Gyokushin	white/pink	upright
Jennifer	red	medium
Macrantha Pink	dark pink	upright, vigorous

Carter Taylor, owner of Condon Gardens in Houston, uses thousands of azaleas each year in landscapes. He advises that the basic Southern Indicas are the toughest and easiest to care for, and he mentions Formosa, Salmon Formosa, Judge Solomon, George L. Taber, and Mrs. G. G. Gerbing, but he adds, "many of the others are almost as easy and add color to other times in the season. Salmon Formosa doesn't revert back to the Formosa color like the Salmon Solomon variety does."

Carter says that lacebugs can be brought under control with organic sprays like Neem oil or molasses spray. "Petal blight fungus isn't the problem it used to be since we began using organic treatments. A popular molasses spray formula for azalea pests is 3 Tbsp. agricultural grade molasses, 1 Tbsp. garlic oil, and 1 Tbsp. seaweed extract per one gallon of spray solution."

NATIVE AZALEAS

Texas does have a few native azaleas—the Piedmont azalea (*Rhododendron canescens*) or Texas azalea (*Rhododendron oblongifolium*). Several others native to the Southeast are worth trying. These species are rather severe in their requirements. In East Texas, these plants are found on acid, sandy mounds in the forest. These soils contain a good bit of organic matter, and frequent rains insure plentiful moisture most of the year. This would not be an easy environment to create, even in Houston. More than a few horticulturists would suggest you enjoy these species on a field trip to East Texas rather than try to grow them in your garden. Having proffered that challenge, let's just say these plants are for the enthusiast! All are for trial in the eastern zones of Central and Coastal South Texas.

Alabama Azalea (*Rhododendron alabamense*)
Sweet Azalea (*Rhododendron arborescens*)
Flame Azalea (*Rhododendron austrinum*)
Piedmont Azalea (*Rhododendron canescens*)
Oconee Azalea (*Rhododendron flammeum*)

Texas Azalea (*Rhododendron oblongifolium*)
Plumleaf Azalea (*Rhododendron prunifolium*)
Millais Sweet Azalea (*Rhododendron serrulatum*)
Swamp Azalea (*Rhododendron viscosum*)

"Like many other people, my interest in native plants was inspired by my father-in-law, the late Lynn Lowrey," says Mike Anderson, who owns Anderson Landscape and Nursery in Spring Branch. "Adding beauty and diversity, native plants can be incorported into a traditional garden, or they may be used to create a more natural landscape."

SHRUBS FOR ALKALINE SOIL

When working up beds for the landscape, it's always a good idea to amend the soil with organic matter, and you might even try tilling 5 pounds of sulfur per 100 square feet into the soil. However, if you live in an area where the soils tend to be alkaline, your efforts to lower the pH won't be permanent. It may be a good idea to keep trying, especially with plants that are marginally tolerant, but it is a never-ending process in an area with alkaline soils. Alkaline water is another factor in this equation, and it tends to raise the pH of the soil. Soils that are alkaline also tend to be dry, so check the list of plants for dry sites too.

Glossy Abelia (*Abelia* x *grandiflora*), All
Barberry (*Berberis* spp.), N, C
Agarita (*Berberis* [*Mahonia*] *trifoliolata*]), C, CS, V
Littleleaf Boxwood (*Buxus microphylla*), All
Bottlebrush (*Callistemon rigidus*), CSs, V
Flowering Quince (*Chaenomeles speciosa*), All
Feather Dalea (*Dalea formosa*), Cs, CS, V
Black Dalea (*Dalea frutescens*), CS, V
Pineapple Guava (*Feijoa sellowiana*), CS, V
Althaea (*Hibiscus syriacus*), N, C, CS
Burford Holly (*Ilex cornuta 'burfordii'*), All
'Needlepoint' Holly (*Ilex cornuta*), C, CS
Yaupon (*Ilex vomitoria*), All
Nellie Stevens Holly (*Ilex* x *hybrida*), N, C
Winter Jasmine (*Jasminum nudiflorum*), N, C, CS
Creosote Bush (*Larrea tridentata*), Cw, CSw, V
Texas Sage (*Leucophyllum frutescens*), C, CS, V
Japanese Privet (*Ligustrum japonicum*), All
Wax-Leaf Privet (*Ligustrum lucidum*), C, CS, V

Winter Honeysuckle (*Lonicera fragrantissima*), N, C
Mahonia (*Mahonia* spp.), N, C, CS
Mimosa (*Mimosa* spp.), Cw, CSw, V
Nandina (*Nandina domestica*), All
Mock Orange (*Philadelphus coronarius*), N, C, CS
Texas Pistache (*Pistacia texana*), CSw, V
Firethorn (*Pyracantha* spp.), All
India Hawthorn (*Rhaphiolepis indica*), C, CS, V
Yedda Hawthorn (*Rhaphiolepis umbellata*), C, CS, V
Littleleaf Sumac (*Rhus microphylla*), Cw, CSw, V
Desert Yaupon (*Schaefferia cuneifolia*), CSsw, V
Texas Mountain Laurel (*Sophora secundiflora*), C, CS, V
Bridal-Wreath Spiraea (*Spiraea prunifolia*), N, C, CS
Coralberry (*Symphoricarpos orbiculatus*), N, C, CS
Sandwanka Viburnum (*Viburnum suspensum*), CS, V
Laurustinus Viburnum (*Viburnum tinus*), Cs, CS, V
Chaste Tree (*Vitex agnus-castus*), All

"The Midland/Odessa area got 7 inches of rain in 1999, so you have to work a little harder here, but you can grow almost anything. Some of the older, inner-city neighborhoods have soils that have been improved over the years, and it's easier to grow challenging plants here compared to trying these plants in new housing additions on the bald prairies. There is a strong interest beginning to develop in the use of natives, and they can be really tough, yet still attractive. Some, unfortunately, are hard to find, and they can also be hard to transplant because of long taproots."
—Karen Schneider, manager of Alldredge Gardens, Midland

LOW SHRUBS THAT WON'T COVER WINDOWS

Low-growing, compact shrubs won't grow tall enough to obscure the view from your windows. We could use a lot more plants in this category. They save on pruning chores, and they work in lots of places. To this end, nurseries are always on the lookout for dwarf variations of common shrubs.

'Crimson Pygmy' Barberry (*Berberis thunbergii 'atropurpurea'*), N, C

Dwarf Gardenia (*Gardenia jasminoides 'radicans'*), Ce, CSe

Shrubby St. John's Wort (*Hypericum patulum*), Ce, CSe

Carissa Holly (*Ilex cornuta 'carissa'*) , All

Rotunda Holly (*Ilex cornuta 'rotunda'*), All

Helleri Holly (*Ilex crenata 'helleri'*), N, C

Stokes Holly (*Ilex crenata 'stokes'*), N, C, CS

'Nana,' 'Schelling's Dwarf,' 'Stokes Dwarf' Dwarf Yaupon (*Ilex vomitoria*), All (N protected)

Showy Jasmine (*Jasminum floridum*), CS, V

Shore Juniper cultivars (*Juniperus conferta*), N, C, CS

Creeping Juniper cultivars (*Juniperus horizontalis*), N, C

Coastal Leucothoe (*Leucothoe axillaris*), Ce, CSe

Drooping Leucothoe (*Leucothoe fontanesiana*), Ce, CSe

Dwarf Wax Myrtle (*Myrica pusilla*), Ce, CSe

Dwarf Myrtle (*Myrtus communis 'microphylla'* or *'compacta'*), CSs, V

'Fire Power,' 'Gulf Stream,' 'Harbour Dwarf' Dwarf Nandina (*Nandina domestica*), All

'Wheeler's Dwarf' Pittosporum (*Pittosporum tobira*), CS, V

'Snow,' 'Enchantress,' 'Ballerina,' 'Clara' Dwarf India Hawthorn (*Rhaphiolepis indica*), C, CS, V

Gumpo Azalea (*Rhododendron 'gumpo'*), Ce, CSe

Serissa (*Serissa foetida*), CSs, V

Coralberry (*Symphoricarpos orbiculatus*), N, C, CS

SHRUBS THAT ADAPT TO SUN OR PARTIAL SHADE

Though the plants on this list are tolerant, in too much shade they tend to stretch and will bloom less than they would with more sun. Most would probably like morning sun and afternoon shade. Wouldn't we all? Unless you can get by with just planting on one side of the house, you may need to consult a few of the other lists before finalizing your garden design plan.

SUMMERSWEET

Glossy Abelia (*Abelia* x *grandiflora*), All

Littleleaf Boxwood (*Buxus microphylla*), All

American Boxwood (*Buxus sempervirens*), All

Beautyberry (*Callicarpa americana*), N, C, CS

Sweet Shrub (*Calycanthus floridus*), Ce, CSe

Mexican Orange (*Choisya ternata*), CSsw, V

Summersweet (*Clethra alnifolia*), Ce, CSe

Sky Flower, Golden Dewdrop (*Duranta repens* [*erecta*]), CSs, V

Thorny Elaeagnus (*Elaeagnus pungens*), All

Pineapple Guava (*Feijoa sellowiana*), CS, V

Gardenia (*Gardenia jasminoides*), Ce, CSe

'Tardiva' Hydrangea (*Hydrangea paniculata*), C, CS

Anise (*Illicium* spp.), Ce, CSe

Virginia Sweetspire (*Itea virginica*), Ce, CSe

Florida Jasmine (*Jasminum floridum*), CS, V

Primrose Jasmine (*Jasminum mesnyi*), C, CS, V

Pinwheel Jasmine (*Jasminum nitidum*), V, Tropical

Winter Jasmine (*Jasminum nudiflorum*), N, C, CS

Variegated Privet (*Ligustrum sinense 'variegatum'*), All

Loropetalum (*Loropetalum chinense*), Ce, CSe

Burmese Mahonia (*Mahonia lomariifolia*), CSs, V

Wax Myrtle (*Myrica cerifera*), Ce, CSe

Nandina (*Nandina domestica*), All

Sweet Olive (*Osmanthus fragrans*), CS, V

Pittosporum (*Pittosporum tobira*), CS, V

Cherry Laurel (*Prunus caroliniana*), All
English Laurel (*Prunus laurocerasus*), C, CS
India Hawthorn (*Rhaphiolepis indica*), C, CS, V
Yedda Hawthorn (*Rhaphiolepis umbellata*), C, CS, V
Needle Palm (*Rhapidophyllum hystrix*), C, CS, V
Elderberry (*Sambucus canadensis*), All
Vanhoutte Spiraea (*Spiraea vanhouttei*), N, C, CS

Cleyera (*Ternstroemia gymnanthera*), Ce, CSe
Windmill Palm (*Trachycarpus fortunei*), CS, V
Viburnum (*Viburnum nitidum*), Ce, CSe
Double-File Viburnum (*Viburnum plicatum 'tomentosum'*), C
Leatherleaf Viburnum (*Viburnum rhytidophyllum*), Ce, CSe

SHRUBS WITH ORNAMENTAL FRUIT OR BERRIES

Shrubs are almost expected to have berries. They look great in the landscape, and birds love them too. A number of species, notably the hollies (*Ilex* spp.), require both a male and female plant in the landscape if you expect berries. Fortunately, some Asian species like the Burford holly are an exception.

Chokeberry (*Aronia arbutifolia*), N, C
Beautyberry (*Callicarpa americana*), N, C, CS
Buttonbush (*Cephalanthus occidentalis*), Ce, CSe
Rockspray Cotoneaster (*Cotoneaster horizontalis*), N, Cw, CSw
Clusterberry (*Cotoneaster lacteus*), N, Cw, CSw
Sky Flower, Golden Dewdrop (*Duranta repens [erecta]*), CSs, V
Winged Euonymus (*Euonymus alatus*), Ce, CSe
Strawberry Bush (*Euonymus americanus*), Ce, CSe
Red-Wing (*Heteropterys glabra*), CS, V
Dahoon Holly (*Ilex cassine*), Ce, CSe
Burford Holly (*Ilex cornuta 'burfordii'*), All

Deciduous Holly (*Ilex decidua*), All
Yaupon (*Ilex vomitoria*), All
Oregon Grape (*Mahonia aquifolium*), N, C
Leatherleaf Mahonia (*Mahonia bealei*), C, CS
Nandina (*Nandina domestica*), All
Scarlet Firethorn (*Pyracantha coccinea*), All
Firethorn cultivars (*Pyracantha coccinea*), All
Formosa Firethorn (*Pyracantha koidzumii*), All
Carolina Buckthorn (*Rhamnus caroliniana*), C, CS, V
Arrowwood Viburnum (*Viburnum dentatum*), Ce, CSe

SHRUBS THAT DEER RARELY EAT

A hungry deer will eat almost anything. Plants that are toxic, have an unpleasant flavor, or have serious thorns and prickles at least have a chance. Fortunately, many of these plants are not only deer-resistant but attractive in the landscape as well.

Glossy Abelia (*Abelia × grandiflora*), All
Aucuba (*Aucuba japonica*), C, CS, V
Japanese Barberry (*Berberis thunbergii*), N, C
Agarita (*Berberis [Mahonia] trifoliolata*), C, CS, V
Butterfly Bush (*Buddleia alternifolia*), N, C, CS
Boxwood (*Buxus* spp.), All
Sweetshrub (*Calycanthus floridus*), Ce, CSe
Mexican Orange (*Choisya ternata*), CSsw, V
Brasil (*Condalia hookeri*), CSs, V
Smoke-Tree (*Cotinus obovatus*), Cw, CSw
Cotoneaster (*Cotoneaster* spp.), N, Cw, CSw
Thorny Eleagnus (*Eleagnus pungens*), All
Mexican Silk-Tassel (*Garrya lindheimeri*), CSw, V
Guayacan (*Guaiacum [Porlieria] angustifolia*), CSw, V
Chinese Holly (*Ilex cornuta*), All
Dwarf Yaupon (*Ilex vomitoria*), All (N protected)
Juniper (*Juniperus* spp.), All
Lantana (*Lantana camara*), CS, V, Annual

COTONEASTER

Creosote Bush (*Larrea tridentata*), Cw, CSw, V
Texas Sage, Cenizo (*Leucophyllum frutescens*), C, CS, V
Fragrant Mimosa (*Mimosa borealis*), Cw, CSw, V
Wherry Mimosa (*Mimosa wherryana*), V
Wax Myrtle (*Myrica cerifera*), Ce, CSe
Nandina (*Nandina domestica*), All
Oleander (*Nerium oleander*), CSs, V
Mexican Oregano (*Poliomintha longiflora*), CSs, V, Annual

Cherry Laurel (*Prunus caroliniana*), All
Firethorn (*Pyracantha* spp.) , All
Evergreen Sumac (*Rhus virens*), Cw, CSw

Rosemary (*Rosmarinus officinalis*), CSs, V, Annual
Texas Mountain Laurel (*Sophora secundiflora*), C,
CS, V

A SAMPLER OF SHRUBS FOR INTEREST IN EACH SEASON

Fall

Chokeberry (*Aronia arbutifolia*)	berries	N, C
Japanese Aucuba (*Aucuba japonica*)	berries	C, CS, V
Japanese Barberry (*Berberis thunbergii*)	berries	N, C
Beautyberry (*Callicarpa americana*)	berries	N, C, CS
Sasanqua Camellia (*Camellia sasanqua*)	flowers	Ce, CSe
Senna (*Cassia splendida*)	flowers	CS, V
Cotoneaster (*Cotoneaster* spp.)	berries	N, Cw, CSw
Thorny Elaeagnus (*Elaeagnus pungens*)	flowers	All
Winged Euonymous (*Euonymus alatus*)	fall color	Ce, CSe
Dwarf Winged Euonymus (*Euonymus alatus 'compacta'*)	fall color	Ce, CSe
Strawberry Bush (*Euonymus americana*)	berries, fall color	Ce, CSe
Confederate Rose (*Hibiscus mutabilis*)	flowers	CSs, V
Oakleaf Hydrangeaa (*Hydrangea quercifolia*)	fall color	Ce, CSe
Burford Holly (*Ilex cornuta 'burfordii'*)	berries	All
Yaupon (*Ilex vomitoria*)	berries	All
Virginia Sweetspire (*Itea virginica*)	fall color	Ce, CSe
Nandina (*Nandina domestica*)	berries	All
Sweet Olive (*Osmanthus fragrans*)	flowers	CS, V
Holly-Leaf Osmanthus (*Osmanthus heterophyllus*)	flowers	Ce, CSe
Fortune's Osmanthus (*Osmanthus* x *fortunei*)	flowers	Ce, CSe
Firethorn (*Pyracantha* spp.)	berries	All
Sumac (*Rhus* spp.)	berries	All
Sumac (*Rhus* spp.)	fall color	All
Arrowwood (*Viburnum dentatum*)	berries	Ce, CSe

Winter

Camellia (*Camellia japonica*)	flowers	Ce, CSe
Flowering Quince (*Chaenomeles speciosa*)	flowers	All
Oakleaf Hydrangea (*Hydrangea quercifolia*)	bark	Ce, CSe
Holly (*Ilex* spp.)	berries	All
Winter Jasmine (*Jasminum nudiflorum*)	flowers	N, C, CS
Winter Honeysuckle (*Lonicera fragrantissima*)	flowers	N, C
Oregon Grape (*Mahonia aquifolium*)	flowers	N, C
Leatherleaf Mahonia (*Mahonia bealei*)	flowers	C, CS
Chinese Mahonia (*Mahonia fortunei*)	flowers	CSs, V
Sweet Olive (*Osmanthus fragrans*)	flowers	CS, V

Spring

Ti Ti, Leatherwood (*Cyrilla racemiflora*)	flowers	Ce, CSe
Forsythia (*Forsythia* x *intermedia*)	flowers	N, C
French Hydrangea (*Hydrangea macrophylla*)	flowers	N, C, CS
Virginia Sweetspire (*Itea virginica*)	flowers	Ce, CSe
Japanese Kerria (*Kerria japonica*)	flowers	Ce, CSe
Loropetalum (*Loropetalum chinense*)	flowers	Ce, CSe
Banana Shrub (*Michelia figo*)	flowers	CS, V
Mock Orange (*Philadelphus coronarius*)	flowers	N, C

India Hawthorn (*Rhaphiolepis indica*)	flowers	C, CS, V
Yedda Hawthorn (*Rhaphiolepis umbellata*)	flowers	C, CS, V
Azalea (*Rhododendron* hyb.)	flowers	Ce, CSe
Native Azalea (*Rhododendron* spp.)	flowers	Ce, CSe
Bridal-Wreath Spiraea (*Spiraea prunifolia*)	flowers	N, C, CS
Baby's-Breath Spiraea (*Spiraea thunbergii*)	flowers	N, C, CS
Vanhoutte Spiraea (*Spiraea vanhouttei*)	flowers	N, C, CS
Lilac (*Syringa vulgaris*)	flowers	N, Cn
Snowball (*Viburnum opulus 'roseum'*)	flowers	N, C
Viburnum (*Viburnum* spp.)	flowers	All
Cranberry Bush (*Viburnum trilobum*)	flowers	N

Summer

Chinese Abelia (*Abelia chinensis*)	flowers	C, CS
Glossy Abelia (*Abelia* × *grandiflora*)	flowers	All
Butterfly Bush (*Buddleia davidii*)	flowers	N, C, CS
Bluebeard (*Caryopteris* × *clandonensis*)	flowers	N, C, CS
Senna (*Cassia corymbosa*)	flowers	CS, V
Night-Blooming Jasmine (*Cestrum nocturnum*)	flowers	CSs, V
Willow-Leafed Jasmine (*Cestrum parqui*)	flowers	CSs, V
Ninebark (*Clethra acuminata*)	flowers	Ce, CSe
Summersweet (*Clethra alnifolia*)	flowers	Ce, CSe
Sky Flower, Golden Dewdrop (*Duranta repens* [*erecta*])	flowers	CSs, V
Gardenia (*Gardenia jasminoides*)	flowers	Ce, Cse
Dwarf Gardenia (*Gardenia jasminoides 'radicans'*)	flowers	Ce, CSe
Tropical Hibiscus (*Hibiscus rosa-sinensis*)	flowers	CSs, V, Annual
Althaea (*Hibiscus syriacus*)	flowers	N, C, CS
Hydrangea (*Hydrangea* spp.)	flowers	N, C, CS
Showy Jasmine (*Jasminum floridum*)	flowers	CSs, V
Oleander (*Nerium oleander*)	flowers	CS, V
Pomegranate (*Punica granatum*)	flowers	C, CS, V
India Hawthorn (*Rhaphiolepis indica*)	flowers	C, CS, V
Yedda Hawthorn (*Rhaphiolepis umbellata*)	flowers	C, CS, V
Chaste Tree (*Vitex agnus-castus*)	flowers	All

TREES

Trees are an investment—more so than any other living element in the landscape. They can live for hundreds, if not thousands of years. Where you plant them is thus extremely critical. If they are too close to the house or under power lines, their potential is limited. If they are very susceptible to insect or disease pests or if they are weak wooded and trashy, the landscape is handicapped until the situation is resolved.

A silver maple in a Gulf Coast landscape is a liability. At best it might grow to an average-looking, medium-sized tree before it begins to attract scale insects, develop dead limbs, and generally look like the ill-adapted species that it is. If you planted it for shade, then plant a good species close by and cut down the silver maple after the good tree begins to fill in. Don't pump chemical pesticides into the air trying to kill insects or control diseases on a trash tree. It's immoral—in fact, there are few excuses for spraying any landscape plant that has recurrent pests. This usually means it's prone to these problems and a better species should be selected.

Some tree species like the red maple (*Acer rubrum 'drummondii'*) grow from Canada to Mexico. Trees grown from seed close to home will generally do best. The term used to describe this phenomenon is *provenance*. Red maples are fast growing and not very long lived, but they make for a decent "fast growing tree." In a Gulf Coast landscape, it's still best to plant *Acer rubrum 'drummondii'* from seed collected in South Texas rather than order seedlings of a similar species from Tennessee. A number of selected red maple cultivars are propagated by grafting or budding, but most were selected in the Northeast, and they really suffer in our hot, humid summers. The caution here is to be careful about ordering woody species from out of state.

Native trees are increasingly popular these days. They are well adapted, and they provide wildlife food and shelter, but because they are native, they also have endemic pests. There are many good introduced species. Mexican oaks are really catching on in South Texas. The late Lynn Lowrey and Benny Simpson started bringing plants up from Mexico over thirty years ago, and because the plants often were found growing at high altitudes, many have proven very hardy. Carl Max Schoenfeld and John Fairey of Yucca Do Nursery and Peckerwood Gardens, respectively, are continuing that tradition today.

As much as we love giant oak trees, today's landscape is often too diminutive for big trees, so the demand for small to medium-sized trees is increasing. Landscape designers are finding that large shrubs such as wax myrtle (*Myrica cerifera*) and pineapple guava (*Feijoa sellowiana*) make interesting multi-trunk trees.

The lists that follow are a starting point. Check with local nurseries, landscapers, and County Extension agents. Don't hesitate to make notes in this book; that will only make it more valuable.

Basic Cultural Requirements

If you're in a hurry for shade, have someone plant large trees with a tree spade. In some cases, building a patio shade cover until better species can take off is a good idea. Resist the temptation to plant a fast-growing trash tree, however—they're a poor investment. If you're not in a hurry, plant trees when they are small—even seeds or acorns.

Container growing has made it possible to plant trees almost any time of the year. However, root girdling is a common problem if plants are left in containers too long. Unless you pull the roots apart and even cut some, the tree may remain stunted for years and eventually die. At the Harris County Extension office, one bur oak (*Quercus macrocarpa*) had been planted from a five-gallon container, whereas another was planted a year later from an acorn. The container-grown tree (obviously root bound) barely grew, aphids attacked it, and for years it stayed about the same height. The seedling bur oak grew like a weed. In ten years it was over 20 feet tall. The container-grown specimen eventually died.

The old adage "dig a ten-dollar hole for a two-dollar tree" doesn't apply in the high-rainfall areas of East Texas. You'll end up with a ten-dollar sink to drown a two-dollar tree in. Dig the planting hole no deeper than necessary to set the plant at its original soil level or 1 to 2 inches high. The old dirt line is usually very obvious on a nursery tree trunk. Also, make the hole 12 to 18 inches wider than the natural spread of the root system (or root ball, since most trees will be container grown or balled and burlapped). Put the native soil back into the bottom two-thirds of the hole, and save any organic matter for the last one-third of backfill. You don't want a bunch of organic matter in the bottom of the hole, since it may stay too wet and damage the roots. In most cases you can't amend the entire root-zone area, so the tree will eventually have to adapt to the native soil.

It's also a good idea to take soil samples from several sites in the landscape, just to see what you are starting with. If the soil seems uniform, take one composite sample made from several locations. If you suspect a problem area, take a separate sample. See the "Resources" section for information on soil tests.

Weed-and-feed fertilizers are another potential problem. Atrazine, in particular, is often used in these formulations, and it can cause root damage to trees and shrubs that have roots extending out into the turf. It's a more subtle damage than one would expect with the hormone weed killers such as 2,4,D. There's no twisting or distortion of the foliage, just the dieback and marginal leaf burn you would anticipate with damaged roots. If you forget and use one of these materials, there's no practical antidote. You will just have to wait for time and microorganisms to break the chemicals down.

TREES FOR THE COASTAL BAY AREA

Trees on this list have to be able to tolerate wind, salt spray, downpours in some seasons, drought in others. It's difficult to create a microclimate for trees because of their large size. In some cases, a windbreak may help them get established.

FRINGE TREE

Huisache (*Acacia farnesiana*)	orange flowers; thorns
Red Maple (*Acer rubrum 'drummondii'*)	red spring color
Texas Buckeye (*Aesculus arguta*)	red flowers by early summer
White Orchid Tree (*Bauhinia forficata*)	white flowers in summer
Purple Orchid Tree (*Bauhinia purpurea*)	purple flowers
River Birch (*Betula nigra*)	exfoliating bark
Gum Elastic (*Bumelia lanuginosa*)	attracts birds
Pride-of-Barbados (*Caesalpinia pulcherrima*)	yellow/red flowers in summer
Sasanqua Camellia (*Camellia sasanqua*)	blooms in fall
Buttonbush (*Cephalanthus occidentalis*)	white ball-shaped blooms in summer
Redbud (*Cercis canadensis*)	rose-pink flowers in spring
Mediterranean Fan Palm (*Chamaerops humilis*)	multi-trunk palm
Fringe Tree (*Chionanthus virginicus*)	white flowers in spring
Chitalpa (*Chitalpa tashkentensis*)	pink flowers all summer
Native Hawthorn (*Crataegus* spp.)	white flowers in spring; berries
Ti Ti, Leatherwood (*Cyrilla racemiflora*)	white flowers in spring
Texas Persimmon (*Diospyros texana*)	black fruit; gray-white bark
Anaqua (*Ehretia anacua*)	white flowers
Texas Kidneywood (*Eysenhardtia texana*)	white fragrant flowers
Swamp Privet (*Forestiera acuminata*)	yellow flowers in spring
Loblolly Bay (*Gordonia lasianthus*)	white flowers in summer
Althaea (*Hibiscus syriacus*)	flowers in summer
Dahoon Holly (*Ilex cassine*)	berries
Deciduous Holly, Possumhaw (*Ilex decidua*)	berries
'Savannah,' 'East Palatka' American Holly (*Ilex opaca*)	berries
Yaupon (*Ilex vomitoria*)	berries
Japanese Anise (*Illicium anisatum*)	small yellow flowers

Eastern Red Cedar (*Juniperus virginiana*)	exfoliating bark
'Little Gem' Magnolia (*Magnolia grandiflora*)	white flowers in summer, red seeds
Southern Wax Myrtle (*Myrica cerifera*)	waxy white fruit
Parkinsonia (*Parkinsonia aculeata*)	yellow flowers in summer; thorns
Red Bay (*Persea borbonia*)	black berries
Loblolly Pine (*Pinus taeda*)	interesting bark; native
Cherry Laurel (*Prunus caroliniana*)	white flowers in spring; black berries
Mexican Plum (*Prunus mexicana*)	white flowers in spring; fruit
Swamp Chestnut Oak (*Quercus michauxii*)	good fall color; large acorns
Nuttall Oak (*Quercus nuttallii*)	fast growth
Live Oak (*Quercus virginiana*)	reliable evergreen
Carolina Buckthorn (*Rhamnus caroliniana*)	red berries in late summer
Flame-Leaf Sumac (*Rhus copallina*)	fall color; seeds
Louisiana Sabal Palm (*Sabal louisiana*)	small white flowers
Elderberry (*Sambucus canadensis*)	white flowers in spring; black berries
Texas Mountain Laurel (*Sophora secundiflora*)	purple flowers in spring
Texas Snowbell (*Styrax texana*)	white flowers in spring
Montezuma Cypress (*Taxodium mucronatum*)	no knees, like bald cypress
Windmill Palm (*Trachycarpus fortunei*)	yellow flowers; blue-black fruit
'Drake' Elm (*Ulmus parvifolia*)	interesting bark
Mexican Buckeye (*Ungnadia speciosa*)	pink flowers in spring
Luzon Viburnum (*Viburnum luzonicum*)	white flowers; black berries
Possumhaw Viburnum (*Viburnum nudum*)	white flowers; pink berries
Walter's Viburnum (*Viburnum obovatum*)	white flowers in spring
Chaste Tree (*Vitex agnus-castus*)	lavender flowers all summer
Cut-Leaf Vitex (*Vitex negundo* 'Heterophylla')	pale blue flowers all summer

TREES FOR HEAVY CLAY SOIL

Heavy soils are a fact of life for many Texas gardeners. When planting annuals or perennials, we can build raised beds or add organic matter and significantly change the soil environment these plants will be growing in. Trees, however, have to deal with the pervasive soil environment on the site. Their roots are going to grow well beyond the planting hole, so they either adapt to the existing soil or grow so poorly we eventually replace them with a better adapted species.

Beech trees (*Fagus grandifolia*), for example, are native to East Texas. Take them out of their forest environment and away from an acid soil and watch them turn yellow with iron chlorosis. Plant a tree that's adapted to an upland, sandy soil into heavy clay and you will likely end up with a sick tree. Even the same species can have trouble with different soil types. Trees dug with large tree spades should come from areas with similar soils. Take a live oak (*Quercus virginiana*) that's been grown in a sandy soil and spade it into a heavy clay and it often dies or is stunted. The sandy root ball collects water like a sink when surrounded by the clay.

Small, nursery plants are less sensitive to this problem. The planting hole is smaller, for one thing. Also, young trees are more tolerant, and they have more time to acclimate. Assuming, of course, that the tree species can adapt to a heavy soil.

Red Maple (*Acer rubrum* 'drummondii'), Ce, CSe
Mexican Pink Orchid Tree (*Bauhinia macranthera*), CSs, V
River Birch (*Betula nigra*), N, C, CS
American Hornbeam, Ironwood (*Carpinus caroliniana*), Ce, CSe
Chinese Fringe Tree (*Chionanthus retusus*), C, CS, Mayhaw (*Crataegus aestivalis, C. opaca*), Ce, CSe
Parsley Hawthorn (*Crataegus marshallii*), Ce, CSe
Green Ash (*Fraxinus pennsylvanica*), N, C, CS

'Savannah' Holly (*Ilex* x *attenuata*) , Ce, CSe
Crape Myrtle (*Lagerstroemia indica* and hyb.), All (N protected)
Sweetgum (*Liquidambar styraciflua*), Ce, CSe
Tulip Poplar (*Liriodendron tulipifera*), Ce, CSe
Southern Magnolia (*Magnolia grandiflora*), All
'Little Gem' Magnolia (*Magnolia grandiflora*), All
Bigleaf Magnolia (*Magnolia macrophylla*), Ce, CSe
Oriental Magnolia (*Magnolia soulangiana* hyb.), All
Sweet Bay Magnolia (*Magnolia virginiana*), Ce, CSe

Banana Shrub (*Michelia figo*), CS, V
Slash Pine (*Pinus elliottii*), Ce, CSe
Spruce Pine (*Pinus glabra*), Ce, CSe
Loblolly Pine (*Pinus taeda*), Ce, CSe
Sawtooth Oak (*Quercus acutissima*), Ce, CSe
Overcup Oak (*Quercus lyrata*), C, CS
Bur Oak (*Quercus macrocarpa*), N, C, CS
Swamp Chestnut Oak (*Quercus michauxii*), Ce, CSe
Nuttall Oak (*Quercus nuttallii*), N, Ce, CSe
Monterrey Oak (*Quercus polymorpha*), CS, V
Loquat-Leafed Oak (*Quercus rhizophylla*), CSe

Shumard Oak (*Quercus shumardii*), N, Ce, CSe
Live Oak (*Quercus virginiana*), All
Willow (*Salix* spp.), All
Bald Cypress (*Taxodium distichum*), All
Pond Cypress (*Taxodium distichum* 'nutans', *T. ascendens*), All
Montezuma Cypress (*Taxodium mucronatum*), CSs, V
Cedar Elm (*Ulmus crassifolia*), All
Chinese Elm (*Ulmus parvifolia*) , All
'Drake Elm' (*Ulmus parvifolia*), All

"The best advice we can give gardeners that are new to the Amarillo area is to choose plant materials adapted to our hardiness zone and alkaline soils. That means shopping with a reputable nursery instead of going for bargains at some cash-and-carry outlet. Also, our soils are primarily clay loam, and we recommend the addition of organic matter prior to planting. Finally, the main weather threat to plants in the Panhandle occurs because we often have early warm spells in the spring followed by a hard freeze."
—Brian Bellinghausen, manager, Love & Son Nursery, Amarillo

TREES FOR DRY SITES

Benny Simpson and Lynn Lowrey, two great Texas plantsmen, now deceased, were plant exploring in Texas and Mexico for native plants long before native plants were in fashion. They were contributors to the "Trees for Dry Sites" list in *The Southern Gardener's Book of Lists*. The following list is a continuation of their original work. (For trees that do well in arid regions, see the separate list of "Trees for West Texas.")

Huisache (*Acacia farnesiana*), C, CS, V
Lost Maple, Big-Tooth Maple (*Acer grandidentatum*), N, C, CS
Chalk Maple (*Acer leucoderme*), Ce, CSe
Box Elder (*Acer negundo*), All
Caddo Maple (*Acer saccharum* 'saccharum'), N, C, CSn
Mimosa (*Albizia julibrissin*), All
Fragrant Mimosa (*Albizia borealis*), C, CS, V
Brazil Orchid Tree (*Bauhinia forficata*), CSs, V
Anacacho Orchid Tree (*Bauhinia congesta* [*lunaroides*]), CSs, V
Pata-de-vaca (*Bauhinia macranthera*), CSs, V
Chinese Chestnut (*Castanea mollissima*), N, C, CS
Chinquapin (*Castanea pumila*), Ce, CSe
Western Catalpa (*Catalpa speciosa*), All
Atlas Cedar (*Cedrus atlantica*), N, C, CS
Deodar Cedar (*Cedrus deodara*), N, C, CS
Common Hackberry (*Celtis occidentalis*), All
Plum Yew (*Cephalotaxus harringtonia*), Ce, CSe
Mexican Redbud (*Cercis canadensis mexicana*), All
Texas Redbud (*Cercis canadensis texensis, C. reniformis*), All
Curlleaf Mountain Mahogany (*Cercocarpus ledifolius*), N

Chitalpa (*Chitalpa tashkentensis*), All
Camphor Tree (*Cinnamomum camphora*), CSs, V
Wild Olive (*Cordia boissieri*), CSs, V
Leyland Cypress (*Cupressocyparis leylandii*), C, CS
Texas Persimmon (*Diospyros texana*), All
Anaqua (*Ehretia anacua*), Cs, CS, V
Eucalyptus (*Eucalyptus* spp.), CSs, V
Texas Ash (*Fraxinus texensis*), All
Kentucky Coffee Tree (*Gymnocladus dioica*), N
Little Black Walnut, Nogalito (*Juglans microcarpa*), N, C, CS
Southern Red Cedar (*Juniperus silicicola*), Ce, CSe
Eastern Red Cedar (*Juniperus virginiana*), N, C
Golden-Rain Tree (*Koelreuteria* spp.), All
Osage Orange (*Maclura pomifera*), All
Arroyo Sweetwood (*Myrospermum sousamum*), CSs, V
Jerusalem Thorn, Retama (*Parkinsonia aculeata*), CSs, V
Parrotia (*Parrotia persica*), All
Scotch Pine (*Pinus sylvestris*), N
Chinese Pistache (*Pistacia chinensis*), All
Texas Pistache (*Pistacia texana*), CS, V
Texas Ebony (*Pithecellobium flexicaule*), V
Japanese Yew (*Podocarpus macrophyllus*), C, CS, V

Mesquite (*Prosopis glandulosa*), C, CS, V
Carolina Cherry Laurel (*Prunus caroliniana*), All
Mexican Plum (*Prunus mexicana*), All
Black Cherry (*Prunus serotina*), All
Flatwoods Plum (*Prunus umbellata*), Ce, CSe
Callery Pear (*Pyrus calleryana*), All
Escarpment Live Oak (*Quercus fusiformis*), All
Lacey Oak (*Quercus glaucoides*), C, CS, V
Chisos Red Oak (*Quercus gravesii*), C, CS
Bur Oak (*Quercus macrocarpa*), N, C, CS
Chinquapin Oak (*Quercus muehlenbergii*), N, C, CS
Monterrey Oak (*Quercus polymorpha*), CS, V
Vasey Oak (*Quercus pungens 'vaseyana'*), C, CS, V
Loquat-Leafed Oak (*Quercus rhizophylla*), CSe
Texas Red Oak (*Quercus texana*), N, C, CS

Live Oak (*Quercus virginiana*), All
Black Locust (*Robinia pseudoacacia*), N, C, CS
Western Soapberry (*Sapindus drummondii*), All
Sassafras (*Sassafras albidum*), Ce, CSe
Eve's Necklace (*Sophora affinis*), All
Montezuma Cypress (*Taxodium mucronatum*), CS, V
Arbor Vitae (*Thuja* spp.), N, C, CS
Cedar Elm (*Ulmus crassifolia*), All
Chinese Elm, Lacebark Elm (*Ulmus parvifolia*), All
Mexican Buckeye (*Ungnadia speciosa*), All
Chaste Tree (*Vitex agnus-castus*), All
Prickly-Ash (*Zanthoxylum clava-herculis*), CS, V
Lime Prickly-Ash (*Zanthoxylum fagara*), CSs, V
Jujube (*Ziziphus jujuba*), All

"My greatest frustration as a researcher at Texas Tech," says David L. Morgan, the editor of *Nursery Management & Production,* "was establishing an irrigated field only to observe the steady winds desiccate my collection of beautiful Southwestern maples. After several seasons and considerable losses, I made the following conclusions regarding maples: (1) Windbreaks are essential. (2) Small trees, such as 1-gallon sized, will not survive even if irrigated. (3) You must plant larger trees with good root systems in a backyard or other protected space, and water regularly throughout the growing season. (4) Don't guarantee anything."

TREES FOR WEST TEXAS

These trees require even less precipitation or irrigation than the trees listed for dry sites. They should be limited to the more arid regions of Texas. Most of these trees grow too well in the high-rainfall areas of Texas (more than 30 inches of rain in a year), where they either become so straggly that they're just plain ugly, or they seem to grow themselves to death. The heavy soils in the high-rainfall areas are another factor, causing them to die out from root rot.

Texas Madrone (*Arbutus texana*), Cw, CSw
Netleaf Hackberry (*Celtis reticulata*), N, Cw, CSw
Blue Paloverde (*Cercidium floridum*), CSsw, V
Foothills Paloverde (*Cercidium microphyllum*), CSsw, V
'Bubba,' 'White Storm' Desert Willow (*Chilopsis linearis*), N, Cw, CSw, V
Native Smoke-Tree (*Cotinus obovatus*), Cw, CSw
Russian Hawthorn (*Crataegus ambigua*), N, Cw, CSw
Arizona Cypress (*Cupressus arizonica*), Cw, CSw
Italian Cypress (*Cupressus sempervirens*), CSw
Fragrant Ash (*Fraxinus cuspidata*), N, Cw, CSw
Little-Leaf Ash (*Fraxinus greggii*), CSw
Arizona Ash (*Fraxinus velutina*), N, Cw, CSw
Thornless Honeylocust (*Gleditsia triacanthos 'inermis'*), N, Cw, CSnw
Ashe Juniper (*Juniperus ashei*), N, Cw, CSw

Alligator Juniper (*Juniperus deppeana*), N, Cw, CSw
Weeping Juniper (*Juniperus flaccida*), N, Cw, CSw
One-seeded Juniper (*Juniperus monosperma*), CSw
Rocky Mountain Juniper (*Juniperus scopulorum*), N, Cw
Goldenball Leadtree (*Leucaena retusa*), CSsw, V
Mexican Piñon (*Pinus cembroides*), CSw
Piñon Pine (*Pinus edulis*), N, Cw, CSw
Afghan Pine (*Pinus eldarica*), N, Cw, CSw
Italian Stone Pine (*Pinus pinea*), CSw
Remote Piñon (*Pinus remota*), Cw, CSw
Japanese Black Pine (*Pinus thunbergiana*), N, Cw, CSw
Mt. Atlas Pistache (*Pistacia atlantica*), CSw
Screwbean Mesquite (*Prosopis pubescens*), CSw, V
Hop-Tree (*Ptelea trifoliata*), N, Cw, CSw
Emory Oak (*Quercus emoryi*), Cw, CSw
Gambel's Oak (*Quercus gambelii*), N, Cw

Holly Oak (*Quercus ilex*), CSw

Blackjack Oak, western (*Quercus marilandica*), Cw, CSw

Cork Oak (*Quercus suber*), CSsw

Pink Locust (*Robinia ambigua 'decaisneana'*), N, Cw, CSw

Idaho Locust (*Robinia ambigua 'idahoensis'*), N, Cw, CSw

Mexican Elderberry (*Sambucus mexicana*), CSw, V

Chisos Rosewood (*Vauquelinia corymbosa 'augustifolia'*), CSsw, V

Betty Winningham, owner of Natives of Texas in Kerrville, offers the following advice as "the secret to planting a madrone (*Arbutus*) tree and having it survive."
1. Pick a well-drained site; a slope is best.
2. Dig the hole only as large as the pot, and do not enrich the soil.
3. Water well and deeply after planting the tree.
4. Protect from the west sun and deer.
5. Water only every three to four weeks when there is no rain. Madrones are very sensitive to overwatering.
6. Mulch with juniper litter or loose organic matter.
7. Do not pamper or ignore it after two years unless we have a severe drought.
8. Plant only in alkaline soils west of I-35.

"El Paso isn't really as desert-like as most people think," comments Vicky Black Walker, the owner of Black's Nursery. "We use lots of ash trees, mesquite, and mondel (Afghan) pine. The need for irrigation is basic, of course, and we use peat moss to lower the pH in landscape beds. Native plants like Mexican elderberry are just being discovered, and they are mostly being used in commercial landscapes."

NATIVE SMALL TREES AND SHRUBS FOR EAST TEXAS

The person behind this list, Dave Creech, has been the driving force behind the development of an excellent horticulture department at Stephen F. Austin University. Simultaneously as director of the SFA Mast Arboretum, he has carved out one of the best new arboretums in the South. Development began in 1999 on an eight-acre azalea garden that will feature more than 5,000 azaleas, over 200 Japanese maple cultivars, and more than 300 camellia cultivars. Sprinkled in will be deciduous magnolias and other rarely encountered species.

Next on his agenda is developing the SFA Pineywoods Native Plant Center, a new forty-acre patriarch forest resource at the north end of the campus. Most of it will be left as a natural area, but four acres will feature the best of the native plants for East Texas.

Florida Maple (*Acer barbatum*)

Chalk Maple (*Acer leucoderme*)

Texas Buckeye (*Aesculus arguta*)

Red Buckeye (*Aesculus pavia*)

Redbud (*Cercis canadensis*)

Fringe Tree (*Chionanthus virginicus*)

Dogwood (*Cornus florida*)

Blueberry Hawthorn (*Crataegus brachycantha*)

Ti Ti, Leatherwood (*Cyrilla racemiflora*)

Texas Persimmon (*Diospyros texana*)

Two-Winged Silverbell (*Halesia diptera*)

Witch Hazel (*Hamamelis virginiana*)

Possumhaw Holly (*Ilex decidua*)

American Holly (*Ilex opaca*)

Yaupon (*Ilex vomitoria*)

Southern Wax Myrtle (*Myrica cerifera*)

Mexican Plum (*Prunus mexicana*)

American Snowbell (*Styrax americanus*)

Arrowwood Viburnum (*Viburnum dentatum*)

Rusty Blackhaw Viburnum (*Viburnum rufidulum*)

"In East Texas, the first two years after planting are the most critical; get past that and most trees and many shrubs can survive on rainfall. Plant in the fall, and go with a wide planting hole but don't dig it any deeper than the container. Apply bark mulch, 2 inches deep, and use glyphosate herbicide to keep a wide circle free of competing weeds, but avoid any fertilizer if drought is anticipated in the near future."
—Dave Creech, director of the SFA Mast Arboretum, Nacogdoches.

TREES WITH FRAGRANT BLOSSOMS

Trees with fragrance can have a dramatic impact on the entire garden. The Mexican plums (*Prunus mexicana*) at Bayou Bend Garden in Houston scent the air in sync with the spectacular azaleas during the River Oaks Garden Club annual Azalea Trail. Banana shrubs (*Michelia figo*) planted near the patio will be particularly noticeable on a warm evening. A satsuma tree planted on the south side of the house for winter protection will spill its sweet scent over the backyard in the spring. The trees on this list will add another dimension to your landscape.

Huisache (*Acacia farnesiana*), C, CS, V
Amur Maple (*Acer ginnala*), N, C
Mimosa (*Albizia julibrissin*), All
Serviceberry (*Amelanchier arborea*), Ce, CSe
Fringe Tree (*Chionanthus virginicus*), Ce, CSe
Citrus (*Citrus* spp.), CSs, V
Russian Olive (*Elaeagnus angustifolia*), N, C, CS
Loquat (*Eriobotrya japonica*), CS
Loblolly Bay (*Gordonia lasianthus*), Ce, CSe
Kentucky Coffee Tree (*Gymnocladus dioica*), N
Southern Magnolia (*Magnolia grandiflora*), All
Sweet Bay Magnolia (*Magnolia virginiana*), Ce, CSe
Southern Crabapple (*Malus angustifolia*), N, C, CS
Sargent Crabapple (*Malus sargentii*), N, C
Banana Shrub (*Michelia figo*), CS, V

Fogg's Michelia (*Michelia* x *foggii*), CS, V
Arroyo Sweetwood (*Myrospermum sousamum*), CSs, V
Sweet Olive (*Osmanthus fragrans*), CS, V
Mesquite (*Prosopis glandulosa*), C, CS, V
Mexican Plum (*Prunus mexicana*), All
Japanese Flowering Cherry (*Prunus serrulata* and cvs.), N, C
Black Locust (*Robinia pseudoacacia*), N, C, CS
Eve's Necklace (*Sophora affinis*), All
Texas Mountain Laurel (*Sophora secundiflora*), C, CS, V
Little-Leaf Linden (*Tilia cordata*), C, CS
Jujube (*Ziziphus jujuba*), All

SPECIMEN TREES

Even the rambling estate landscape has a need for specimen trees, but the ordinary home landscape really cries out for small but stunning trees. They don't have to be truly stunning to make this list, but small to medium stature is a requirement. These trees might be used to frame the corners of a house, or to accent a patio planting. They can add height to a shrub border, or they just may be the largest tree that will fit into your patio home landscape. If you're looking for a year-round screen, try the evergreens.

Not every tree on this list is readily available at the local nursery. In particular, some of the natives—such as chalk maple, pawpaw, chittamwood, native smoke-tree, and screwbean mesquite—may be hard to find. If you're a plant lover, the quest will be worth it. Look in the yellow pages for native plant nurseries, and check with members of the local native plant society for sources of these trees. Expect to settle for small seedlings, possibly even seeds.

Deciduous
Berlandier's Acacia (*Acacia berlandieri*), C, CS, V
Huisache (*Acacia farnesiana*), C, CS, V
Blackbrush Acacia (*Acacia rigidula*), CSw, V
Wright's Acacia (*Acacia wrightii*), C, CS, V
Lost Maple, Big-Tooth Maple (*Acer grandidentatum*), N, C, CS

Chalk Maple (*Acer leucoderme*), Ce, CSe
Japanese Maple (*Acer palmatum*), Ce, CSe
Texas Buckeye (*Aesculus arguta*), All
Red Buckeye (*Aesculus pavia*), All
Hazel Alder (*Alnus serrulata*), Ce, CSe
Texas Madrone (*Arbutus texana*), Cw, CSw
Pawpaw (*Asimina triloba*), Ce, CSe

Orchid Tree (*Bauhinia* spp.), CSs, V

River Birch (*Betula nigra*), N, C, CS

La-Coma (*Bumelia celastrina*), CSs, V

Chittamwood (*Bumelia lanuginosa*), All

Camptotheca (*Camptotheca acuminata*), V

American Hornbeam, Ironwood (*Carpinus caroliniana*), Ce, CSe

Redbud (*Cercis canadensis*), All

Texas Redbud (*Cercis canadensis 'texensis'*), C, CS, V

Desert Willow (*Chilopsis linearis*), N, Cw, CSw, V

Chinese Fringe Tree (*Chionanthus retusus*), C, CS

Fringe Tree (*Chionanthus virginicus*), Ce, CSe

Chitalpa (*Chitalpa tashkentensis*), All

Starleaf Mexican Orange (*Choisya dumosa*), V

Fiddlewood (*Citharexylum berlandieri*), V

Wild Olive (*Cordia boissieri*), CSs, V

Dogwood (*Cornus florida*), Ce, CSe

Native Smoke-Tree (*Cotinus obovatus*), Cw, CSw

Parsley Hawthorn (*Crataegus marshallii*), Ce, CSe

Mayhaw (*Crataegus opaca, C. aestivalis*), Ce, Cse

Green Hawthorn (*Crataegus viridis*), C, CS

Asian Persimmon (*Diospyros kaki*), All

Texas Persimmon (*Diospyros texana*), All

Anaqua (*Ehretia anacua*), Cs, CS, V

Blueberry, Horuto-no-ki Zoko (*Elaeocarpus decipiens*), CS, V

Fireman's-Hat (*Erythrina crista-galli*), CSs, V

Chinese Parasol-Tree (*Firmiana simplex*), C, CS, V

Fragrant Ash (*Fraxinus cuspidata*), N, Cw, CSw

Honey Locust (*Gleditsia triacanthos*), N, Cw, CSnw

Two-winged Silverbell (*Halesia diptera*), Ce, CSe

Possumhaw (*Ilex decidua*), All

Golden-Rain Tree (*Koelreuteria* spp.), All

Crape Myrtle (*Lagerstroemia indica* and hyb.), All

Goldenball Leadtree (*Leucaena retusa*), CSsw, V

Oriental Magnolia (*Magnolia soulangiana* hyb.), All

Star Magnolia (*Magnolia stellata*), Ce, CSe

Sweet Bay Magnolia (*Magnolia virginiana*), Ce, CSe

Southern Crabapple (*Malus angustifolia*), C, CS

Crabapple (*Malus floribunda*), N, C

American Hop Hornbeam (*Ostrya virginiana*), Ce, CSe

Jerusalem Thorn, Retama (*Parkinsonia aculeata*), CSs, V

Chinese Pistache (*Pistacia chinensis*), All

Texas Pistache (*Pistacia texana*), CSw, V

'Flying Dragon' Trifoliate Orange (*Poncirus trifoliata*), CS, V

Mesquite (*Prosopis glandulosa*), C, CS, V

Screwbean Mesquite (*Prosopis pubescens*), CSs, V

Dwarf Screwbean Mesquite (*Prosopis reptans*), CSs, V

Mexican Plum (*Prunus mexicana*), All

Black Cherry (*Prunus serotina*), All

Flatwoods Plum (*Prunus umbellata*), Ce, CSe

Chinese Quince Tree (*Pseudocydonia sinensis*), C, CS, V

Hop-Tree (*Ptelea trifoliata*), N, Cw, CSw

Callery Pear (*Pyrus calleryana*), All

Evergreen Pear (*Pyrus kawakami*), CSs, V

Evergreen Sumac (*Rhus virens*), Cw, CSw, V

Black Locust (*Robinia pseudoacacia*), N, C, CS

Mexican Elderberry (*Sambucus mexicana*), CSw, V

Western Soapbery (*Sapindus drummondii*), All

Sassafras (*Sassafras albidum*), Ce, CSe

Chinese Snowbell (*Sinojackia rehderiana*), CS, V

Eve's Necklace (*Sophora affinis*), All

Winged Elm (*Ulmus alata*), Ce, CSe

Cedar Elm (*Ulmus crassifolia*), All

Chinese Elm (*Ulmus parvifolia*), All

Mexican Buckeye (*Ungnadia speciosa*), All

Farkleberry (*Vaccinium arboreum*), Ce, CSe

Rusty Blackhaw Viburnum (*Viburnum rufidulum*), C, CS

Vitex (*Vitex agnus-castus*), All

Prickly-Ash (*Zanthoxylum clava-herculis*), CSs, V

Zelkova (*Zelkova serrata*), N, C, CS

Jujube (*Ziziphus jujuba*), All

Evergreen

Paloverde (*Cercidium microphyllum*), V

Camphor-Tree (*Cinnamomum camphora*), CSs, V

Citrus (*Citrus* spp.), CSs, V

Cryptomeria (*Cryptomeria japonica*), Ce, CSe

China Fir (*Cunninghamia lanceolata*), CS

Leyland Cypress (*Cupressocyparis leylandii*), C, CS

Yuzuri-ha (*Daphniphyllum macropodum*), CS, V

Silver-Dollar Eucalyptus (*Eucalyptus cinerea*), CSs, V

Dahoon Holly (*Ilex cassine*), Ce, CSe

Nepal Holly, Mochi Noki (*Ilex integra*), CS, V

American Holly (*Ilex opaca*), Ce, CSe

Yaupon (*Ilex vomitoria*), All

Tabu-no-ki (*Machilus thunbergii*), CS, V

Banana Shrub (*Michelia figo*), CS, V

Japanese Silver-Tree (*Neolitsia sericea*), CS, V

European Olive (*Olea europaea*), CSsw, V

Red Bay (*Persea borbonia*), Ce, CSe

Spruce Pine (*Pinus glabra*), Ce, CSe

Mugo Pine (*Pinus mugo*), N

Japanese Black Pine (*Pinus thunbergia*), N, Cw, CSw

Ebony Ape's-Earring (*Pithecellobium flexicaule*), V

Japanese Yew (*Podocarpus macrophyllus*), C, CS, V

Cherry Laurel (*Prunus caroliniana*), All

Lime Prickly-Ash (*Zanthoxylum fagara*), CSs, V

"When people ask us what plants to use, we first ask whether they live in the city or in the more exposed suburbs. The variations in soils, temperatures, and exposure to drying winds make a tremendous difference. In the exposed area, we suggest they pick trees adapted to dryer Texas climates, such as bur oak and the West Texas oaks.
—Mike Ilse, landscape architect, Vernon G. Henry & Associates, Houston

TREES THAT CAST LIGHT SHADE

Trees are typically planted for the shade they cast, but sometimes just a little shade is plenty. Trees that don't cast heavy shade allow perennials, wildflowers, ferns, caladiums, and impatiens to flourish at their base. For more ideas, see the list of palms in the "Tropicals, Succulents, and Exotics" chapter.

Native Acacias (*Acacia* spp.), All
Red Buckeye (*Aesculus pavia*), C, CS
Devil's Walking Stick (*Aralia spinosa*), Ce, CSe
Texas Madrone (*Arbutus texana*), Cw, CSw
River Birch (*Betula nigra*), N, C, CS
Mexican Caesalpinia (*Caesalpinia mexicana*), V
Texas Paloverde (*Cercidium texanum*), CSs, V
Desert Willow (*Chilopsis linearis*), N, Cw, CSw, V
Brasil (*Condalia hookeri*), CSs, V
Honey Locust (*Gleditsia triacanthos 'inermis'*), N, Cw, CSnw

Goldenball Leadtree (*Leucaena retusa*), CSsw, V
Jerusalem Thorn, Retama (*Parkinsonia aculeata*), CSs, V
Mesquite (*Prosopis glandulosa*), C, CS, V
Screwbean Mesquite (*Prosopis pubescens*), CSw, V
Texas Palmetto (*Sabal texana*), CS, V
Western Soapberry (*Sapindus drummondii*), All
Eve's Necklace (*Sophora affinis*), All
Chisos Rosewood (*Vauquelinia angustifolia*), CSsw, V

TREES WITH ORNAMENTAL BERRIES OR SEEDPODS

Tree fruits (whether big like apples or small like holly berries) add a great deal of interest to the landscape. Typically these fruits appear in the fall and winter when we need something of interest to brighten the day. Hollies are a mainstay because the berries last so long. Eventually the color begins to fade in late winter and the cedar waxwings finish them off. Perhaps birds find holly berries toxic or not very tasty early in the season. People certainly should not eat them, because they induce vomiting.

Lots of folks worry about poisonous plants, and it is a concern, but few people die from plant toxins accidentally ingested. Kids and pets are a worry because they tend to put things in their mouths. Start your kids out right by discouraging the consumption of wild plants until they are old enough to identify edible plants. Keep the number of the area poison control center near the phone with other important numbers.

Red or Orange Fruit or Berries	Season	Region
Serviceberry (*Amelanchier arborea*)	summer	Ce, CSe
Flowering Dogwood (*Cornus florida*)	fall	Ce, CSe
Hawthorn (*Crataegus* spp.)	fall	C, CS
Asian Persimmon (*Diospyros kaki*)	fall	All
Deciduous Holly, Possamhaw (*Ilex decidua*)	winter	All
Large-Leaf Holly (*Ilex latifolia*)	winter	Ce, CSe
American Holly (*Ilex opaca*)	winter	Ce, CSe
Foster Holly (*Ilex* x *attenuata* 'fosteri')	winter	Ce
'Savannah' Holly (*Ilex* x *attenuata*)	winter	Ce, CSe
Yaupon (*Ilex vomitoria*)	winter	All
'Saratoga Gold,' 'Wiggins,' 'Sandy Hook' Yellow-Fruited Yaupon (*Ilex vomitoria*)	winter	All
Weeping Yaupon (*Ilex vomitoria* 'pendula')	winter	All
Flowering Crabapple (*Malus* hyb.)	fall	N, C
Carolina Buckthorn (*Rhamnus caroliniana*)	late summer	C, CS, V
Sumac (*Rhus* spp.)	fall	All

Interesting Cones or Seedpods

Amur Maple (*Acer ginnala*)	summer	N, C
Red Maple (*Acer rubrum 'drummondii'*)	spring	Ce, CSe
Red Buckeye (*Aesculus pavia*)	fall	C, CS
True Cedar (*Cedrus* spp.)	winter	N, C, CS
Flamegold Golden-Rain Tree (*Koelreuteria elegans*)	fall	V
Golden-Rain Tree (*Koelreuteria paniculata*)	fall	All
Evergreen Stone Oak (*Lithocarpus henryi*)	fall	C, CS
Southern Magnolia (*Magnolia grandiflora*)	fall	All
Pine (*Pinus* spp.)	fall	All
Bur Oak (*Quercus macrocarpa*)	fall	N, C, CS
Chinese Tallow Tree (*Sapium sebiferum*)	fall	CS
Mexican Buckeye (*Ungnadia speciosa*)	fall	All

TREES FOR WET SITES

Landscape situations that include wet areas are usually best if the drainage is corrected either with subsurface drain tiles or by filling in the low areas. However, wetlands or bog gardens are popular these days, so if you have the room to leave a wet area in the landscape, here are some trees to include.

Red Maple (*Acer rubrum 'drummondii'*), Ce, CSe
Tung-Oil Tree (*Aleurites fordii*), CS, V
False Indigo (*Amorpha fruticosa*), Ce, CSe
Devil's Walking-Stick (*Aralia spinosa*), Ce, CSe
River Birch (*Betula nigra*), N, C, CS
American Hornbeam, Ironwood (*Carpinus caroliniana*), Ce, CSe
Catalpa (*Catalpa bignonioides*), Ce, Cse
Sugar Hackberry (*Celtis laevigata*), All
Rough-Leaf Dogwood (*Cornus drummondii*), All
Mayhaw (*Crataegus aestivalis, C. opaca*), Ce, CSe
Parsley Hawthorn (*Crataegus marshallii*), Ce, CSe
Green Haw (*Crataegus viridis*), C, CS
Ti Ti, Leatherwood (*Cyrilla racemiflora*), Ce, CSe
Persimmon, male (*Diospyros virginiana*), Ce, CSe
Swamp Privet (*Forestiera acuminata*), CSe
Dahoon Holly (*Ilex cassine*), Ce, CSe
Deciduous Holly, Possumhaw (*Ilex decidua*), All
Tulip Poplar (*Liriodendron tulipfera*), Ce, CSe
Staggerbush (*Lyonia ferruginea*), CS, V
Southern Magnolia (*Magnolia grandiflora*), All
Sweet Bay Magnolia (*Magnolia virginiana*), Ce, CSe
Evergreen Sweet Bay (*Magnolia virginiana 'australis'*), Ce, Cse
Swamp Tupelo (*Nyssa aquatica*), Ce, CSe
Black Gum (*Nyssa sylvatica*), Ce, CSe
Red Bay (*Persea borbonia*), Ce, CSe

Mexican Sycamore (*Platanus mexicana*), C, CS, V
Sycamore (*Platanus occidentalis*), All
White Oak (*Quercus alba*), Ce, CSe
Laurel Oak (*Quercus laurifolia*), Ce, CSe
Overcup Oak (*Quercus lyrata*), Ce, CSe
Bur Oak (*Quercus macrocarpa*), N, C, CS
Swamp Chestnut Oak (*Quercus michauxii*), Ce, CSe
Nuttall Oak (*Quercus nuttallii*), Ce, CSe
Weeping Willow (*Salix babylonica*), N, C
Snowbell (*Styrax americana*), C, CS
Sweetleaf (*Symplocos tinctoria*), Ce, CSe
Bald Cypress (*Taxodium distichum*), All
Montezuma Cypress (*Taxodium mucronatum*), CSs, V
Water Elm (*Ulmus aquatica*), Ce, CSe
Farkleberry, Tree Huckleberry (*Vaccinium arboreum*), Ce, CSe
Rusty Blackhaw Viburnum (*Viburnum rufidulum*), C, CS

SWAMP TUPELO

TREES WITH BRANCHES PRIZED FOR ARRANGEMENTS

Branches cut from the trees in this list lend an artistry to indoor arrangement either because of their sculptural form or their interesting flowers, foliage, or fruit. What you put in an arrangement is limited only by your imagination, so consider the list below as a beginning. Cut branches from your favorite trees and see how they hold up.

Texas Madrone (*Arbutus texana*), Cw, CSw
Citrus (*Citrus* spp.), CSs, V
American Beech (*Fagus grandifolia*), Ce, CSe
American Holly (*Ilex opaca*), Ce, CSe
Golden-Rain Tree (*Koelreuteria* spp.), All
Sweet Gum (*Liquidambar styraciflua*), Ce, CSe
Southern Magnolia (*Magnolia grandiflora*), All
Oriental Magnolia (*Magnolia soulangiana* hyb.), All

Staghorn Sumac (*Rhus typhina*), All
Weeping Willow (*Salix babylonica*), N, C
Florist's Willow (*Salix caprea*), N, C
Dragon's-Claw Willow (*Salix matsudana 'tortuosa'*),
   N
Winged Elm (*Ulmus alata*), Ce, CSe
Lacebark Elm (*Ulmus parvifolia*), All

LONG-LIVING TREES YOUR GRANDCHILDREN WILL ENJOY

Who doesn't want to leave a legacy? Making your mark in business or as an educator may be an unachievable goal, but planting a tree is a piece of cake. You just have to plant the right one! No silver maples or Arizona ash trees, and you can hardly take much credit for planting a Chinese tallow or a chinaberry. The words majestic and oak just seem to go together, and for good reason. Most oak species tend to live for hundreds of years. Majestic may not seem to be an appropriate adjective to use with small trees, but some of them live a long time, too. Trees that live for a long time often grow slowly, with a few exceptions. Bald cypress starts out fast, but then it slows down and lives a long time. Another fairly fast-growing but long-living tree is the overcup oak.

BALD CYPRESS

   The following trees may give you a bit of gardening immortality.

Small to Medium Trees
Huisache (*Acacia farnesiana*), C, CS, V
Texas Madrone (*Arbutus texana*), Cw, CSw
La-Coma (*Bumelia celastrina*), CSs, V
Chittamwood (*Bumelia lanuginosa*), All
Brasil (*Condalia hookeri*), CSs, V
Texas Persimmon (*Diospyros texana*), All
Anaqua (*Ehretia anacua*), Cs, CS, V
Mexican Piñon (*Pinus cembroides*), CSw
Piñon (*Pinus edulis*), N, Cw, CSw
Texas Pistache (*Pistacia texana*), CSw, V
Texas Ebony (*Pithecellobium flexicaule*), V
Mesquite (*Prosopis glandulosa*), C, CS, V
Screwbean Mesquite (*Prosopis pubescens*), CSw, V
Western Soapberry (*Sapindus drummondii*), All
Eve's Necklace (*Sophora affinis*), All
Cedar Elm (*Ulmus crassifolia*), All

Large Trees
Pecan (*Carya illinoensis*), All
Hickory (*Carya* spp.), All
Nogalito (*Juglans microcarpa*), N, C, CS
Southern Magnolia (*Magnolia grandiflora*), All
White Oak (*Quercus alba*), Ce, CSe
Escarpment Live Oak (*Quercus fusiformis*), All
Lacey Oak (*Quercus glaucoides*), C, CS, V
Overcup Oak (*Quercus lyrata*), C, CS
Bur Oak (*Quercus macrocarpa*), N, C, CS
Swamp Chestnut Oak (*Quercus michauxii*), Ce, CSe
Chinkapin Oak (*Quercus muehlenbergii*), N, C, CS
Durand Oak (*Quercus sinuata*), C, CS
Live Oak (*Quercus virginiana*), All
Bald Cypress (*Taxodium distichum*), All
Montezuma Bald Cypress (*Taxodium mucronatum*),
   CSs, V

TREES WITH WEAK WOOD OR STRUCTURAL PROBLEMS

In spite of the fact that these trees may have weak limbs that break under certain circumstances, many of them—like river birch, pecan, and green ash—have redeeming qualities. In some areas of west Texas they may be the only trees you can grow.

Use Only as a Last Resort
Box Elder (*Acer negundo*), All
Silver Maple (*Acer saccharinum*), N, C
Tree-of-Heaven (*Ailanthus altissima*), N
Paper Mulberry (*Broussonetia papyrifera*), N, Cw, CSw

Chinaberry (*Melia azedarach*), C, CS, V
White Poplar (*Populus alba*), N, C
Cottonwood (*Populus deltoides*), All
Siberian Elm (*Ulmus pumila*), N, C, CS

Good Trees That Could Break in Severe Storm
River Birch (*Betula nigra*), N, C, CS
Pecan (*Carya illinoinensis*), All
Hackberry (*Celtis occidentalis*), All
Leyland Cypress (*Cupressocyparis leylandii*), C, CS
Green Ash (*Fraxinus pennsylvanica*), N, C, CS

Golden-Rain Tree (*Koelreuteria paniculata*), All
Tulip Poplar (*Liriodendron tulipifera*), Ce, CSe
Pine (*Pinus* spp.), All
'Bradford' Pear (*Pyrus calleryana*), N, C
Water Oak (*Quercus nigra*), Ce, CSe
Chinese Elm (*Ulmus parvifolia*), All

TREES WITH SHOWY BARK

One of the most spectacular new trees with interesting bark color is the Japanese crape myrtle (*Lagerstroemia fauriei*). A number of hybrids between this species and the standard crape myrtle (*Lagerstroemia indica*) have been developed. The bark on these trees can be cinnamon red, with contrasting patches of light brown.

Several Texas natives, such as Texas madrone (*Arbutus texana*), have beautiful bark. Too bad it's been so difficult to transplant, even in the Hill Country where it is adapted. Flatwoods plum (*Prunus umbellata*) has shiny, burgundy-red bark, and the peeling bark of the Mexican plum is pretty spectacular as well. Western soapberry (*Sapindus drummondii*) develops an exfoliating bark as it ages.

Texas Madrone (*Arbutus texana*), Cw, CSw
River Birch (*Betula nigra*), N, C, CS
European Birch (*Betula pendula*), N
Shagbark Hickory (*Carya ovata*), Ce, CSe
Chinese Fringe Tree (*Chionanthus retusus*), C, CS
Hawthorn (*Crataegus* spp.), C, CS
Chinese Quince (*Cydonia sinensis*), N, C, CS
Texas Persimmon (*Diospyros texana*), All
American Beech (*Fagus grandifolia*), Ce, CSe
Franklin Tree (*Franklinia altamaha*), Ce, CSe
Crape Myrtle (*Lagerstroemia indica*, *L.* x *fauriei*), All

Cucumber Magnolia (*Magnolia acuminata*), Ce, CSe
Sourwood (*Oxydendrom arboreum*), Ce
Chinese Pistache (*Pistacia chinensis*), All
Sycamore (*Platanus occidentalis*), All
Mexican Plum (*Prunus mexicana*), All
Flatwoods Plum (*Prunus umbellata*), Ce, CSe
White Oak (*Quercus alba*), Ce, CSe
Swamp Chestnut Oak (*Quercus michauxii*), Ce, CSe
Western Soapberry (*Sapindus drummondii*), All
Lacebark Elm, Chinese Elm (*Ulmus parvifolia*), All

"Trees are like big dogs; they need plenty of room in order to be happy. Remember, trees take up most of their water at the dripline. So consider the planting location in relation to other plants and structures, not just climate, when selecting a species of tree for your landscape."
—**Carol Cammack, County Extension horticulturist, Houston**

WEEPING TREES

The trees on this list have graceful, pendulous limbs that often reach to the ground. They are eye-catching, powerful forms in the landscape to be used as specimens or accents. Occasionally, the evergreens such as weeping yaupon may be used as a departure from the ordinary for a light screen. You will find weeping forms of many upright trees, not just the ones below. Generally they are specialty items, but the ones below are among the most common and will be the easiest to find.

'Jacmonti' European Birch (*Betula pendula*), N
Weeping Yaupon (*Ilex vomitoria* 'pendula'), All
Weeping Juniper (*Juniperus flaccida*), N, Cw, CSw
'Jade' Weeping Crabapple (*Malus sylvestris*), N, C
'Chaparral' Weeping Mulberry (*Morus alba*), N, C
Mesquite (*Prosopis glandulosa*), C, CS, V
Weeping Willow (*Salix babylonica*), N, C

EUROPEAN
BIRCH

FAST-GROWING TREES THAT AREN'T TOTAL LOSERS

Most fast-growing trees are short lived, weak wooded, insect and disease prone, and just plain ugly. Sometimes the only good thing you can say about them is "they are easy to transplant." In fact, they would probably grow in the ditch if they fell off a truck on the way to your landscape. Then why do so many people want fast-growing trees? Many people are in a hurry, desperate for shade, or impatient. Most fast-growing trees aren't worth planting, but the following trees deserve consideration.

Red Maple (*Acer rubrum 'drummondii'*), Ce, CSe

Desert Willow (*Chilopsis linearis*), N, Cw, CSw, V

Chitalpa (*Chitalpa tashkentensis*), All

Leyland Cypress (*Cupressocyparis leylandii*), C, CS

Chinese Parasol Tree (*Firmiana simplex*), C, CS, V

Green Ash, male (*Fraxinus pennsylvanica*), N, C, CS

Japanese Crape Myrtle (*Lagerstroemia fauriei*), CSs, V

Hybrid Crape Myrtle (*Lagerstroemia fauriei* hyb.), C, CS, V

Dawn Redwood (*Metasequoia glyptostroboides*), Ce, CSe

Empress Tree (*Paulownia tomentosa*), N, C

Mexican Sycamore (*Platanus mexicana*), C, CS, V

Cherry Laurel (*Prunus caroliniana*), All

Overcup Oak (*Quercus lyrata*), C, CS

Monterrey Oak (*Quercus polymorpha*), CS, V

Bald Cypress (*Taxodium distichum*), All

Pond Cypress (*Taxodium distichum 'nutans'*, *T. ascendens*), All

Montezuma Bald Cypress (*Taxodium mucronatum*), CSs, V

"Before planting any tree, consider what it will become in the next fifteen years," advises Alan D. Dreesen, a County Extension forestry specialist in Conroe. "Will it have surface roots and cause problems in the landscape? How extensive is the root system; how close can you come to a tree during construction and not damage it? After you've transplanted the perfect tree, be careful not to kill it with excess fill dirt or with root-cutting excavations for underground utilities, sprinkler systems, and forms for walkways. If you plant in the right spot and use the right planting techniques, plus follow up with good post-planting care, a tree can add significant aesthetic and economic value to your landscape."

TREES FOR THE SOUTH PLAINS

David Morgan, editor of *Nursery Management & Production* magazine, and formerly an associate professor of horticulture at Texas Tech, put together this list of trees for the South Plains (south of Plainview). "It is commonly believed that there are no trees native to Lubbock County," he notes, "and that's probably a fair assumption, though some historians will argue that the old hackberries found along the breaks and ravines are progeny of plantings by pre-Columbian Native Americans. So I guess that makes hackberries native trees. But it's still an odd thought as you look over the Texas Tech campus and appreciate the canopy of green that shades the grounds."

One spring, David and two Texas Tech graduate students, Ann Hild and Marvin Hatter, documented 103 woody plant species on campus and another fifty at the nearby arboretum. "Some of them, like the Siberian elm (*Ulmus pumila*) and the fruitless white mulberry (*Morus alba*), were planted out of desperation by settlers who believed what they had been told: In Lubbock you grow cotton, so be thankful for the shadeless sky. But the fact that we were able to introduce so many species should tell us that we had not made the best selections, and there was work to be done." David also points out that fruit trees grow in the South Plains. "You will see occasional orchards of pecans, peaches, apples, and apricots, though hail takes out crops about one out of every three years. The limiting factors to tree survival in the South Plains are drying winds and sudden temperature extremes. Crape myrtles and maples thrive much farther north, but often do not survive in Lubbock."

Pecan (*Carya illinoinensis*)

'Pawnee,' 'Caddo,' 'Shoshoni,' 'Maramec,' 'Osage' varieties

Texas Redbud (*Cercis canadensis 'texensis'*)

native; magenta color in early spring

Mexican Redbud (*Cercis canadensis 'mexicana'*)

native to extreme Southwest Texas

Eastern Redbud (*Cercis canadensis*)	native to East Texas
Desert Willow (*Chilopsis linearis*)	large white to burgundy flowers
Chitalpa (*Chitalpa tashkentensis*)	a cross of *Chilopsis* x *Catalpa*
Honeylocust (*Gleditsia triacanthos*)	select only thornless, fruitless cultivars
Nogalito or River Walnut (*Juglans microcarpa*)	native of the Hill Country
Eastern Red Cedar (*Juniperus virginiana*)	'Canaertii,' 'Keteleeri'
Golden-Rain Tree (*Koelreuteria paniculata*)	yellow spring flowers; fall fruit
Crape Myrtle (*Lagerstroemia indica*)	some cultivars may freeze
Crabapple (*Malus* spp.)	drought hardy; spring flowers
Pinyon Pine (*Pinus cembroides* var. *edulis*)	compact, small
Remote Pinyon Pine (*Pinus cembroides* 'remota')	grows in the Edwards Plateau
Afghan Pine (*Pinus eldarica*)	desert species
Austrian Pine (*Pinus nigra*)	some good specimens
Chinese Pistache (*Pistacia chinensis*)	lovely reddish to yellow fall color; fast growing
Mesquite (*Prosopis glandulosa*)	for dry sites; flowers, thorns, seed pods
Flowering Peach, Plum, Apricot (*Prunus* spp.)	spring flowers
Mexican Plum (*Prunus mexicana*)	native to Central and East Texas
Callery Pear (*Pyrus calleryana*)	'Aristocrat,' 'Capital'
Prairie Crabapple (*Pyrus ioensis* 'texana')	'Blanco'
Plateau, Hill Country Live Oak (*Quercus fusiformis*)	native, hardy
Bur Oak (*Quercus macrocarpa*)	tough, stately; resistant to oak wilt
Blackjack Oak (*Quercus marilandica*)	stately, xeric form from Central Texas
Chinkapin Oak (*Quercus muhlenbergii*)	native to river bottoms; not for xeriscapes
Texas Red Oak (*Quercus texana*)	tough, stately; red to crimson fall foliage
Western Soapberry (*Sapindus drummondii*)	native, tough; yellowish fall color
Bald Cypress (*Taxodium distichum*)	for wet, well-watered sites
American Elm (*Ulmus americana*)	grow a Texas native
Cedar Elm (*Ulmus crassifolia*)	hardy; yellow fall color
Chinese Lacebark Elm (*Ulmus parvifolia*)	pinkish bark; drought tolerant
Rusty Blackhaw (*Viburnum rufidulum*)	native to Central and East Texas; white flowers
Chaste Tree (*Vitex agnus-castus*)	aromatic; lavender or white flowers
Zelkova (*Zelkova serrata*)	stately shade tree; yellow fall foliage color
Jujube (*Ziziphus jujuba*)	plant three or more for good show

David Morgan, editor of *Nursery Management & Production* magazine and a former associate professor of horticulture at Texas Tech in Lubbock, says that several native Texas or Mexican oaks brought into production by Lone Star Growers have done very well in the South Plains. "Of particular interest are the Sierra oak (*Quercus canbyi* or *Quercus graciliformis*), *Quercus polymorpha*, *Quercus rhysophylla*, and the Texas Hill Country's lacey oak (*Quercus laceyi*), a straight-trunked tree of exceptional landscape appearance."

He also notes, "Many junipers thrive in the South Plains, and native species should be introduced, such as Ashe juniper (*Juniperus ashei*), alligator juniper (*Juniperus deppeana*), one-seed juniper (*Juniperus monosperma*), Pinchot juniper (*Juniperus pinchotii*), and Rocky Mountain juniper (*Juniperus scopulorum*)."

TREES THAT RESEED EVERYWHERE

In South Texas, gardeners know that you don't have to plant a Chinese tallow tree in your yard; sooner or later a bird will do it for you. The same is true for a number of tree species, and we can't blame birds for all of the seedlings. Some seeds are carried on the wind; others wash along with the rain. The trees in this list aren't all bad—they just reseed heavily.

Although most trees have male and female flowers in the same tree or within the same flower, in some cases there are gender preferences. Ash trees, for example, come in male and female forms. Botanists call them dioecious plants because the male and female flowers develop on separate plants. Other dioecious trees include cottonwood, willow, mulberry, pistache, and holly. In the case of hollies, we want the female trees with their beautiful berries, but most other dioecious species are best in the male form because they don't produce seed. This list of dioecious species indicates if only the female form reseeds heavily.

Box elder (*Acer negundo*), N, C, CSn
Mimosa (*Albizia julibrissin*), All
Hackberry (*Celtis* spp.), All
Persimmon, female (*Diospyros virginiana*), Ce, CSe
Ash, female (*Fraxinus* spp.), All
Golden-Rain Tree (*Koelreuteria* spp.), All

Sweetgum (*Liquidambar styraciflua*), Ce, CSe
Chinese Pistache, female (*Pistacia chinensis*), All
Cottonwood, female (*Populus deltoides*), All
Willow, female (*Salix* spp.), All
Chinese Tallow Tree (*Sapium sebiferum*), CSe
Elm (*Ulmus* spp.), All

TREES WITH CHARACTER

Some gardeners will call these trees ugly; others may note that they show their age. A few of these trees become that way because they have inherently weak branches, while others such as the hackberry harbor gall insects. Some just have an awkward growth habit.

Sometimes trees from the drier climates of West Texas grow with a different characteristic than in high-rainfall areas like Houston. The Texas pistache is a classic example of a tree that grows rank and unruly in high-rainfall areas.

Huisache (*Acacia farnesiana*), C, CS, V
Hackberry (*Celtis occidentalis*), All
Russian Olive (*Elaeagnus angustifolius*), N
Fireman's-Hat (*Erythrina crista-galli*), CSs, V
Silver-Dollar Eucalyptus (*Eucalyptus cinerea*), CSs, V
Ginkgo (*Ginkgo biloba*), Ce, CSe
Honey Locust (*Gleditsia triacanthos*), N, Cw, CSnw
Chinese Witch Hazel (*Hamamelis mollis*), Ce, CSe
Cedar (*Juniperus* spp.), All
Mulberry (*Morus* spp.), All

Jerusalem Thorn, Retama (*Parkinsonia aculeata*), CSs, V
Paulownia (*Paulownia tomentosa*), N, C
Piñon Pine (*Pinus cembroides*), CSw
Spruce Pine (*Pinus glabra*), Ce, CSe
Longleaf Pine (*Pinus palustris*), Ce, CSe
Virginia Pine (*Pinus virginiana*), Ce, CSe
Chinese Pistache, female (*Pistacia chinensis*), All
Texas Pistache (*Pistacia texana*), CSw, V
Mesquite (*Prosopis glandulosa*), C, CS, V

Peter Loos, owner of Ecovirons Nursery in Conroe, stresses using native plants in Texas gardens. "Utilizing native plants not only helps preserve the surrounding natural heritage, but natives tend to require less attention and maintenance. They're an important factor in the natural plant diversity that encourages a better balance in nature." Peter's love for native plants came out in several of the plant lists he reviewed. "I wouldn't mention tallow at all; environmental concerns outweigh any ornamental benefits." About Bradford pear, Peter noted: "Overused and people seem to ignore its pest problems." We agree with Peter, but like the imported fire ant, these imported plants aren't going away.

TREES WITH INCONVENIENT LITTER

Anyone who has ever walked barefoot over sweetgum balls will think twice about planting one in their next landscape. But we certainly wouldn't want to give up magnolias just because they have big leaves. Oaks have redeeming qualities, as do river birch, sycamore and Mexican buckeye. If the following faults don't pose a problem in your estimation, then incorporate these trees into your design plan. Remember to keep them away from swimming pools or walkways where the mess will be significant.

Big Leaves Hard to Rake
Catalpa (*Catalpa bignonioides*), Ce, CSe
Chinese Parasol-Tree (*Firmiana simplex*), C, CS, V
Magnolia (*Magnolia* spp.), All
Empress Tree (*Paulownia tomentosa*), N, C
Sycamore (*Platanus occidentalis*), All
Blackjack Oak (*Quercus marilandica*), C, CS

Narrow Leaves Quick to Clog Gutters
Willow Oak (*Quercus phellos*), Ce, CSe

Drop Twigs
Mimosa (*Albizia julibrissin*), All
River Birch (*Betula nigra*), N, C, CS
Pecan (*Carya illinoinensis*), All
Sugar Hackberry (*Celtis laevigata*), All
White Poplar (*Populus alba*), N, C
Water Oak (*Quercus nigra*), Ce, CSe
Willow Oak (*Quercus phellos*), Ce, CSe
Weeping Willow (*Salix babylonica*), N, C

Seeds and Pods Hard to Walk Over
Hickory (*Carya* spp.), All
Pecan (*Carya* spp.), All
Honey Locust (*Gleditsia triacanthos*), N, Cw, CSnw
Kentucky Coffee Tree (*Gymnocladus dioica*), N, C

Black Walnut (*Juglans nigra*), N, C, CS
Sweet Gum (*Liquidambar styraciflua*), Ce, CSe
Osage Orange, female (*Maclura pomifera*), All
Empress Tree (*Paulownia tomentosa*), N, C
Pine (*Pinus* spp.), All
Sycamore (*Platanus occidentalis*), All
Bur Oak (*Quercus macrocarpa*), N, C, CS
Black Locust (*Robinia pseudoacacia*), N, C,CS
Mexican Buckeye (*Ungnadia speciosa*), All

Messy Fruit and Seed Drop
Persimmon, female (*Diospyros virginiana*), Ce, CSe
Ash, female (*Fraxinus* spp.), All
Ginkgo, female (*Ginkgo biloba*), N, Ce, CSe
Flowering Crabapple (*Malus* hyb.), N, C
Chinaberry (*Melia azedarach*), C, CS, V
Mulberry (*Morus rubra*), All
Cottonwood (*Populus deltoides*), All
Mexican Plum (*Prunus mexicana*), All
Chinese Tallow Tree (*Sapium sebiferum*), CS

BLACKJACK OAK

A SAMPLER OF TREES BY FLOWER COLOR

Flowering trees make a dramatic statement in the landscape. Maybe it is because of their stature. But for whatever reason, they can't be ignored, nor should they be left out. The following categories may seem contradictory in that a number of trees appear in different lists, but many of these trees come with different flower colors.

White	Bloom season	Region
Anacacho Orchid Tree (*Bauhinia congesta/lunaroides*)	spring	CSs, V
Brazilian Orchid Tree (*Bauhinia forficata*)	spring/summer	CSs, V
White Bud (*Cercis canadensis*)	early spring	All
Chinese Fringe Tree (*Chionanthus retusus*)	late spring	C, CS
Fringe Tree (*Chionanthus virginicus*)	late spring	Ce, CSe
Flowering Dogwood (*Cornus florida*)	midspring	Ce, CSe
Native Hawthorn (*Crataegus* spp.)	spring	C, CS
Loblolly Bay (*Gordonia lasianthus*)	all summer to early fall	Ce, CSe
Two-Winged Silverbell (*Halesia diptera*)	late spring	Ce, CSe
Crape Myrtle (*Lagerstroemia indica*)	summer to early fall	All
Ashe Magnolia (*Magnolia ashei*)	all summer	Ce
Southern Magnolia (*Magnolia grandiflora*)	all summer to early fall	All
Oriental Magnolia (*Magnolia soulangiana* hyb.)	late winter/early spring	All
Star Magnolia (*Magnolia stellata*)	early spring	Ce, CSe
Sweet Bay Magnolia (*Magnolia virginiana*)	all summer to early fall	Ce, CSe
Sargent Crabapple (*Malus sargentii*)	early spring	N, C
Callery Pear (*Pyrus calleryana*)	early spring	All
Sinojackia (*Sinojackia rehderana*)	late summer	CS, V
Japanese Pagoda-Tree (*Sophora japonica*)	late summer	N

Wild Stewartia (*Stewartia malacodendron*)	spring	Ce, CSe
Japanese Snowbell (*Styrax japonica*)	summer	C, CS

Blue, Violet, or Lavender

Native Smoke-Tree (*Cotinus obovatus*)	all summer	Cw, CSw
Crape Myrtle (*Lagerstroemia indica*)	summer to early fall	All
Oriental Magnolia (*Magnolia soulangiana* hyb.)	late winter/early spring	All
Texas Mountain Laurel (*Sophora secundiflora*)	late summer	C, CS, V
Chaste Tree (*Vitex agnus-castus*)	summer	All

Yellow

Huisache (*Acacia farnesiana*)	spring	C, CS, V
Mexican Poinciana (*Caesalpinia mexicana*)	all	V, Annual
Pride-of-Barbados (*Caesalpinia pulcherrima*)	summer/fall	CSs, V, Annual
Senna (*Cassia corymbosa*)	summer	CS, V
Shower Tree (*Cassia splendida*)	fall	CS, V
Chinese Golden-Rain Tree (*Koelreuteria bipinnata*)	late summer/early fall	CS, V
Flamegold Golden-Rain Tree (*Koelreuteria elegans*)	midsummer	V
Golden-Rain Tree (*Koelreuteria paniculata*)	midsummer	All
Jerusalem Thorn, Retama (*Parkinsonia aculeata*)	late spring	CSs, V

Pink

Orchid Tree (*Bauhinia purpurea*)	summer/fall	V
Redbud (*Cercis*)spp.	early spring	All
Flowering Dogwood (*Cornus florida*)	midspring	Ce, CSe
Native Smoke-Tree (*Cotinus obovatus*)	spring	Cw, CSw
Chinese Quince (*Cydonia sinensis*)	midspring	N, C, CS
Crape Myrtle (*Lagerstroemia indica*)	summer to early fall	All
Oriental Magnolia (*Magnolia soulangiana* hyb.)	early spring	All
Flowering Crabapple (*Malus* hyb.)	spring	N, C
Persian Parrotia (*Parrotia persica*)	spring	All
Taiwan Cherry (*Prunus campanulata*)	late winter/early spring	CS
Flowering Peach (*Prunus persica*)	early spring	All
Eve's Necklace (*Sophora affinis*)	spring	All
Salt Cedar (*Tamarix* spp.)	midspring	All

Red/Purple

Red Maple (*Acer rubrum 'drummondii'*)	late winter	Ce, CSe
Red Buckeye (*Aesculus pavia*)	late spring	C, CS
Pata-de-Vaca (*Bauhinia macranthera*)	summer/fall	CSs, V
Red Bauhinia (*Bauhinia punctata*)	summer/fall	CSs, V
Purple Orchid Tree (*Bauhinia purpurea*)	summer/fall	V
Bottlebrush (*Callistemon rigidus*)	summer to fall	CSs, V
Crape Myrtle (*Lagerstroemia indica*)	summer to early fall	All
Flowering Crabapple (*Malus* hyb.)	spring	N, C

A SAMPLER OF TREES BY THEIR FALL COLOR

Fall color is a rare commodity in most areas of Texas. The northeastern part of the state sometimes puts on a spectacular show, and the lost maples (*Acer grandidentatum*) and escarpment black cherries (*Prunus serotina 'eximia'*) can be beautiful in the Hill Country. Sometimes, though, we have warm weather right up to the first hard freeze, so many trees don't get the signal to develop fall color.

Yellow or Gold

Japanese Maple (*Acer palmatum*), Ce, CSe
Red Maple, yellow form (*Acer rubrum 'drummondii'*), Ce, Cse
Southern Sugar Maple (*Acer saccharum, A. barbatum*), Ce, CSe
Pawpaw (*Asimina triloba*), Ce, CSe
Pecan and Hickory (*Carya* spp.), All
Eastern Redbud (*Cercis candensis*), All
Chinese Fringe Tree (*Chionanthus retusus*), C, CS
Ginkgo (*Ginkgo biloba*), N, Ce, CSe
Little-Nut Walnut (*Juglans microcarpa*), N, C, CS
Black Walnut (*Juglans nigra*), N, C, CS
Crape Myrtle (*Lagerstroemia* x *hybrida*), All
Sweet Gum (*Liquidambar styraciflua*), Ce, CSe
Escarpment Black Cherry (*Prunus serotina 'eximia'*), All
Western Soapberry (*Sapindus drummondii*), All
Chinese Tallow (*Sapium sebiferum*), CSe
Cedar Elm (*Ulmus crassifolia*), All

Orange

Trident Maple (*Acer buergeranum*), C, CS
Lost Maple, Big-Tooth Maple (*Acer grandidentatum*), N, C, CS
Chalk Maple (*Acer leucoderme*), Ce, CSe
American Hornbeam, Ironwood (*Carpinus caroliniana*), Ce, CSe
Crape Myrtle (*Lagerstroemia indica*), All
Chinese Pistache (*Pistacia chinensis*), All
Chinese Tallow (*Sapium sebiferum*), CSe
Sassafras (*Sassafras albidum*), Ce, CSe

Red

Japanese Maple (*Acer palmatum*), Ce, CSe
Red Maple (*Acer rubrum 'drummondii'*), Ce, CSe
Flowering Dogwood (*Cornus florida*), Ce, CSe
Swamp Tupelo (*Nyssa aquatica*), Ce, CSe
Black Gum (*Nyssa sylvatica*), Ce, CSe
Chinese Pistache (*Pistacia chinensis*), All
Callery Pear (*Pyrus calleryana*), All
Shining Sumac (*Rhus copallina*), Ce, CSe
Staghorn Sumac (*Rhus typhina*), All
Chinese Tallow (*Sapium sebiferum*), CSe

Bronze

Japanese Maple (*Acer palmatum*), Ce, CSe
Chinese Chestnut (*Castanea mollissima*), N, C, CS
American Beech (*Fagus grandifolia*), Ce, CSe
Crape Myrtle (*Lagerstroemia indica* and hyb.), All
Dawn Redwood (*Metasequoia glyptostroboides*), Ce, CSe
White Oak (*Quercus alba*), Ce, CSe
Swamp Chestnut Oak (*Quercus michauxii*), Ce, CSe
Bald Cypress (*Taxodium distichum*), All

Rust, Maroon, and Burgundy

Japanese Maple (*Acer palmatum*), Ce, CSe
Flowering Dogwood (*Cornus florida*), Ce, CSe
Asian Persimmon (*Diospyros kaki*), All
American Persimmon (*Diospyros virginiana*), All
Sweetgum (*Liquidambar styraciflua*), Ce, CSe
Black Gum (*Nyssa sylvatica*), Ce, CSe
White Oak (*Quercus alba*), Ce, CSe
Rusty Blackhaw Viburnum (*Viburnum rufidulum*), C, CS

VINES

Vines are to a landscape what icing is to a cake. They add interest, and they are just plain fun. Sometimes we use them to hide an ugly chain-link fence, but even better, we can use them as an excuse to build an arbor or a trellis to showcase a vine. Annual vines can grow on most any trellis, but for perennial vines like wisteria or climbing roses, you will need something substantial. Rough cedar logs make a rustic arbor, or you can opt for treated 4 by 4s.

Vines come in many forms—annuals, perennials, woody vines, attack vines that can cover the house in a single season. Most have beautiful flowers. Some are worth growing for their foliage. A few, such as grapes, even produce fruit. Best of all, they bring these features to eye level and higher. Avid gardeners soon realize that no garden is large enough, so employing vertical space not only makes for an interesting landscape, but it allows us to grow more species.

Most home owners see vines as a potential nuisance on one hand and a mystery on the other. Everyone knows that Japanese honeysuckle can take over the landscape, yet there are lots of mystery vines—Rangoon creeper, garlic vine, sandpaper vine, and more—that gardeners aren't quite sure about. They're great fun. Do a little research and give them a try.

Basic Requirements

- Vines are no different from other landscape plants in that they like good soil preparation with lots of organic matter. Work 6 to 8 inches of compost into the bed before planting, and then jump back. Most vines are extremely vigorous.
- Make sure you have an adequate support. A few bamboo canes or a willow trellis will work for sweet peas, but for wisteria you'll need 6-inch posts or a structure that involves welding.
- Some vines climb by twining, others by tendrils or clinging. You will need to know which so you can provide the necessary support. Big poles work fine for twiners, but vines with tendrils will need plastic mesh, a section of chain-link fence, or small bamboo canes to wrap their tendrils around.
- You will also need a sharp set of pruning shears, loppers, and maybe even a pruning saw. Vines need renewal pruning every year during the dormant season, and some gardeners like to do a bit of snipping all summer long.

EASY VINES FOR A MAILBOX OR FENCE POST

The vines in this list tend to be less vigorous than others, so they work on short structures like a mailbox pole or fence post. Clematis is perhaps the perfect vine for this use, but even the honeysuckle can be kept in bounds with a little shearing.

Allamanda (*Allamanda cathartica*), Tropical
Climbing Aster (*Aster carolinianus*), C, CS
Cross Vine (*Bignonia capreolata*), C, CS
Henryi Clematis (*Clematis henryi*), N, C, CS
Scarlet Clematis (*Clematis texensis*), All
Hybrid Clematis (*Clematis x hybrida*), N, C, CS

Carolina Jessamine (*Gelsemium sempervirens*), C, CS, V
Goldflame Honeysuckle (*Lonicera heckrottii*), All
Trumpet Honeysuckle (*Lonicera sempervirens*), All

CAROLINA
JESSAMINE

Japanese Climbing Fern (*Lygodium japonicum*), C, CS, V

Chilean Jasmine (*Mandevilla laxa*), Tropical

Dipladenia (*Mandevilla splendens*), Tropical

Pink Mandevilla (*Mandevilla x amabilis*), Tropical

Blue Crown Passion Vine (*Passiflora caerulea*), CS, V

Maypop (*Passiflora incarnata*), All

Stephanotis (*Stephanotis floribunda*), Tropical

TROPICAL AND SEMI-TROPICAL VINES FOR COLOR

Most Texas gardeners should think of the plants in this list as annual vines, or vines to grow in a container and protect in the greenhouse during the winter. Even in the lower Rio Grande Valley, some of these vines can be frozen out in a hard winter. Fortunately they all get off to a quick start in the spring. Whether you're starting with a new plant from the nursery or a half-dead one you've overwintered, the Texas summer will soon breathe new life into these vines.

Vines marked with an asterisk (*) are extremely cold sensitive.

Allamanda (*Allamanda cathartica*)

Madeira Vine (*Anredera cordifolia*)

Coral Vine (*Antigonon leptopus*)

Araujia (*Araujia sericofera*)

Wooly Morning-Glory (*Argeryia nirvosa*)*

Orchid Vine (*Bauhinia yunnanensis*)

Bougainvillea (*Bougainvillea spectabalis*)*

Bleeding-Heart Vine (*Clerodendron thomsoniae*)*

Lavender Trumpet Vine, Argentine (*Clytostoma callistegioides*)

Garlic Vine (*Cydista aequinoctialis* [*Pseudocalymma alliacea*])

Winged Beauty (*Dalechampia dioscoraefolia*)

Angel-Wing Jasmine (*Jasminum nitidum*)*

Pink Jasmine (*Jasminum polyanthum*)*

Hyacinth Bean (*Lablab purpurea* [*Dolichos lablab*])

Chilean Jasmine (*Mandevilla laxa*)

Mandevilla, Dipladenia (*Mandevilla splendens*)*

Pink Mandevilla (*Mandevilla x amabilis*)

Bower Vine (*Pandorea jasminoides*)

Snail-flower Vine (*Phaseolus caracalla*)

Raspberry Vine (*Podranea ricasoliana*)

Rangoon Creeper (*Quisqualis indica*)

Mexican Flame Vine (*Senecio confusus*)

Stephanotis (*Stephanotis floribunda*)*

Butterfly Vine (*Stigmaphyllon ciliatum*)

Purple Thunbergia (*Thunbergia battiscombei*)

Cape Honeysuckle (*Tecomaria capensis*)

Corkscrew Flower (*Vigna caracalla*)

"Gardeners in the Rio Grande Valley often forget we really aren't in the tropics. They plant mandevilla, allamanda, and other tropicals thinking we won't have another freeze like we had in '83 or '89. They even plant ficus trees in the yard. Someday they are going to freeze out. We encourage people to plant in large pots so they can bring the plants in if a hard freeze makes its way this far south. Native plants have potential, but most of the ones in this area have thorns and people are reluctant to plant them."
—Don Giffen and Ann Campbell, Grimsell Seed Company, Harlingen

HARDY EVERGREEN VINES

Evergreen is a relative term. Even in the semi-tropical Texas zones, evergreen plants don't always look their best. Usually in late winter they have lost a few leaves, and the foliage may have turned purplish as with cross vine (*Bignonia capreolata*). Farther north they may lose all their leaves. The hardy evergreen plants in this list can be used to cover a trellis or chain-link fence to provide a year-round screen.

Cross Vine (*Bignonia capreolata*), C, CS

Armand Clematis (*Clematis armandii*), N, C, CS

Wintercreeper (*Euonymus fortunei*), N, C

Creeping Fig (*Ficus pumila*), CS, V

Carolina Jessamine (*Gelsemium sempervirens*), C, CS, V

Algerian Ivy (*Hedera canariensis*), CS, V

Persian Ivy (*Hedera colchica*), C, CS, V

English Ivy (*Hedera helix*), All

Variegated Kadsura (*Kadsura japonica* 'variegata'), C, CS, V

Goldflame Honeysuckle (*Lonicera heckrottii*), All

Evergreen Wisteria (*Millettia reticulata*), CS, V

Blue Crown Passion Vine (*Passiflora caerulea*), CS, V

Cherokee Rose (*Rosa laevigata*), C, CS, V

Catbrier (*Smilax glauca*), C, CS, V

Stauntonia Vine (*Stauntonia hexaphylla*), CSs, V
Asian Jasmine (*Trachelospermum asiaticum*), C, CS, V

Confederate Jasmine (*Trachelospermum jasminoides*), CS, V

VINES WITH FRAGRANT FLOWERS

Fragrance is such a subtle, fleeting feature in the landscape. Anything we can do to bring it into play should be encouraged. Because vines can be encouraged to grow around a window or to cover an arbor, they can be directed to concentrate their fragrance where it will be most appreciated. See the rose chapter for climbing roses. Not all roses have fragrance, but many do.

White Flowers
Armand Clematis (*Clematis armandii*), N, C, CS
Sweet Autumn Clematis (*Clematis maximowicziana*), N, C, CS
Moonflower (*Ipomoea alba*), Annual
Angel-Wing Jasmine (*Jasminum nitidum*), V, Tropical
Poet's Jasmine (*Jasminum officinale*), CSs, V
Pink Jasmine (*Jasminum polyanthum*), Tropical
Hall's Japanese Honeysuckle (*Lonicera japonica 'halliana'*), All
Chilean Jasmine (*Mandevilla laxa*), Tropical
Silver Lace Vine (*Polygonum aubertii*), N, C
White Lady Banks Rose (*Rosa banksiae 'alba plena'*), CS, V
Stephanotis (*Stephanotis floribunda*), Tropical
Confederate Jasmine (*Trachelospermum jasminoides*), CS, V

Purple Flowers
Five-Leaf Akebia (*Akebia quinata*), C, CS, V
'Incense' Passion Vine (*Passiflora incarnata* x *cincinnata*), CS, V
Japanese Wisteria (*Wisteria floribunda*), N, C
American Wisteria (*Wisteria frutescens*), C, CS

Yellow Flowers
Chalice Vine (*Solandra maxima*), Tropical

Red Flowers
Rangoon Creeper (*Quisqualis indica*), CSs, V

Flowers Hidden Under Foliage
Five-Leaf Akebia (*Akebia quinata*), C, CS, V
Madeira Vine (*Anredera cordifolia*), Tropical

VINES WITH SHOWY FLOWERS

Most vines are planted for the spectacular flowers they produce. The following include mostly perennials, but don't forget that the tropical vines and annual vines have beautiful flowers, too.

Variety of Colors
Italian Clematis (*Clematis viticella*), N, C, CS
Hybrid Clematis (*Clematis* x *hybrida*), N, C, CS

Yellow
Yellow Trumpet Vine (*Campsis radicans 'flava'*), All
Swamp Jessamine (*Gelsemium rankinii*), CSe
Carolina Jessamine (*Gelsemium sempervirens*), C, CS, V
Yellow Trumpet Honeysuckle (*Lonicera sempervirens 'sulphurea'*), All
Cat's-Claw Vine (*Macfadyena unguis-cati*), CS, V
Butterfly Vine (*Mascagnia macroptera*), CSs, V
Yellow Passion Vine (*Passiflora lutea*), Ce, CSe
Butterfly Vine (*Stigmaphyllon ciliatum*), CSs, V
Black-Eyed Susan Vine (*Thunbergia alata*), Annual

Orange to Red
Cross Vine (*Bignonia capreolata*), C, CS
Trumpet Creeper (*Campsis radicans*), All
Trumpet Honeysuckle (*Lonicera sempervirens*), All
Mexican Flame Vine (*Senecio confusus*), CSs, V, Annual

Pink to Red
'Cherries Jubilee' Allamanda (*Allamanda cathartica*), Tropical
Coral Vine (*Antigonon leptopus*), CS, V
Clematis (*Clematis montana 'rubens'*), N, C
Scarlet Clematis (*Clematis texensis*), All
Trumpet Honeysuckle (*Lonicera sempervirens*), All
Pandorea (*Pandorea jasminoides*), Tropical
Red Passion Vine (*Passiflora coccinea*), CSs, V
Texas Scarlet Passion Vine (*Passiflora vitifolia*), CS, V

Raspberry Vine (*Podranea ricasoliana*), CSs, V
Rangoon Creeper (*Quisqualis indica*), CSs, V
Carolina Rose (*Rosa carolina*), All

Blue
Climbing Aster (*Aster carolinianus*), C, CS
Blue Butterfly Pea (*Clitoria ternatea*), Annual
Snapdragon Vine (*Maurandya grandiflora*), All
Blue Crown Passion Vine (*Passiflora caerulea*), CS, V
Maypop (*Passiflora incarnata*), All
Potato Vine (*Solanum seaforthianum*), CSs, V
Blue Trumpet Vine (*Thunbergia grandiflora*), CSs, V

White
White Coral Vine (*Antigonon leptopus 'alba'*), CS, V
Clematis (*Clematis montana 'grandiflora'*), N, C
Armand Clematis (*Clematis armandii*), N, C, CS
Sweet Autumn Clematis (*Clematis maximowicziana*), N, C, CS
Climbing Hydrangea (*Hydrangea anomala*), Ce
Angel-Wing Jasmine (*Jasminum nitidum*), V, Tropical
Bower Vine (*Pandorea jasminoides 'alba'*), Tropical
Mexican Mock Orange (*Philadelphus mexicanus*), CS, V

Silver Lace Vine (*Polygonum aubertii*), N, C
Cherokee Rose (*Rosa laevigata*), C, CS, V
Memorial Rose (*Rosa wichuraiana*), C, CS, V
Confederate Jasmine (*Trachelospermum jasminoides*), CS, V

Purple
India Rubber Vine (*Cryptostegia grandiflora*), V
Purple Hyacinth Bean (*Lablab purpurea* [*Dolichos lablab*]), Annual
Purple Orchid Vine (*Mascagnia cilacina*), V
Evergreen Wisteria (*Millettia reticulata*), CS, V
'Incense' Passion Vine (*Passiflora* x *alatocaerulea*, *P. incarnata* x *cincinnata*), CS, V
Sand-Paper Vine (*Petrea volubilis*), Tropical
Japanese Wisteria (*Wisteria floribunda*), N, C
American Wisteria (*Wisteria frutescens*), C, CS

Bicolor
Cross Vine (*Bignonia capreolata*), C, CS
Garlic Vine (*Cydista aequinoctialis* [*Pseudocalymma alliacea*]), CSs, V
Goldflame Honeysuckle (*Lonicera heckrottii*), All
Trumpet Honeysuckle (*Lonicera sempervirens*), All

"Vines have a way of making their own way in a landscape, whether you want them to or not," notes David Creech, director of the SFA Mast Arboretum in Nacogdoches. "The arboretum is home to a number of rambunctious vines mixed into the varied landscapes of twenty-two theme gardens, and not all of them are well behaved." In fact, David says some are now firmly placed on their "how do we kill them" list.

Among the vines being evaluated at the arboretum for ornamental use are twenty-three clones of wisteria, a dozen honeysuckles, six Carolina jessamine cultivars, four clones of cross vine, and a few rare vines. "We have a diminutive relative of the wisteria (*Milletia japonica 'alba'*); silk vine (*Periploca gracea*), which is a strong climber with dark shiny foliage; and finally *Agdestris clematidea*, which has tropical-looking, redbud-like foliage and white flowers in the early fall."

TEAS NURSERY VINES FOR THE GULF COAST

This list of vines is a collection of those that the horticulturists at Teas Nursery in Houston have found work well in the Gulf Coast area. Some are woody; others are tropical or perennials. Vines in this list marked with an asterisk (*) are considered tropical.

Kris Engel-Bitner of Teas Nursery advises, "Do not combine annual and perennial vines because the fall clean-up is disastrous, unless you intend to prune everything to the ground." Kris recommends combining different kinds of plants for interesting effects. "To visually expand an area, try combining a similar looking plant in front of a vine. For instance, plant Mexican sunflower (*Tithonia rotundifolia*) in front of a flame vine (*Senecio confusus*) or a wedelia (*Wedelia trilobata*) above, below, or behind yellow alder (*Turnera ulmifolia*) or kerria (*Kerria japonica*). My favorite vine trick is to combine evergreen vines with similar leaf colors and shapes in one area. This creates an ever-changing display of color by season. I usually combine Chinese evergreen wisteria (*Millettia taiwanensis*), cross vine

BLACK-EYED
SUSAN VINE

(*Bignonia capreolata*), butterfly vine (*Mascagnia macroptera*), and Carolina jessamine (*Gelsemium semper-virens*). Another attractive combination is Chinese evergreen wisteria (*Millettia taiwanensis*) grown with five-leaf akebia (*Akebia quinata*)."

Allamanda (*Allamanda cathartica*)*
Coral Vine (*Antigonon leptopus*)
Dutchman's-Pipe Vine (*Aristolochia durior*)
Calico Flower (*Aristolochia elegans*)
Malabar Spinach (*Basella alba, B. rubra*)
Cross Vine (*Bignonia capreolata*)
'Tangerine Beauty' Cross Vine (*Bignonia capreolata*)
Bougainvillea (*Bougainvillea spectabalis*)
Yellow Trumpet Creeper (*Campsis flava*)
Chinese Trumpet Creeper (*Campsis grandiflora*)
'Madame Galen' Trumpet Vine (*Campsis* x tagliabuana)
Evergreen Clematis (*Clematis armandii*)
Downy Clematis (*Clematis macropetala*)
Sweet Autumn Clematis (*Clematis maximowicziana*)
Jackman Clematis (*Clematis* x *jackmanii*)
Bleeding-Heart Vine (*Clerodendron thomsoniae*)*
Lavender Trumpet Vine, Argentine (*Clytostoma callistegioides*)
Rubber Vine (*Cryptostegia* spp.)
Cup-and-Saucer Vine (*Cobea scandens*)
Scarlet Trumpet Vine (*Distictus buccinatoria*)*
Royal Trumpet Vine (*Distictus* x *riversii*)*
Creeping Fig Vine (*Ficus pumila*)
Swamp Jessamine (*Gelsemium rankinii*)
Carolina Jessamine (*Gelsemium sempervirens*)
Gloriosa Lily (*Gloriosa* spp.)
Algerian Ivy (*Hedera canariensis*)
English Ivy (*Hedera helix*)
Angel-Wing Jasmine (*Jasminum nitidum*)*
Pink Jasmine (*Jasminum polyanthum*)*
'Grand Duke' Arabian Jasmine (*Jasminum sambac*)
Giant Burmese Honeysuckle (*Lonicera hildebrandiana*)*
Hall's Japanese Honeysuckle (*Lonicera japonica* 'halliana')
Purple-Leaf Honeysuckle (*Lonicera purpurea*)
Trumpet Honeysuckle (*Lonicera sempervirens*)

Cat's-Claw Vine (*Macfadyena unguis-cati*)
Chilean Jasmine (*Mandevilla laxa*)
'Red Riding Hood' Mandevilla (*Mandevilla sanderi*)*
'Alice du Pont' Mandevilla (*Mandevilla* x *amabilis* [*Dipladenia amoena*])*
'Summer Snow' Mandevilla (*Mandevilla* x *amabilis*)*
Butterfly Vine (*Mascagnia macroptera*)
Evergreen Wisteria (*Millettia reticulata*)
Chinese Evergreen Wisteria (*Millettia taiwanensis*)
Pandora Vine, Bower Vine (*Pandorea jasminoides*)*
Virginia Creeper (*Parthenocissus quinquefolia*)
Boston Ivy (*Parthenocissus tricuspidata*)
Red Passion Vine (*Passiflora coccinea*)*
Texas Scarlet Passion Vine (*Passiflora vitifolia*)*
Incense Passion Vine (*Passiflora* x *alatocaerulea, P. incarnata* x *cincinnata*)
Lady Banks Rose (*Rosa banksiae*)
Mexican Flame Vine (*Senecio confusus*)
Potato Vine (*Solanum jasminoides*)*
Stephanotis (*Stephanotis floribunda*)*
Cape Honeysuckle (*Tecomaria capensis*)
Orange Clock Vine (*Thunbergia gregorii*)*
Grapes (*Vitis* spp.)
Chinese Wisteria (*Wisteria chinensis*)
Japanese Wisteria (*Wisteria floribunda*)

Vines to Grown From Seed
Climbing Snapdragon (*Asarina antirrhinifolia*)
Blue Pea Vine (*Clitoria ternatia*)
Moon Vine (*Ipomoea alba*)
Cypress Vine (*Ipomoea quamoclit*)
Morning-Glory (*Ipomoea tricolor*)
Cardinal Climber (*Ipomoea* x *multifida*)
Hyacinth Bean (*Lablab purpurea* [*Dolichos lablab*])
Scarlet Runner Bean (*Phaseolus coccineus*)
Black-Eyed Susan Vine (*Thunbergia alata*)
Clock Vine, Sky Flower (*Thunbergia grandiflora*)
Snail Vine (*Vigna caracalla*)

VINES FOR THE BEACH

Vines need a little protection at the beach. It's best to plant them on the leeward side of a structure. This doesn't mean they can't be used on a trellis to provide quick shade, since most will do best in the sun. It just means that the constant bombardment of the wind may make them so ragged you'll wish you had never plant-ed them on the windy, salty side.

Allamanda (*Allamanda cathartica*), Tropical
Bougainvillea (*Bougainvillea spectabilis*), Tropical
Trumpet Creeper (*Campsis radicans*), All

Wintercreeper (*Euonymus fortunei*), N, C
Carolina Jessamine (*Gelsemium sempervirens*), C, CS, V

Algerian Ivy (*Hedera canariensis*), CS, V
Virginia Creeper (*Parthenocissus quinquefolia*), All
Lady Banks Rose (*Rosa banksiae*), CS, V

Confederate Jasmine (*Trachelospermum jasminoides*), CS, V

 "Bougainvillea wants to grow too much in high-rainfall areas. As a result, it often forgets to bloom. To force it to bloom: (1) Plant it in full sun and keep it root bound. I plant it in the ground pot and all, though I may split the pot in a few places to give it some room to grow. If planted directly in the ground (no pot), pack rocks or brick chips around the roots to insure they don't escape too soon into the surrounding soil. (2) Feed it only lightly with Hibiscus Food, and let it get droopy dry between waterings. (3) Most importantly, *pinch, pinch, pinch* the tips off, as this promotes flowering."
—Kris Engel-Bitner, Teas Nursery, Houston

VINES FOR THE COASTAL BAY AREA

Vines will need extra support and attention in bayside gardens. The often unrelenting winds and salt spray can take a toll on any plant, but vines are up in the air, vulnerable and exposed. Trellises and arbors need to be extra strong to withstand the wind and elements.

Five-Leaf Akebia (*Akebia quinata*)	white or purple flowers
Coral Vine (*Antigonon leptopus*)	pink flowers in late summer
Dutchman's-Pipe Vine (*Aristolochia durior*)	exotic purple and cream flowers
Aster Vine (*Aster carolinianus*)	lavender daisy-like flowers
Cross Vine (*Bignonia capreolata*)	red and yellow flowers
Trumpet Creeper (*Campsis radicans*)	orange flowers
Curly Clematis (*Clematis crispa*)	purple flowers
Fatshedera (x *Fatshedera lizei*)	lustrous foliage
Carolina Jessamine (*Gelsemium sempervirens*)	yellow spring flowers
Red-Wing Vine (*Heteropterys alata*)	yellow flowers, red seeds
Climbing Hydrangea (*Hydrangea anomala*)	white flowers
Cypress Vine (*Ipomoea quamoclit*)	scarlet flowers in late summer
Variegated Kadsura (*Kadsura japonica* 'variegata')	glossy foliage, red fruit
Trumpet Honeysuckle (*Lonicera sempervirens*)	red flowers, spring/summer
Mexican Butterfly Vine (*Mascagnia macroptera*)	yellow flowers
Evergreen Wisteria (*Millettia reticulata*)	purple flowers
Virginia Creeper (*Parthenocissus quinquefolia*)	fall color
Passion Vine (*Passiflora* spp.)	many different flower colors
Raspberry Vine (*Podranea ricasoliana*)	pink flowers
Climbing Roses (*Rosa* spp.)	many different flower colors
Mexican Flame Vine (*Senecio confusus*)	orange daisy-like flowers
Thunbergia (*Thunbergia* spp.)	white or blue flowers
Confederate Jasmine (*Trachelospernum jasminoides*)	white spring flowers

VINES THAT MAKE GOOD GROUND COVERS

Many vines will trail rather well on the ground, and the following do it well enough to make good ground covers. Algerian and English ivy are easily kept looking fresh by simply going over them with a lawn mower in late winter just before spring growth begins. Yes, you really can do this. Just set the mower at its highest setting. Or you may use a pair of large hedge shears or a heavy-duty line trimmer (some can use a metal blade) to give any of these vines an efficient trim.

Five-Leaf Akebia (*Akebia quinata*), C, CS, V
Cross Vine (*Bignonia capreolata*), C, CS
Wintercreeper (*Euonymus fortunei*), N, C
Carolina Jessamine (*Gelsemium sempervirens*), C,
  CS, V
Algerian Ivy (*Hedera canariensis*), CS, V
English Ivy (*Hedera helix*), All
'Blackie,' 'Tricolor,' 'Marguerite' Sweet Potato Vine
  (*Ipomoea batatas*) CS, V

Japanese Honeysuckle (*Lonicera japonica*), All
Virginia Creeper (*Parthenocissus quinquefolia*), All
Boston Ivy (*Parthenocissus tricuspidata*), N, C
Memorial Rose (*Rosa wichuraiana*), C, CS, V
Asian Jasmine (*Trachelospermum asiaticum*), C, CS,
  V
Confederate Jasmine (*Trachelospermum jasminoides*),
  CS, V

VINES FOR ALKALINE SOIL

Often we amend the soil for vines and add lots of peat moss or other organic materials, but that's not always practical. Even when we do go to great lengths to improve the soil, alkaline water can soon negate our efforts. Besides, nothing looks sicker than a plant with yellow interveinal chlorosis caused by iron deficiency. This list of plants that tolerate alkaline conditions was developed by garden writer and avid gardener Scott Ogden.

Porcelain Ampelopsis (*Ampelopsis brevipedunculata*),
  C
Madeira Vine (*Anredera cordifolia*), Tropical
Coral Vine (*Antigonon leptopus*), CS, V
Dutchman's-Pipe (*Aristolochia durior*), CS, V
Cross Vine (*Bignonia capreolata*), C, CS
Trumpet Creeper (*Campsis radicans*), All
Armand Clematis (*Clematis armandii*), N, C, CS
Scarlet Clematis (*Clematis texensis*), All
Italian Clematis (*Clematis viticella*), N, C, CS
Creeping Fig (*Ficus pumila*), CS, V
Morning-Glory (*Ipomoea* spp.), Annual
Perennial Morning-Glory (*Ipomoea lindheimeri*), CS,
  V
Cypress Vine (*Ipomoea quamoclit*), Annual
Cardinal Climber (*Ipomoea* x *multifida*), Annual
Hyacinth Bean (*Lablab purpurea* [*Dolichos lablab*]),
  Annual
Perennial Pea (*Lathyrus latifolius*), C
Trumpet Honeysuckle (*Lonicera sempervirens*), All
Sponge Gourd (*Luffa aegyptiaca*), Annual

Pink Mandevilla (*Mandevilla* x *amabilis*),
  Tropical
Seven-Leaf Creeper (*Parthenocissus
  heptaphylla*), All
Virginia Creeper (*Parthenocissus
  quinquefolia*), All
Boston Ivy (*Parthenocissus
  tricuspidata*), N, C
Passion Vine (*Passiflora* spp.), CS,
  V, Annual
Grecian Silk Vine (*Periploca
  graeca*), CS, V
Silver Lace Vine (*Polygonum
  aubertii*), N, C
Rangoon Creeper (*Quisqualis
  indica*), CSs, V
Mexican Flame Vine (*Senecio
  confusus*), CSs, V, Annual
Potato Vine (*Solanum jasminoides*), CS, V
Bunch Grapes (*Vitis* spp.) , All
Wisteria (*Wisteria sinensis*), N, C, CS

TRUMPET
HONEYSUCKLE

VINES THAT DO WELL IN POOR, DRY SOIL

Most gardeners will try to improve the soil before planting, but sometimes you need a tough plant for a tough site. It might be for a public area that you won't have much opportunity to change or keep track of. Maybe it's a recommendation for a friend that you know isn't a garden enthusiast. Whatever the circumstances, these are toughies.

Porcelain Ampelopsis (*Ampelopsis brevipedunculata*),
  C
Coral Vine (*Antigonon leptopus*), CS, V
Orchid Vine (*Bauhinia yunnanensis*), CSs, V
American Bittersweet (*Celastrus scandens*), N, C
Carolina Jessamine (*Gelsemium sempervirens*), C,
  CS, V

Perennial Morning-Glory (*Ipomoea purpurea*),
  Annual
Cypress Vine (*Ipomoea quamoclit*), Annual
Hyacinth Bean (*Lablab purpurea* [*Dolichos Lablab*]),
  Annual
Hall's Japanese Honeysuckle (*Lonicera japonica
  'halliana'*), All

Cat's-Claw Vine (*Macfadyena unguis-cati*), CS, V
Maypop (*Passiflora incarnata*), All
Silver Lace Vine (*Polygonum aubertii*), N, C

Lady Banks Rose (*Rosa banksiae*), CS, V
Potato Vine (*Solanum jasminoides*), CS, V

VINES THAT CLIMB BY CLINGING

The vines below grab walls, wood fences, and even tree trunks with adhesive pads that sprout from their stems, so they seem to be glued to their support. Trying to pull one off is like ripping packing tape from a box, only it requires more strength. Plant these vines where you know they won't have to be pulled off in a year or two, or ever for that matter. They are great for covering low walls—especially ones made from concrete blocks with no façade. Be careful about letting them grow up the wall of your house or up trees. If you do, keep their tops in check so you don't have to rip them off the gutter or upper windowsills in a few years. They will also pull off paint if you tug, and they often leave pieces of their adhesive structures clinging to a wall. If all this sounds ominous, it's not intended to deter you from using the vine, but to prompt you to put it somewhere it can be left alone except for occasional pruning.

Cross Vine (*Bignonia capreolata*), C, CS
Trumpet Creeper (*Campsis radicans*), All
Wintercreeper (*Euonymus fortunei*), N, C
Creeping Fig (*Ficus pumila*), CS, V
Persian Ivy (*Hedera colchica*), C, CS, V

English Ivy (*Hedera helix*), All
Climbing Hydrangea (*Hydrangea anomala*), Ce
Virginia Creeper (*Parthenocissus quinquefolia*), All
Boston Ivy (*Parthenocissus tricuspidata*), N, C

According to Kris Engel-Bitner of Teas Nursery in Houston, creeping fig, or fig ivy (*Ficus pumila*), will help cool an area by reducing the amount of heat absorbed by a brick surface. "The variegated fig ivy is beautiful but much less vigorous and cannot be counted on to rapidly cover walls or topiaries. I encourage people to look for unusual objects to train their vines on. They can use old basketball hoops, street lamps, utility poles, and wattles woven from grape vine or crape myrtle branches. Discarded wrought-iron panels (from 1950s tract houses) are my absolute favorite though."

VINES THAT CLIMB BY TWINING

At least half of the vines mentioned in this book climb by wrapping their stems around or through a support. Sometimes they'll twine themselves into a wad by growing atop themselves rather than reaching out. What this means is that you'll need to help these twiners stretch in the direction you want them to go by occasionally taking the shoots and winding them through lattice or whatever structure you've provided for their support. If you held your finger out in front of a real twiner long enough, it would wrap around your finger like a coiled spring. Shrubby, sprawling vines, such as some of the jasmines, don't really twine in the strictest sense, but their long, woody stems need the same kind of training and perhaps fastening to their given support. In addition to the ones below, there are many annual and tropical vines.

Five-Leaf Akebia (*Akebia quinata*), C, CS, V
Dutchman's-Pipe (*Aristolochia durior*), CS, V
Armand Clematis (*Clematis armandii*), N, C, CS
Hybrid Clematis (*Clematis* x *hybrida*), N, C, CS
Swamp Jessamine (*Gelsemium rankinii*), CSe
Carolina Jessamine (*Gelsemium sempervirens*), C, CS, V
Goldflame Honeysuckle (*Lonicera heckrottii*), All
Trumpet Honeysuckle (*Lonicera sempervirens*), All
Firecracker Vine (*Manettia cordifolia*), CSs, V
Evergreen Wisteria (*Millettia reticulata*), CS, V
Silver Lace Vine (*Polygonum aubertii*), N, C
Smilax (*Smilax* spp.), C, CS, V

SMILAX

Confederate Jasmine (*Trachelospermum jasminoides*),
CS, V
Japanese Wisteria (*Wisteria floribunda*), N, C

American Wisteria (*Wisteria frutescens*), C, CS
Chinese Wisteria (*Wisteria sinensis*), N, C, CS

VINES THAT CLIMB WITH TENDRILS

Vines with tendrils are great for covering a chain-link fence or any support that isn't too large to wrap around. They won't cling to a wall without a lattice or something like wire or fishing line strung zigzag fashion on the surface, but they are worth the effort. Technically, clematis don't have tendrils; they have leaves that grab like tendrils.

Porcelain Ampelopsis (*Ampelopsis brevipedunculata*),
C
Madeira Vine (*Anredera cordifolia*), Tropical
Coral Vine (*Antigonon leptopus*), CS, V
Cross Vine (*Bignonia capreolata*), C, CS
Sweet Autumn Clematis (*Clematis maximowicziana*),
N, C, CS
Scarlet Clematis (*Clematis texensis*), All

Hybrid Clematis (*Clematis* x *hybrida*), N, C, CS
Cup-and-Saucer Vine (*Cobaea scandens*), Annual
Sweet Peas (*Lathyrus odoratus*), Annual
Sponge Gourd (*Luffa aegyptiaca*), Annual
Cat's-Claw Vine (*Macfadyena unguis-cati*), CS, V
Passion Vine (*Passiflora* spp.), CS, V, Annual
Muscadine Grapes (*Vitis rotundifolia*), Ce, CSe
Bunch Grapes (*Vitis* spp.), All

VINES THAT REACH A LONG, LONG WAY

When you need to cover an arbor, or your house for that matter, many of these vines can do the job. They all respond to sharp pruning shears if things get out of hand, and some, such as the muscadine grape, will reward you with more and better quality fruit if they get some pruning. Some, however, are downright dangerous. They will attack siding, mortar, fences and slow-moving pets. Consult with local nurseries and other gardeners to find out which vines can be particularly vigorous in your area.

50 Feet or Longer
Clematis (*Clematis montana*), N, C
Virginia Creeper (*Parthenocissus quinquefolia*), All
Boston Ivy (*Parthenocissus tricuspidata*), N, C
Muscadine Grape (*Vitis rotundifolia*), Ce, CSe
Japanese Wisteria (*Wisteria floribunda*), N, C
American Wisteria (*Wisteria frutescens*), C, CS

40 Feet
Five-Leaf Akebia (*Akebia quinata*), C, CS, V
Dutchman's-Pipe (*Aristolochia durior*), CS, V
Cross Vine (*Bignonia capreolata*), C, CS
Trumpet Creeper (*Campsis radicans*), All
Silver Lace Vine (*Polygonum aubertii*), N, C
Mustang Grape (*Vitis candicans*), Cw, CSw

20 to 30 Feet
Porcelain Ampelopsis (*Ampelopsis brevipedunculata*),
C
Clematis (*Clematis montana* 'rubens'), N, C

15 to 20 Feet
Armand Clematis (*Clematis armandii*), N, C, CS
Jackman Clematis (*Clematis jackmanii*), N, C, CS
Scarlet Clematis (*Clematis texensis*), All
Carolina Jessamine (*Gelsemium sempervirens*), C,
CS, V
Lady Banks Rose (*Rosa banksiae*), CS, V
'Reve d'Or,' 'Climbing Pinkie' Rose (*Rosa* spp.), All

VINES FOR SHADE

Some vines tolerate shade and grow well in full sun, too. Others must have shade or they'll suffer. The first five on this list will do well in deep shade where there is never a direct ray of sunlight, such as a shaded north side or under trees that form a dense canopy.

Plants don't conform to neat formulas, so for the purposes of this book, we will call partial shade (1) a shade that is broken up by mottled sunlight peeping through a tree canopy or under tall limbs or (2) part-time exposure to sun on the east or west sides of a home. Remember, the west side gets the hottest afternoon sun.

Vines for Deep Shade

Air Potato Vine (*Dioscorea bulbifera*), CSs, V, Annual
Ornamental Yam (*Dioscorea discolor*), CS, V
Creeping Fig (*Ficus pumila*), CS, V
Algerian Ivy (*Hedera canariensis*), CS, V
English Ivy (*Hedera helix*), All
Climbing Fern (*Lygodium japonicum*), C, CS, V
Confederate Jasmine (*Trachelospermum jasminoides*), CS, V

Vines for Partial Shade

Five-Leaf Akebia (*Akebia quinata*), C, CS, V
Porcelain Ampelopsis (*Ampelopsis brevipedunculata*), C
Armand Clematis (*Clematis armandii*), N, C, CS
Air Potato Vine (*Dioscorea bulbifera*), CSs, V, Annual
Wintercreeper (*Euonymus fortunei*), N, C

Creeping Fig (*Ficus pumila*), CS, V
Algerian Ivy (*Hedera canariensis*), CSs, V
Persian Ivy (*Hedera colchica*), C, CS, V
English Ivy (*Hedera helix*), All
Climbing Hydrangea (*Hydrangea anomala*), Ce
Variegated Kadsura (*Kadsura japonica 'variegata'*), C, CS, V
Trumpet Honeysuckle (*Lonicera sempervirens*), All
Virginia Creeper (*Parthenocissus quinquefolia*), All
Boston Ivy (*Parthenocissus tricuspidata*), N, C
Smilax (*Smilax* spp.), C, CS, V
Confederate Jasmine (*Trachelospermum jasminoides*), CS, V

BOSTON IVY

A VINE SAMPLER BY SEASON OF BLOOM

Spring

Cross Vine (*Bignonia capreolata*), C, CS
Hybrid Clematis (*Clematis* x *hybrida*), N, C, CS
Carolina Jessamine (*Gelsemium sempervirens*), C, CS, V
Sweet Pea (*Lathyrus odoratus*), Annual
Goldflame Honeysuckle (*Lonicera heckrottii*), All
'Pam's Pink' Honeysuckle (*Lonicera* x *hybrida*), All
Evergreen Wisteria (*Millettia reticulata*), CS, V
Lady Banks Rose (*Rosa banksiae 'lutea'* or *'alba'*), CS, V
Cherokee Rose (*Rosa laevigata*), C, CS, V
Japanese Wisteria (*Wisteria floribunda*), N, C
Chinese Wisteria (*Wisteria sinensis*), N, C, CS

Summer

Coral Vine (*Antigonon leptopus*), CS, V
'Tangerine Beauty' Cross Vine (*Bignonia capreolata*), Ce, CSe
Trumpet Creeper (*Campsis radicans*), All
Scarlet Clematis (*Clematis texensis*), All
Goldflame Honeysuckle (*Lonicera heckrottii*), All
Japanese Honeysuckle (*Lonicera japonica*), All
Trumpet Honeysuckle (*Lonicera sempervirens*), All
Cat's-Claw Vine (*Macfadyena unguis-cati*), CS, V

Butterfly Vine (*Mascagnia macroptera*), CSs, V
Passion Vine (*Passiflora* spp.), CS, V, Annual
Raspberry Vine (*Podranea ricasoliana*), CSs, V
Butterfly Vine (*Stigmaphyllon ciliatum*), CSs, V
Confederate Jasmine (*Trachelospermum jasminoides*), CS, V
American Wisteria (*Wisteria frutescens*), C, CS

Late Summer

Climbing Aster (*Aster carolinianus*), C, CS
Sweet Autumn Clematis (*Clematis maximowicziana*), N, C, CS
Scarlet Clematis (*Clematis texensis*), All
Hybrid Clematis (*Clematis* x *hybrida*), N, C, CS
Goldflame Honeysuckle (*Lonicera heckrottii*), All
Silver Lace Vine (*Polygonum aubertii*), N, C
Blue Clock Vine, Sky Flower (*Thunbergia grandiflora*), CSs, V

Fall

Coral Vine (*Antigonon leptopus*), CS, V
Scarlet Clematis (*Clematis texensis*), All
Swamp Jessamine (*Gelsemium rankinii*), CSe
Rangoon Creeper (*Quisqualis indica*), CSs, V
Everblooming Climbing Rose (*Rosa* spp.), All

SPECIAL LISTS AND GARDENS

This catch-all chapter was inevitable. There are simply too many interesting plants and specialty gardens that don't fit into one of the other chapters. For example, this chapter includes a list of Mexican plants (see "South of the Border Plants"), many of which are still rare but so very worthy of trial that they have to be mentioned. Lists of plants that attract butterflies or hummingbirds might be broken into annuals and perennials, but they are more useful when considered together, as they are here. Our state is famous for its wildflowers, so no *Lone Star Gardener's Book of Lists* would be complete without a list of "Wildflowers of Texas." Nor could we leave out a list of the heirloom plants our ancestors used in their cottage gardens. There are other lists too. This is certainly the most eclectic chapter, but we also think it is one of the most interesting.

HEIRLOOM PLANTS FOR TEXAS

Heirloom plants are living symbols of success from generations of Texas gardeners. Many have been lovingly handed down from one gardener to another within the families that contribute cultural diversity and richness to our gardens. The fact that these plants have been time tested makes their use in today's gardens a compelling choice. In addition to being adapted and easy to grow, many of these plants add fragrance, color, and historical importance to our gardens. More detailed discussion concerning the history and culture of these plants and many others may be found in *The Southern Heirloom Garden* (Welch and Grant, Taylor Publishing, Dallas). This list of Texas heirlooms comes from William C. Welch, one of that book's authors.

BLACKBERRY LILY

Heirloom Roses
Archduke Charles
Cécile Brunner
Cécile Brunner Climber
Cramoisi Superieur
Duchesse de Brabant
Eugene Boerner
Felicia
La Marne
Marie Pavié

Marquise Bocella
Mme. Alfred Carrière
Monsieur Tillier
Mrs. B. R. Cant
Mrs. Dudley Cross
Mutabilis, Butterfly Rose
Old Blush
Paul Neyron
Perle d'Or
Rêve d'Or
Souvenir de la Malmaison
Swamp Rose

Trier Rambler
White Lady Banks Rose
Yellow Lady Banks Rose
Zépherine Drouhin

Found Roses
Caldwell Pink
Georgetown Tea
Maggie
McClinton Tea
Natchitoches Noisette

Heirloom Bulbs and Corms

Blackberry Lily (*Belamcanda chinensis*)
Crinum Lily (*Crinum* spp.)
Byzantine Gladiolus (*Gladiolus byzantinus*)
Parrot Gladiolus (*Gladiolus natalensis*)
Hardy Red Amaryllis (*Hippeastrum* × *johnsonii*)
Roman Hyacinth (*Hyacinthus orientalis*)
Louisiana Iris (*Iris brevicaulis, I. fulva, I. nelsonii*)
Giant Blue Lousiana Iris (*Iris giganticaerulea*)
Cemetery White Iris (*Iris* × *albicans*)
Snowflake (*Leucojum aestivum*)
Spider Lily (*Lycoris radiata*)
Grand Primo Narcissus (*Narcissus jonquilla*)
Campernelle Jonquil (*Narcissus* × *odorus*)
Tuberose (*Polianthes tuberosa*)

Heirloom Shrubs

Alba Plena Camellia (*Camellia japonica 'alba plena'*)
'Pink Perfection' Camellia (*Camellia japonica*)
'Purple Dawn' Camellia (*Camellia japonica*)
Flowering Quince (*Chaenomeles speciosa*)
Kumquat (*Fortunella* spp.)
Gardenia, Cape Jasmine (*Gardenia jasminoides*)
Hip Gardenia (*Gardenia thunbergia*)
Confederate Rose (*Hibiscus mutabilis*)
Althaea (*Hibiscus syriacus*)
French Hydrangea (*Hydrangea macrophylla*)
Greek Laurel, Cooking Bay (*Laurus nobilis*)
Winter Honeysuckle (*Lonicera fragrantissima*)
Banana Shrub (*Michelia figo*)
Dwarf Myrtle (*Myrtus communis 'compacta'*)
Nandina, Heavenly Bamboo (*Nandina domestica*)
Sweet Olive (*Osmanthus fragrans*)
Mock Orange (*Philadelphus coronarius*)
Trifoliate Orange (*Poncirus trifoliata*)
Flowering Almond (*Prunus glandulosa*)
Pomegranate (*Punica granatum*)
Rosemary (*Rosmarinus officinalis*)

Heirloom Fruits

Mayhaw (*Crataegus opaca*)
Japanese Persimmon (*Diospyros kaki*)

Fig (*Ficus carica*)
Kumquat (*Fortunella japonica*)
Chinese Quince (*Pseudocydonia sinensis*)
Muscadine (*Vitis rotundifolia*)
Champanel Grape (*Vitis* × 'Champanel')
Chinese Date, Jujube (*Ziziphus jujuba*)

Heirloom Perennials

Coral Vine (*Antigonon leptopus*)
Autumn Aster (*Aster oblongifolius*)
Cannas (*Canna generalis*)
Oxeye Daisy (*Chrysanthemum leucanthemum*)
Gaura (*Gaura lindheimeri*)
Daylilies (*Hemerocallis* spp.)
Spider Lily (*Hymenocallis liriosme*)
Philippine Lily (*Lilium formosanum 'philippinense'*)
Turk's-Cap Lily (*Malvaviscus arboreus 'drummondii'*)
Four-O'clock (*Mirabilis jalapa*)
Lindheimer's Muhly Grass (*Muhlenbergia lindheimeri*)
Brazos Penstemon (*Penstemon tenuis*)
Summer Phlox (*Phlox paniculata*)
Prairie Phlox (*Phlox pilosa*)
Gregg's Salvia (*Salvia greggii*)
Mexican Bush Sage (*Salvia leucantha*)
'Indigo Spires' Salvia (*Salvia*)
Bouncing Bet (*Saponaria officinalis*)
Butterfly Vine (*Stigmaphyllon ciliatum*)
Mexican Marigold Mint (*Tagetes lucida*)
White Rain Lily (*Zephyranthes candida*)

Fragrant Heirlooms

Crinum Lily (*Crinum* spp.)
Cape Jessamine (*Gardenia jasminoides*)
Hip Gardenia (*Gardenia thunbergia*)
Carolina Jessamine (*Gelsemium sempervirens*)
Roman Hyacinth (*Hyacinthus orientalis*)
Winter Honeysuckle (*Lonicera fragrantissima*)
Jonquils (*Narcissus jonquilla*)
'Grand Primo' Narcissus (*Narcissus tazetta*)
Campernelle Jonquil (*Narcissus* × *odorus*)
Sweet Olive (*Osmanthus fragrans*)
Tuberose (*Polianthes tuberosa*)

"Early Texas gardens were as practical as they were beautiful. Many of the plants were useful in some way; rosemary, wormwood, dill, thyme, and borage often appeared along with a host of other culinary and medicinal herbs. Settlers often planted soapberry (*Sapindus drummondi*) and bouncing Bet (*Saponaria officinalis*) for the sake of convenience as well as beauty, since the soapberry's fruits and the bouncing Bet's roots furnished home-grown substitutes for soap. Native plants were gathered from the wild and planted because they were beautiful, available, and easily grown. Any imported plants must naturalize easily and be available at low cost, since survival was the first order of business."
—William C. Welch, Extension landscape specialist, Texas A&M, College Station.

TEXAS SUPERSTARS

One of the most frustrating things for gardeners is to buy plants that aren't adapted to their growing conditions and have them die within a few months or weeks. It's also important to know the best season for planting certain varieties and when they will give their peak performance. Steve George, a County Extension landscape horticulturist in Dallas, has been testing landscape plants for a number of years and tries to deal with another gardening frustration: hearing about a wonderful plant but not being able to find a source for it. The Texas Superstars aren't promoted until they're tested and available in nurseries.

Steve explains that plants receive superstar status based on their exemplary performance in extensive statewide testing by horticulture experts with the Texas A&M Agriculture Program. "Texas Superstar plants play a crucial role in helping consumers create beautiful, productive landscapes which provide maximum protection for the environment, yet require much less maintenance." The plants in this list are highly recommend as superstars. Given proper care, they are truly outstanding, proven performers for Texas landscapes and gardens. Unless otherwise noted, the plants in this list are adapted throughout the state.

Annuals

SPRING PERFORMERS (plant in late winter or early spring)
'VIP' Petunia (*Petunia violacea*) — vigorous; various shades of violet
'Laura Bush' Petunia (*Petunia* x 'Laura Bush') — vigorous; intense pink violet
'Plum Parfait' Coleus (*Coleus* x 'Plum Parfait') — sun tolerant; plum and pink foliage
'Burgundy Sun' Coleus (*Coleus* x 'Burgundy Sun') — sun tolerant; burgundy foliage

SUMMER PERFORMERS (plant in late spring or early summer)
'New Wonder' Fan Flower (*Scaevola aemula*) — sun tolerant; lavender flowers
Large-Flowered Purslane (*Portulaca* x Yubi™) — varied intense colors
Trailing Lantana (*Lantana montevidensis*) — lavender, purple, or white flowers
'New Gold' Lantana (*Lantana* x 'New Gold') — golden-yellow flowers
Firebush (*Hamelia patens*) — red-orange tubular blooms; fall color
'Gold Star' Esperanza (*Tecoma stans*) — golden-yellow trumpet flowers

FALL PERFORMERS (plant in late spring to summer)
'Antigua' Mari-Mum (*Tagetes erecta*) — double-flowered marigold blooms
Mexican Bush Sage (*Salvia leucantha*) — purple and white flower spikes

EARLY SPRING PERFORMERS (plant in late summer to fall)
Texas Bluebonnet (*Lupinus texensis*) — classic blue, white, or pink flowers
'Texas Maroon' Bluebonnet (*Lupinus texensis*) — maroon and white blooms
Bunny Bloom Larkspur (*Consolida ambigua*) — purple, pink, or white flower spikes

Perennials

SPRING PERFORMERS
Blue Princess Verbena (*Verbena* x 'Blue Princess') — lavender-blue flowers
'Texas Gold' Columbine (*Aquilegia chrysantha*) — long-spurred yellow blossoms

SUMMER PERFORMERS
'Flare' Hibiscus (*Hibiscus* x 'Flare') — fuchsia-colored flowers
'Moy Grande' Hibiscus (*Hibiscus* x 'Moy Grande') — dinner-plate-sized pink blossoms
'Lord Baltimore' Hibiscus (*Hibiscus* x 'Lord Baltimore') — stunning red flowers
'John Fanick' Phlox (*Phlox paniculata*) — light-pink with darker throats
'Victoria' Phlox (*Phlox paniculata*) — magenta-pink blossoms

Roses

‘Belinda’s Dream’ (*Rosa* x ‘Belinda’s Dream’) fragrant, double pink blossoms
‘Marie Daly’ (*Rosa* x *polyantha*) few thorns; fragrant, double pink

Vines

‘Pam’s Pink’ Honeysuckle (*Lonicera* x *americana*) pink and white trumpet flowers

Trees

Deciduous Holly (*Ilex decidua*) showy red or orange berries
Shantung Maple (*Acer truncatum*) red-orange fall color, East Texas
Chinese Pistache (*Pistacia chinensis*) red-orange fall color
Lacey Oak (*Quercus glaucoides*) bluish-green foliage, West Texas

Vegetables

SPRING/SUMMER PERFORMERS
‘Merced’ Tomato (*Lycopersicon lycopersicum*) medium/large red fruit

SPRING/SUMMER/FALL PERFORMERS
‘Surefire’ Tomato (*Lycopersicon lycopersicum*) firm, meaty red fruit

Citrus

Satsuma Mandarin (*Citrus reticulata*) almost seedless, sweet, slipskin fruit

A CHILD'S GARDEN

Frances Robeson and Jan Gisler, two Harris County Master Gardeners, contributed this list of plants that can be used to create a child's garden. They explain, "Master Gardener volunteers wanted a special garden to entertain and educate children, parents, and even grandparents who might visit our display gardens. We had seen the delight on small faces as they bent to look into the face of a johnny-jump-up or to open the mouth of a snapdragon. We saw their happiness when told they could pick a flower for themselves. We remembered our own childhood— days in a garden in the presence of a loved family member. We decided to create this special garden for the children as well as for Master Gardeners (gardeners still feel the child within). Our goal was to pass on fond memories of the gardening experiences of childhood, to plant the seed of a lifelong pleasure in these children as it had been planted in us, and to help them experience the natural world."

Frances and Jan say that one thing they did was make a bean teepee from bamboo poles and string on which to grow sugar snap peas, and later sweet peas, scarlet runner beans, blue morning glories, and cypress vine, which is covered with tiny bright-red flowers. They even placed two small chairs inside the teepee, so visitors could have a place for a private conversation. The volunteers also made a butterfly-shaped bed, outlined in rocks, in which to plant butterfly-attracting pentas, salvia, verbena, and zinnia. A small vegetable garden was equipped with a scarecrow, who was in charge of menacing a topiary rabbit. A toad abode was established, to teach the value of small and maybe not so pretty but very helpful animals.

PEANUR

Teepees, Tunnels, Towers, and Hiding Places

Giant Sunflower (*Helianthus giganteus*)
Hops (*Humulus lupulus*)
Morning Glory (*Ipomoea purpurea*)
Cypress Vine (*Ipomoea quamoclit*)
Cardinal Climber (*Ipomoea* x *multifida* [*I. quamoclit*])
Scarlet Runner Bean (*Phaseolus coccineus*)
Edible Podded Peas (*Pisum sativum*)

Quick, Easy, Fun to Watch and Harvest

Chard (*Beta vulgaris*)
Beet (*Beta vulgaris*)

Carrot (*Daucus carota 'sativus'*)
Lettuce (*Lactuca sativa*)
Bush Bean (*Phaseolus vulgaris*)
Radish (*Raphanus sativus*)

Fun to Dig, Pick, or Use
Peanut (*Arachis hypogaea*)
Cotton (*Gossypium hirsutum*)
Gourd (*Lagenaria* and *Luffa* spp.)
Money Plant (*Lunaria annua*)
Potato (*Solanum tuberosum*)
Four-Leaf Clover (*Trifolium repens*)

Inviting Imagination, Creativity, and Pretending
Hollyhock (*Alcea rosea*)
Snapdragon (*Antirrhinum majus*)
Milkweed (*Asclepias* spp.)
Bleeding Hearts (*Dicentra spectabilis*)
Poppy (*Papaver* spp.)
Obedient Plant (*Physostegia* spp.)
Rose (buds) (*Rosa* spp.)
Pussywillow (*Salix caprea*)
Wooly Lamb's-Ear (*Stachys* spp.)
Dandelion (*Taraxacum officinale*)
Pansy (*Viola* X *wittrockiana*)
Daisy (many spp.)

"Part of the success of our child's garden lies in the future, as children who visit it continue their joy in the garden—whether ours, theirs, or any other—from the seed that we planted. It is successful now as a garden from which the gardeners who created it take great delight in caring for it week by week and welcoming all visitors of whatever age."
—Frances Robeson and Jan Gisler, Harris County Master Gardeners, Houston

NECTAR-PRODUCING BUTTERFLY PLANTS

If you hope to enjoy butterflies, you will need a special selection of plants to attract and hold them in your garden for a while. Flowering plants that produce lots of easy-to-reach nectar are the key. Most plants that are attractive to butterflies have colorful small- to medium-size flowers with showy heads, such as pentas and zinnias. Many red, tubular flowers such as firebush attract both butterflies and hummingbirds. Lantana is also good for both butterflies and hummingbirds—it is easy to grow, flowers almost constantly, and tolerates drought. Perhaps because one common lantana species is considered invasive, it is often left off "Plants That Attract" lists.

Most gardeners don't think about attracting moths, but they can be fun and interesting to watch in the evening hours. Hawk or sphinx moths are the nocturnal equivalent of hummingbirds, and it's sometimes hard to distinguish them from a bird! Evening- or night-blooming flowers such as moonflowers (*Ipomoea alba*), four-o'clocks (*Mirabilis jalapa*), and evening primrose (*Oenothera speciosa*) do a great job of attracting these moth species.

BUTTERFLY WEED

Chinese Abelia (*Abelia chinensis*), C, CS
'Sunset' Hyssop (*Agastache rupestris*), All
Wild Ageratum (*Ageratum* spp.) , All
Mimosa (*Albizia julibrissin*), All
White Almond Bush (*Aloysia virgata*), CS, V
Milkweed (*Asclepias* spp.), All
Mexican Butterfly Weed (*Asclepias curassavica*), CS, V
Butterfly Weed (*Asclepias tuberosa*), Ce, CSe
Aster (*Aster* spp.), All
Bouvardia (*Bouvardia ternifolia*), CS, V
Butterfly Bush (*Buddleia* spp.), N, C, CS

Bottlebrush (*Callistemon rigidus*), CSs, V,
Feather Celosia (*Celosia cristata*), Annual
Basket Flower (*Centaurea americana*), C, CS
Buttonbush (*Cephalanthus occidentalis*), Ce, CSe
Tickseed (*Coreopsis* spp.), Annual
Cosmos (*Cosmos* spp.), All
Mexican Heather (*Cuphea* spp.), CSs, V, Annual
Pink (*Dianthus* spp.), Annual/biennial
Golden Dewdrop (*Duranta repens* [*erecta*]), CSs, V
Purple Coneflower (*Echinacea purpurea*), All
Hardy Ageratum (*Eupatorium coelestinum*), All

Gregg's Blue Mist Flower (*Eupatorium greggii*), All
Joe Pye Weed (*Eupatorium maculatum*), All
Hardy Gynura (*Gynura bicolor*), CS, V
Firebush (*Hamelia patens*), CSs, V, Annual
False Creeping Blue Curls (*Heliotropium amplexicaule*), CS, V
Jatropha (*Jatropha* spp.), V, Annual
Orange Jacobinia (*Justicia fulvicoma*), CSs, V
Lantana (*Lantana* x *hybrida*), CS, V, Annual
Gayfeather (*Liatris* spp.) , All
Alyssum (*Lobularia maritima*), Annual
Barbados Cherry (*Malpighia glabra*), CSs, V
Mimosa Bush (*Mimosa martindelcampi*), V
Horsemint, Beebalm (*Monarda* spp.), All,
Flowering Tobacco (*Nicotiana* spp.), Annual
Pentas, Star Flower (*Pentas lanceolata*), V, Annual
Phlox (*Phlox* spp.), All
Pickerelweed (*Pontederia cordata*), Ce, CSe

Azalea (*Rhododendron*)spp., Ce, CSe
Black-Eyed Susan (*Rudbeckia hirta*), All
Coral Fountain Plant (*Russelia equisetiformis*), CS, V
Scarlet Sage (*Salvia splendens*), Annual
Mexican Flame Vine (*Senecio confusus*), CS, V, Annual
Goldenrod (*Solidago* spp.), All
Porter Weed (*Stachytarpheta jamaicensis*), CSs, V, Annual
Stokes' Aster (*Stokesia laevis*), All
Marigold (*Tagetes* spp.), Annual
Green Shrimp Plant (*Tetrameria nervosa*), Cs, CS, V
Mexican Sunflower (*Tithonia rotundifolia*), Annual
Garden Verbena (*Verbena* spp.), Annual
Vervain (*Verbena bipinnatifida*), CS, V
Ironweed (*Vernonia* spp.), All
Vitex (*Vitex negundo 'heterophylla'*), CSs, V, Annual
Zinnia (*Zinnia* spp.), Annual

"Butterfly gardening is a richly rewarding experience," says Nancy Greig, director of the Cockrell Butterfly Center at Houston's Museum of Natural Science. "Not only will you add color and movement to your garden; you will be enriching the environment and making the world a healthier place. Because using chemical pesticides is 'verboten' in a butterfly garden, you will soon see many other beneficial insects and other animals (birds, lizards, etc.) that also avoid toxin-laden plants."

BUTTERFLY HOST PLANTS

Butterflies do not flock just to nectar. In fact, female butterflies are often more interested in finding a place to lay their eggs. Gardeners often forget that the larval stage of a butterfly is a caterpillar that eats leaves of its food plant, or host, to grow and eventually become a butterfly. Most butterflies are quite picky about the plants they eat as caterpillars, concentrating on one species or a few related species (so you don't need to worry about them eating up your roses). So be prepared to plant some host plants and let them get eaten down. Fortunately, most butterfly hosts can tolerate a lot of chewing and still come back. Monarch caterpillars, for example, often eat butterfly weed (*Asclepias curassavica*) down to mere stems. However, by the time they emerge from their chrysalis, those same plants will already have plenty of orange and yellow flowers that provide the adult butterflies with nectar.

Host Plant	Guest Caterpillar	
Dutchman's-Pipe Vine (*Aristolochia* spp.)	Pipevine Swallowtail	CS, V
Milkweed (*Asclepias* spp.)	Monarch, Queen	All
Pawpaw (*Asimina triloba*)	Zebra Swallowtail	Ce, CSe
Aster (*Aster* spp.)	Pearl Crescent	All
Wild Senna (*Cassia* spp.)	Cloudless Sulphur	All
Hackberry (*Celtis laevigata, C. occidentalis*)	Hackberry Butterfly, Snout Butterfly	All
Texas Thistle (*Cirsium texanum*)	Painted Lady	CS, V
Citrus (*Citrus* spp.)	Giant Swallowtail	CSs, V
Green Ash (*Fraxinus pennsylvanica*)	Eastern Tiger Swallowtail	N, C, CS
Spicebush (*Lindera benzoin*)	Spicebush Swallowtail	C, CS
Litsea (*Litsea aestivalis*)	Spicebush Swallowtail	CSs, V
Passionflower (*Passiflora* spp.)	Gulf Fritillary	CS, V, Annual

Red Bay (*Persea borbonia*)	Palamedes Swallowtail, Spicebush Swallowtail	Ce, CSe
Hop-Tree (*Ptelea trifoliata*)	Giant Swallowtail	N, Cw, CSw
Locust (*Robinia* spp.)	Silver-Spotted Skipper	N, C, CS
Black Willow (*Salix nigra*)	Viceroy	All
Sassafras (*Sassafras albidum*)	Palamedes Swallowtail, Spicebush Swallowtail	Ce, CSe
Fennel, Dill, Parsley (*Umbelliferae* spp.)	Black Swallowtail	Annual
Nettle (*Urtica* spp.)	Red Admiral	All
Wisteria (*Wisteria* spp.)	Skipper Butterfly	All
Prickly-Ash (*Zanthoxylum clava-herculis*)	Giant Swallowtail	CS, V

PLANTS THAT ATTRACT HUMMINGBIRDS

Hummingbird plants also attract a lot of insects, including bees and butterflies. Fortunately they all seem to get along fine, and bees are not defensive while they are busy working. Many hummingbird-attracting flowers are red and tubular. Makes sense. They also have lots of nectar.

Pink Abutilon (*Abutilon pictum*), CSs, V, Annual

Buckeye (*Aesculus* spp.), C, CS

'Sunset' Hyssop (*Agastache rupestris*)', All

Hollyhock (*Alcea rosea*), All

Narrow-Leafed Hummingbird Bush (*Anisacanthus linearis*), Csw, CSw, V

Anisacanthus (*Anisacanthus wrightii*), Cw, CSw, V

Butterfly Bush (*Buddleia officinalis*), CS, V

Indian Paintbrush (*Castilleja coccinea*), All

Cleome (*Cleome hasslerana*), Annual

Sky Flower, Golden Dewdrop (*Duranta repens* [*erecta*]), CSs, V

Coral Bean (*Erythrina herbacea*), All

Hummingbird Bush (*Hamelia patens*), CSs, V, Annual

Red Yucca (*Hesperaloe parviflora*), All

Tropical Hibiscus (*Hibiscus rosa-sinensis*), CSs, V, Annual

Impatiens (*Impatiens* x *hybrida*), Annual

Cardinal Climber, Cypress Vine (*Ipomoea quamoclit*), Annual

Morning-Glory (*Ipomoea tricolor*), Annual

Shrimp Plant (*Justicia brandegeana*), CS, V, Annual

Jacobinia (*Justicia* spp.), CSs, V, Annual

Lantana (*Lantana camara*), CS, V, Annual

False Turk's-Cap (*Malvaviscus arboreus*), All

Monkey Flower (*Mimulus hybridus*), CSe, Annual

Four-O'clock (*Mirabilis jalapa*), All

Nicotiana, Flowering Tobacco (*Nicotiana alata*), Annual

Firespike (*Odontonema strictum*), CSs, V, Annual

Golden Shrimp Plant (*Pachystachys lutea*), CSs, V, Annual

Geranium (*Pelargonium* x *hybrida*), V, Annual

Star Flower, Pentas (*Pentas lanceolata*), V, Annual

Petunia (*Petunia hybrida*), Annual

Annual Phlox (*Phlox drummondii*), Annual

Scarlet Sage (*Salvia splendens*), Annual

Salvia (*Salvia* spp.), All

Texas Betony (*Stachys coccinea*), C, CS, V

Hybrid Yellow Bells (*Tecoma alata* [*Stenolobium alatum*]), CSs, V

Nasturtium (*Tropaeolum majus*), Annual

Zinnia (*Zinnia* x *hybrida*), Annual

BOG GARDENS

Including a bog garden in the landscape is a relatively new concept. Perhaps it's because of our recent interest in wetlands. Suddenly it's "cool" to have a small piece of the swamp in your landscape—and for good reason. Wonderful plants like pitcher plants (*Sarracenia* spp.) and swamp lily (*Crinum americanum*) grow in bogs.

The plants listed below are adapted to bogs, wetlands, marshes, prairie potholes, and swamps. The definition for a bog is a wetland situation characterized by waterlogged, hydric soils and dominated by spongy mosses. While many of these plants like wetlands and anaerobic conditions, others (like the grasses) are more adapted to drier conditions part of the time. They are found higher up the bank of a bog garden, creek, ditch, or swale.

Creating a bog garden in Odessa may require a pond liner and a windbreak, while in Liberty your backyard very well may *be* a bog. Actually, bog gardens almost anywhere in Texas are easier to manage with a liner.

Bog gardens can effectively be used as natural filters for a water garden, too. Simply locate them up from the deeper water garden, with channels for the water to flow back into the deeper water, and use a recirculating pump to move the water back through the bog. With the exception of the pump, the whole process is very natural.

Accent plants can be added to the bog garden during warm summer months. Just place water-tolerant plants (left in containers) in the bog. Good examples would be calla lilies (*Zantedeschia aethiopica*), walking iris (*Neomarica gracilis*), Chinese evergreens (*Aglaonema* spp.), philodendrons, and other water-loving houseplants. The interest in bog gardens is just beginning to escalate, so don't be surprised if some of these plants, especially natives, are hard to find.

This list is divided into groups of bog plants, shoreline plants, and invasive bog plants. Many of the shoreline plants can be grown in the water, but they all thrive on the shoreline.

PITCHER PLANT

Bog Plants

Dwarf Variegated Sweetflag (*Acorus gramineus 'variegatus'*)

Elephant-Ear, Taro (*Alocasia* spp., *Colocasia* spp.)

Ruby Creeper (*Alternanthera reineckii*)

Canna (*Canna* spp.)

Swamp Lily (*Crinum americanum*)

Umbrella Palm (*Cyperus alternifolius*)

Dwarf Papyrus (*Cyperus isocladus*)

Star Grass (*Dichromena colorata*)

Giant Melon Sword (*Echinodorus cordata*)

Spike Rush (*Eleocharis montevidensis*)

Chinese Water Chestnut (*Eleocharis tuberosa*)

Dwarf Horsetail (*Equisetum scirpoides*)

Chameleon Plant (*Houttuynia cordata 'variegata'*)

Spider Lily (*Hymenocallis* spp.)

Louisiana Iris (*Iris brevicaulis, I. fulva, I. hexagona*)

Giant Blue Louisiana Iris (*Iris giganticaerulea*)

Japanese Iris (*Iris kaempferi*)

Siberian Iris (*Iris sibirica*)

Creeping Jenny (*Lysimachia nummularia*)

Macbridea (*Macbridea caroliniana*)

Marsh Trefoil, Bogbean (*Menyanthes trifoliata*)

Milfoil (*Myriophyllum* spp.)

Yellow Water Lotus (*Nelumbo lutea*)

Yellow Water Lily (*Nuphar luteum*)

Fragrant White Water Lily (*Nymphaea odorata*)

Floating Heart (*Nymphoides aquatica*)

Water Celery (*Oenanthe javanica*)

Ribbon Grass (*Phalaris arundinacea*)

Pickerelweed (*Pontederia cordata*)

Pondweed (*Potamogeton crispus, P. densus*)

Red-Stemmed Sagittaria (*Sagittaria lancifolia 'ruminoides'*)

Arrowhead (*Sagittaria lancifolia*)

Ruby-Eye Arrowhead (*Sagittaria montevidensis*)

Lizard's-Tail (*Saururus cernuus*)

White Bullrush (*Scirpus lacustris 'albescens'*)

Zebra Rush (*Scirpus lacustris 'tabernaemontani'*)

Powdery Thalia (*Thalia dealbata*)

Red-Stemmed Thalia (*Thalia geniculata*)

Shoreline Plants

Sweetflag (*Acorus calamus*)

Elephant-Ear, Taro (*Alocasia* spp., *Colocasia* spp.)

Ruby Creeper (*Alternanthera reineckii*)

Indigobush Amorpha (*Amorpha fructicosa*)

Bushy Bluestem (*Andropogon glomeratus*)

Broomsedge Bluestem (*Andropogon virginicus*)

Giant Cane (*Arundo donax*)

Lady Fern (*Athyrium filix-femina*)

Angel Trumpet (*Brugmansia versicolor*)

Wild Calla, Water-Dragon (*Calla palustris*)

Canna Lily (*Canna* spp.)

Sedges (*Carex* spp.)

Buttonbush (*Cephalanthus occidentalis*)

Turtlehead (*Chelone obliqua*)

Spider Plant (*Chlorophytum comosum*)

Swamp Lily (*Crinum americanum*)

Australian Tree Fern (*Cyathea cooperi*)

Umbrella Grass (*Cyperus alternifolius*)

Ti Ti, Leatherwood (*Cyrilla racemiflora*)

Blue Ginger (*Dichorisandra thyrisiflora*)

White Top Sedge (*Dichromena colorata*)

Himalayan Wood Fern (*Dryopteris wallichiana*)

Spike Rush (*Eleocharis montevidensis*)

Horsetail (*Equisetum hyemale*)

Tiny Horsetail (*Equisetum scirpoides 'striatum'*)

Sugarcane Plumegrass (*Erianthus giganteus*)

Joe Pye Weed (*Eupatorium purpureum*)

Water Locust (*Gleditsia aquatica*)

Butterfly Ginger (*Hedychium* spp.)

Swamp Sunflower (*Helianthus angustifolius*)

Waterleaf (*Hydrolea ovata*)

Spider Lily (*Hymenocallis* spp.)

Louisiana Iris (*Iris brevicaulis, I. fulva, I. hexagona*)

Giant Blue Louisiana Iris (*Iris giganticaerulea*)

Japanese Iris (*Iris kaempferi*)

Siberian Iris (*Iris sibirica*)

Soft Rush (*Juncus effusus*)

Spotted Dead Nettle (*Lamium maculatum 'variegatum'*)

Leopard Plant (*Ligularia tussilaginea 'aureo-maculata'*)

Cardinal Flower (*Lobelia cardinalis*)
Primrose Creeper (*Ludwigia palustris*)
Water Primrose, tropical (*Ludwigia peploides*)
Red Ludwigia (*Ludwigia repens*)
Creeping Jenny (*Lysimachia congestiflora*)
Barbara's-Buttons (*Marshallia grandiflora*)
Marsh Trefoil (*Menyanthes trifoliata*)
Partridgeberry (*Mitchella repens*)
Sensitive Fern (*Onoclea sensibilis*)
Royal Fern (*Osmunda regalis*)
Maidencane (*Panicum hemetomon*)
Vine Mesquite (*Panicum obtusum*)
Longtom (*Paspalum lividum*)
Vasey Grass (*Paspalum urvillei*)
Tuckahoe (*Peltandra virginica*)
Smartweed (*Polygonum* spp.)
Pickerelweed (*Pontederia cordata*)
Primrose (*Primula bulleyana, P. japonica*)
Arrowhead (*Sagittaria lancifolia*)
Native Pitcher Plant (*Sarracenia alata, S. flava*)

Lizard's-Tail (*Saururus cernuus*)
Bullrush (*Scirpus lacustris*)
Powdery Thalia (*Thalia dealbata*)
Meadow Rue (*Thalictrum* spp.)
Wedelia (*Wedelia trilobata*)
Chain Fern (*Woodwardia areolata*)
Virginia Chain Fern (*Woodwardia virginica*)
Yellow-Root (*Xanthorhiza simplicissima*)
Calla Lily (*Zantedeschia aethiopica*)

Invasive Bog Plants
Elephant-Ear (*Colcasia* spp.)
Swamp Lily (*Crinum americanum*)
Horsetail (*Equisetum hyemale*)
Yellow Iris (*Iris pseudacorus*)
Aquatic Mint (*Mentha aquatica*)
Parrot's-Feather (*Myriophyllum aquaticum*)
Lizard's-Tail (*Saururus cernuus*)
Cattail (*Typha* spp.)

"Bog plants make for a rather eclectic plant community," observes Steve Wood, a Master Gardener/Naturalist and a water garden designer in Rosenberg. "Some are quite common, and they might be found in a ditch bordering your property; others are exotic but worth searching for and ordering by mail if necessary. The creative gardener will have a wonderful experience designing a bog garden—it can be large or small, with a liner or with an earthen bottom. Plant combinations might include tropicals, grasses, and natives. The true reward, though, is the experience of observing an ever-changing, wetland ecosystem."

"Bog plants are great for wet spots in the landscape," says Anita Nelson, who with her husband Rolf owns Nelson Water Gardens in Katy. "Typically, they like to have wet feet and dry ankles. Most, however, are very tolerant, and they can grow in a standard perennial bed. As container plants, they're the plants you can't overwater!"

MARSHA HARLOW'S FAVORITE XERISCAPE PLANTS

This list is from Marsha Murray Harlow, a writer and Master Gardener in San Antonio, who says, "Xeriscaping just makes good sense in Texas, or anywhere water is precious. Savvy gardeners know that a xeric garden can be as vibrant in color and texture as a water-guzzling garden. As a bonus, many low-water-use plants attract butterflies and hummingbirds. Keep in mind that plants appropriate for a West Texas xeriscape may vary from those in a Houston xeriscape, so choose wisely for your specific location."

Xeriscape plants are tough, but they need regular watering to get established, and some supplemental water in droughts. The plants in this list offer reliable color, and drought and heat tolerance, which is important for Texas summers. Most of these plants are readily available, and they blend easily into home landscapes. For lists of trees, shrubs, and vines to use in a xeriscape planting, refer to those chapters for lists of plants for dry sites or for West Texas.

Hinckley's Columbine (*Aguilegia hinckleyana*), All

Coral Vine (*Antigonon leptopus*), CS, V

Butterfly Weed (*Asclepias tuberosa*), Ce, CSe

Hardy Blue Aster (*Aster oblongifolius*), All

Poinciana (*Caesalpinia* spp.), CSs, V

Coreopsis (*Coreopsis lanceolata*), All

Purple Coneflower (*Echinacea purpurea*), All

Blanket Flower (*Gaillardia* x *grandiflora*), All

Firebush (*Hamelia patens*), CSs, V, Annual

Daylily (*Hemerocallis* x *hybrida*), All

Shrimp Plant (*Justicia brandegeana*), CS, V, Annual

Lantana (*Lantana* hybrids), CS, V, Annual

Texas Sage, Cenizo (*Leucophyllum frutescens*), C, CS, V

Trumpet Honeysuckle (*Lonicera sempervirens*), All

Turk's-Cap (*Malvaviscus arboreus*), All

Blue Plumbago (*Plumbago auriculata* [*capensis*]), CSs, V

Moss Rose (*Portulaca grandiflora*), Annual

Yellow Lady Banks Rose (*Rosa banksiae 'lutea'*), CS, V

'Indigo Spires' Salvia (*Salvia*), All

Autumn Sage (*Salvia greggii*), All

Texas Mountain Laurel (*Sophora secundiflora*), C, CS, V

Mexican Mint Marigold (*Tagetes lucida*), CSs, V, Annual

Yellow Bells (*Tecoma stans 'angustata'*), CSs, V

"The beauty of xeriscape emerges during the heat of a Texas summer. Even faced with drought and threat of water restrictions, you know your landscape will not only survive, but keep right on blooming."
—Marsha Murray Harlow, writer and Master Gardener, San Antonio

According to John White, formerly a County Extension agent in El Paso and currently an Extension horticulturist in Las Cruces, New Mexico, "Water is a major concern for El Paso residents, especially if they garden. Underground water has been the primary source of drinking water for many years, but these sources are not being recharged and may not last more than twenty-five years. Now, about half of the drinking water comes from processed river water. El Paso has a population of 750,000 and a neighbor, Juarez, Mexico, has 1.4 million people. That's a lot of thirst to quench, and water conservation ordinances leave comparatively little for landscapes."

John says that lawn grass is being phased out and replaced with native plants requiring little water. Also, low-volume irrigation systems are being encouraged. "The water that is available, especially if it is well water, is very salty with lots of chlorides, sodium, boron, and calcium carbonate." In the future, El Paso landscapes will have to rely on more native plants as well as introduced plants with low water requirements. "The popular term for El Paso landscaping is *xeriscaping*," John notes, "but we like to call it *sunscaping*."

COOL-SEASON FLOWERS FOR A WINTER GREENHOUSE

The nurseries always seem to be filled with geraniums for sale in the spring. This is great if you live in an area with cool summer temperatures—maybe in Alpine—but for most Texans, geraniums are a bust in the summer. The time to grow them is in the fall and winter. In a mild winter we can grow them outside from the Upper Gulf Coast south, but it's impossible to predict these things, so the best alternative is to fill the winter greenhouse with plants that like cool weather but can't take a frost.

If you want to really get crazy, string a line of lightbulbs over the bench and put them on a time clock set to come on from 10 P.M. until 2 A.M. You should now be able to grow tuberous-rooted begonias. That is, if you ordered tubers in the spring and stored them in the refrigerator until October. Why do you need the lightbulbs? Tuberous-rooted begonias are long-day plants, and they like cool weather—an unlikely scenario to find in Texas. Actually, they are short-night plants, stimulated to bloom when the nights are short (or if the night is interrupted by light).

You can also grow some of the cool-season plants that survive outdoors in the winter—plants such as pansies, snapdragons, dianthus, linaria, and stock.

Calendula (*Calendula officinalis*)
Godetia (*Clarkia amoena*)
Wallflower (*Erysimum cheiri*)
Sweet Pea (*Lathyrus odoratus*)
Blue Lobelia (*Lobelia erinus 'compacta'*)
Monkeyflower (*Mimulus hybridus*)

Nemesia (*Nemesia strumosa*)
Geranium (*Pelargonium* × *hortorum*)
German Primrose (*Primula obconica*)
Painted-Tongue (*Salpiglossis sinuata*)
Schizanthus (*Schizanthus pinnatus*)
Nasturtiums (*Tropaeolum majus*)

REALLY, REALLY TOUGH CONTAINER PLANTS

Most of these plants are frost tender, and in a container they are even more cold sensitive, essentially because the roots are more tender than the top of the plants, and in a container the roots are more exposed to cold damage. So, tough as they are, they will need some protection in the winter. Otherwise they laugh at the occasional lack of water, limited fertilizing, and benign care most gardeners are sometimes capable of.

Chinese Evergreen (*Aglaonema commutatum*)
Lazy Daisy (*Aphanostephus skirrhobasis*)
Meyer Asparagus (*Asparagus densiflorus 'meyerii'*)
Asparagus Fern (*Asparagus densiflorus 'sprengeri'*)
Airplane Plant (*Chlorophytum comosum*)
Pencil Cactus (*Euphorbia tirucalli*)

Sedum (*Hylotelephium* [*Sedum*] *sieboldii*)
Donkey-Ear Kalanchoe (*Kalanchoe gastonis-bonnieri*)
Lantana (*Lantana* spp.)
Peperomia (*Peperomia* spp.)
Dahlberg Daisy (*Thymophylla* [*Dyssodia*] *tenuiloba*)

WILDFLOWERS OF TEXAS

Wildflowers are a Texas tradition. Our highways are resplendent in the spring with bluebonnets (*Lupinus texensis*), annual phlox (*Phlox drummondii*), and Indian paintbrush (*Castilleja indivisa*). By early summer the palette changes to Indian blanket (*Gaillardia pulchella*), lemon mint (*Monarda citriodora*), Mexican hat (*Ratibida columnaris*), and coreopsis (*Coreopsis tinctoria*). It's no wonder we want to plant these wildflowers in our gardens. When we finally get that place in the country, we want them to grow in the fields and along the roads that lead to our home.

Most of the more popular native Texas wildflowers should be planted in the fall months (September, October, and November) to become established and growing before winter sets in. Planting in the spring or summer usually creates disappointing results, unless you are planting live plants and not seed.

Planting wildflowers isn't always the great success we want it to be. First, we need to select varieties adapted to the area, then plant them in the proper place—most need full sun and good drainage—and make sure the seeds have soil contact. Too many disappointments have been experienced by folks walking through the pasture and slinging a couple of pounds of wildflower seeds. It's best if the ground can be lightly tilled or raked first. Sow the seed evenly by broadcasting it in two different directions. Then the seed needs to be pressed into the soil by walking over or rolling the area.

PLAINS
COREOPSIS

Wildflower seed planting is usually more successful when you plant a variety of species at one time in the same location. This will increase your chances that some of the varieties will grow on your site and will be happy. After the first blooms have occurred, take note of the varieties that performed well, and plant more of the successful varieties next fall to increase the size of your wildflower meadow.

Of course gardeners have been planting wildflowers in their flowerbeds for years. Many a Texas wildflower has been turned into a popular garden flower by plant breeders. Most recently, the Texas bluebell (*Eustoma grandiflora*) has been dubbed lisianthus by Japanese plant breeders and the once single, purple flower is now available in a myriad of colors and forms. Bluebonnet plants are often available in the nursery for those who forgot to plant seed in the fall, and as long as you plant them in sunny raised beds, they can be gorgeous.

If you're determined to have the wildflower look in your garden or in a pasture close to the house, here are some of the ones that are most successful. There are two lists—the native wildflowers and introduced species. The introduced species listed make a good wildflower show without threatening to take over.

Native Wildflowers

Plains Coreopsis (*Coreopsis tinctoria*)	full sun, moist areas
Indian Blanket (*Gaillardia pulchella*)	full sun, anywhere
Texas Bluebonnet (*Lupinus texensis*)	full sun, good drainage
Lemon Mint (*Monarda citriodora*)	full sun, anywhere
Showy Primrose (*Oenothera speciosa*)	full sun, anywhere
Drummond Phlox (*Phlox drummondii*)	full sun, sandy soil
Mexican Hat (*Ratibida columnaris*)	full sun, anywhere
Black-Eyed Susan (*Rudbeckia hirta*)	full sun, anywhere
Scarlet Sage (*Salvia coccinea*)	part sun, anywhere
Moss Verbena (*Verbena tenuisecta*)	part sun, good drainage

Introduced Species

Cornflower (*Centaurea cyanus*)	full sun, anywhere
Oxeye Daisy (*Chrysantemum leucanthemum*)	full sun, sandy soils
Cosmos (*Cosmos bipinnatus*)	full sun, anywhere; plant in spring
Rocket Larkspur (*Delphinium ajacis*)	part sun, good drainage
Candytuft (*Iberis umbellata*)	full sun, good drainage
Toadflax (*Linaria maroccana*)	full sun, good drainage
Scarlet Flax (*Linum rubrum*)	full sun, drought tolerant
Sweet Alyssum (*Lobularia maritima*)	full sun, anywhere
Shirley Poppy (*Papaver rhoeas*)	full sun, deep soils, good drainage
Johnny Jump-Up (*Viola cornuta*)	part sun, anywhere

"As wildflower enthusiasts, we want to produce in two to three years a display of color to match that which has taken Mother Nature hundreds of years to achieve," says John R. Thomas, owner of Wildseed Farms in Fredericksburg. "Nature plays an important role in the success or failure of all wildflower plantings. Adverse weather conditions such as drought, hail, or excessive rainfall—obviously beyond human control—may seriously affect the success of your wildflowers."

STRATEGIES FOR BENEFICIAL INSECTS

Planting a lot of *Apaciae* like cilantro, Italian parsley, dill, and fennel is probably the most important single thing an organic food gardener can do to reduce pests," says Bob Randall, director of Urban Harvest in Houston. He advises that the main way to encourage beneficial insects is to grow plants that beneficials need in their life cycle. Bob makes these basic points about beneficial gardening:

- **Plant the right plants**—native beneficial insects are adapted first to native flowering plants.
- **Diversify** by planting many different types of herbs, flowers, and other plants so there will be nectar and pollen, resting places, and breeding areas for the adult forms. Different flower shapes and different colors attract a diversity of beneficials. For example, drab-colored flowers (white, brown, off-white) encourage night-flying insect predators, and highly colored flowers encourage daytime predators. Also, different insects need different shaped flowers in order to use the nectar, so you get many different types of predators with a panoply of differently shaped flowers at all seasons.
- **Intercrop** plants attractive to beneficials so that beneficials are near pest-prone plants. This duplicates the natural landscape.

- **Humidify** with close spacing of plants and drip irrigation, so that small predators don't lose body moisture. Provide groundwater through bird baths, ponds, seasonal vernals, low boggy areas, but also include some dry, hot places.
- **Keep blooms year round** so that insects will have what they need when their life cycles need it.

The Parsley Family (*Apiaceae*)

A large number of Texas wildflowers happen to be either related to parsley or to sunflowers, so many of our native beneficial insects are adapted to feeding on nectar of plants in one of these families. Many of the following will self-seed.

Cilantro, Coriander (best at attracting beneficials)	Italian Parsley
Fennel (best for long season of bloom)	Queen Anne's Lace
Dill	

The Daisy-Sunflower Family (*Compositæ*)

The sunflower family includes asters, blanket flower (gaillardia), coneflowers, coreopsis, cosmos, ox-eye and other daises, Texas dandelion, goldenrod (solidago), liatris, Mexican hat, mist flowers (wild ageratum), rudbeckia, sneezeweed, sunflowers, thistles, and yarrow. Goldenrod attracts seventy-five species of predatory insects. It does not cause hay fever, but it blooms at the same time as ragweed and therefore gets blamed. Goldenrod spreads by wind-blown seed and runners, and it gets 6 feet tall, so it can become a minor weed.

Goldenrod, Solidago	Cosmos
Tansy	Blanket flower
Yarrow	Maximillian and other native sunflowers

The Mint Family

Basil, especially African Blue	
Mint	Lemon Balm
Oregano	
Rosemary	

Specific Beneficials and the Plants They Prefer

Wolf, Jumping, and Lynx Spiders	Sweet Allysum, Asters
Ladybug Beetles	Mint Marigold, Yarrow, Butterfly Weed
Assassin Bugs	Sunflowers
Hover Flies	Cosmos, Mint Marigold, Marigolds, Spearmint
Robber Flies	Flowers of almost any description, year round
Tachinid Flies	Buckwheat
Ant Lions, Owl Flies, Mantidflies, Green Lacewings	Goldenrod, Red Cosmos, Coreopsis, Tansy, Queen Anne's Lace, Citrus
Parasitic Braconid Wasps	Single-blossom wildflowers, Mints
Ichneumon, Chalcid, Tiphiid, Pelecinid Parasitic Wasps	Buckwheat, Southern Peas, Fava Beans
Predatory Wasps	Ox-eye Daisy, Black-Eyed Susan, Goldenrod, Yarrow

THE LAZY GARDENER'S LIST OF PLANTS

Brenda Beust Smith, known as the Lazy Gardener, writes for the *Houston Chronicle* and has a TV show on Channel 8/PBS in Houston. Her motto is: "If a plant has insect/disease problems, don't treat it! Take it out and replace it with a plant that doesn't have insect/disease problems in your area."

The Lazy Gardener advises, "The following are some great-for-Houston plants that should be insect and disease free, or—if they do have problems—are strong enough so we can ignore temporary invasions. Don't ignore drainage stipulations; these are vital!"

This list is adapted from *The Lazy Gardener's Guide* and *The Lazy Gardener's Calendar* (River Bend Company, Houston).

Plants for Sun—Excellent Drainage
(For sites raised 8 to 12 inches above ground level or on sloping areas)

Butterfly Weed (*Asclepias curassavica*)
Orchid Trees (*Bauhinia* spp.)
Butterfly Bush (*Buddleia davidii*)
Poinciana (*Caesalpinia pulcherrima*)
Summer-Blooming Flowery Senna (*Cassia corymbosa*)
Fall-Blooming Flowery Senna (*Cassia splendida*)
Wheat Celosia (*Celosia spicata*)
Orange Cestrum (*Cestrum aurantiacum*)
Chrysanthemum (*Chrysanthemum* spp.)
Cigar Plant (*Cuphea ignea*)
Gaura (*Gaura lindheimeri*)
Hummingbird Bush (*Hamelia patens*)
Lantana (*Lantana* spp.)
Fern Leaf Lavender (*Lavandula* spp.)
Lion's-Ear (*Leonotis* spp.)
Loropetalum (*Loropetalum chinense*)
Spider Lily (*Lycoris radiata*)
Oleander (*Nerium oleander*)
Rock Rose (*Pavonia lasiopetala*)
Frangipani, Lei Flower (*Plumeria* spp.)
Antique Roses (*Rosa* spp.)
Salvia (*Salvia* spp.)
Bridal-Wreath Spiraea (*Spiraea prunifolia*)
Copper Canyon Daisy (*Tagetes lemmonii*)
'Angustata' Yellow Bells (*Tecoma stans*)
Verbena (*Verbena* spp.)
Vitex (*Vitex agnus-castus*)

Plants for Sun—Good Drainage
(For sites raised 3 to 4 inches above ground or on slightly sloping areas)

Yesterday-Today-&-Tommorow (*Brunfelsia australis*)
Cleome (*Cleome hasslerana*)
Cosmos (*Cosmos* x *hybrida*)
Coneflowers (*Echinacea* and *Rudbeckia*)
Blue Daze (*Evolvulus glomeratus*)
Indian Blanket (*Gaillardia* spp.)
Byzantine Gladiolus (*Gladiolus byzantinum*)
Daylily (*Hemerocallis* spp.)
Althaea (*Hibiscus syriacus*)
Amaryllis (*Hippeastrum* spp.)
Dutch Iris (*Iris* x *hybrida*)
Gayfeather, Blazing Star (*Liatris* spp.)
Allyssum (*Lobularia maritima*)

Banana Shrub (*Michelia figo*)
'Fortune' Daffodil (*Narcissus* spp.)
Firespike (*Odontonema strictum*)
Evening Primrose (*Oenothera* spp.)
Cat's Whiskers (*Orthosiphon stamineus*)
Black-Eyed Susan (*Rudbeckia hirta*)
Fan Flower (*Scaevola aemula*)

Plants for Sun—Ground Level
(But no standing water after rains)

Four-O'clocks (*Mirabilis jalapa*)
Rain Lily (*Zephyranthes* spp.)

Vines for Sun—Excellent Drainage
'Mme. Galen' Trumpet Creeper (*Campsis tagliabuana*)
Carolina Jessamine (*Gelsemium sempervirens*)
Morning Glory (*Ipomoea purpurea*)
Cypress Vine (*Ipomoea quamoclit*)
Jasmine (*Jasminum* spp.)
Coral Honeysuckle (*Lonicera sempervirens*)
Black-Eyed Susan Vine (*Thunbergia alata*)

Shade Plants—Good Drainage
(Sites raised 3 to 4 inches above ground or on slope)

Lily-of-the-Nile (*Agapanthus africanus*)
'Texas Gold' Columbine (*Aquilegia chrysantha*)
Begonia (*Begonia* spp.)
Ground Orchid (*Bletilla striata*)
Coreopsis (*Coreopsis* spp.)
Hydrangea (*Hydrangea macrophylla*)
Polka Dot Plant (*Hypoestes phyllostachya*)
Impatiens (*Impatiens* spp.)
Indigo (*Indigofera* spp.)
Brazilian Plume (*Justicia carnea*)
Snowflake (*Leucojum aestivum*)
Toadflax (*Linaria maroccana*)
Cardinal Flower (*Lobelia cardinalis*)
Rock Rose (*Pavonia* spp.)
Pentas (*Pentas lanceolata*)
Old-Fashioned Petunias (*Petunia violacea*)
Mock Orange (*Philadelphus* spp.)
Summer Phlox (*Phlox paniculata*)
Obedient Plant (*Physostegia* spp.)
Blue Plumbago (*Plumbago auriculata*)
Chocolate Plant (*Pseuderanthemum alatum*)
Pigeonberry (*Rivina humilis*)

Shade Plants—Ground Level
(*No standing water after rains*)

'Alabama Sunset' Coleus (*Coleus hybridus*)
'Duck's Foot' Coleus (*Coleus hybridus*)
Crinum Lily (*Crinum* spp.)
Strawberry Bush (*Euonymus americanus*)
Native Hibiscus (*Hibiscus moscheutos*)
Hosta (*Hosta* spp.)
Peacock Ginger (*Kaempferia* spp.)
Turk's-Cap (*Malvaviscus arboreus 'drummondii'*)
Oxalis (*Oxalis* spp.)
'Katie's Compact' Ruellia (*Ruellia Brittoniana*)

Persian Shield (*Strobilanthes dyeranus*)
Torenia (*Torenia fournieri*)
Calla Lily (*Zantedeschia aethiopica*)
Ginger (*Zingiber, Hedychium, Costus, Alpinia, Curcuma*)

Vines for Shade
Cross Vine (*Bignonia capreolata*)
Hyacinth Bean Vine (*Lablab purpurea* [*Dolichos lablab*])
Butterfly Vine (*Stigmaphyllon ciliatum*)
Black-Eyed Susan (*Thunbergia alata*)

Among the plants recommended by Brenda Beust Smith, the *Houston Chronicle*'s Lazy Gardener, is the spider lily (*Lycoris radiata*). The spring foliage disappears, and single spidery flowers appear in fall. "Don't overwater!" she cautions. Another plant she favors is wheat celosia (*Celosia spicata*), which "grows 6 feet tall with purplish-red flowers, and it reseeds. Most of all, I love it and it's growing at Mercer Arboretum." Other good reseeders that Brenda recommends are rock rose (*Pavonia lasiopetala*), obedient plant (*Physostegia*), and cleome (*Cleome hasslerana*). Cleome she describes as tall and elegant. "If it likes you," she says, "it will reseed."

SOUTH OF THE BORDER PLANTS FOR TEXAS GARDENS

Mexico might not seem like the most likely place to find landscape plants for Texas gardens, but even though many areas of Mexico are quite tropical, other areas, at higher altitudes, are confronted with temperature extremes that mirror the lowest temperatures experienced in the Lone Star State. Recognizing this similarity, plant explorers like the late Lynn Lowrey and Benny Simpson began importing trees, shrubs, and herbaceous plants decades ago for trial in Texas. Today this work is carried on through people like Carl Max Schoenfeld (Yucca Do Nursery) and John Fairey (Peckerwood Garden). Carl contributed this list of Mexican plants that are becoming available for Texas gardens.

As Carl explains, "Texas is caught between the Great Plains to our north, the Chihuahuan desert to our southwest, and the Gulf of Mexico to the southeast. Also, stretching across portions of the state in a loose patchwork are the remnant populations of a once immense woodland forest that reached from the Appalachian Mountains to Guatemala. These climatic regions forged our distinct landscape, and their constant repositioning affords the opportunities necessary for a rich flora. In addition to this diverse natural resource, we have an immense untapped source of desirable plants to the southwest in northern Mexico.

"By a stroke of good luck, I had the pleasure of befriending one of Texas's great plantsmen, Lynn Lowrey. He introduced John Fairey, owner of Peckerwood Garden, and me to the wonderful world of Texas natives and then to the Mexican flora. Working at Peckerwood Garden for sixteen years afforded me the opportunity to experience firsthand many of these new plants as they were being introduced from Mexico—during this time, more than seventy trips were made into the remote mountainous areas of northeastern Mexico. After thirteen years of testing, the following plants have shown great hardiness and ornamental qualities. Many are quite different from what we have grown up with, and since they do not yet have common names, they sound foreign. However, they are perfectly at home here."

AGAVE AMERICANA

Trees

Acer skutchii, All
Clethra pringlei, CS, V
Diospyrus palmeri, CS, V
Juniperus flaccida, C, CS, V
Magnolia macrophylla 'dealbata', C, CS, V
Magnolia tamaulipana, C, CS, V
Myrospermum sousanum, Cs, CS, V
Nectandra salicifolia, V
Persea podadenia, CS, V
Pinus arizonica 'stormae', Cs, CS, V
Pinus moctezumae, C, CS, V
Pinus patula, Cs, CS, V
Pinus pseudostrobis, C, CS, V
Platanus mexicana, C, CS, V
Podocarpus matudai 'reichei', CS, V
Quercus canbyi, All
Quercus germanae, Cs, CS, V
Quercus polmorpha, All
Quercus rhizophylla, All
Quercus sartorii, C, CS, V
Taxodium mucronatum, CS, V

Shrubs

Amyris madrensis, CS, V
Amyris texana, CS, V
Anisacanthus linearis, Cs, CS, V
Anisacanthus puberlus, Cs, CS, V
Bauhinia macranthera, C, CS, V
Bauhinia ramosissima, CS, V
Buddleia cordata, Cs, CS, V
Buddleia marrubifolia, Cs, CS, V
Caesalpinia mexicana, CS, V
Calliandra californica, CSs, V
Calliandra coulteri, CS, V
Calliandra eriophylla, CS, V
Callicarpa acuminata, Cs, CS, V
Casimora pringlei, CS, V
Ceanothus coeruleus, C, CS, V
Chiococca alba, CS, V
Cordia boissieri, CS, V
Cordia parviflora, C, CS, V
Coursetia glandulosa, CS, V
Crataegus greggii, C, CS, V
Dalea bicolor, CS, V
Dalea formosa, Cs, CS, V
Dalea frutescens, CS, V
Dectropsis bicolor, CS, V
Esenbeckia berlandieri, CSs, V
Eupatorium viburnioides, Cs, CS, V
Fraxinus greggii, Cs, CS
Helietta parvifolia, Cs, CS, V
Leucophyllum laevigatum, CS, V
Leucophyllum langmanae 'Lynn's Everblooming', Cs, CS, V

Leucophyllum xyzophyllum 'Desert Dazzler', Cs, CS, V
Litsea glaucenscens, Cs, CS, V
Litsea parvifolia, CS, V
Mahonia chochoca, C, CS, V
Mahonia gracilis, C, CS, V
Mahonia lanceolata, C, CS, V
Malomeles denticulata, Cs, CS, V
Mimosa martindelcampoi, CSs, V
Morkillia acuminata, CSs, V
Mortonia greggii, Cs, CS, V
Osmanthus salicifolia, Cs, CS, V
Philadelphus calciocolus, C, CS, V
Philadelphus mexicana, Cs, CS, V
Pinus pinceana, Cs, CS, V
Pistacia texana, C, CS, V
Porlieria angustifolia, Cs, CS, V
Rhus muellerii, Cs, CS, V
Rhus pachyrrhachis, CS, V
Senecio aeschenborianus, Cs, CS, V
Staphylea pringlei, Cs, CS, V
Styrax platanifolia subsp. mollis, C, CS, V
Trixis californica, Cs, CS, V
Ungnadia speciosa, Ns, C, CS, V
Vauquelinia angustifolia, Cs. CS, V

Palms

Brahea armata, CS, V
Brahea bella, CS, V
Brahea berlandieri, CS, V
Brahea decumbens, CS, V
Brahea dulcis, Cs, CS, V
Brahea moorei, CS, V
Chamaedorea microspadix, CS, V
Chamaedorea radicalis, CS, V
Sabal mexicana, C, CS, V
Sabal uresana, C, CS, V

Perennials

Aquilegia skinneri, Cs, CS, V
Asclepias linaria, CS, V
Asclepias subulata, CS, V
Begonia nelumbifolia, CSs, V
Begonia heracieifolia, CSs, V
Bouchea linifolia, Cs, CS, V
Callirhoe involucrata 'tenuissima', Ns, C, CS
Dicliptera resupinata, CSs, V
Eryngium venustrum, Ns, C, CS, V
Justicia fulvicoma, CS, V
Justicia leonardii, Cs, CS, V
Justicia runyonii, CS, V
Lobelia laxiflora, Cs, CS, V
Melochia pyramidata, CS, V
Monarda bartlettii, Ns, C, CS, V
Monarda pringlei, Ns, C, CS, V
Oenothera macrosceles, Ns, C, CS, V

Salvia blepharophylla 'Painted Lady', CS, V
Salvia blepharophylla 'Diablo', CS, V
Salvia coulteri, CSs, V
Salvia madrensis, C, CS, V
Salvia mexicana, C, CS, V
Salvia microphylla 'San Carlos Festival', C, CS, V
Salvia molissidora, CS, V
Salvia sinaloansis, CS, V
Scutellaria seleiana, CSs, V
Scutellaria suffrutescens, Ns, C, CS, V
Tephrosia potosii, Cs, CS, V
Tetrameria nervosa, C, CS, V
Trichosacme lanata, CS, V
Vigethia mexicana, C, CS, V
Zinnia martianus, CS, V, Annual

"Woody Lilies"
Agave americana 'marginata', CS, V
Agave americana 'protoamericana', CS, V
Agave applanata, CSs, V
Agave bovicornuta, V
Agave bracteosa, Cs, CS, V
Agave celsii, Cs, CS, V
Agave ferox 'Green Goblet', Cs, CS, V
Agave inaequidens, V
Agave macroacantha, V
Agave maximiliana, V
Agave montana, Cs, CS, V
Agave ocahui, CS, V
Agave parrasana, C, CS, V
Agave parryi 'truncata', C, CS, V
Agave pelona, Cs, CS, V
Agave polyacantha, V
Agave potrerana, Cs, CS, V
Agave salmiana, Cs, CS, V
Agave schidigera, Cs, CS, V
Agave striata 'falcata', C, CS, V
Agave striata 'striata', C, CS, V
Agave weberi, CS, V
Agave zebra, Cs, CS, V
Beschorneria decosteriana, CSs, V
Beschorneria septentrionalis, C, CS, V
Dasylirion berlandieri, C, CS, V
Dasylirion longissimum, CS, V
Hechtia texensis, CS, V
Hesperaloe campanulata, C, CS, V
Hesperaloe funifera, C, CS, V
Hesperaloe funifera 'chungii', Cs, CS, V
Manfreda longiflora, Cs, CS, V
Manfreda maculosa, Cs, CS, V
Manfreda sileri, Cs, CS, V
Manfreda undulata, C, CS, V
Manfreda variegata, C, CS, V

Nolina beldingii, CS, V
Nolina longifolia, CS, V
Nolina matapensis, CS, V
Nolina nelsoni, C, CS, V
Yucca australis, CS, V
Yucca rigida, Cs
Yucca schottii, C, CS, V

Vines
Agdestea clematidea, CSs, V
Aristolochia elegans, CSs, V
Mascagnia macroptera, CS, V
Maurandya grandiflora, Cs, CS, V
Merremia aurea, CSs, V
Vigna populena, CS, V

Bulbs
Achimenes grandiflora, Cs, CS, V
Alophia veracruzana, Cs, CS, V
Amoreuxia wrightii, Cs, CS, V
Arisaema macrospathum, C, CS, V
Cipura paludosa, CS, V
Habranthus howardii, Cs, CS, V
Hymenocallis harrisiana, Cs, CS, V
Hymenocallis maximiliani, Cs, CS, V
Hypoxis decumbens, Cs, CS, V
Polianthes geminiflora, Cs, CS, V
Polianthes graminifolia, Cs, CS, V
Polianthes howardii, CS, V
Polianthes nelsoni, Cs, CS, V
Polianthes platyphylla, CS, V
Polianthes pringlei, CS, V
Polianthes X brundrandtii 'Mexican Firecracker', Cs, CS, V
Tigridia pavonia, Ns, C, CS, V
Zephyranthes chichimeca, Cs, CS, V
Zephyranthes insularum, CSs, V
Zephyranthes labuffarosa, C, CS, V
Zephyranthes lindleyana, Cs, CS, V
Zephyranthes macrosiphon, C, CS, V
Zephyranthes morrisclintii, Cs, CS, V
Zephyranthes nymphaea, CS, V
Zephyranthes primulina, C, CS, V
Zephyranthes reginae, Ns, C, CS, V
Zephyranthes subflava, CS, V
Zephyranthes traubii, Ns, C, CS, V

Ground Covers
Aristolochia coryi, Cs, CS, V
Dalea greggii, CS, V
Dyschoriste linearis, Cs, CS, V
Orbexilum pedunculatum, Cs, CS, V

Grasses
Muhlenbergia dumosa, Cs, CS, V
Stipa tenuissima, Ns, C, CS, V

Cycads
Ceratozamia hildae, CS, V
Ceratozamia kuersteriana, CS, V

Ceratozamia latifolia, CSs, V
Ceratozamia microstrobila, CS, V
Dioon edule 'angustifolia', CS, V
Dioon edule 'edule', CSs, V
Zamia fischeri, CSs, V
Zamia vasquzii, CS, V

"How could such a vast and unparalleled source of new plants exist at our doorstep and yet remain virtually unknown? Possibly Mexico is too close geographically to be considered exotic, so it has been passed over for more distant hunting grounds. Numerous trips to this under-explored part of the world paved the way for many totally unexpected discoveries that will forever change my attitude about plants, plant relationships, gardening, and designing with them."
—Carl Max Schoenfeld, owner, Yucca Do Nursery, Hempstead

GARDEN ORNAMENTATION

Cindy Appleman, a recycling and decorating enthusiast, suggests: "A garden needs focus to achieve balance. Garden ornamentation achieves this with points of reference that contrast with the flora. You can use the traditional or the whimsical. You don't need expensive items, but you do need to exercise your imagination. During the transition from one growing season to the next, these focal points will come into their own as they draw the eye when the foliage has faded and fallen."

Cindy says, "Garden ornamentation can come from anywhere that your imagination takes you. A few places to get started are antique stores or junk shows, catalogs, craft shows, flea markets, discount stores, garage sales, garden nurseries, hardware stores, salvage companies, and the Internet. In fact, for the flea market nearest you, see http://www.fleamarketguide.com."

The lists that follow are some of Cindy's ideas for embellishing your garden with ornamentation.

Light: Decide whether you want to provide light or reflect it. Recycling compact disks into light catchers by hanging them from tree limbs may keep squirrels out of fruit trees. A hanging disco ball that twirls with the breeze creates a fabulous effect as it splashes light around your garden. Prisms can give a similar effect. After dark, bring the moon down to your garden with light strings coiled within a grapevine sphere (a loosely woven ball made with grapevines).

Citronella candles	Fireplace or fire pit	Light strings
Compact disks	Garden torches or smudge pots	Ponds
Disco or millennium balls	Gazing balls	Prisms
	Lamps or lanterns	

Sound: Sound generated within your garden will insulate you from the rest of the world. Attract birds and find entertainment in the range of their delightful chatter. Scatter wind chimes and bells throughout the garden. Go Texan! Build a water fountain by pairing an old cowboy bathtub with a vintage hand-water-pump spout and hook it together with a recycling water pump.

Aviary	Fountains	Waterwall
Bells	Streams	Waterwheel
Dovecote	Waterfalls	Wind chimes

Supports: Enhance plants that require support by providing them with something interesting to climb on. Don't throw away that old step ladder—give it a new lease on life and see how charming it will look with morning glories growing on it. Give a vintage door a final hurrah by planting it in your garden; allow a honeysuckle vine to meander up the sides and form a cloud on top.

Arbors and arches	Recycled ladder trellis	Vintage bedspring trellis
Obelisks	Tricycle	Vintage door or window trellis
Porch columns	Tuteur or steeple trellis	

Planters: An old bicycle with hanging gardens on the front bar or in the back wheel baskets can be made even more eye-catching if painted bright yellow. Partially sink a decorative tire planter to control invasive plants. A wrought-iron chair minus its round seat provides a wonderful place to hang a flowerpot. Use a weathered metal bedframe to outline a garden bed.

Clawfoot bathtub	Stone water trough	Weathered metal bedframe
Pedestal sink	Tire planter	Wheelbarrow
Red wagon	Topiary frame	Wrought-iron chair
Retired bicycle	Urns	Yard cart
	Watering can	

Motion: Create movement in your garden by making it wildlife friendly. Provide food, water, and shelter for birds, bees, and butterflies. Butterflies need water to drink, so make a butterfly puddle by piling stones in very shallow water in a birdbath. Build a train garden by combining large-scale model train railroading with miniature gardening. Kick back and just watch the action.

Bee hives	Ladybug house	Stepping stones
Birdbaths, birdfeeders, birdhouses	Mobiles	Swings
Butterfly puddle	Nesting boxes	Toad abode
Flag or windsock	Pinwheels and whirligigs	Walkways
Garden train	Pond fish	Weather vane
	Rocking chair	

Art Elements: Take a traditional garden ornament and go a step further, like the interactive sundial at Terry Hershey Park in Houston. As you step onto the stone named for the current month, your body casts a shadow to the hour point.

Adirondack and twig chairs	Obelisk	Shells
Armillary sphere	Park bench	Statuary
Bee skep	Rocks	Sundial

Garden Structures: Recycle an old garden tool into a door handle for the potting shed. Mismatch a 4-foot picket fence with a regular-size door and doorframe. Add a fanciful element to your garden with a theme like the Wizard of Oz—make that walkway a yellow brick road and plant a pair of red shoes sticking out from under the potting shed. Recycle materials into a Tin Man and a Scarecrow and include a topiary Lion.

Cold frame	Foot bridge	Greenhouse
Fencing	Garden gate	Shed
Folly	Gazebo	Treehouse

Yard Art: Yard-art connoisseur Felder Rushing quipped, "Yard art makes me feel better. Not you, me!" Just as outdoor Christmas decorations can easily move from delightful to gaudy, yard art wavers between artistic and tacky—and it's simply individual perspective. Deck a pole with decorative birdhouses, recycle an old outhouse into a tool shed, mount old garden tools as a potting-shed wall collage, or park a carousel beast in your flowerbed. Whether it produces laughter because it's amazing or appalling, it's a good thing. Let the whimsy begin.

Carousel animal	Stone face	Ceramic or glass balls
Clay pot people	Garden gnome	Grapevine or wire spheres
Recycled tool creature	Scarecrow	Stepping stones
Fairy rings	Metal insect creation	Wire sculpture
Garden angel	Outhouse	Yard-tool collage
	Downspouts	

"Recycling with your compost pile enriches the soil your garden grows in. Recycling mundane items into your garden settings enriches you with another avenue for creativity. Open your eyes, your mind, and have fun!"
—Cindy Appleman, decorating and recycling enthusiast, Houston

RESOURCES

Hopefully this book has you excited about plants. That's the idea. Start your research with this book and then design your garden. Not being able to find a plant can sure spoil your fun, though. For this reason, we have included a few sources for plants and supplies. Many of them are in Texas, but not all. Some specialty plants are hard to find, and even though we recommend you buy locally first, then shop Texas mail order second, it would be unfair to leave out some of the wonderful mail-order sources listed here that are out of state.

The gardener that finds the most compost wins, so it is only right to list as many compost sources as possible. Want to start your garden project right? Then you'll want to send a soil sample to one of the Texas A&M University diagnostic labs. Sick plants? Contact the Plant Disease Diagnostic Lab.

This section includes sources for ferns, orchids and orchid supplies, and seed catalogs. There are also lists of mail-order companies and garden-related websites. If you're a plant lover and not connected to the web, you are missing out on a wonderful source of plant information. Moreover, you can probably buy most of what you need for the garden online.

COMPOST PRODUCERS IN TEXAS

Finding good compost is one of the main challenges that gardeners face everywhere. Too often products sold as compost are partially decomposed wood chips that may still have a tremendous nitrogen affinity. If you mix this product with your soil, plants will be stunted and turn yellow from a lack of available nitrogen. The microorganisms trying to break down the wood chips are using most of it. John Ferguson of Nature's Way Resources put this list of Texas composters together as an aid to gardeners looking for this magic black stuff. Also, look around for stables, cow lots, chicken yards, and rabbit producers. Finding an old pile of rotted manure is like finding gold.

Private Operations
Agronomic Management Group (compost bio-solids for Fort Worth and Arlington), P.O. Box 120306, Arlington, TX 76012; 817-571-9391.
Creative Wood Products, P.O. Box 28410, Dallas, TX 75228; 214-801-DIRT.
Earth Works Compost, Grapevine, TX 76051; 817-424-0540.
Earthly Treasures, 1416 S Loop 256, Palestine, TX 75801, P.O. Box 130, Neches, TX 75779; 903-584-3566.
Garden-Ville Fertilizer Company, Inc., 7561 E. Evans Rd., San Antonio, TX 78266; 210-651-6115.
Kaderli Materials, 8200 I-35 N., New Braunfels, TX 78130; 830-625-1400.
Lawn Lovers, 1319 Galveston St., Laredo, TX 78040; 956-727-5743.
Living Earth Technology, 5625 Crawford, Houston, TX 77041; 713-466-1111, 713-466-7360.
Mulch King, 12622 Boudreaux Rd., Tomball, TX 77375; 281-351-5422.
Nature's Way Resources, Inc., 1945 F.M. 1488, Conroe, TX 77384; 409-273-1200 (Conroe Local), 409-321-6990 (Houston).
Oma's Haus & Garten (turkey-litter compost), 12194 E. US Hwy 290, Fredericksburg, TX 78624-5758; 830-644-5506.
Organic "By Gosh" (bag Dillo Dirt for city of Austin), 1306 West St. John's Ave., Austin, TX 78757; 512-908-7284.

Rabbit Hill Farm (vermi-compost and worms), 288 SW CH0020, Corsicana, TX 75110; 903-872-4289.

Ramrod Enterprises, Inc. (sheep-manure compost), P.O. Box 1106, Hwy. 190 West, Menard, TX 76859; 915-396-4518.

Silver Creek Materials Recycling and Compost, 2251 Silver Creek Rd., Fort Worth, TX; 817-246-2426.

Soil Building Systems, Inc., 1770 "Y" Street, Dallas, TX 75229; 972-831-8181.

South Plains Compost (cow-manure and cotton-burr compost), 5407 Slaton Hwy., P.O. Box 9, Slaton, TX 79364; 806-745-3559.

Texas Organic Recovery, P.O. Box 17126, Austin, TX 78760-7126; 512-243-4100.

Twin Oaks Farms Organic Greenhouse (worms and vermi-compost), Rt. 1, Box 78A, Purdon, TX 76679-9801; 817-578-1272.

Waste Reduction Systems, 100 Genoa Red Bluff Rd., Houston, TX 77034; 281-922-1000.

Municipal Composting Operations

Brazos Valley Solid Waste Managment Agency, 2700 East Bypass, Suite 4300, P.O. Box 9960, College Station, TX 77842; 409-764-3832.

City of Austin (Dillo-Dirt bio-solids compost), Hornsby Bend Waste Water Treatment Facility, 2210 South F.M. 973, Austin, TX 78725; 512-929-1016.

City of Baytown, 2123 Market St., P.O. Box 424, Baytown, TX 77522-0424; 281-420-5300.

City of Beaumont (green-waste compost), 4955 Lafin Rd., Beaumont, TX 77705; 409-842-1483.

City of Bryan (bio-solid compost), P.O. Box 1000, Bryan, TX 77805; 409-361-3699.

City of College Station, 2613 Texas Ave. S., College Station, TX 77842; 409-764-3691.

City of Irving, Public Health and Environmental Services, 825 Irving Blvd., Irving, TX 75060; 972-721-2349.

City of LaPorte, 2963 N. 23rd St., P.O. Box 1115, LaPorte, TX 77572-1115; 281-471-9369.

City of Pflugerville, 100 E. Main, Suite 100, P.O. Box 589, Pflugerville, TX 78691-0589; 512-251-9935 #708.

City of Plano (green-waste compost), P.O. Box 860358, Plano, TX 75074; 972-964-4150.

City of San Antonio (bio-solid compost, brush, wood, and yard waste), 1800 Bitter Rd., San Antonio, TX; 210-822-1779.

City of Temple-Belton-Brazos River Authority (bio-solid compost), 2405 E. 6th St., Belton, TX 76513; 254-939-6471.

City of Waco, Solid Waste Services, P.O. Box 2570, Waco, TX 76702-2570; 254-751-8590.

City of Wichita Falls (bio-solid compost), 130 7th St., Wichita Falls, TX 78307; 940-761-7977.

Kingsland Municipal Utility District (bio-solid compost), P.O. Box 748, Kingsland, TX 78639; 915-388-2097.

LCRA (Cities of Burnett, Marble Falls, and Kingsland), P.O. Box 220, Austin, TX 78767-0220; 512-217-8856.

SOIL TESTS

Soil-test kits actually work quite well for home garden projects. They are based on color charts or other visual reactions caused by reagent chemicals added to soil solutions. Since they require the user to make a judgment based on sometimes subtle differences, it might seem that they shouldn't be relied on. In reality, you learn to work with the system and base your fertility needs on experience.

It's still good to have a soil test analyzed by the Texas A&M University soils lab in College Station or Lubbock. This gives you a reliable mark to compare your home test-kit results to. Other agricultural universities, even community colleges, may also offer this service.

It's also a good idea to have your water tested for irrigation quality. Find out if it contains high soluble salts or if the pH is high. Forms for these tests are available from the local Extension office in your county. The current prices are about $15 to $20.

Extension Soil, Water, and Forage Testing Laboratory, Texas A&M University, 345 Soil and Crop Sciences, Heep Center, College Station, TX 77843-2474; 409-845-4816.

Plains Soil, Water, and Plant Testing Laboratory, Texas Ag. Ext. Service, Rt. 3, Box 213AA, Lubbock, TX 79401-9746; 806-746-6101.

DISEASE DETECTION

You can have plants analyzed for diseases, and soils (including root tissue) can be checked for nematodes (microscopic round worms). The current charge for these services is about $15. An information sheet on how to sample and submit plants or soils for disease analysis is available from the County Extension office. However, testing a soil sample for any and all diseases isn't practical. Neither is the disease lab set up to test soil for toxic substances like herbicides that may have been added to the soil. These investigations can be very expensive, so it helps to know what substance you suspect has caused the plant damage.

Texas Plant Disease Diagnostic Laboratory, Texas Agricultural Extension Service, Room 101, L. F. Peterson Bldg., College Station, TX 77843.

FERN SOURCES

Ferns can be one of the most frustrating groups of plants to locate. To make it a bit easier, here are some fern specialists to try.

Eco-Gardens
Dr. Don Jacobs
P.O. Box 1227
Decatur, GA 30031

Fancy Fronds
P.O. Box 1090
Goldbar, WA 98251
Catalog $2.00

The Fernery
94 Magellan Way
Covington, KY 41015
Catalog SASE

Foliage Gardens
2003 128th Ave. S.E.
Bellevue, WA 98005
Catalog $2.00

Russell Graham
4030 Eagle Crest Rd. N.W.
Salem, OR 97304
Catalog $3.00

Plant Delights Nursery
9241 Sauls Rd.
Raleigh, NC 27603
Catalog 10 stamps

Roslyn Nursery
211 Burrs Lane
Dix Hills, NY 11746
Fax 516-643-0894

ORCHID PLANTS AND SUPPLIES

Orchid supplies aren't available at every nursery, and they are somewhat specialized. You can use regular pots, but there are special shallow pots with larger holes for air circulation that work well with orchids. Then there are the special bark and fiber root mediums, clips to hold new plants in the pot, and cork for epiphytic species. The list goes on and on, so it pays to shop with an orchid specialist. They are also helpful if you have cultural questions.

Orchid Supplies and Potting Material

OFE International
P.O. Box 161302
Miami, FL 33116
305-253-7080

Tropical Plant Products
P.O. Box 547754
Orlando, FL 32854-7754
407-293-2451

Plants
Butterfly Orchid
One Arroyo Pl.
San Benito, TX 78586
210-748-4240

D & B Orchids
Dotty and Berry Woodson
(By appointment only)
5608 Boat Club Rd.
Fort Worth, TX 76135
817-731-0397
dwoodson@airmail.net

Flowering Fingers
Steve Eagle
(By appointment only)
11 Chase Ct.
Fort Worth, TX 76110
817-921-3343
flfngrs@flash.net

Gunther's Greenhouse
Gunther Schnetzinger
513 W. Campbell Rd.
Richardson, TX 75080
214-234-6017
gunther@intex.net

It's A Jungle
Juanice Davis
907 Kramer Ln.
Austin, TX 78758
214-837-1205
jdavis@onramp.com

La Selva Orchids
Dan and Eddie Ruth Chadbourne
3910 Harvey Rd.
College Station, TX 77843
409-774-4775
LaSelvaOrc@aol.com

Mansfield Orchid Mart
Dave and Donna Maggard
(By appointment only)
2391 N. Main
Mansfield, TX 76063
817-478-6961
donna.maggard@Imco.com

Orchid Gardens
9748 Brockbank Dr.
Dallas, TX 75220
214-350-4985
orgdns@swbell.net

Orchid Konnection
Meir Moses
(By appointment only)
6812 Gold Dust Trail
Dallas, TX 75252
972-407-1885
orchidkonn@aol.com

Orchids by Hopkins
509 Bellevue
Cleburne, TX 76031
817-645-6750

Orchids & Ferns
7802 Bellaire
Houston, TX 77036
713-774-0949

Palmer Orchids
1308 E. Broadway
Pasadena, TX 77501
713-472-1364
palmer@flash.net

Siam Orchids
735 Crenshaw
Pasadena, TX 77504
713-487-1047

Sundance Orchids
(By appointment only)
Galveston, TX
409-744-4878

Teas Nursery Company
P.O. Box 1603
Houston, TX 77402-1603
800-446-7723

Van Horn Orchids
1316 Peden
Houston, TX 77006
713-520-7443

The Wright Company
223 Larkwood
San Antonio, TX 78209-2909
210-824-0823
orched@texas.net

Xanadu Orchids
14003 Dublin Square
San Antonio, TX 78217
210-653-8100

SEED CATALOGS

This is a partial list of firms. The inclusion of a firm does not guarantee reliability, and an absence does not imply disapproval. These addresses were viable at the time this book was written, but some may have changed and some firms may be no longer active.

Bountiful Gardens, 18001 Shafer Ranch Rd., Willits, CA 95490-9626; 707-459-6410, Fax: 707-459-1925, bountiful@sonic.net, www.bountifulgardens.org. Source for open-pollinated and untreated seeds.

Burpee (W. Atlee) & Co., 300 Park Ave., Warminster, PA 18991-0001; 800-888-1447, Fax 800-487-5530, www.burpee.com. Free catalog. Quality seed company offering many specialty vegetables like Charantai melons, Purple Blush eggplant, and Roly Poly squash.

The Chile Pepper Institute, NMSU, Box 30003, Dept. 3Q, Las Cruces, NM 88003. 505-646-3028, hotchile@nmsu.edu, www.nmsu.edu/~hotchile/index.html. Hot-pepper seeds and information.

The Cook's Garden, P.O. Box 535, Londonderry, VT 05148; 800-457-9703, Fax 800-457-9705. Free catalog. Gourmet varieties and recipes.

Enchanted Seeds, P.O. Box 6087, Las Cruces, NM 88006; www.tvfuture.com/enchanted. Hot-pepper seeds.

Evergreen Y.H. Enterprises, P.O. Box 17538, Anaheim, CA 92817; 714-637-5769, Fax 714-637-5769, EEseeds@aol.com, evergreenseeds.com. Asian vegetable seeds, books, and cooking supplies.

Field's (Henry) Seed & Nursery Co., 415 N. Burnet, Shenandoah, IA 51602-0001, www.myseasons.com. Phone Orders: 800-235-0845, Customer Service: 800-798-7842, Fax: 800-357-4149; Internet Orders: www.henryfields.com. This old standby catalog is still going strong with good seed and services, and new, interesting varieties.

Gardener's Supply Co., 128 Intervale Road, Burlington, VT 05401; 800-863-1700, Fax: 800-551-6712, info@gardeners.com, www.gardeners.com. Supplies, including organic pest controls.

Gurney's Seed & Nursery Co., 110 Capital St., Yankton, SD 57079, www.gurneys.com. Phone Orders: 605-665-1930, Customer Service: 605-665-1671, Fax: 605-665-9718. Free catalog, unusual varieties, and varieties recommended for the South.

Harris Seeds, 60 Saginaw Dr., P.O. Box 22960, Rochester, NY 14692-2960, www.harrisseeds.com. Phone Orders: 800-514-4441, Fax: 716-442-9386. Free catalog, good historical and growing tips for most vegetables, many commercial and specialty selections like the Mexican herb epazote.

Hudson (J. L.) Seedsman, Star Route 2, Box 337, La Honda, CA 94020. Catalog: $1; many plant seeds, from shrubs to vegetables.

Johnny's Selected Seeds, 1 Foss Hill Rd., RR 1, Box 2580, Albion, ME 04910-9731. Phone Orders: 207-437-4301, Fax: 800-437-4290, customerservice@johnnyseeds.com. Free catalog, heirloom and open-pollinated varieties, hybrids. Good prices and service.

Kilgore Seed Co., 1400 W. First St., Sanford, FL 32771; 407-323-6630. Catalog: $1; good cultural information for gardeners in the South to extreme South, hard-to-find Dade pole beans and Cuban vegetables.

Native American Seed, Junction, TX; 800-728-4043, www.seedsource.com. Free catalog, Texas native grass and wildflower seed.

Native Seeds, 526 N. 4th Ave., Tucson, AZ 85705; 520-622-5561, Fax: 520-622-5591, nss@azstarnet.com, www.azstarnet.com/~nss. Southwestern varieties, including hot peppers.

Nichols Garden Nursery, 1190 North Pacific Hwy., Albany, OR 97321; 541-928-9280. Great source for herbs, Asian and European vegetables.

Pacific Coast Tropicals, 1259 El Camino Real #297, Menlo Park, CA 94025, steve@pctgardens.com, www.pctgardens.com. Seed source for tropical plants.

Park Seed Co., 1 Parkton Ave., Greenwood, SC 29647-0001, www.parkseed.com. Phone Orders: 800-845-3369, Fax: 864-941-4206, info@parkseed.com. Free catalog, good service and quality.

Peaceful Valley Farm Supply, P.O. Box 2209, Grass Valley, CA 95945; 530-272-4769. Phone Orders: 888-784-1722, Fax: 530-272-4794. Catalog: $2; organic gardening supplies and organically grown, open-pollinated seeds.

Pepper Joe's, Inc., 1650 Pembrooke Rd., Norristown, PA 19403, www.pepperjoe.com. Catalog: $2; unusual peppers and tomatoes.

Pinetree Garden Seeds, Box 300, New Gloucester, ME 04260; 207-926-3400, superseeds@worldnet.att.net, www.superseeds.com. Free catalog, extensive selection of books, too.

Plants of the Southwest, 1812 Second St., Santa Fe, NM 87501, www.plantsofthesouthwest.com. Phone Orders: 800-788-7333, Fax 505-438-8800, mark@plantsofthesouthwest.com. Catalog: $1; chilies and Southwestern plants, including grasses.

Redwood City Seed Co., P.O. Box 361, Redwood City, CA 94064; 650-325-7333, www.ecoseeds.com. Catalog: $1; unusual vegetables, including Asian and Mexican special collections.

Renee's Garden, 7389 West Zayante Rd., Felton, CA 95018; 888-880-7228, Fax: 831-335-7227, Reneesgarden.com. Gourmet vegetable varieties.

SC Foundation Seed Assoc., 1162 Cherry Rd., Box 349952, Clemson, SC 29634-9952; 864-656-2520, Fax: 864-656-1320, seedw@clemson.edu, www.clemson.edu/seed. Heirlooms, plus varieties developed for South Carolina but great for Texas too.

Seed Savers Exchange, 3076 North Winn Road, Decorah, IA 52101; 319-382-5990, Fax: 319-382-5872. Heirloom varieties.

Seeds of Change, P.O. Box 15700, Santa Fe, NM 87506-5700, www.seedsofchange.com. Phone Orders: 888-762-7333, Fax: 888-329-4762, gardener@seedsofchange.com. Organic seeds—flowers, herbs, vegetables. Gardening accessories and books.

Seeds of Texas Seed Exchange, P.O. Box 9882, College Station, TX 77842; 409-693-4485, jackrowe@compuserve.com, http://csf.colorado.edu/perma/stse. Seed source for plants adapted to Texas—antique flowers, vegetables, trees, shrubs, vines, fruits, gourds. Contact Jack Rowe for membership information.

Seeds West Garden Seeds, 317 14th Street NW, Albuquerque, NM 87104; 505-843-9713, seeds@nmia.com, www.seedswestgardenseeds.com. Dry-land varieties, native plant seeds.

Select Seeds, 180 Stickney Hill Road, Union, CT 06076-4617; 860-684-9310, Fax: 800-653-3304. Antique flower seeds.

Shepherd's Garden Seeds, 30 Irene St., Torrington, CT 06790; 860-482-3638, Fax 860-482-0532, www.shepherdseeds.com. Catalog: $1; gourmet vegetable and herb varieties.

Southern Exposure Seed Exchange, P.O. Box 460, Mineral, VA 23117; 540-894-9480, Fax 540-894-9481. Catalog: $2; unusual and heirloom varieties.

Stokes Seeds, Inc., Box 548, Buffalo, NY 14240-0548; 800-263-7233. Customer Service: 716-695-6980, Fax: 888-834-3334, stokes@stokesseeds.com. Free catalog, many varieties great in Southern gardens.

Thompson & Morgan, Inc., P.O. Box 1308, Jackson, NJ 08527-0308; 800-274-7333, Fax: 888-466-4769, www.thompson-morgan.com. Free catalog. English company with U.S. distributor, so the seed is rather expensive.

Tomato Growers Supply Company, P.O. Box 2237, Fort Myers, FL 33902; 888-478-7333. Customer Service: 941-768-1119, Fax: 888-768-3476. Tomato varieties and extensive list of sweet and hot peppers.

Totally Tomatoes, P.O. Box 1626, Augusta, GA 30903-1626; 803-663-0016, Fax: 888-477-7333, www.totallytomato.com. Specialty catalog, tomatoes and peppers.

Twilley (Otis S.) Seed Co., Inc., P.O. Box 65, Trevose, PA 19053-0065; 800-622-7333, Fax: 864-227-5108. Free catalog, good selection and quality.

Wildseed Farms, 425 Wildflower Hills-P.O. Box 3000, Fredericksburg, TX 78624-3000; 800-848-0078, Fax: (830) 990-8090, www.wildseedfarms.com. Catalog: $2; wonderful source for wildflower seeds, great as reference guide.

Willhite Seed Co., P.O. Box 23, Poolville, TX 76487; 817-599-8656, 800-828-1840 (orders only), Fax: 817-599-5843. Free catalog, melons and vegetable varieties adapted to Texas, wildflowers, and more.

MAIL-ORDER RESOURCES

This is a partial list of firms selling plants and gardening supplies. These addresses were viable at the time this book was written, but some may have changed and some firms may be no longer active.

The Antique Rose Emporium, 9300 Lueckemeyer Rd., Brenham, TX 77833-6453; 800-441-0002, Fax: 409-836-0928. Source for old-fashioned roses, perennials, herbs.

Berdoll Pecan Nursery, Rte. 1, Box 605A, Cedar Creeks, TX 78612; 512-321-6157. Pecan trees—bare root and in containers.

Brent and Becky's Bulbs, 7463 Heath Trail, Gloucester, VA 23061; (toll-free) 877-661-2852, www.brentandbeckybulbs.com. Lots and lots of bulbs, including many adapted to Texas.

Camellia Forest Nursery, 9701 Carrie Rd., Chapel Hill, NC 27516; 919-968-0504, http://camforest.com. Camellias.

Crystal Palace Perennials, P.O. Box 154, St. John, IN 46373; 219-374-9419, GSpeichert@aol.com. Water plants.

Edible Landscaping, P.O. Box 77, Afton, VA 22920; 800-524-4156, Fax: 804-361-1916, EL@cstone.net, www.eat-it.com. Unusual fruits, nice assortment of figs, mayhaws.

Flowerfield Enterprises, 10332 Shaver Rd., Kalamazoo, MI 49024; 616-327-0108, Fax: 616-327-7009, www.wormwoman.com. Earthworms and vermiculture supplies.

Glasshouse Works, Church St., Stewart, OH 45778-0097; 800-837-2142, www.rareplants.com. Rare greenhouse and semi-tropical plants.

Gossler Farms Nursery, 1200 Weaver Rd., Springfield, OR 97478-9691; 541-766-3922. Rare and hybrid magnolias, other specialty plants.

Ison Nursery and Vineyard, P.O. Box 190, Brooks, GA 30205; 770-599-6970. Phone Orders: 800-733-0324. Muscadine grapes.

A.M. Leonard, Inc., 241 Fox Drive, PO Box 816, Piqua, OH 45356; 800-543-8955, Fax: 800-433-0633, www.amleo.com. Grafting knives, dibbles, and other garden tools.

Lilypons Water Gardens, 839 FM 1489 Rd., Brookshire, TX 77423; 281-391-0076, www.lilypons.com. Mail Order: 7000 Lilypons Rd., Buckeystown, MD 21717. Phone Orders: 800-999-5459. Water plants and supplies.

Logee's Greenhouses, 141 North St., Danielson, CT 06239-1939; 888-330-8038, Fax: 888-774-9932, logeeinfo@logees.com, www.logees.com. Greenhouse plants, including tropicals that can often be grown outdoors in South Texas.

Louisiana Nursery, 5853 Hwy. 182, Opelousas, LA 70570; 337-948-3696, Fax: 337-942-6404. Rare landscape plants. Catalog: $6; Daylily & Louisiana Iris catalog: $4; Crinum catalog: $5; Clivia catalog: $3.

Roger and Shirley Meyer Nursery, 16531 Mt. Shelley, Fountain Valley, CA 92708; 714-839-0796, exoticfruit@95net.com. Jujubes and other rare fruits.

Nelson Water Gardens and Nursery, 1502 Katy Ft. Bend Co. Rd., Katy, TX 77493; 281-391-4769. Water plants and supplies.

Niche Gardens, 1111 Dawson Rd., Chapel Hill, NC 27516; 919-967-0078, Fax: 919-967-4026, www.nichegdn.com. Perennials, pitcher plants (*Sarracenia* spp. and hybrids).

Old House Gardens, 536 Third St., Ann Arbor, MI 48103-4957, OHGbulbs@aol.com. Heirloom bulbs.

Plant Delights Nursery, Inc., 9241 Sauls Rd., Raleigh, NC 27603; 919-772-4794, plantdel.com. Rare landscape plants.

Raintree Nursery, 391 Butts Rd., Morton, WA 98356-9700; 360-496-6400, Fax: 888-770-8358, order@raintreenursery.com, www.raintreenursery.com. Rare fruit varieties, including Petite Negri fig.

Sandy Mush Herbs, 316 Surrett Cove Rd., Leicester, NC 28748-5517; 828-683-2014. Herbs.

Stokes Tropicals, P.O. Box 9868, New Iberia, LA 70562-9868; 800-624-9706, www.stokestropicals.com. Gingers and other rare tropical and semi-tropical plants.

Strawn Water Gardens, L.L.C., P.O. Box 10255, College Station, TX 77842-0255; 409-696-6644, Fax 409-696-0379. Hardy water lilies, tropical water lilies, lotus, Louisiana iris, and other aquatic plants. Wholesale only.

Texas Pecan Nursery, P.O. Box 306, Chandler, TX 75758; 214-849-6203. Fruit and pecan trees.

Bob Wells Nursery, Box 606, Lindale, TX 75771; 903-882-3550, Fax: 903-882-8030. Nut, fruit, and shade trees, berries, grapes, roses, flowering shrubs.

Womack Nursery Co., RR 1, Box 80, De Leon, TX 76444-9631; 254-893-6497, Fax 254-893-3400. Pecan and fruit trees, pecan graftwood, landscape trees, shrubs, roses.

Woodlanders Inc., 1128 Colleton Ave., Aiken, SC 29801; 803-648-7522. Catalog: $2; rare woody plants and sub-tropicals, bulbs, perennials.

Yucca Do Nursery Inc., Route 3, Box 104, Hempstead, TX 77445; 409-826-4580, yuccado@nettexas.net. Catalog: $4; native plants, plants from Mexico and worldwide.

GARDENING INTERNET SITES

This is just a sprinkling of what is available today on the Internet in the gardening realm—enough to whet your appetite for virtual gardening.

General Gardening Information

E-Answers—Extension Publication Search Engine: www.e-answers.org

Extension Service Urban Gardening Program: www.bright.net/~gardens

Florida Tropicals: www.floridaplants.com/tropics.htm

Garden Net: gardennet.com/

Gardening in the Gulf South: members.aol.com/cucryer/lagardeners.html

Horticulture in Virtual Perspective: www.hcs.ohio-state.edu/hcs/hcs.html

Le Jardin Ombragé (ginger information): www.nettally.com/skinnerd/ombrage.html

Museum of Garden History: www.compulink.co.uk/~museumgh

Oklahoma State Univ. Entomology and Plant Pathology: www.ento.okstate.edu

Ornamental Horticulture for Houston and the Gulf Coast Area: www.ghgcorp.com/beyer/ornament.htm

Plants: The Biggest and Best New Garden Plants: www.aquil.demon.co.uk/index.html

Rare Plants: rareplants.co.uk

Seed Catalog Source: www.b-and-t-world-seeds.com

Southern Gardening: www.southerngardening.com

Texas A&M Aggie Horticulture: aggie-horticulture.tamu.edu

Texas A&M Entomology: entowww.tamu.edu

Texas Plant Disease Handbook: cygnus.tamu.edu/texlab/tpdh.html

Texas Seed Exchange: csf.colorado.edu/perma/stse

Tropical Gardening: www.tropicalgardening.com
USDA Plant Hardiness Zone Map: www.ars-grin.gov/ars/Beltsville/na/hardzone/ushzmap.html
Variegated and Colored Leaves: www.rareplants.com/abg

Links to Other Sites
Botanic Garden and Arboreta Links: www.helsinki.fi/kmus/botgard.html
Botany Related Websites: www.botany.org/bsa/www-bot.html
Fern Links: www.home.aone.net.au/byzantinum/ferns/links.html
Internet Directory for Botany: www.helsinki.fi/kmus/botmenu.html
My Garden: hal-pc.org/~trobb/horticul.html
The Gardening Launch Pad: www.tpoint.net/neighbor/
The Trellis Gardening Links on the Internet: www.wormsway.com/trellis.html

Master Gardeners
Harris County Master Gardener Association: harris-cnty.tamu.edu/mg/
Master Gardener Programs in the USA: www.hal-pc.org/~trobb/mastgar.html
Texas Master Gardeners: aggie-horticulture.tamu.edu/mastergd/mg.html

Gardens to Visit on the Web
Arnold Arboretum (Massachusetts): arboretum.harvard.edu/
Atlanta Botanical Garden (Georgia): www.atlantabotanicalgarden.org/
Birmingham Botanical Gardens (Alabama): www.bbgardens.org/
Birmingham Botanical Gardens (UK): www.bham-bot-gdns.demon.co.uk/
Boggy Creek Farm (Texas): boggycreekfarm.com/
Brooklyn Botanic Garden (New York): www.bbg.org/
Calloway Gardens (Georgia): www.callawaygardens.com/
Canadian Gardens : www.hedgerows.com
Chicago Botanic Garden (Illinois): www.chicago-botanic.org/
Cleveland Botanical Garden (Ohio): www.cbgarden.org
Dallas Arboretum (Texas): www.thepeachtree.com/ent/texas/dallas/aboretum
Daniel Stowe Botanical Garden (North Carolina): www.stowegarden.org/
Davis Arboretum (California): www.aes.ucdavis.edu/outreach/univout/programs/arbor.htm
Denver Botanic Gardens (Colorado): www.botanicgardens.org/
Desert Botanical Garden (Arizona): www.dbg.org/
Fairchild Tropical Garden (Florida): www.ftg.org/
GardenNet's Guide to Gardens of the USA: gardennet.com/InformationDirectory/destinations.idc
Harvard University Herbaria (Massachusetts): www.herbaria.harvard.edu
Holden Arboretum (Ohio): www.holdenarb.org/
Houston Arboretum and Nature Center (Texas): www.neosoft.com/~arbor/
Huntington Library, Art Collections & Botanical Gardens (California): www.huntington.org/
JC Raulston Arboretum (North Carolina): arb.ncsu.edu/
Kew Gardens (UK): www.kewgardens.org
Leu Botanic Garden (Florida): www.ci.orlando.fl.us/departments/leu_gardens/index
Longwood Gardens (Pennsylvania): www.longwoodgardens.org/
Marie Selby Botanical Garden (Florida): www.selby.org
Mercer Arboretum and Botanic Gardens (Texas): www.houston-guide.com/guide/attract/attractmercer.htm
Missouri Botanical Garden : www.mobot.org/welcome.html
Moody Gardens (Texas): www.moodygardens.com/
New York Botanical Garden : www.nybg.org/
Rio Grande Botanic Gardens and Conservatory (Texas): www.cabq.gov/biopark/garden/index.html
Royal Botanic Garden Edinburgh (Scotland): www.rbge.org.uk/
Royal Botanic Gardens Kew (UK): www.rbgkew.org.uk/
San Antonio Botanical Gardens (Texas): www.sabot.org/
St. Andrews Botanic Garden (Scotland): www.gardenweb.com/gotw/standrew.html

State Botanical Garden of Georgia: www.uga.edu/~botgarden/
Stephen F. Austin Univ. Mast Arboretum (Texas): www.sfasu.edu/ag/arboretum/index.htm
Strybing Arboretum (California): www.strybing.org
The Conservatory in Golden Gate Park (California): www.netins.net/showcase/novacon/cyphaven/foundtn1.htm
The National Garden (Washington D.C.): www.nationalgarden.org/
Tohono Chul Park (Arizona): www.tohonochulpark.org/
Tucson Botanical Gardens (Arizona): www.azstarnet.com/~tbg/
U.S. Botanic Garden (Washington D.C.): www.aoc.gov/pages/usbgpage.htm
United States National Arboretum (Washington D.C.): www.ars-grin.gov/ars/Beltsville/na
University of California Botanical Garden : www.mip.berkeley.edu/garden
Zilker Botanical Garden (Texas): www.zilker-garden.org

Horticultural Organizations
African Violet Society of America: avsa.org
American Association of Botanical Gardens and Arboreta: www.aabga.org/
American Azalea Society: www.theazaleaworks.com/asa.htm
American Bamboo Society: www.bamboo.org/abs
American Camellia Society: www.peach.public.lib.ga.us/ACS
American Community Gardening Association: www.communitygarden.org/index.html
American Dahlia Society: www.dahlia.org
American Fern Society: www.visuallink.net/fern
American Hemerocallis Society: www.daylilies.org
American Hibiscus Society: Americanhibiscus.org
American Horticultural Society: eMall.com/ahs/ahs5.html
American Horticultural Therapy Association: www.ahta.org/
American Hosta Society: www.hosta.org
American Orchid Society: Orchidweb.org
American Rose Society: www.ars.org
American Society for Horticultural Science: www.ashs.org
American Society of Botanical Artists: Huntbot.andrew.cmu.edu/ASBA/ASBotArtists.html
American Society of Landscape Architects: www.asla.org/asla
Hardy Fern Foundation: www.hardyferns.org/
Herb Research Foundation: www.herbs.org
International Bulb Society: www.bulbsociety.com
International Oleander Society: www.oleander.org/
International Society of Arboriculture: www2.champaign.isa-arbor.com
Lady Bird Johnson Wildflower Center: www.wildflower.org/
Lone Star Chapter of the American Hibiscus Society: www.lonestarahs.org/
National Gardening Association: www.garden.org/
New England Wildflower Society: www.newfs.org
North American Lily Society: www.lilies.org/
North American Rock Garden Society: www.nargs.org/
Palm Society of South Texas: www.raingardens.com/psst.htm
Pennsylvania Horticultural Society: www.libertynet.org/~phs/
Plumeria Society of America: www.theplumeriasociety.org/
Royal Horticultural Society: www.rhs.org.uk/
Seeds of Texas Seed Exchange: http://csf.colorado.edu/perma/stse/
Texas Bamboo Society: www.bamboo.org/abs/TexasChapterInfo.html
Texas Botanical Garden Society: admin.inetport.com/~texasbot/
Texas Rose Rustlers: www.texas-rose-rustlers.com/
The Herb Society – United Kingdom: sunsite.unc.edu/herbmed/HerbSociety
The Mushroom Council: www.mushroomcouncil.com

Youth Gardening
Composting for Kids: Aggie-horticulture.tamu.edu/sustainable/slidesets/kidscompost/cover.html
Growing With Plants: www.pierce.wsu.edu/text/proggwp.htm
Junior Master Gardener Program: Juniormastergardener.tamu.edu/
KinderGarden: aggie-horticulture.tamu.edu/kindergarden/kinder.htm
National Gardening Association's Kids and Classrooms: www.garden.org/edu/home.asp
Nutrition in the Garden: aggie-horticulture.tamu.edu/nutrition/index/index.html
Youth Gardening Information Source: ag.arizona.edu/maricopa/garden/html/youth/youth.htm

INDEX